The Insider's Guide to
Venture Capital

The Insider's Guide to Venture Capital, 2002

Who the Key Players Are, What They're Looking for, and How to Reach Them

Dante Fichera, CPA

Prima Venture
An Imprint of Prima Publishing
3000 Lava Ridge Court • Roseville, California 95661
(800) 632-8676 • www.primalifestyles.com

Library of Congress Cataloging-in-Publication Data
Fichera, Dante.
    The insider's guide to venture capital, 2002 : who the key players are, what they're looking for, and how to reach them / Dante Fichera
        p. cm.
    Includes index.
    ISBN 0-7615-3239-0
    1. Venture capital. 2. Venture capital—Directories. I. Title.
    HG4751 .F53 2000
    332.66—dc21   00-069215

01 02 03 04 DD 10 9 8 7 6 5 4 3 2 1
Printed in the United States of America

Visit us online at www.primalifestyles.com

To my father, the late Salvatore Fichera,
whose philosophy was that with hard work, persistence,
a good sense of humor, and a little luck, you can
accomplish anything you set your mind to.

Contents

Acknowledgments   ix

How to Use This Book   xi

Part One
Directory of Venture Capital Funds   **1**

Part Two
Insider Secrets and Tools You Can Use   **265**

The 10 Things a Company Needs to Do to Get Venture
*   Capital Funding*   267
      Bill Stensrud and David Lee

Angels on Earth: Seeking Venture Capital from
*   Private Investors*   271
      Joe Sullivan

From Seed Round to "C" Round: The Early-Stage Build-Out   281
      Wade H. Bradley

An Early-Stage Venture Capitalist's Perspective on
*   Risk Management*   289
      Larry Kubal

How to Fund That Compelling Business Idea   299
      Robert F. Kibble

The Capital-Raising Process   307
      Benjamin E. N. Blumenthal

The Venture Valuation Process: Arriving at a Value for
*   Your Business*   313
      Standish M. Fleming

The Role of the Board   325
      Vincent Occhipinti

Venture Leasing   331
      Richard C. Walker

Business Incubation: An Evolving Model for Launching
   Successful Enterprises   343
      L. Tyler Orion

Critical Employment Issues for Start-Ups   351
      Jennifer A. Kearns

Venture Capital Marriage—Until Money Do Us Part?   361
      Ben R. Neumann

What to Be Prepared for—The Inside Story   367
      Nick Desai

Danger Ahead: Success   375
      David A. Kay and Michael Dedina

What It Takes to Lead Your Company from Start-Up
   to Liquidity   379
      Robert J. Harrington

A Biotech CEO's Perspective   383
      Walter H. Moos, Ph.D.

Hear This! What You Must Know When Raising
   Venture Capital   393
      R. Michael Jones

What It Means to Take VC Money—Is the Vision Still Yours?   399
      Nick Desai

Part Three
Indexes   **407**

Investment Terms   409
      Kurt L. Kicklighter

Funds in Alphabetical Order   415

Funds by Industry Preference   421

Funds by Geographical Area of Interest   433

Index for Part Two   441

About the Author   449

Acknowledgments

I thank my wife, Teri Fichera, for living the life of an entrepreneur which, as many of you know, is not easy! Thank you for taking several months away from your career to work on the compilation of this book.

I also thank all of my interns who worked on this project, with a special thanks to the following: Matt Bottalico, Grossmont College; Jennifer Chu, University of California, San Diego; Neal Hamovitch, University of California, Los Angeles; Oliver Hollender, Darmstadt University of Technology, Germany; Nedim Ozyel, National University; and Jason Weiner, University of California, San Diego.

How to Use This Book

The Insider's Guide to Venture Capital, 2002, is the most up-to-date and complete source for raising venture capital. As venture funds are constantly changing hands, merging, separating, and branching into additional funds, this publication keeps you ahead of the game.

The alphabetical directory to venture capitalists includes active funds only. Thus, you will not spend numerous hours pursuing dead funds. Each entry specifies industry, geographical, and other critical preferences so you can find the venture funds that are especially tailored to your specifications.

The collection of essays that follow the directory of funds is an awesome sample of the know-how of venture capitalist insiders from many different business backgrounds. You will be engrossed by their timely thoughts and ideas.

The numerous indexes provide you with several options to make your research as seamless as possible.

This practical guide is a superb resource, whether you are an entrepreneur, a finance student, or simply someone with a strong interest in venture capital funds.

WHAT'S INSIDE

This easy-to-use guide contains three parts:

1. A comprehensive directory of more than 400 current venture funds.
2. Eighteen informative essays covering major topics all entrepreneurs should know about when starting their company.
3. Five indexes for easy reference.

Part One: Directory of Venture Capital Funds

Part One is an alphabetical directory of venture capital funds. Each profile includes the name of the fund, its address(es), telephone and fax numbers, Web site address, total assets under management, initial investment size, year founded, a summary about the company, and a listing of portfolio companies. The summary provides the fund's industry preference, geographical focus, and other investment criteria.

Part Two: Insider Secrets and Tools You Can Use

The essays in Part Two are written by some of the most reputable professionals in their arena, with each chapter specifically tailored with the individual entrepreneur in mind. The result is a fabulous collection of helpful tips and inside glimpses of the venture capital world.

Part Three: Indexes

Part Three contains five indexes including an index of investment terms; three indexes broken down into venture capital funds in alphabetical order, by industry preference, and by geographical area of interest; as well as a general index.

PART ONE

Directory of
Venture Capital Funds

ABN AMRO PRIVATE EQUITY

208 S. LaSalle Street, 10th Floor
Chicago, IL 60604
312-885-7292   fax: 312-553-6648
www.abnequity.com

David L. Bogetz, Managing Director
Daniel J. Foreman, Managing Director
Keith A. Walz, Managing Director
Donna C. E. Williamson, Managing Director

total assets under management	*initial investment*	*year founded*
$300 Million	$1–10 Million	1996

ABN AMRO Private Equity (AAPE) is one of the leading venture capital firms in the Midwest. AAPE invests in privately held companies exclusively in North America and focuses on early- to later-stage ventures. AAPE primarily invests in four broad industries, including business services, communications, information technology, and health-care services. Specific target markets within these broad industry segments include B2B electronic commerce, traditional and e-business services, communications services and infrastructure, Internet applications, and traditional and e-health companies.

   Portfolio Companies: CoreChange; Dental One, Inc.; ecom.xml; eCredit.com; Phone.com; Tavve; UpShot.com; and WellMed.

ABS CAPITAL PARTNERS

101 California Street, 47th Floor
San Francisco, CA 94111
415-477-3297   fax: 415-477-3229

Andrew T. Shoehan, General Partner

John D. Stobo Jr., General Partner

total assets under management	*initial investment*	*year founded*
$450 Million	$10–30 Million	1993

ABS Capital Partners makes privately negotiated equity investments in acquisitions, recapitalizations, and expansion financings of companies in selected industry segments. ABS Capital Partners seeks to invest in established companies with experienced and proven management teams. ABS Capital Partners also has an office in the Baltimore area.

AC VENTURES

1661 Page Mill Road   2 Arundel Street
Palo Alto, CA 94025   London WC2R 3LT
650-213-2500   UK
fax: 650-213-2222   44-(0)-20-7844-3333
www.ac-ventures.com

Jackson L. Wilson Jr., Managing General Partner

Cherine Chalaby, London

total assets under management	*initial investment*	*year founded*
$132.1 Million	$2–30 Million	1999

AC Ventures is a venture capital unit of Accenture, formerly Andersen Consulting, through which it has a superb network of relationships with established industry leaders and governments worldwide. AC Ventures also has access to the firm's renowned intellectual capital—leading-edge technology skills, business strategy and process knowledge, industry insight, and the many other capabilities found in the world's leading global management and technology consulting firm. AC Ventures is able to draw on Accenture's brand name, reputation, and scale to support its portfolio companies.

Its focus is to make investments primarily in early-stage e-commerce companies with the potential for superior economic returns. The majority of investments are focused on business-to-business e-commerce companies, including industry exchanges, and product and service companies; e-infrastructure companies, together with software and other e-commerce technology-focused companies; plus a smaller portion of investments focusing on breakthrough business-to-consumer e-commerce.

AC Ventures looks at opportunities across all major industries, including financial services, retail, transportation and travel services, automotive, food and consumer packaged goods, energy, chemicals, utilities, communications, new media, and high technology. They deliberately spread their investments geographically to achieve balanced coverage of the fund across Europe, the Americas, and the Asia-Pacific region.

Portfolio Companies: Adaytum; Asera; Avanade Inc.; B2Emarkets; Biztro, Inc.; Blue Martini; Calico; Channelpoint; ChemConnect; Click Commerce, Inc.; Covation; Data Distilleries; Docent, Inc.; E*Advisor; Entrust; Epylon; Everypath; FuelQuest, Inc.; GameChange; Gamut Interactive; Imagine Broadband; iSuppli; MimEcom; Moai; OneSwoop; Portal Software, Inc.; Portum GmbH; PRA Solutions; PrimeResponse; Qpass; Quaris; RealMed Corporation; Retek Inc.; S1; Seals GmbH; ServiceNet; Sharepeople Ltd.; ShopLink; Siebel Systems, Inc.; Silicon Energy; Software Technologies Corporation; Swift Rivers, Inc.; via World Network; and xwave solutions.

ACACIA VENTURE PARTNERS

101 California Street, Suite 3160
San Francisco, CA 94111
415-433-4200   fax: 415-433-4250
www.acaciavp.com

C. Sage Givens, Managing Director
David S. Heer, Managing Director
Bruce A. Keller, Managing Director
Brian J. Roberts, Managing Director
P. Christian Hester, Principal

total assets under management	*initial investment*	*year founded*
$200 Million	$1–8 Million	1995

Acacia Venture Partners is a San Francisco–based venture capital firm dedicated to building world-class health-care companies. Acacia specializes solely in identifying and building leading service businesses in health care and related industries.

Acacia Venture Partners invests in all stages of company formation—from start-up through expansion and later-stage financing. Acacia provides seed capital to test the viability of a business plan and also invests in more mature companies that are in need of additional capital to expand their business or geographic presence.

Portfolio Companies: Acacia's private investments include Abaton.com; AmeriGroup Corporation; Data Critical Corporation; Medical Logistics, Inc.; and Simpata.

ACCEL PARTNERS

428 University Avenue
Palo Alto, CA 94301
650-614-4800   fax: 650-614-4880
www.accel.com

Jim Breyer, Managing Partner

Bud Colligan, Partner

Jim Flach, Partner

Jim Goetz, Partner

Bruce Golden, Partner

Mitch Kapor, Partner

Bill Lanfri, Partner

Arthur Patterson, General Partner, Founder

Theresia Ranzetta, Partner

Joe Schoendorf, Partner

Carter Sednaoui, Partner, CFO

Jim Swartz, General Partner, Founder

Peter Wagner, General Partner

total assets under management	*initial investment*	*year founded*
$3 Billion	N/A	1984

Accel Partners invests in companies at various stages of development. In order to bring greater understanding and experience to Accel's portfolio companies, the firm focuses exclusively on two sectors of technology: communications Internet/Intranet.

With this focus, Accel Partners believes it can contribute more deeply to the development of winning companies. Its contributions extend well beyond financing and include strategic guidance, recruiting, business development, and partnering.

Portfolio Companies: Auici Systems; iBeam Broadcasting; North Point Communications; Portal Software; RedBack Networks; and Support.com.

ACCESS VENTURE PARTNERS

4133 Mohr Avenue, Suite H
Pleasanton, CA 94566
925-426-9574   fax: 925-426-4398
www.accessventurepartners.com

John (Jay) E. Campion, Managing Director
Frank Mendicino Sr., Managing Director
Frank Mendicino Jr., Managing Director
Robert (Bob) W. Rees, Managing Director

total assets under management	*initial investment*	*year founded*
$34 Million	$250,000–1 Million	1999

Access Venture Partners is a seed- and early-stage venture capital firm. The Firm invests in technology companies with hyper-growth potential; particularly Web-based business applications, e-commerce infrastructure, communications equipment and services, and semiconductors. The four broad criteria for investments include high energy, driven founders/management, large emerging markets, innovative technologies, and attraction to public markets.

Access Venture Partners has offices in Austin, Denver, and Silicon Valley and invests primarily in those regions, alongside top-tier technology funds.

Portfolio Companies: BizBlast.com; Bionumerik; Brightware; Broadcloud; Digital Microwave; EnterpriseLink; Evan & Sutherland; HotRail; Infinitec Communications; Intertrust Technologies; IQ Destination; Media Prise; Mobilize; Myelos; Neon; Netfront; Osteobiologics; Product Buzz; QuickArrow; Quiniles; Sirros Networks; Street Fusion; Tian Software Company; Topaz Technology; TriVida Corporation; and USA Retama.

ADVANCED TECHNOLOGY VENTURES

485 Ramona Street   281 Winter Street, Suite 350
Palo Alto, CA 94301   Waltham, MA 02451
650-321-8601   781-290-0707
fax: 650-321-0934   fax: 781-684-0045
www.atvcapital.com

Steven Baloff, General Partner
Michael Carusi, General Partner

Michael Frank, General Partner

Jack Harrington, General Partner

Jos Henkens, General Partner

Wes Raffel, General Partner

Pieter Schiller, General Partner

April Evans, Partner, CFO

total assets under management	*initial investment*	*year founded*
N/A	N/A	1979

Advanced Technology Ventures (ATV) is a leading venture capital firm focused on early-stage opportunities in the information technology and health-care markets. ATV offers emerging companies an unparalleled breadth and depth of industry, market, operational, and technical expertise. Since 1979, ATV's combination of management experience, world-class technical talent, extensive global network, and international reach has helped more than 100 emerging companies develop winning strategies.

Portfolio Companies: Accord Networks; Annuncio Software; Cepheid; CollaGenex; Cytyc; DataSage; Epigram; garage.com; RF Micro Devises; TranSwitch Corporation; ViryaNet; and Webline.

ADVENT INTERNATIONAL CORPORATION

2180 Sand Hill Road, Suite 420
Menlo Park, CA 94025
650-233-7500   fax: 650-233-7515
www.adventinternational.com

Peter A. Brooke, Founder and Chairman

John J. Rockwell, Partner

Gwendolyn M. Phillips, Principal

Gregory C. Smitherman, Principal

total assets under management	*initial investment*	*year founded*
$3.5 Billion	$5–50 Million	1984

Advent International is one of the world's largest and most experienced global private equity investment firms. Advent's founder and chairman, Peter A. Brooke, began investing internationally in the early 1970s. Advent manages about $3.5 billion; has 16 offices in Europe, North America, Asia, and Latin America; and employs over 90 investment professionals. Advent invests globally and will consider investments in almost any industry but has particular expertise in high-growth or countercyclical sectors such as cable TV and media, IT, specialty chemicals, health care, consumer products, and retailing.

Portfolio Companies: Advanced Radio Telecom Corp.; Primacom; Synergon; and Worldgate.

AD-VENTURES, LLC

11288 Ventura Boulevard, Suite 443
Studio City, CA 91604
323-993-8664   fax: N/A
www.ad-ventures.com

Ben R. Neumann, President and CEO
Andrea Seimer, CFO

total assets under management	*initial investment*	*year founded*
$35 Million	$100,000–3 Million	1999

Ad-Ventures, LLC, acts as an investor and an entrepreneurial force, which enables it to provide financial knowledge and management expertise to its portfolio companies. The Firm is interested in technology and real estate, with a secondary interest in entertainment venues. Ad-Ventures seeks a majority position in its investments, usually taking charge of the company's management and structure. Ad-Ventures will only consider companies located in the United States.

Portfolio Companies: iboost Technology, Inc.; Internet Communications; McCormick Office Plaza, LLC.; Modern Living, LLC.; and Zeus Entertainment.

ALEXANDER HUTTON VENTURE PARTNERS

999 Third Avenue, Suite 3700
Seattle, WA 98104
206-341-9800   fax: 206-341-9810
www.alexanderhutton.com

Kent L. Johnson, Managing Director
Jerry Keppler, Managing Director
Mark Klebanoff, Managing Director
Tom Johnston, Managing Director

total assets under management	*initial investment*	*year founded*
$100 Million	$3–5 Million	1999

Alexander Hutton Venture Partners is a leading venture capital firm that focuses on equity investments in the Pacific Northwest's most promising technology companies. The Firm's roots can be traced to its predecessor, Alexander Hutton Capital, LLC, a regional investment banking firm that focused on raising capital for technology start-ups.

Portfolio Companies: Activate.net; Advanced Marine Technology; Appliant.com; Asterion.com; F5 Networks, Inc.; Halosource Corp.; Health Sense Int'l., Inc.; InfoSpace; Medifor, Inc.; Metrika Labs; NetUPDATE; nPassage; Oralis.com; Pro2Net; RevX.net, Inc.; SelfCharge, Inc.; Smarterville; TelcoOnline; and Tidemark Computer Systems.

ALLIED CAPITAL CORPORATION
One Maritime Plaza, Suite 1750
San Francisco, CA 94111-3507
415-399-2980   fax: 415-986-8922
www.alliedcapital.com

William L. Walton, Chairman and CEO

Phillip A. McNeill, Managing Director

John M. Scheurer, Managing Director

Joan M. Sweeney, Managing Director

G. Cabell Williams III, Managing Director

total assets under management	*initial investment*	*year founded*
$800 Million	$250,000–25 Million	1958

Allied Capital Corporation is principally engaged in lending to and investing in private small- to medium-sized businesses. For 40 years, Allied Capital Corporation has been dedicated to financing growing businesses nationwide in a wide variety of industries. Allied Capital Corporation is unique in that it creatively structures investments to meet the needs of each individual borrower and business, and is committed to servicing to maturity the vast majority of the loans it originates. Allied Capital Corporation focuses on providing loans and investments in three areas: mezzanine finance, commercial real estate finance, and small business loans.

ALLOY VENTURES
480 Cowper Street, 2nd Floor
Palo Alto, CA 94301
650-687-5000   fax: 650-687-5010
www.alloyventures.com

Craig Taylor, General Partner
John Shoch, General Partner

total assets under management	*initial investment*	*year founded*
$400 Million	$1–10 Million	1977

Alloy Ventures is an investment firm with a special interest in seed- and early-stage companies in the information technology, life sciences, bioinformatics, and e-health sectors of the economy. Alloy Ventures will draw upon its considerable experience and knowledge to assist companies with strategies, recruitment, business development opportunities, and financial capital. Alloy Ventures invests in the United States.

Portfolio Companies: Adiana; Alacritech; AllAdvantage.com; BioSpace.com; Boldfish; Camitro; Cbyon; Chimeric Therapies; Conductus; Ellie Mae; Etranslate; Fusion Medical Technologies; Galileo Laboratories; Integrated Biosystems; K2 Optronics; Kasenna; Knowledge Networks; Lynx Therapeutics; MadeToOrder.com; MontaVista Software; Network Elements; Novocell; Nuance; Orquest; Packetcom; Personify; Pharmacyclics; Pharsight; PostX; Rainfinity; Remedy; Sapient (now WebMD); Surromed; Targesome; UpShot.com; Zing; and Zyomyx.

ALPINE TECHNOLOGY VENTURES

20300 Stevens Creek Boulevard, Suite 495
Cupertino, CA 95014
408-725-1810   fax: 408-725-1207
www.alpineventures.com

Chuck Chan, General Partner
David A. Lane, General Partner

total assets under management	*initial investment*	*year founded*
$72 Million	$500,000–5 Million	1995

Alpine Technology Ventures invests in California-based companies, preferably those with headquarters in Silicon Valley. Investments are made in seed- and early-stage technology companies that desire venture capital partners with strong operational backgrounds and hands-on experience in building successful companies.

ALTA PARTNERS

One Embarcadero Center, Suite 4050
San Francisco, CA 94111
415-362-4022   fax: 415-362-6178
www.altapartners.com

Farah Champsi, Managing Director

Jean Deleage, Managing Director

Garrett Gruener, Managing Director

Daniel Janney, Managing Director

Dr. Alix Marduel, Managing Director

Guy Paul Nohra, Managing Director

Marino R. Polestra, Managing Director

Khaled Nasr, Director

Robert Simon, Director

total assets under management	*initial investment*	*year founded*
$525 Million	$1–10 Million	1996

Alta Partners invests primarily in early-stage businesses led by experienced management teams with exceptional product concepts. Alta Partners prefers to act as a lead investor and active Board Member, providing assistance to the company as it develops. Although primarily focused on early-stage investments, Alta also makes later-stage investments to balance the investment portfolio. While West Coast focused, Alta makes investments worldwide.

Alta Partners specializes in life sciences and information technologies, which allows it to accurately assess investment opportunities. Alta is well positioned to use its established networks within each area of concentration to facilitate rapid review of prospective investments and conduct thorough due diligence. Furthermore, its ability to consistently add value to its investments is largely dependent upon its access to information, talent, and strong relationships, which are available to Alta Partners only through its deep, long-term commitment to each industry.

ALTOS VENTURES

2882 Sand Hill Road, Suite 100
Menlo Park, CA 94025
650-234-9771   fax: 650-233-9821
www.altosvc.com

Brandon S. Kim, General Partner

Han J. Kim, General Partner

Ho Nam, General Partner

Anthony P. Lee, Principal

Paul J. Marsili, CFO

total assets under management	*initial investment*	*year founded*
N/A	$500,000–2 Million	1993

Altos Ventures generally prefers to take a lead position and an active Board seat. It works with entrepreneurs to plan with foresight, recruit the best people, find customers, build alliances, and access capital. The Firm acts as a sounding board and provides an outside perspective.

Altos Ventures seeks early-stage investments, including seed rounds, and prefers opportunities in business-to-business e-commerce and software, e-tailing and Internet community, networking, and communications.

ALTOTECH VENTURES, LLC

707 Menlo Avenue, Suite 120
Menlo Park, CA 94025
650-330-0881   fax: 650-330-0885

Walter Lee, General Partner

Thanos Triant, General Partner

Gloria Wahl, General Partner

total assets under management	*initial investment*	*year founded*
$100 Million	$500,000–2 Million	2000

Headquartered in Menlo Park, California, AltoTech Ventures, LLC, is a $100 million early-stage firm focusing on enabling technologies and software for communications, networking products, and service in the business-to-business market. Priority is given to broadband and wireless applications.

AltoTech is an active participant in some of the companies in which it invests and is an SBIC company.

AMERICAN RIVER VENTURES, LP

1699 East Roseville Parkway
Roseville, CA 95661
916-783-5565   fax: 916-783-9038

John Kunhart, General Partner

Corley Phillips, General Partner

total assets under management	*initial investment*	*year founded*
N/A	$100,000–1 Million	2000

American River Ventures, LP provides equity capital to early-stage technology companies, with special emphasis on opportunities in Central California from Contra Costa to Nevada Counties and Northern Nevada. They invest primarily in companies that are engaged in various information technology industries, including telecommunications hardware and applications, business productivity applications including enterprise software, small business software, and B2B e-commerce, and outsourcing firms. They look for characteristics such as strong management teams, potentially large markets with strong market demand and attractive growth, the opportunity to create a unique and sustainable competitive advantage, and an industry that supports high valuations in both acquisitions and the public market.

Portfolio Companies: The Firm has prior investments in the following representative companies: Customer Link Systems; Flextronics; igo Corp (IGOC); Integrated Aviation Systems; Itronics; Netmosphere/Critical Path; Salu.net; Storactive; Telestream; Varatouch Corporation; Virtual Ink; and YY Software.

AMERICAN SECURITIES CAPITAL PARTNERS, L.P.

Chrysler Center
666 Third Avenue, 29th Floor
New York, NY 10017-4011
212-476-8000   fax: 212-697-5524
www.american-securities.com

Michael G. Fisch, Managing Director

David L. Horing, Managing Director

Charles D. Klein, Managing Director

Paul Rossetti, Managing Director

Glen B. Kaufman, Principal

total assets under management	*initial investment*	*year founded*
$1 Billion	$25–100 Million	1947

American Securities Capital Partners, L.P. (ASCP), a private investment firm, makes equity investments in privately and publicly held profitable companies. ASCP invests in the United States and Canada, with an interest in becoming a major stockholder in its investments. It funds the following types of transactions: majority positions in private companies, leveraged recapitalizations, minority positions in private and public companies, and off-balance sheet joint ventures with public companies. ASCP does not have an industry preference.

Portfolio Companies: Anthony International; Cambridge International, Inc.; Caribbean Restaurants, Inc.; CTB International Corp.; DRL Holdings, Inc.; El Pollo Loco, Inc.; Miltex Instrument Company, Inc.; and VUTEk Inc.

AMERIMARK CAPITAL CORPORATION

1111 West Mockingbird Lane, Suite 1111
Dallas, TX 75247
214-638-7878   fax: 214-638-7612
www.amcapital.com

Charles R. Martin, Managing Principal and CEO
Neil C. Marsh, Principal
James R. Normal, Principal

total assets under management	*initial investment*	*year founded*
$30 Million	$500,000–10 Million	1988

Amerimark Capital Corporation is a merchant and investment banking firm serving private and public companies in the manufacturing, distribution, and service industries. It will consider a majority or minority position in established, profitable companies with strong potential for growth. Amerimark Capital Corporation provides financial capital and solutions to business owners who require funding for growth or personal liquidity. Amerimark Capital funds companies in the United States.

Portfolio Companies: Amerimark Capital has more than 17 portfolio companies.

AMPERSAND VENTURES

162 South Rancho Santa Fe Road, Suite B70
Encinitas, CA 92024
760-632-0626   fax: 760-632-0284
www.ampersandventures.com

David J. Parker, General Partner
David L. Lyon, Executive in Residence

total assets under management	*initial investment*	*year founded*
$200 Million	$2–10 Million	1988

Ampersand's portfolio companies include early expansion-stage companies seeking capital for product development and growth. Ampersand also supplies capital to established businesses for acquisitions, recapitalizations, and providing liquidity to existing owners.

Ampersand's partners actively support the management teams of its portfolio companies. Its partners possess a unique combination of operational experience within the Firm's targeted industry sectors. Past positions held by members of Ampersand's team include president of Pacific Communication Sciences, Inc. (PCSI); president of Union Carbide's Electronics Division; chairman and CEO of Cabot Corporation; and president of AMAX Performance Materials Corporation. Ampersand also has an office in Wellesley, Massachusetts.

ANILA FUND

400 Channing Avenue	119 University Avenue	9973 Valley View Road,
Palo Alto, CA 94301	Palo Alto, CA 94301	Suite 100
650-833-5790		Eden Prairie, MN 55344
fax: 650-833-0590		
www.anila.com		

Moses Joseph, Managing Partner

Steve Bowden, Venture Partner

Gary Schlageter, Venture Partner

total assets under management	*initial investment*	*year founded*
$100 Million	$1–5 Million	1999

Anila Fund, a full-service venture capital firm, believes in nurturing early-stage companies in the optical and broadband communications market. Anila works closely with its portfolio companies to assist with marketing, finance and accounting, recruitment, engineering and technical consulting, and operations. Portfolio companies are co-located within Anila's offices, giving entrepreneurs immediate and ongoing contact with Anila's resources. Anila Fund will only consider investments in the United States.

Portfolio Companies: Bravida; eTrango; Napali Networks; and World Citizen.

ANTARES CAPITAL CORPORATION

7900 Miami Lakes Drive West
Miami Lakes, FL 33016
305-894-2888   fax: 305-894-3227

Randall E. Poliner, Managing Partner

total assets under management	*initial investment*	*year founded*
N/A	$500,000–3 Million	1993

Antares Capital Corporation is a private venture capital firm that invests equity capital in developmental and expansion-stage companies and in management buyout opportunities. Candidates for investment should have good management teams in place, have established sales, and be serving large and growing markets. There is no industry restriction, with the exclusion of real estate and mineral-exploration projects. Antares focuses on the Southeast and Texas areas and specializes in expansion financing, management buyouts of existing businesses, buyouts of minority shareholder positions, developmental capital, and special situations in which the management team desires an equity-oriented, experienced partner to be involved with the company.

ANTHEM CAPITAL, L.P.

16 South Calvert Street
Baltimore, MD 21202-1305
410-625-1510   fax: 410-625-1735
www.anthemcapital.com

William M. Gust, Managing General Partner

Gerald A. Schaafma, General Partner

C. Edward Spiva, General Partner

total assets under management	*initial investment*	*year founded*
$43 Million	$500,000–3 Million	1995

Anthem Capital invests regionally, with a general industry focus that includes information technology, technology, telecommunications, and life sciences.

Anthem prefers equity-expansion financing for small-growth businesses but may participate in other types of investments if deemed suitable.

Anthem invests alone or as a member of a larger financing syndicate.

APEX VENTURE PARTNERS

225 W. Washington, Suite 1450
Chicago, IL 60606
312-857-2800   fax: 312-857-1800
www.apexvc.com

James A. Johnson, Partner

George M. Middleman, Partner

Lon H. H. Chaw, Partner

Babu Ranganathan, Partner

Wayne Boulais, Principal

Amando Parker, Principal

total assets under management	*initial investment*	*year founded*
$200 Million	$500,000–3 Million	1998

Apex Venture Partners manages four Chicago-based private equity funds totaling $300 million. Apex invests primarily in early-stage companies that are devoted to products and services in the telecommunications, information technology, and software industries. Apex originates or leads 70 percent of its transactions and expects to work with entrepreneurial management in all phrases of building a successful business. Apex is a global investor, with emphasis on the United States.

APPLIED TECHNOLOGY

One Cranberry Hill
Lexington, MA 02421
781-862-8622   fax: 781-862-8367

Fred Bamber, Managing Director

total assets under management	*initial investment*	*year founded*
$75 Million	$250,000–1.5 Million	1983

Applied Technology identifies companies bringing significant innovations in the use of information technologies—innovations that will create substantial market opportunities. The investments primarily exploit the advantages of early-stage engagement, with first-round investments in the $250,000 to $1.5 million range.

The Firm seeks to maximize returns, while adhering to fundamental risk-minimization strategies: focusing on the specific areas where knowledge of the market and access to industry participants enables validation of product potential and performance; providing stage investments and including milestones for each investment phase; and staying active, typically taking a Board seat at each portfolio company.

The objective of Applied Technology's investment philosophy is to exploit the high returns available in early-stage venture investing while controlling the risk present in such situations. The Firm's investments are focused on the information industry, where the potential for high returns comes from three channels: sustained strong growth in the traditional industry; new markets emerging from the convergence of computing, communications, and media; and structural industry changes creating new opportunities.

APV TECHNOLOGY PARTNERS

535 Middlefield Road, Suite 150
Menlo Park, CA 94025
650-327-7871   fax: 650-327-7631
www.apvtp.com

Pete Bodine, General Partner

Jim Hinson, General Partner

William Stewart, General Partner

Spencer Tall, General Partner

total assets under management	*initial investment*	*year founded*
$210 Million	$1–10 Million	1995

APV Technology Partners is a venture capital firm based in Menlo Park, California, with funding primarily from large technology corporations. The firm is focused on seed- and early-stage investments in information technology companies with proprietary and leading-edge technologies. The APV Technology Partners funds have a unique structure that allows information technology corporations to gain access to and invest in cutting-edge, developmental technologies.

APV Technology Partners is one of a shrinking number of venture capital firms concentrating the vast majority of its financial and professional resources on early-stage information technology companies. Each investment is carefully selected to provide superior returns based on the following characteristics: a significant, growing market; a strong, experienced management team; a business model that addresses specific needs of the market; and a technology or product that represents a proprietary innovation or improvement that provides a sustainable competitive advantage. The Firm's intensive selection process is combined with active, hands-on investment management to reduce risk and build strong, successful companies.

Portfolio Companies: APV Technology Partners has invested in over 40 portfolio companies in the wireless, semiconductor, Internet, infrastructure, telecommunications, and software industries. Notable investments have included WebTV; E.piphany; and Lexar Media.

AQUA INTERNATIONAL PARTNERS, L.P.
345 California Street, Suite 3300
San Francisco, CA 94104
415-743-1505   fax: 415-743-1504
www.waterfund.com

William K. Reilly, CEO and Founder
John G. Sylvia, Partner

total assets under management	*initial investment*	*year founded*
$232 Million	$5–25 Million	1997

Aqua International Partners, L.P., an investment firm, makes private equity investments in companies that provide water or water-related products and services to the water sector. It will invest in operating and special purpose companies that are devoted to: bottled water; water purification and treatment operations; manufacturing equipment or products for commercial, industrial, and residential water users; and other related activities or services regarding the purification, treatment, and supply of water. Aqua International Partners invests in common equity, preferred stock, or debt with warrants or conversion features. It invests worldwide.

ARBOR PARTNERS, LLC
130 South First Street
Ann Arbor, MI 48104
734-668-9000   fax: 734-669-4195
www.arborpartners.com

Stephen A. Swanson, Managing Director
Richard L. Crandall, Managing Director
Donald J. Walker, Managing Director
Richard P. Eldwick, Managing Director
Peter D. Gray, Technology Partner

total assets under management	*initial investment*	*year founded*
$37.8 Million	$500,000–5 Million	1995

Arbor Venture Partners, LLC, invests primarily, but not exclusively, in companies based in the Midwest, with emphasis on opportunities in electronic commerce. The Firm acts as lead investor in some local opportunities and also co-invests in other appropriate opportunities nationwide.

Portfolio Companies: BeautifulIsland.com; BlueGill Technologies; Bulbs.com; CMS Technologies; E-time; Genitor Corporation; Global Music Network; MaxFunds.com; Solid Speed Inc.; Steeplechase Software, Inc.; and US Internetworking Inc.

ARCH VENTURE PARTNERS

1000 Second Avenue, Suite 3700
Seattle, WA 98104
206-674-3028   fax: 206-674-3026
www.archventure.com

Steve Lazarus, Managing Director
Keith L. Crandell, Managing Director
Robert T. Nelsen, Managing Director
Clinton W. Bybee, Managing Director
Karen Kerr, Managing Director
Alex Knight, Managing Director

total assets under management	*initial investment*	*year founded*
$600 Million	$250,000–10 Million	1992

ARCH Venture Partners invests in the development of seed- and early-stage technology companies that have the potential to grow rapidly into successful businesses. It invests primarily in companies co-founded with leading scientists and entrepreneurs, concentrating on bringing to market innovations in the Internet and e-commerce, information technology, life sciences, and physical sciences.

ARCH currently manages five funds totaling over $600 million and has invested in the founding venture round for more than 75 companies.

Portfolio Companies: ARCH Venture Partners has over 75 portfolio companies.

ASPEN VENTURES

1000 Fremont Avenue, Suite 200
Los Altos, CA 94024
650-917-5670   fax: 650-917-5677
www.aspenventures.com

Alex Cliento, General Partner

E. David Crockett, Partner

Debra L. Schiling, Partner

Thaddeus J. Whalen, Partner

total assets under management	*initial investment*	*year founded*
$75 Million	$1.5 Million	1985

Aspen Ventures is a venture capital firm focused on early-stage information technology investments. Aspen has offices in both Northern and Southern California. Its major investment theme is software solutions bought by commercial customers. The Firm does not focus on consumer products or the medical/health markets. The General Partners of Aspen Ventures combine extensive business and venture capital backgrounds and are active investors.

ASSET MANAGEMENT COMPANY

2275 East Bayshore Road, Suite 150
Palo Alto, CA 94303
650-494-7400   fax: 650-856-1826
www.assetman.com

Franklin P. Johnson Jr., Founding Partner

Bennett S. Dubin, Partner

Dr. Graham Crooke, Partner

total assets under management	*initial investment*	*year founded*
$500 Million	$500,000–3 Million	1965

Asset Management Company focuses on high-potential, technology-based seed- and early-stage companies in the biological and information sciences. Areas of interest in the biological sciences include biopharmaceuticals, gene and cell therapies, medical devices, diagnostics, research and clinical laboratory instrumentation, and health-care information services. Areas of interest in the information sciences include multimedia, Intra- and Internet applications, networking, telecommunications, mobile computing, and tools.

Portfolio Companies: Airflash; Amgen; Applied Micro Circuits Corporation; Boole & Baggage; IDEC Pharmaceuticals Corporation; KillerBiz, Libritas; Noosh; Novare Surgical; Searchbutton; Prime Advantage; Simplexity; Tandem; and VetCentric.

ASSOCIATED VENTURE INVESTORS

1 First Street, Suite 2
Los Altos, CA 94022
650-949-9862   fax: 650-949-8510
www.avicapital.com

Brian J. Grossi, General Partner
Barry M. Weinman, General Partner
Peter L. Wolken, General Partner

total assets under management	*initial investment*	*year founded*
$75 Million	$500,000–4 Million	1982

Associated Management Partners III (AVI Management) is the general partner of a family of professionally managed venture capital partnerships specializing in seed- and early-stage investments in high-technology companies that are positioned for high-growth segments of the information technologies market. Active participation in the seed and start-up phases has been a hallmark of the AVI general partners. In addition to capital, the Firm brings extensive operating experiences and a network of contacts in the financial, business, and technical worlds to assist the emerging company in developing to its full potential.

AVI, by focusing on new information technology companies, will profit from the impending convergence of computers and communications. Investment areas include software, enabling hardware, publishing and electronic distribution, mobile computing and communications, and multimedia. Its vision is to share the dreams of visionary entrepreneurs and to create major new industrial companies.

Portfolio Companies: 3COM; Apple Computer; Altera; ASK Group; Bell Microelectronics; Cadnetix; Caere; Cypress Semiconductor; Extreme Networks; Information Storage Devices; Microchip; Network Peripherals; Pinnacle Systems; Qualix Group; Radius; S3; Tokos Medical; and Ventritex.

AUSTIN VENTURES

701 North Brazos Street, Suite 1400
Austin, TX 78701
512-485-1900   fax: 512-476-3952
www.austinventures.com

Joe Aragona, General Partner
Ken Deangelis, General Partner
Jeff Garvey, General Partner

Ed Olkkola, General Partner

John Thornton, General Partner

Blaine Wesner, General Partner

total assets under management	*initial investment*	*year founded*
$768 Million	$100,000–25 Million	N/A

Austin Ventures invests in management teams of early-stage technology and services firms with high growth potential. Austin Ventures's investment focus is on applications and infrastructure, business-to-business e-commerce and services, business-to-consumer commerce and media, communications, and semiconductors.

Portfolio Companies: Austin Ventures has more than 80 portfolio companies.

AXIOM VENTURE PARTNERS, L.P.

One Post Street, Suite 2525
San Francisco, CA 94104
415-434-9999   fax: 415-434-0505
www.axiomventures.com

Barry Bronfin, General Partner

Samuel McKay, General Partner

Alan M. Mendelson, General Partner

Linda Sonntag, Ph.D., General Partner

total assets under management	*initial investment*	*year founded*
$97 Million	$1–5 Million	1994

Axiom focuses on venture capital investments in the medical/health-care and media/communications/information areas. Its investments range from seed to late stage, with a concentration on later stage.

Each investment opportunity receives the attention of an Axiom partner and is evaluated on its specific merits through a comprehensive due diligence process. Due diligence focuses on management, technology, intellectual property, market potential, product positioning, and financial projections. Axiom prefers working with management teams who have experience in venture-like situations, who are developing platform technologies, and who provide a significant barrier to competitive entry or at least offer a meaningful lead time to market. The company must also have substantial revenue and earning potential. Axiom considers deals on a national level.

AZTEC VENTURE NETWORK, LLC

3104 Fourth Avenue
San Diego, CA 92103
619-725-4947   fax: 619-239-5125

Joe Sullivan

Bob Cerasoli

Bob Watkins

total assets under management	*initial investment*	*year founded*
N/A	$50,000–1 Million	1999

Aztec Venture Network, LLC (AVN), is a San Diego–based seed capital and mentoring firm available to qualified early-stage Southern California companies in need of financing and/or business coaching expertise. Generally, AVN seeks those companies operating in the technology sectors of communications, telecommunications, Internet, computer hardware, software, or peripherals.

AVN takes its role as an Angel capital resource well beyond providing early investment support. Many times, start-up teams are equally in need of mentoring assistance in order to complete their business plan. AVN provides portfolio companies with access to the professional experience of its investors in all areas of business, including manufacturing, executive and board recruitment, operations, engineering, finance, marketing, product development, and strategic planning.

BACHOW & ASSOCIATES, INC.

Three Bala Plaza East, Suite 502
Bala Cynwyd, PA 19004
610-660-4900   fax: 610-660-4930
www.bachow.com

Paul S. Bachow, Senior Managing Director

Sal A. Grasso, Managing Director

Frank H. Nowaczek, Managing Director

Jay D. Seid, Managing Director

total assets under management	*initial investment*	*year founded*
$200 Million	$5–25 Million	1985

Bachow & Associates, Inc. seeks investment opportunities in high-growth businesses within the United States. It is particularly interested in: technology, communications, service businesses, manufacturing, and vertical software. Bachow & Associates prefers that its portfolio companies already have products or services with a proven market demand and should be profitable in the near future.

Portfolio Companies: Acme Paging, Anadigics; Bachtel Cellular; Bentley Systems; Coastel; GoCom Communications; Digital Access, Inc.; Digital Microwave; Discovery Schools; Genus; OutSource International; Paradigm Geophysical; VertiCom; and VISTA Information Solutions.

BANCBOSTON VENTURES, INC.

175 Federal Street, 10th Floor
Boston, MA 02110
617-434-2509   fax: 617-434-1153
www.bancbostonventures.com

Frederick M. Fritz, President

Marcia Bates, Managing Director

total assets under management	*initial investment*	*year founded*
$1.5 Billion	$2–10 Million	1959

BancBoston Ventures is the venture capital investment arm of BancBoston, providing early-stage venture capital to emerging-growth companies in the information technology and health-care sectors. Its sister company, BancBoston Capital, provides later-stage capital options, from equity sponsorship to co-investment and mezzanine capital for buyouts, recapitalization, and expansion of mid-size. For 40 years, BancBoston Capital and BancBoston Ventures have invested $3 billion in over 400 companies around the world and are supported by offices in Boston, London, Hong Kong, Buenos Aires, and San Paulo.

Portfolio Companies: BancBoston Ventures invests in over 90 portfolio companies.

BATTERSON VENTURE PARTNERS, LLC

303 West Madison Street, Suite 1110
Chicago, IL 60606
312-269-0300   fax: 312-269-0021
www.battersonvp.com

Leonard Batterson, Chairman

total assets under management	*initial investment*	*year founded*
N/A	N/A	1995

Batterson Venture Partners, LLC (BVP), is a Chicago-based venture capital management firm that invests in high-technology opportunities throughout the United States. Leonard Batterson founded BVP in late 1995, together with a group of high net worth investors, successful entrepreneurs, and venture capitalists. They invest and build major high technology companies through the application of classic venture capital techniques. BVP actively invests and manages venture capital for its high net worth investors on a transaction-by-transaction basis.

BATTERY VENTURES

901 Mariner's Island Boulevard, Suite 475
San Mateo, CA 94404
650-372-3939 fax: 650-372-3930
www.battery.com

20 William Street, Suite 200
Wellesley, MA 02481
781-577-1000 fax: 781-577-1001

Anthony M. Abate, General Partner

Thomas J. Crotty, General Partner

Oliver D. Curme, General Partner

Todd A. Dagres, General Partner

Michael B. Darby, General Partner

Richard D. Frisbie, General Partner

Morgan M. Jones, General Partner

Kenneth F. Lawler, General Partner

Ravi Mohan, General Partner

Mark H. Sherman, General Partner

Scott R. Tobin, General Partner

total assets under management	*initial investment*	*year founded*
$1.8 Billion	$5–25 Million	1983

Battery Ventures invests nationally in high-technology companies, primarily in the communications and software industries. Most investments are made in both early-stage and emerging companies (revenues from $1–10 million), although both start-ups and later-stage companies are considered. After an investment is made, Battery is an active investor though its position on the Board of Directors.

In addition to strategic advice, Battery typically provides guidance with respect to management additions, financings, and mergers/acquisitions.

Portfolio Companies: Battery Ventures has over 60 portfolio companies.

BAY PARTNERS

10600 North De Anza Boulevard, Suite 100
Cupertino, CA 95014-2031
408-725-2444   fax: 408-446-4502
www.baypartners.com

Neal Dempsey, General Partner

John Freidenrich, General Partner

Loring Knoblauch, General Partner

Chris Noble, General Partner

Bob Williams, General Partner

total assets under management	*initial investment*	*year founded*
$121 Million	$1–10 Million	1976

Bay Partners offers financial operating and strategic planning expertise of partners, board membership, banking assistance, acting as lead investor in raising initial or second-round capital, form action of equity partnerships for seed and start-up financings. Bay Partners invests mainly in the Southwest and Northwest but predominantly in California.

Bay Partners considers deals in various industries, although Internet-related industries are preferred. Some deals that have been funded by Bay Partners include Exodus Communication, Audio Base, NetManage, Concord Communication, and more.

Portfolio Companies: Bay Partners has over 50 portfolio companies.

BENCHMARK CAPITAL

2480 Sand Hill Road, Suite 200
Menlo Park, CA 94025
650-854-8180   fax: 650-854-8183
www.benchmark.com

Alex Balkanski, General Partner

Dave Beirne, General Partner

Bruce Dunlevie, General Partner

Bill Gurley, General Partner

Kevin Harvey, General Partner

Bob Kagle, General Partner

Andy Rachleff, General Partner

total assets under management	*initial investment*	*year founded*
N/A	$3–5 Million	N/A

Benchmark's investment strategy is to be the first venture investor in technology companies that seek to create new markets. It focuses on early-stage investing and takes a labor-intensive, service-oriented approach in markets where it has direct experience. These markets include consumer devices, e-commerce, application services, networking equipment, semiconductor, software, and telecommunications services.

    Portfolio Companies: Benchmark Capital has over 45 portfolio companies.

BERKELEY INTERNATIONAL CAPITAL CORPORATION

650 California Street, Suite 2800
San Francisco, CA 94108-2609
415-249-0450   fax: 415-392-7617
www.berkeleyvc.com

Arthur I. Trueger, Chairman

Michael J. Mayer, President

total assets under management	*initial investment*	*year founded*
$4.6 Billion	$5–15 Million	N/A

Berkeley International Capital Corporation (BICC) arranges private placement investments into rapidly growing technology and medical companies. It is a wholly owned subsidiary of London Pacific Group Limited, a diversified international financial services firm. Its investments typically serve as development capital for later-stage companies that are profitable or within six months of achieving profitability.

    Portfolio Companies: 3Com Corporation; Cirrus Logic, Inc.; LSI Logic Corporation; and Oracle.

Bertelsmann Ventures

111 El Paseo
Santa Barbara, CA 93101
805-568-1514   fax: 805-568-1534
www.bvfund.com

Jan Henric Buettner, General Partner

Thomas Gieselmann, General Partner

Wolfgang Rose, General Partner

Mathias Schilling, General Partner

total assets under management	*initial investment*	*year founded*
N/A	$2–5 Million	N/A

Bertelsmann Ventures (BV) focuses solely on C2C and B2B services, enabling technologies, and wireless applications. BV typically invests between $10 million and $20 million over the life cycle of an investment. BV invests nationwide, primarily in early-stage firms.

Portfolio Companies: Ants.com; BeMANY.com; Done.com; ExertCity.com; and eGroups.com.

Bessemer Venture Partners

535 Middlefield Road, Suite 245
Menlo Park, CA 94025
650-853-7000   fax: 650-853-7001
www.bvp.com

David Cowan, Managing Partner

Rob Soni, Managing Partner

Felda Hardymon, General Partner

Bob Buescher, General Partner

Joanna Strober, General Partner

Bruce Graham, General Partner

Bob Goodman, General Partner

Gautam Prakash, General Partner

total assets under management	*initial investment*	*year founded*
N/A	$100,000–10 Million	1911

Bessemer Venture Partners invests approximately $400 million each year, while other Bessemer entities manage more than $2 billion of investments in public and private non–venture capital assets. BVP is an autonomous entity of 25 professionals with offices in California, Massachusetts, and New York. Its efforts are entirely devoted to financing and building young companies.

Portfolio Companies: Circe Biomedical; eMed.com; eToys.com; Furniture.com; HotJobs.com; LightLogic; MindSpring; MotherNature.com; PowerTel; Register.com; Staples; and Traffic.com.

BioVentures West

101 N. Wilmot Road, Suite 600
Tucson, AZ 85711-3365
520-748-4400   fax: 520-748-0025
www.rctbvw.com

Fred G. Voinsky, M.D., President

total assets under management	*initial investment*	*year founded*
$30 Million	$100,000–1 Million	1997

BioVentures West exclusively invests in companies operating in the life-science arena. BioVentures West invests in Southern California companies, with a focus on technologies derived from research institutions.

Technologies targeted are those that effectively address important market needs, show reasonable cost to gain proof of principle, demonstrate significant competitive advantage, exhibit acceptable profitability projections, or offer reasonable prospects for valuable patents.

The initial objective for a particular invention is to increase its attractiveness by reducing its economic uncertainty, typically through investment in research to obtain additional proof of principle, to perfect patent monopolies, or to asses regulatory requirements.

In addition to technology enhancement, BioVentures West may develop comprehensive business plans, nurture the early-stage enterprise, recruit a management team, and syndicate or invest in additional venture funding.

Blue Capital Management, L.L.C.

1925 Century Park East, Suite 2320   152 West 57th Street, 11th Floor
Los Angeles, CA 90067   New York, NY 10019
310-286-2186   fax: 310-286-2187   212-956-0500   fax: 212-245-6520
www.bluecapital.com

Rick Beckett, Managing Director

Chris Gagnon, Managing Director
Chip Hughes, Managing Director
Robert Taylor, Managing Director

total assets under management	*initial investment*	*year founded*
$112 Million	$8–20 Million	1997

Blue Capital Management L.L.C., a private equity investment firm, prides itself in its expertise with growth opportunities, "created" opportunities, operational turnarounds, and analytically complex opportunities. It is interested in: healthcare provision and insurance, telecommunications, lodging and leisure, medical devices and supplies, basic manufacturing, lifestyle brands, and print media. It is also interested in companies that have or can create a "franchise" value. Blue Capital Management seeks opportunities throughout the United States.

    Portfolio Companies: AirClic, Inc.; Decorative Concepts, Inc.; FNX Limited; Great Lakes Computer Source, Inc.; M2 Automotive, Inc.; and Quivox Systems.

BLUEFISH VENTURES

990 Avenue of the Americas, Suite 17J
New York, NY 10018
212-290-5317   fax: 212-695-3449
www.bluefishventures.com

Alex Millar, Partner
David Istock, Partner

total assets under management	*initial investment*	*year founded*
N/A	N/A	N/A

Bluefish Ventures is a venture capital firm based in New York City that invests in seed- and early-stage Internet and technology companies. Bluefish targets markets with significant growth potential and specifically companies involved in, but not limited to, Internet infrastructure, broadband capacity solutions, business-to-business e-commerce systems, and wireless applications. Key criteria when making an investment decision include the strength of the management team, the potential size of the company's target market, and its competitive advantages.

BOSTON FINANCIAL & EQUITY CORPORATION

20 Overland Street
Boston, MA 02215
617-267-2900   fax: 617-437-7601

Adolf F. Monosson, President

Deborah Monosson, Senior Vice President

total assets under management	*initial investment*	*year founded*
N/A	$100,000–5 Million	1968

Boston Financial & Equity Corporation is a venture leasing business for seed-, start-up, and later-stage growth companies. Spot factoring for venture-backed and publicly traded companies is also available. The Firm's geographical investment strategy allows it to invest in all areas of the United States across various industries.

Industry preferences are as follows: biotechnology, broadcasting/cable/radio, business services, communications equipment, computer hardware/software/services, electronic equipment and components, medical-health devices and services, pharmaceuticals, and publishing/advertising.

BOSTON MILLENNIA PARTNERS

30 Rowes Wharf, Suite 330
Boston, MA 02110
617-428-5150   fax: 617-428-5160
www.millenniapartners.com

Dana Callow Jr., Managing General Partner

Martin J. Hernon, General Partner

Robert S. Sherman, Partner

Suresh Shaqnmugham, Partner

Frank P. Pinto, Partner

Robert W. Jevon, Partner

Thomas A. Penn, Partner

Jean Yves Lagarde, Principal

Enmi Sung, Associate

Mike P. Larsen, Associate

Robert Dyer, Analyst

Sean Riley, Analyst

total assets under management	*initial investment*	*year founded*
$600 Million	$5–15 Million	1997

Boston Millennia Partners provides private equity financing to high-growth companies in the telecommunications, information technology, and health-care and life sciences industries. The Firm shares a common goal with its investors and the management teams in which it invests: to build enduring, successful companies that result in personal fulfillment and superior financial returns.

Boston Millennia Partners invests in companies at various stages of development, from the first round of institutional funding to later-stage expansion opportunities. It seeks investments in which the risks associated with technology development and market development have been adequately addressed. Typically, these companies will have ongoing revenues from an existing product or service.

Portfolio Companies: Brooks Fiber Properties; Deltagen; Double Twist; ECCubed; Entigo; HotJobs; Inventa; iVillage; NetGenesis; Parexel International; TriVergent Communications; UniSite; Verio, Inc.; VIA Networks; and Yantra.

BOULDER VENTURES LIMITED
500 Washington Street, Suite 720
San Francisco, CA 94111
415-374-8721   fax: 415-381-6125
www.boulderventures.com

Peter Roshko, General Partner

Andy Jones, General Partner

Kyle Lefkoff, General Partner

Lawrence Macks, General Partner

Josh Fidler, General Partner

Todd Jaguez-Fissori, Associate

Sara Gutterman, Associate

total assets under management	*initial investment*	*year founded*
$115 Million	$2–8 Million	1995

Boulder Ventures Limited manages a venture capital fund out of offices in San Francisco, California; Boulder, Colorado; and Baltimore, Maryland. Boulder

Ventures identifies qualified entrepreneurs and provides the funding, contacts, and experience needed to succeed in today's highly competitive environment. Boulder Ventures is dedicated to helping start-up, early-stage, and emerging-growth companies.

Approximately 80 percent of its investments are in information technology. Another area of interest is life sciences. Its Partners believe that exceptional investment opportunities will be available in these sectors in the next decade, especially in the geographic areas in which Boulder Ventures has offices.

Portfolio Companies: Cogent Communication; Entelos, Inc.; Entevo Corp.; Finali; Interland; Medical Business Applications, Inc.; Restaurant Pro; and YAFO.

BRAD PEERY CAPITAL INC.

145 Chapel Drive
Mill Valley, CA 94941
415-389-0625   fax: 415-389-1336
www.peery-inc.com

total assets under management	*initial investment*	*year founded*
$50 Million	$100,000 Million	1993

Brad Peery Capital Inc. is an investment advisory firm that provides investment management in the communications industry. It seeks to invest globally in communications companies, including service providers, equipment, the Internet, software, and semiconductors. Brad Peery Capital invests in both private and public early-stage companies worldwide.

Portfolio Companies: @Motion; AccessLan; Amber Networks; Anda Networks; Centillium; Ceon; Cignal Global; Colo.Com; Com 21; e.spire; eCharge; eFusion; LongBoard; Manage.com; Mayan Networks; Packet Engines; Pluris; Sonoma Systems; TopLayer; Tut Systems; VeloCom; and WavTrace.

BRANTLEY PARTNERS, L.P.

20600 Chagrin Boulevard, Suite 1150
Cleveland, OH 44122
216-283-4800   fax: 216-283-5324

Kevin J. Cook, Associate

total assets under management	*initial investment*	*year founded*
$300 Million	$5–10 Million	1987

Brantley Partners is a private equity organization with offices in Ohio and California. Since the Firm's inception in 1987, it has been a lead investor in companies in a variety of manufacturing, technology and service industries throughout the United States. Brantley always acts as an originator and lead investor in its investments. Its professionals have extensive experience in identifying, evaluating, selecting, negotiating, and closing investments in privately held companies over the last 10 years. Brantley has established a significant track record in successfully building businesses.

While Brantley has invested in companies in all stages of development, it focuses almost exclusively on acquisition-strategy investments. This investment approach entails identifying large, highly fragmented industries that are being driven toward consolidation by economic and competitive market forces. Once these industries have been identified, Brantley attempts to back superior management teams and establish a platform company.

Typically, Brantley's equity in a company represents the initial round of institutional capital. Brantley commits between $5 million and $10 million and can invest up to $15 million in any company. BVP will invest funds throughout the United States in a variety of industries that meet its acquisition template.

BRENTWOOD VENTURE CAPITAL

1920 Main Street, Suite 820
Irvine, CA 92614-7227
949-251-1010   fax: 949-251-1011
www.brentwoodvc.com

William J. Link, Ph.D., General Partner

total assets under management	initial investment	year founded
$408 Million	$500,000–8 Million	1972

Over the past 25 years, Brentwood Venture Capital has invested over $400 million in more than 300 entrepreneurial companies. Brentwood takes an active, hands-on approach to selecting and building its investments, helping to create leading-edge companies in today's most important industries: computer networking, the Internet, enterprise software, and health care. Its geographic focus is primarily California.

Brentwood currently has 18 employees and prefers to make equity investments in start-up and development-stage companies. However, it also makes seed investments and participates in later rounds in companies with exceptional growth and profitability potential.

Portfolio Companies: Brentwood Venture Capital has over 95 portfolio companies.

BRISTOL INVESTMENT GROUP, INC.

300 Park Avenue
New York, NY 10022
212-571-6306   fax: 212-705-4292

Alan P. Donenfeld, President

total assets under management	*initial investment*	*year founded*
$35 Million	$500,000–10 Million	1990

Bristol Investment Group, Inc., is an equity capital provider. Specializing in second-stage, mezzanine, bridge, and buyouts, Bristol has experience in financing later-stage companies. Bristol will invest in companies needing immediate capital in order to take a lead role in the company raising capital. Bristol will also assist with other bridge capital or IPOs.

BROADVIEW CAPITAL PARTNERS LLC

950 Tower Lane, 18th Floor
Foster City, CA 94404-2130
650-356-6000   fax: 650-356-6001
www.broadviewcapital.com

Stephen Bachmann, Managing Director
Steven Brooks, Managing Director
John Helm, Managing Director

total assets under management	*initial investment*	*year founded*
N/A	$10–50 Million	N/A

Broadview Capital Partners's philosophy is to help build world-class enterprises in the IT, communications, and digital media industries by seeking and supporting outstanding management teams with bold aspirations and strategic vision. Broadview Capital Partners provides not only capital but also the deep industry experience, relationships, and knowledge necessary to help achieve shared long-term success.

Broadview Capital Partners is committed to the success of the management teams of its portfolio companies and of entrepreneurs driven to build world-class companies.

Portfolio Companies: Business Engine Software Corporation; Extricity; RedHerring; Cogent Communication; and Xuma.

BURRILL & COMPANY

120 Montgomery Street, Suite 1370
San Francisco, CA 94104
415-743-3160   fax: 415-743-3161
www.burrillandco.com

Roger E. Wyse, Ph.D., Managing Director
Michael K. Ullman, Managing Director

total assets under management	*initial investment*	*year founded*
$250 Million	$1–5 Million	1997

Burrill & Company, a San Francisco–based life sciences–focused merchant bank, is the general partner of several venture capital funds: the Burrill Biotechnology Capital Fund, the Burrill Agbio Capital Fund, the Burrill Animal Health Capital Fund, and the Burrill Nutraceuticals Capital Fund. These funds invest in companies having bio-based technologies broadly applicable to the life sciences industry (biotechnology, pharmaceuticals, agriculture, animal health, nutraceuticals, biomaterials and bioprocesses, and related bio-based technologies) at two stages of development: in the early venture capital financing stage but generally not "seed-round" investments; and at the mezzanine round, often in spinouts from established entities.

CALLIER INTERESTS

950 Echo Lane, Suite 335
Houston, TX 77024
713-973-7722   fax: 713-973-8237

James T. Callier, General Partner

total assets under management	*initial investment*	*year founded*
$90 Million	$250,000–10 Million	1982

Callier Interests is interested in companies with industrial/commercial product lines or services requiring marketing, production, or general management expertise; and meaningful market share or potential in its industry niche.

It has no interest in retail, real estate, or extractive industries, offered with characteristics of turnaround. Venture investments include software and biotechnology.

The Cambria Group

1600 El Camino, Suite 155
Menlo Park, CA 94025
650-329-8600 fax: 650-329-8601
www.cambriagroup.com

Paul L. Davies III, Managing Principal
Christopher Sekula, Principal

total assets under management	*initial investment*	*year founded*
N/A	$250,000–5 Million	1996

The Cambria Group is a private investment company that acquires and invests in small- and mid-sized businesses with established operating histories. Cambria was established to fill a void in the private equity markets to pursue businesses that are fundamentally attractive but that lack both the high-growth characteristics sought by traditional venture capitalists and the scale required to interest most fund-based buyout firms. Cambria's industry focus includes manufacturing, processing, distribution, transportation, resource, or service businesses.

Cambria focuses on stable, profitable businesses with revenues of under $40 million and valuations of under $20 million. The Firm seeks four critical elements in every situation—a fundamentally sound and durable business; availability of a strong management team; a fair purchase price in relation to historical performance and profitability; and opportunities for management and Cambria to add value to the business over time.

Portfolio Companies: Classroom Connect; Cobblestone Golf Group; Crossbow Technology; DSA/Phototech; FleetPride; and WorldPoint Logistics.

Canaan Partners

2884 Sand Hill Road, Suite 115
Menlo Park, CA 94025
650-854-8092 fax: 650-854-8127
www.canaan.com

Harry T. Rein, Founder

Deepak Kamra, General Partner

total assets under management	*initial investment*	*year founded*
1.2 Billion	$5–25 Million	1987

Canaan's investment strategy focuses on providing capital for growth, and the Firm is comfortable working with entrepreneurial companies across three major industry sectors: information technology, health care and medical, and financial services.

   Portfolio Companies: Capstone Turbine; CommerceOne; Copper Mountain; Double Click; E-stamp Intraware; iPrint.com; Mortgage.com; ONI System; and Saleslogix.

CAPITAL INSIGHTS

P.O. Box 27162
Greenville, SC 29616-2162
864-423-3060   fax: N/A
www.capitalinsights.com

John Warner

total assets under management	*initial investment*	*year founded*
$15 Million	N/A	1982

Capital Insights invests in high-growth companies with outstanding leadership in the Carolinas. Key managers in the organization should have previous experience with successful high-growth companies. Capital Insights has no industry preference, but the company should be able to demonstrate that its industry provides an opportunity for the company to achieve a premium valuation. Capital Insights does not have a stage of development preference, but the company should have a clear strategy for creating liquidity through a strategic sale or IPO within five years. A description of portfolio companies can be found at its Web site.

THE CAPITAL NETWORK INCORPORATED

3925 West Baker Lane, Suite 406
Austin, TX 78759-5321
512-305-0826   fax: 512-305-0836
www.thecapitalnetwork.com

David H. Gerhardt, President

George Watson, Chairman of the Board of Directors

George Kozmetsky, Chairman of the Advisory Board

total assets under management	*initial investment*	*year founded*
$300 Million	$100,000–5 Million	1989

The Capital Network, Inc., is an economic development organization that introduces entrepreneurial ventures to investors. The Capital Network, Inc., has a comprehensive network throughout the entire United States.

CAPITAL SOUTHWEST CORPORATION

12900 Preston Road, Suite 700
Dallas, TX 75230
972-233-8242   fax: 972-233-7362

William R. Thomas, President

Howard Thomas, Investment Associate

Patrick F. Hamner, Vice President

Tim M. Smith, Vice President and Treasurer

total assets under management	*initial investment*	*year founded*
$324 Million	$1–6 Million	1961

Capital Southwest Corporation is a venture capital investment company whose objective is to achieve capital appreciation through businesses believed to have favorable growth potential. The company and its wholly owned small business investment company subsidiary have provided capital to support the growth and development of small- and medium-sized businesses in varied industries throughout the United States. Capital Southwest Corporation will invest anywhere in the United States.

CAPITOL HEALTH PARTNERS LP

2620 P. Street NW
Washington, D.C. 20007
202-342-6300   fax: 202-342-6399

Debora Guthrie, General Partner

Joseph F. Kelly Jr., General Partner

total assets under management	*initial investment*	*year founded*
$57 Million	$500,000–38 Million	1995

Capitol Health Partners LP is a $57 million venture capital firm that provides growth equity financing and business experience to entrepreneurial private health-care services companies on a national basis. Capitol Health is presently raising a second fund of $200 million of private equity. The second fund will make equity heath-care services investments in the United States and Western Europe.

Capitol Health Partners LP invests in early-stage companies, with an emphasis on health care and related industries.

CAPSTONE VENTURES

3000 Sand Hill Road, Building 1, Suite 290
Menlo Park, CA 94025
650-854-2523   fax: 650-854-9010
www.capstonevc.com

Eugene L. Fischer, General Partner
Barbara L. Santry, General Partner

total assets under management	*initial investment*	*year founded*
$54 Million	$500,000–2 Million	1996

Capstone Ventures is a venture capital firm focused on investing in early-stage companies that target health-care markets or that use enabling information technology, including Internet technology, to improve productivity in rapidly growing vertical markets. Capstone Ventures prefers to invest in companies located in the West or upper Midwest.

Capstone Ventures invests in early-stage health-care companies that provide an improved level of care compelling cost/benefit dynamics. It is particularly interested in businesses where health care and information technology come together.

Capstone Ventures also invests in early- to expansion-stage companies that apply known technology, via a distinctive service model, to new markets such that their customers achieve a significant increase in productivity. It particularly likes businesses with a "toll" transaction fee or other types of recurring revenue streams that are the result of long-term customer relationships.

CELERITY PARTNERS

11111 Santa Monica Boulevard, Suite 1127
Los Angeles, CA 90025
310-268-1710   fax: 310-268-1712
www.celeritypartners.com

Stephen E. Adamson, President
Mark R. Benham, Co-Founder
Clifford A. Lyon, CFO

total assets under management	*initial investment*	*year founded*
$250 Million	$5–20 Million	1995

Celerity Partners knows the importance of expert management and seeks long-term partnerships with the management teams of its portfolio companies. The Firm is involved with management buyouts and recapitalizations and seeks investment returns through a sale, recapitalization, or initial public offering within a three- to five-year range. Celerity Partners will fund companies in the United States.

   Portfolio Companies: Advanced Accessory Systems; AKrion; Chaparral Network Storage; Dynamic Details; Financial Pacific; Imperial Technology; Mediaplex; Pinnacle Automation; Rapid Design Service; SMTC; and StarCom.

CENTENNIAL VENTURES

1428 Fifteenth Street	600 Congress Park	1330 Post Oak Boulevard
Denver, CO 80202-1318	Suite 200	Suite 1525
303-405-7500	Austin, TX 78701	Houston, TX 77056
fax: 303-405-7575	512-505-4500	713-627-9200
www.centennial.com	fax: 512-505-4500	fax: 713-627-9292

Duncan T. Butler Jr., Managing Principal, Austin
Adam Goldman, Managing Principal, Denver
Steven C. Halstedt, Managing Principal, Denver
David C. Hull Jr., Managing Principal, Houston
Jeffrey H. Schutz, Managing Principal, Denver

total assets under management	*initial investment*	*year founded*
$750 Million	N/A	1981

Centennial Ventures makes impact investments in communications convergence industries. Centennial is more than a source of financing; its Partners provide entrepreneurs with ongoing assistance in each seed-, early-stage, or Centennial-founded company in which it invests. Centennial helps entrepreneurial teams build companies that become industry leaders by offering unique resources in four critical areas facing rapid, high-growth companies: people, plans, money, and partners.

Portfolio Companies: Agilera.com; ATG Group; Broadband Services; ClearSource; Crown Castle International; Cypress Communications; Ecrix Corporation; Evoke Communications; Evolution Networks; Fantasma Networks; Gabriel Communications; Grande Communications; HighGround Systems; InterNAP Network Services; iVAST; SiteShell; Tachyon; UMONGO; Vestor esp; VeloCom; and VIA.NET.WORKS.

CENTERPOINT VENTURES

Two Galleria Tower
13455 Noel Road, Suite 1670
Dallas, TX 75240
972-702-1101   fax: 972-702-1103
www.cpventures.com

Bob Paluck, Managing Partner

Terry Rock, General Partner

total assets under management	*initial investment*	*year founded*
$150 Million	$3–6 Million	1996

CenterPoint Ventures generally invests in early-stage companies in the following areas: computer software, Internet and Intranet products, hardware and software, computer hardware, semiconductors, and high-tech industrial equipment.

CenterPoint normally invests in the first round or second round of venture capital financing. It prefers to invest in early-stage companies, which are normally less than two years old, investing a total of $3 million to $6 million in a single company. This would normally be invested over two to three rounds.

CenterPoint generally invests in companies headquartered in Texas but will consider investments in any location in the United States. It has an additional office in Austin, Texas, with Kent Fuka and Cam McMartin as General Partners.

CEO VENTURE FUND

2000 Technology Drive
Pittsburgh, PA 15219-3109
412-687-3451   fax: 412-687-8139
www.ceoventurefund.com

James Colker, Managing Partner

William R. Newlin, Managing Partner

Gary G. Glauser, General Partner

Ned J. Renzi, General Partner

Glen F. Chatfield, General Partner

Eugene R. Yost, General Partner

total assets under management	*initial investment*	*year founded*
$80 Million	N/A	1985

Formed by successful entrepreneurs, the CEO Venture Fund is a venture capital firm providing equity capital to privately held technology companies in the Mid-Atlantic states.

Industries of interest include: software, communications, biotechnology, business/information services, and manufacturing automation. The Fund's strategy is to lead its investments, but it will also consider investments in deals originated by others. Companies seeking investment capital should forward a full business plan describing their distinctive, proprietary products or services. The Fund will consider investments in new entities and mature firms with expanding market opportunities.

The CEO Venture Fund Partners provide value-added management assistance and growth strategies to the Firm's portfolio companies.

CHANEN & CO. LTD.

1420 5th Avenue, Suite 2975
29th Floor, US Bank Center
Seattle, WA 98101
206-386-5656   fax: 206-386-5376
www.chanenco.com

Stephen Campbell, Principal

Gordon L. Chanen, Principal

J. Scott Painter, Principal

total assets under management	initial investment	year founded
N/A	$2–20 Million	1988

Chanen & Co. Ltd. specializes in corporate finance transactions and does not generally handle publicly traded securities. Chanen consists of five investment bankers with previous transaction and management experience; an advisory board with experience in national, regional, and venture-stage business; and an investor group that acts as additional regional eyes. It focuses on transactions in the size of $2 to 20 million. Transaction types include: institutional venture funding, corporate partnering, foreign joint ventures, debt placements and restructuring, merger and acquisitions, management buyouts, asset-based debt fundings, and investment advising. It invests globally but specializes in the Rocky Mountain area and California.

CHARTERWAY INVESTMENT CORPORATION

9660 Flair Drive, Suite 328
El Monte, CA 91731
626-279-1189   fax: 626-279-9062

Edmund C. Lau, Chairman

total assets under management	initial investment	year founded
$5 Million	$100,000–450,000	1983

Charterway Investment Corporation is a special small business investment company. Charterway invests in only second-stage financings such as mezzanine debt and senior debt. Charterway is only interested in businesses that are based in California. Charterway prefers stock options to be included and has long-term loans (five years) with interest equivalent to 2 to 3 percent over prime.

CHASE CAPITAL PARTNERS

1221 Avenue of the Americas
New York, NY 10020-1080
212-899-3400   fax: 212-899-3401
www.chasecapital.com

Laxdes Munier, Marketing Associate

total assets under management	initial investment	year founded
$18 Billion	N/A	1984

Chase Capital Partners (CCP) is a global private equity organization with over $18 billion under management. Through professionals in the United States, Europe, Asia, and Latin America, CCP provides equity and mezzanine financing for a wide variety of investment opportunities, including management buyouts, recapitalizations, venture capital, and growth equity to reduce excessive debt burdens.

Since its inception in 1984, the Firm has closed more than 950 individual transactions. CCP's primary limited partner is the Chase Manhattan Corporation, one of the largest bank holding companies in the United States, with assets totaling approximately $406 billion. The financial acumen and entrepreneurial diversity of the 140 professionals at CCP are the result of the Firm's broad base of business and geographical investment experience.

CHISHOLM PRIVATE CAPITAL

211 North Robinson, Suite 1910
Oklahoma City, OK 73102
405-605-1111   fax: 405-605-1115
www.chisholmvc.com

C. James Bode, Partner

John B. Frick, Partner

D. Greg Main, Partner

William D. Paiva, Ph.D., Partner

total assets under management	initial investment	year founded
$100 Million	$1 Million	1996

Chisholm Private Capital is a private venture firm with no preference in which stages it will fund. Chisholm is actively seeking new projects in Oklahoma and the adjacent states; however, some other areas in the continental United States will be reviewed.

CHRYSALIS VENTURES

101 South Fifth Street, Suite 1650
Louisville, KY 40202
502-583-7644   fax: 502-583-7648
www.chrysalisventures.com

David A. Jones Jr., Chairman and Senior Managing Director

Robert S. Saunders, Senior Managing Director

Koleman E. Karleski, Principal

James K. Cameron, Associate

Michael Lenihan, Associate

total assets under management	*initial investment*	*year founded*
$193 Million	$3–5 Million	1993

Chrysalis Ventures invests in early-stage companies in the broadband data, service, telecommunications, Internet, health-care, and business services industries. It prefers to invest in the Southeast and Midwest but has and will move outside of this region wherever it can add value.

The Firm typically invests in the form of a convertible preferred stock; and depending on the company's stage and prospects, Chrysalis Ventures can purchase a controlling or minority interest. It does not assume management responsibility for any portfolio company but is generally an active director.

Portfolio Companies: Aperture; Appris; bCatalyst; ClearVision Laser Centers; Construction-Zone.com, Inc.; Dalet S.A.; Darwin Networks, Inc.; Golden State Overnight Delivery Services, Inc.; High Speed Access Corp.; IntelliSeek, Inc.; IronMax.com; Manorhouse, Inc.; MindLeaders.com; NetByTel, Inc.; Network Two; Pathology Consultants of America; PeopleFirst.com, Inc.; Primis, Inc.; ToyCity.com; and Tritel, Inc.

CIVC PARTNERS

231 South LaSalle, 7th Floor
Chicago, IL 60697
312-828-8021   fax: 312-987-0887

Christopher J. Perry, Partner

Daniel G. Helle, Partner

Marcus D. Wedner, Partner

Gregory W. Wilson, Partner

Sue C. Rushmore, Partner

John H. Compall, Partner

Keith H. Yamada, Partner

Michael J. Miller, Principal

total assets under management	*initial investment*	*year founded*
$750 Million	$10–75 Million	1970

CIVC Partners is a private equity firm whose sole limited partner is Bank of America. CIVC Partners, with 30 years' experience in private equity investing, provides growth capital to middle-market companies with a focus on business services, financial services, media and communications, and niche manufacturing.

CLAREMONT CAPITAL CORPORATION

509 Madison Avenue
New York, NY 10022
212-832-2370   fax: 212-832-0474

Nissan Boury, Managing Director

total assets under management	*initial investment*	*year founded*
$120 Million	$500,000–38 Million	1996

Claremont Capital Corporation ("Claremont") is a venture capital and private equity investment firm located in New York, New York. Claremont entertains investment opportunities that range from venture capital and expansion capital to growth-oriented acquisitions of companies with under $100 million in revenues.

Claremont looks to make investments in early- and late-round venture capital situations and in small-growth companies that have the potential for superior capital appreciation.

CLARION CAPITAL CORPORATION

1801 East 9th Street, Suite 1120
Cleveland, OH 44114
216-687-1096   fax: 216-694-3545

Morton A. Cohen, Chairman
Thomas Niehaus, Treasurer

total assets under management	*initial investment*	*year founded*
$40 Million	$250,000–1.35 Million	1968

Clarion Capital Corporation teams financial backing with over 40 years of experience. It funds companies in various stages of development, including: first-stage, second-stage, mezzanine, acquisition, and buyout. Its investments are geographically confined to the Midwest and California.

CMEA VENTURES

235 Montgomery Street, Suite 920
San Francisco, CA 94104
415-352-1520   fax: 415-352-1524
www.cmeaventures.com

Thomas R. Baruch, General Partner

Gordon D. Hull, General Partner

Christine B. Cordaro, General Partner

Karl D. Handelsman, General Partner

David Tuckerman, Partner

Vlad Dabija, Vice President

Meryl Schreibstein, Director of Administration

total assets under management	*initial investment*	*year founded*
$310 Million	$500,000–3 Million	1990

CMEA Ventures is a venture capital partnership focused on making equity investments in high-technology companies serving the information technology and the life sciences industries.

CMEA Ventures's information technology practice focuses its investment activities in companies and technologies that enable the electronics revolution. Currently, its principal interests are in software, hardware, and services that enable Moore's Law, communications, e-commerce, and the Internet.

CMEA Ventures's life sciences group focuses its investment activities on companies and technologies that will radically improve the practice of bioindustries. Currently, the group's principal interests are: agriculture, e-bioindustry, health care, genomics, bioinformatics, and proteomics.

Portfolio Companies: 3DFX; Aclara; Aerogen; Alien Technology; Cadabra Technology; ChemConnect; Cplane; E-markets; Ensim; EpiCyte Pharmaceuticals; Focus Engine; Freshnex; Galileo; i2; Infra Switch; iSuppli; LinuxCare; Magma; Maxygen; Myogen, O-In; Quantum Dot; RAVEN Biotechnologies; Rigel Pharmaceuticals; Silicon Spice; Siros; Stratum8; Symyx; Synopsys; Syrrx; Virologic; and Xeno Port.

CMGI @Ventures

3000 Alpine Road
Menlo Park, CA 94028
650-233-0333   fax: 650-233-0506
www.ventures.com

Jonathan D. Callaghan, Managing Partner

Peter Mills, Managing Partner

Lior Yahalomi, Managing Partner

total assets under management	*initial investment*	*year founded*
$3 Billion	N/A	1995

CMGI @Ventures is a private venture capital firm that takes strategic positions in potentially synergistic Internet and technology companies. The Firm is affiliated with CMGI, Inc., and they work together to leverage new ventures across the established network of CMGI operating companies. Since 1995, the Firm has funded over 65 complementary companies.

CMGI @Ventures focuses on early-stage companies in which the Firm believes it can add significant value to the investment through its network of relationships and experience in helping Internet companies build distribution, develop brands, and capitalize upon an entrepreneurial vision. CMGI @Ventures' portfolio consists of complementary investments in e-commerce, services, enterprise software, Internet appliance companies, wireless, video compression, and voice user interfaces.

Portfolio Companies: Lycos; geoCities; Half.com; Ventro Corporation; MobileLogic; and Dialpad.com.

Coast Business Credit

12121 Wilshire Boulevard, Suite 1400
Los Angeles, CA 90025
888-77-COAST   fax: 310-447-3150
www.coastbusinesscredit.com

Jack Baruch, Chairman and CEO

Scott B. Sampson, President and COO

total assets under management	*initial investment*	*year founded*
$700 Million	$1–30 Million	1954

Coast Business Credit (CBC) is an aggressive asset-based lender providing $1 to $30 million loans to America's emerging-growth companies. CBC specializes in providing financing to companies in the high-technology and telecommunications industries. CBC provides revolving lines of credit as well as term loans. Collateral can include: accounts receivable, inventory, machinery and equipment, and industrial real estate. CBC will lend to companies in diversified industries anywhere in the United States to support their growth, acquisition, recapitalization, and special situation needs.

COLLINSON HOWE & LENNOX, LLC

1055 Washington Boulevard
Stamford, CT 06901
203-324-7700   fax: 203-324-3636
www.chlmedical.com

Jeffrey J. Collinson, Partner
Timothy F. Howe, Partner
Ronald W. Lennox, Partner

total assets under management	initial investment	year founded
$100 Million	$250,000–5 Million	1990

Collinson Howe & Lennox, LLC, is a venture capital manager founded in 1990 that invests principally in start-up and early-stage companies in the medical sector, defined to include biotechnology, pharmaceuticals, genomics, drug delivery technology, medical and diagnostic devices, and health-care service companies.

Collinson Howe & Lennox invests frequently as the lead investor. As its portfolio companies grow, the Firm continues its active support and follow-on financings.

Portfolio Companies: American Renal Associates, Inc.; Boston Medical Technologies, Inc.; Camitro Corporation, Inc.; Cellular Genomics, Inc.; Comprehensive NeuroScience, Inc.; Durect Corporation; InfiMed Therapeutics, Inc.; Molecular Staging, Inc.; Point Biomedical Corporation; Prolifix Medical, Inc.; Revivant, Inc.; RxCentric, Inc.; SemperCare, Inc.; and Targesome, Inc.

COMVENTURES

505 Hamilton Avenue, Suite 305
Palo Alto, CA 94301
650-325-9600   fax: 650-325-9608
www.comventures.com

Cliff Higgerson, General Partner

Roland Van der Meer, General Partner

David Helfrich, General Partner

Jim McLean, Partner

Michael Rolnick, Partner

Paul Vabakos, Partner

total assets under management	*initial investment*	*year founded*
$1 Billion	$500,000–10 Million	1997

ComVentures is a venture capital firm with a focus on early-stage companies with a significant market opportunity and sustainable competitive advantage. The firm is interested in: network infrastructure, which includes optical solutions, wireless solutions, carrier networks, enterprise networks, and management software; communications and IP services, which includes access and transport, value-added networks, and hosting; and Internet applications and services, such as ASPs, content/commerce, and wireless Internet. ComVentures will consider investments in the United States and Europe.

Portfolio Companies: ComVentures has over 50 portfolio companies, including Brix Networks; CoSine Communications, Inc.; Oresis Communications; and Zeus Wireless.

COMCAST INTERACTIVE CAPITAL

1500 Market Street
Philadelphia, PA 19102
215-981-8450   fax: 215-981-8429
www.civentures.com

Julian A. Brodsky, Senior Managing Director

John E. Kole, Managing Director

Samuel H. Schwartz, Managing Director

Kathleen M. Hyneman, Vice President and General Counsel

total assets under management	*initial investment*	*year founded*
$350 Million	$2–10 Million	1999

Comcast Interactive Capital (CIC) is a $350-million venture capital firm affiliated with Comcast Corporation, a diversified global leader in broadband services, telecommunications, electronic commerce, and entertainment. CIC's primary goal is to generate superior financial returns from equity investments in companies involved in the Internet and other interactive technologies. To achieve this goal, CIC works to foster the success of its portfolio companies by bringing to bear the unique resources, experience, and insight of both CIC and the Comcast family of companies. CIC has a portfolio of many of the leaders in defining the new economy.

Comcast Corporation is principally involved in the development, management, and operation of broadband cable networks and in the provision of programming content through majority ownership of QVC, Comcast-Spectacor, Comcast SportsNet, and The Golf Channel, a controlling interest in E! Entertainment Television, and through other programming investments.

CIC will consider investing in promising businesses at any stage of development, from seed- through late-stage (pre-IPO). Although sometimes larger or smaller, investments typically range in size from $2 million to $10 million, with appropriate follow-on financing in later private rounds. CIC can act as a lead investor and often co-invests with other high-caliber venture capital funds or strategic investors.

Portfolio Companies: About.com; BizTravel.com; Bolt.com; Clearway Technologies; Community Connect; CultureFinder.com; Deja.com; Ethentica; Exent Technologies; Expand Networks; eziaz; Garden.com; half.com; Internet Capital Group; KPCB Java Fund; The Lightspan Partnership; LinkShare Corp.; Media Technology Ventures; NDS; NetLibrary; Online Retail Partners; AIG Orion Fund; Persona; Pets.com; PlanSoft; Quantum Bridge; QuickBuy; Quokka Sports; ReplayTV; RespondTV; SupplyFORCE.com; Ticketmaster Online-CitySearch; TiVo; V-SPAN; VeriSign; VerticalNet; WhatsHotNow.com; WIT Soundview; and Yupi Internet.

COMMERCIAL BRIDGE CAPITAL, LLC

4275 Executive Square, Suite 350
La Jolla, CA 92037
858-535-9660   fax: 858-535-9664
www.cbcloans.com

John C. Stiska, Chairman

Carl M. Fredericks, Chief Executive Officer

Richard A. Nance, Vice President, Credit Administration

Brian Mooney, Vice President, Loan

John D. Cambon, Principal

total assets under management	*initial investment*	*year founded*
$5 Million	$50,000–2 Million	1999

Commercial Bridge Capital, LLC (CBC), provides short-term bridge loans to growth companies with an immediate need for capital. These loans typically provide working capital for companies that are in the process of consummating equity of long-term debt financing, the closing of a major business combination, or other business opportunities that require immediate capital. Most loans are secured by a lien on the asset of the borrower and have two distinct pricing components: interest rate and warrants.

CBC provides loans on a nationwide basis, but its primary geographic focus is Southern California and Arizona. The Firm does not have any particular industry preference but differentiates itself from other lenders by making and implementing loan decisions quickly; the kind of fast, decisive turnaround not commonly found in the financial service industry but especially appreciated by fast-growing companies. It also differentiates itself from more traditional lenders by considering the enterprise value of a borrower rather than focusing only on tangible assets.

COMMUNITY TECHNOLOGY FUND, BOSTON UNIVERSITY

108 Bay State Road
Boston, MA 02215
617-353-4550   fax: 617-353-6141
www.bu.edu/ctf/

Matthew J. Burns, Managing Director

Randall C. Crawford, Director, Venture Capital

Roger D. Kitterman, Director, New Ventures

total assets under management	initial investment	year founded
$30 Million	$300,000–750,000	1975

Community Technology Fund (CTF) provides venture capital and access to Boston University's scientific and technical resources to growing businesses. CTF invests directly in entrepreneurial ventures and advises Boston University on its investments in venture capital funds. Direct investment activity is focused on the life sciences and IT industries. CTF generally seeks to make its initial investment in privately held companies at an early stage of development as part of a venture capital syndicate.

Industries of preference include communications, Internet, health care, information technology, and biotechnology.

Portfolio Companies: AtheroGenius; C-Port Corporation; Cytologix; Digital Broadbased Communicationquenom; ExactLabs; Hemagen

Diagnostics, Inc.; Home Wireless Network; NitroMed; Pointshare; and Sequenom.

COMPASS TECHNOLOGY PARTNERS

1550 El Camino Real, Suite 275
Menlo Park, CA 94025
650-322-7595   fax: 650-322-0588
www.compasstechpartners.com

David G. Arscott, Co-Founder

Martha P. E. Arscott, Partner

Sheila Cunningham, Partner

Alain S. Harrus, Ph.D., Partner

total assets under management	*initial investment*	*year founded*
$100 Million	$500,000 and up	1988

Compass Technology Partners is an investment firm with a focus on emerging public and private companies with high-growth potential. The private equity focus is on the Internet, silicon advances, and health-based industries. It will consider investments at all stages of a company's development, with a preference for funding start-up and early-stage companies. Compass Technology Partners will fund companies throughout the United States.

  Portfolio Companies: Compass Technology Partners has over 30 portfolio companies, including: @comm; AvantCom Network Inc.; BlueKite.com; Boxer Cross; CyberStateU.com; Locality; NuvoMedia, Inc.; Oculex Pharmaceuticals; Radio Therapeutics; Response Logic; Ripfire; Softbook Press; Starvox; and Torrex.

COMSTOCK PARTNERS, LLC

9430 Readcrest Drive
Beverly Hills, CA 90210
310-276-8386   fax: 310-276-6409

Jeffrey L. Balash, Chairman

total assets under management	*initial investment*	*year founded*
N/A	$5–100 Million	1992

Comstock Partners, LLC ("Comstock"), is a privately owned merchant bank, headquartered in Los Angeles, California. It combines experience from both operating and investment banking perspectives to provide an integrated approach in addressing its clients' strategic and financial issues. It focuses on the issues that are important to the senior operating and financial officers, working directly with the CEO, the COO, and the CFO.

Comstock works with its clients across a variety of industries in order to increase the value of the company's equity. Initially, this involves defining the company's goals in a cooperative effort with senior management.

Once a set of goals has been identified and articulated, Comstock works with senior management to fashion a strategy to achieve these objectives.

Finally, the Firm takes responsibility for executing the transactions that are necessary to implement this strategy. Comstock has extensive transactional experience in mergers and acquisitions, exclusive sales, joint ventures, public financing (including initial public offerings), private financings, international transactions, and leveraged buyouts.

Comstock enjoys extremely close relationships with the leading sources of private capital, both debt and equity; understands the types of businesses in which it is interested; and can achieve an expedited review and decision at a senior level.

CONNING CAPITAL PARTNERS

CityPlace II, 185 Asylum Street
Hartford, CT 06103
860-527-1131   fax: 860-520-1299
www.conning.com

John B. Clinton, Senior Vice President
Preston B. Kavanagh, CFO
Steven F. Piaker, Senior Vice President

total assets under management	initial investment	year founded
$630 Million	N/A	1985

Conning Capital Partners is a private equity firm that looks for investment opportunities in financial services, insurance, and health-care companies, including supporting services, e-commerce businesses, and technology enterprises. Conning Capital Partners offers research-based investing, strategic advice, and access to the Conning network to its portfolio companies. The Firm will consider funds located in the United States.

Portfolio Companies: AnnuityNet, Inc.; Answer Financial, Inc.; Arlberg Holding Company, Inc.; Axiom8; CapMAC Holdings, Inc.; Clark/Bardes Holdings, Inc.; Collegiate Health Care, Inc.; Commercial Capital Corporation;

Connecticut Surety Corporation; CORE Insurance Holdings, Ltd.; Cox Insurance Holdings Plc; Discover Re Managers, Inc.; Environmental Warranty, Inc.; Etinuum, Inc. (formerly Intek Information, Inc.); E*Trade Bank; Executive Risk Inc.; FamilyMeds.com; FOCUS Healthcare Management, Inc.; The Galtney Group, Inc.; HealthRight, Inc.; Hobbs Group, LLC; Home Financial Network; InfoGlide Corporation; Intersections, Inc.; Investors Insurance Holding Corporation; Medspan, Inc.; The Merallis Company, Inc.; Mid Ocean Limited; MMI Companies, Inc.; Monroe Guaranty Insurance Company; Mutual Risk Management Ltd.; Paradigm Health Corporation; PAULA Financial; PennCorp Financial Group, Inc.; Quester, I.T.; Re Capital Corporation; The Robert Plan Corporation; Sagamore Financial Corporation; SageMaker, Inc.; Spider Technologies, Inc.; SS&C Technologies, Inc.; Sterling Collision Centers, Inc.; Stockton Holdings Limited; Trenwick Group, Inc.; United Capitol Holding Company; U.S.I. Holdings Corporation; and Ward North America, Inc.

CONSOLIDATED FIRSTFUND CAPITAL CORP.

837 West Hastings Street, Suite 304
Vancouver, Canada V6C3N6
604-683-6111   fax: 604-662-8254

William N. Grant, President
W. Douglas Grant, Controller

total assets under management	*initial investment*	*year founded*
$10 Million	$150,000–1.5 Million	1984

Consolidated Firstfund Capital Corp. (CFC Corp.) specializes in companies' needs ranging from fund-raising through equity, debt- or tax-favored instruments, syndication and marketing of investments, and also direct investment. It offers provision for funds for secondary financing and expansion for companies with proven revenue and products. The company prefers debt, equity, and quasi-equity financing, tax-favored limited partnership, and venture capital corporations. CFC Corp. requires board representation in investee companies and can provide marketing, strategic planning, and financial expertise to the management of companies. CFC Corp. invests mainly in second-stage financing, while investing with a geographic focus on Canada and the Northwest.

CONVERGENCE PARTNERS
3000 Sand Hill Road, Building 2, Suite 235
Menlo Park, CA 94025
650-854-3010   fax: 650-854-3015
www.convergencepartners.com

Paul Dali, General Partner
Eric Di Benedetto, General Partner
Russ Irwin, General Partner
Chen Tang, General Partner

total assets under management	*initial investment*	*year founded*
$200 Million	$250,000–6 Million	1997

Convergence Partners is a Silicon Valley–based Internet venture capital firm focused on the needs of B2B entrepreneurs.

Convergence Partners's strategy is to assist a core group of technology start-up founders in building unique world-class companies from the conceptual stage of development through a successful liquidity event. It makes very few investments in order to commit all its resources to the success of its entrepreneurs. Like Convergence Partners, the entrepreneur's ambition is to develop the infrastructure, critical applications, and most-transacted marketplaces of the Internet.

Convergence Partners has helped open world markets for its portfolio companies as early as the first year. The Firm's strong international relationships, investing experience, and strategic partners enable its portfolio companies to enjoy another clear and distinct competitive advantage.

Recognizing the need to address the shortage of information-technology management talent worldwide, Convergence Partners has partnered with the full-service B2B Internet incubator, Campsix, based in San Francisco. Their close relationship provides entrepreneurs with compelling benefits of a virtual management team and a complete portfolio of services. In those specific cases, the Firm's goal is to bring a start-up from concept to execution stage in six months.

Portfolio Companies: AdForce; B2Bworks; Bizfinity; Campsix; Chameleon Systems; CollegeClub.com; Decisive Technology; Entegrity Solutions; FreeGAte; HiFive; iVillage; Magnifi; Music Vision; OneMediaPlace; Signio; Tropian; US Creative; Vectiv; and Villa Montage.

CORAL VENTURES

3000 Sand Hill Road
Building 3, Suite 220
Menlo Park, CA 94025
650-854-5227   fax: 650-854-4625
www.coralventures.com

Yuval Almog, Managing Partner
Pete McNerney, Managing Partner
Karen Boezi, Venture Partner
Mark Headrick, Senior Associate
Linda Watchmaker, CFO

total assets under management	*initial investment*	*year founded*
$300 Million	$200,000–8 Million	1983

Coral Ventures's focus is on investments in the technology and health-care sectors, making equity investments of up to $8 million in start-up businesses and emerging companies at all stages of development. In the technology sector, Coral focuses on telecommunication systems, software, and information-services companies; in health care, it invests in the areas of medical devices, health-care services, and technology and biotechnology/pharmaceuticals. Coral Ventures believes that outstanding entrepreneurial management teams with perseverance and long-term commitment can become the market leaders of tomorrow. Coral Ventures seeks to make investments in companies that can attain a defensible market leadership position.

Coral Ventures typically serves as the lead investor and takes a board position with the majority of its portfolio companies.

CORPORATE ACQUISITIONS, INC.

5430 LBJ Freeway, Suite 1600
Dallas, TX 75240
972-788-5115   fax: 972-788-5462

Allan J. Kvasnicka, President and CEO
Craig W. Wycoff, Managing Director

total assets under management	*initial investment*	*year founded*
$10 Million	$250,000–5 Million	1984

Corporate Acquisitions, Inc., specializes in later-stage financing. Corporate Acquisitions is a merchant banking firm, a private venture capital firm, and an investment banking firm. Corporate Acquisitions, Inc., is a team of seasoned investment bankers with very strong deal-making capabilities. For over 15 years, they have proven to be excellent investor partners for management and/or former ownership. Corporate Acquisitions is highly experienced (at the Board of Directors level) in supporting management as the firm develops a company through its next level of growth.

CRESCENDO VENTURES

480 Cowper Street, Suite 300
Palo Alto, CA 94301
650-470-1200   fax: 650-470-1201
www.iaiventures.com

Roeland Boonstoppel, Partner

John Borchers, Partner

Jean-Charles Charpentier, Partner

Tony Daffer, Partner

Lorraine Fox, Partner

Richard Grogan-Crane, Partner

Jeff Hinck, Partner

David Spreng, Partner

Jeff Tollefson, Partner

total assets under management	*initial investment*	*year founded*
$400 Million	$3–10 Million	N/A

Crescendo Ventures is an early-stage venture capital group dedicated to investing in tomorrow's global leaders in the areas of information technology, communication services, and health care.

Portfolio Companies: Crescendo Ventures has over 25 portfolio companies.

CROSSPOINT VENTURE PARTNERS

18552 MacArthur Boulevard, Suite 400
Irvine, CA 92612
949-852-1611   fax: 949-852-9804
www.crosspointvc.com

Robert A. Hoff, General Partner

Donald B. Milder, General Partner

total assets under management	*initial investment*	*year founded*
$2.5 Billion	$1–50 Million	1963

Crosspoint has $2.5 billion under management and invests in 25 to 30 new projects per year. Crosspoint's focus is in two areas: e-business services and software and broadband infrastructure. In the aggregate, Crosspoint has invested in more than 200 projects and takes an active and early role in building companies. In its early-stage funds, the Firm invests up to $40 million per project and participates in follow-on rounds with late-stage funds by investing up to an additional $10 million per project.

Crosspoint's business goals are creating rapid growth through access to capital; building long-term sustainable value; and providing substantial returns to entrepreneurs, employees, and investors, most often through public stock offerings. Crosspoint's offices are located in Southern and Northern California.

CRYSTAL INTERNET VENTURE FUNDS

1120 Chester Avenue, Suite 418
Cleveland, OH 44114
216-263-5515   fax: 216-263-5518
www.crystalventure.com

Daniel Kellogg, Managing Partner

Joseph Tzeng, Managing Partner

Howard Lee, General Partner

Brian Goncher, General Partner

Richard Kovach, CFO

John Farrall, Associate

total assets under management	*initial investment*	*year founded*
$240 Million	$1–6 Million	1997

Established in January 1997, Crystal Internet Venture Funds (CIVF) was formed to invest solely in Internet and Internet-related opportunities. Internet companies include software, hardware, access, security, content, and vertical applications. CIVF currently has $240 million of capital under management, with the primary concentration being the funding and development of early-stage, domestic, or international companies.

CIVF typically invests in preferred equities and participates actively on the Board of Directors. CIVF focuses on three vital areas before making an investment decision: the evaluation of the company's product/technology, the management team, and the market potential.

Portfolio Companies: About.com; Baby Center; Cobalt Networks; and Sina.com.

CS CAPITAL PARTNERS, LLC

328 Second Street, Suite 200
Lakewood, NJ 08701
732-901-1111   fax: 212-202-5071
www.cs-capital.com

Solomon Lax, Managing Director

Charles Nebenzahl, Managing Director

total assets under management	*initial investment*	*year founded*
$20 Million	$1–3 Million	1998

CS's primary focus is on private or public companies where the technology/business model has achieved proof of concept but has yet to generate significant revenues. Investments are generally made within four weeks of introduction to the Firm and are usually intended to facilitate a development-stage company's transition to a revenue- and income-producing enterprise.

Portfolio Companies: Active Health; Assurenet; Avana Communications; Bathopia; Career Fairs International; Laser Medical Corporation; OpenAuto.com; Pet Assure; TripleHop Technologies; and US Capital.

DAVIS, TUTTLE VENTURE PARTNERS

320 South Boston, Suite 1000
Tulsa, OK 74103
918-584-7272   fax: 918-582-3404

Barry M. Davis, Managing General Partner

Philip A. Tuttle, General Partner

total assets under management	*initial investment*	*year founded*
$100 Million	$1–3 Million	1986

Davis, Tuttle Venture Partners is a private venture capital firm that invests with companies located in the Southern United States. Davis, Tuttle Venture Partners prefers to invest in first and second stages, mezzanine, acquisition, and leverage and management buyouts.

Its industry preferences include: consumer services, communication equipment, diversified education, energy and natural sources, food services/products, industrial equipment, materials and chemicals, and medical health services/devices.

DELPHI VENTURES

3000 Sand Hill Road
Building 1, Suite 135
Menlo Park, CA 94025
650-854-9650   fax: 650-854-2961
www.delphiventures.com

James J. Bochnowski, General Partner
David L. Douglass, General Partner
Donald J. Lothrop, General Partner
Kevin L. Roberg, General Partner
Paul S. Auerbach, M.D., Venture Partner
Douglas A. Roeder, Venture Partner

total assets under management	*initial investment*	*year founded*
$450 Million	$500,000–1.5 Million	1988

Delphi Ventures is a private venture capital firm that provides equity financing and supportive business expertise to young biomedical and health-care companies. Its goal is to contribute added value to the companies it funds by serving as an active investor.

Portfolio Companies: Delphi Ventures has over 50 portfolio companies.

DELTA CAPITAL PARTNERS, LLC

60 Germantown Court, Suite 200
Cordova, TN 38018
901-755-0949   fax: 901-755-0436
www.deltacapital.com

Donald L. Mundie, Managing Partner
C. Kevin Campbell, CFO/Principal
David B. Latham, Principal/Secretary
John A. Bobango, Adviser

total assets under management	initial investment	year founded
$45 Million	N/A	1992

Delta Capital Partners is a $45-million family of two venture capital funds. Both funds are engaged in the high-tech, manufacturing, health-care, and technology markets. Currently, the Firm has invested in 10 companies, ranging from early- to later-stage companies. Delta Capital Partners will consider deals on a national basis.

Portfolio Companies: BioNumerik Pharmaceuticals, Inc.; Compass Intervention Center, LLC; MidSouth Health Plan, Inc.; MidSouth Practice Management, Inc.; Neodyne Corporation; Nextek, Inc.; Outlet Mall Network, Inc.; Soltech, Inc.; Spire, Inc.; and Therapeutic Antibiodies, Inc.

DIGITALVENTURES

50 California Street, 8th Floor
San Francisco, CA 94111
415-354-6200   fax: 415-354-6248
www.dtpnet.com

Dean L. Gardner, Founder and CEO
Stephen Young, President
Mike Severson, Managing Director

total assets under management	initial investment	year founded
N/A	N/A	1995

DigitalVentures (DV), a strategic venture investment and operating company, was formed in 1995 to take advantage of the growth of the Internet market. DV specializes in the digital convergence industry, focusing on the Internet and related enabling technologies. DV focuses on two primary investment strategies: early-stage synergistic investments and core sector investments focused around a consolidation strategy.

Within the Internet industry, DV's focus will include the following: Internet/Intranet enabling technology; network security and authentication; Java tools and software, Java communication and marketing tools; electronic commerce; Internet applications; Java applications; distance learning and telemedicine systems; affiliated technologies, tools, and services; metasearch and advanced database technologies new media infrastructure and services; multimedia content developers and providers; cable television; video on demand; supplementary telecom services and infrastructure; online commercial and information services; and online merchandising and advertising.

Portfolio Companies: AgencyX; DigitalVentures Asia; DigitalVentures Europe; eFounders; eFinance Corporation; FusionStorm; and MarketPing.

DOLL CAPITAL MANAGEMENT CO., LLC

3000 Sand Hill Road, Building 3, Suite 225
Menlo Park, CA 94025
650-233-1400   fax: 650-854-9159
www.dcmvc.com

Dixon Doll, Managing General Partner

David Chao, General Partner

Peter Moran, General Partner

Rob Theis, General Partner

Tom Blaisdell, Partner

Eric Gonzales, Partner

Rudolph Rehm, CFO, Partner

Sandra Kearney, Investor/External Relations, Partner

total assets under management	*initial investment*	*year founded*
$656 Million	N/A	1996

Doll Capital Management Co., LLC (DCM), a venture capital firm, places great importance on a lasting relationship with its portfolio companies. It is focused on communications, networking, and Internet service companies. DCM primarily invests in early-stage companies, although it will also consider later-stage companies. DCM invests in the United States but may selectively invest in international companies.

Portfolio Companies: 2Wire, Inc.; 51net.com; @Motion; About.com; Branders; BravoGifts; Buzzhits; Ecast; ECNet; Embark.com; eDreams.com; Foundry Networks; InterNAP; International Manufacturing Services; iOwn; Ipivot; Japan Communications, Inc.; Luminous Networks; Mayan Networks; NextNet Wireless; nQuire; PeakXV Networks; PlanSoft; Pocket.com; Recourse Technologies; Takira; and VENDAVO.

DOLPHIN COMMUNICATIONS PARTNERS, L.P.

750 Lexington Avenue, 16th Floor
New York, NY 10022
212-446-1600   fax: 212-446-1638
www.dolphinfund.com

Richard J. Brekka, President
Kenneth Kharbanda, Managing Director
Donald Kraftson, Managing Director
Barry W. Stewart, Managing Director

total assets under management	*initial investment*	*year founded*
$300 Million	$10–75 Million	1997

Dolphin Communications Partners, L.P., is an investment firm with an emphasis on established private companies with experienced management teams. It is interested primarily in the communications industry and will invest in the United States and abroad. Dolphin Communications Partners offers an extensive network of financial and industry contacts to help portfolio companies become successful businesses.

Portfolio Companies: CAVU, Inc.; Ceragon Networks Ltd.; Dolphin Networks, Ltd.; Epoch Networks, Inc.; Gigared, Inc.; Gomez, Inc., Inter Digital Networks Limited; Iplan, Inc.; Nava Networks; Norigen Communications Group, Inc.; Pangea Ltd.; Terago Canada, Inc.; VeloCom, Inc.; Western Integrated Networks; and Wired Business, Inc.

DOMAIN ASSOCIATES, LLC

28202 Cabot Road, Suite 200
Laguna Niguel, CA 92677
949-347-2446   fax: 949-347-9729
www.domainvc.com

James C. Blair, General Partner
Brian H. Dovey, General Partner
Arthur J. Klausner, General Partner
Robert J. More, General Partner
Kathleen K. Schoemaker, Administrative General Partner
Richard S. Schneider, General Partner

Jesse I. Treu, General Partner

Olav B. Bergheim, Venture Partner

total assets under management	*initial investment*	*year founded*
$500 Million	$500,000–5 Million	1985

With offices in Laguna Niguel, California, and Princeton, New Jersey, Domain Associates is a venture capital management company that provides seed- and early-stage financing and organization support to technology-based companies focused on life sciences. Total funds managed or advised exceed $500 million. Specific areas of investment interest include biopharmaceuticals, medical devices, drug discovery services, bioinstrumentation, diagnostic devices, new materials as applied to health care, health-care information systems, and e-health. With demonstrated expertise in technology assessment, strategic planning, operations, and finance, Domain's Partners have been involved in the creation and development of more than 100 life sciences ventures. Today these companies generate total annual revenues of greater than $55 billion, employ more than 22,000 people, and have a combined market capitalization exceeding $100 billion.

DOMINION VENTURES, INC.

1656 N. California Blvd.	2400 Sand Hill Road	One Post Office Square
Suite 300	Suite 100	38th Floor, Suite 3820
Walnut Creek, CA 94596	Menlo Park, CA 94025	Boston, MA 02109
925-280-6300	650-234-1800	617-367-8575
fax: 925-280-6338	fax: 650-234-9975	fax: 617-367-0323
www.dominion.com		

Michael Lee, General Partner

Brian Smith, General Partner

Randy Werner, General Partner

Kendall Cooper, General Partner

Renee Baker, Managing Director

James Bratton, Managing Director

total assets under management	*initial investment*	*year founded*
$403 Million	$2–8 Million	1985

Dominion Ventures is a venture capital company uniquely designed to meet the needs of a growing company by providing venture leasing or expansion capital. Founded in 1985, Dominion Ventures was created with the goal of providing capital and value-added resources to private companies in the information technology, communications, life sciences, health-care, and service industries. Dominion has invested more than $260 million in 160 companies.

Dominion is focused on investing in rapidly growing companies in existing or potentially large markets. It places an emphasis on funding companies that are beginning to prove a business model concept and that possess talented management teams that can capably execute their business plan. In addition to providing investment capital, the Firm is a valuable resource for business expertise. Dominion forms close relationships with the firms in which it invests and adds value through active participation, experience, and resources.

DORSET CAPITAL MANAGEMENT, LLC

343 Sansome Street, Suite 1210
San Francisco, CA 94104
415-398-7101   fax: 415-398-7141
www.dorsetcapital.com

John A. Berg, Managing Partner
Mark G. Saltzgaber, Principal
Jeffery S. Mills, Principal
Amanda N. Peterson, Business Manager

total assets under management	*initial investment*	*year founded*
$71 Million	$2–5 Million	1999

Dorset Capital Management will participate in various stages of financing, including growth equity, leveraged recapitalizations, and management buyouts. Dorset looks for situations where the company can have active involvement, typically at the board level. Dorset is currently evaluating North American investments only. Dorset focuses on investing throughout the entire consumer supply chain, including retail, direct marketing, food service, B2C, B2B, consumer products and services distribution, and technology via the Internet.

Portfolio Companies: Pasta Pomodoro; Perksatwork.com; RetailExchange.com; Savi Technology; and Zoots.

DOUGERY VENTURES

165 Santa Ana Avenue
San Francisco, CA 94127
415-566-5220   fax: 415-566-5757
www.dougery.com

John R. Dougery

total assets under management	*initial investment*	*year founded*
N/A	N/A	1997

Dougery Ventures is interested in fast-growing emerging markets, where the company can achieve dominance in its niche. This generally includes high-technology products or services. Some examples of areas would be as follows: Internet content and services, data communications/telecommunications/wireless advances, client-server software applications and tools, electronic design automation advances, telephony software applications, and networking software.

Portfolio Companies: Compression Labs; Cornerstone Imaging, Inc.; DSC Communications; Exodus Communications; FileNet Corporation; FORE Systems; In Focus Systems, Inc.; Intevac, Inc.; MediaWay; MultiPoint Corporation; Novell; Thera Cardia; Unify Corporation; Vanguard Automation, Inc.; VIA Medical Corporation; and Zanza.

DOYLE & BOISSIERE, LLC

330 Primrose Road, Suite 500
Burlingame, CA 94010
650-685-8700   fax: 650-685-8711
www.dbllc.com

Lionel P. Boissiere, President

total assets under management	*initial investment*	*year founded*
$100 Million	$5–15 Million	1997

Doyle & Boissiere, LLC, is an investment firm with a focus on middle-market private and public companies. It works in partnership with the management team of each of its portfolio companies and assists with strategic and financial advice. Doyle & Boissiere targets the manufacturing, marketing, service, and distribution industries and will consider investments on a nationwide level.

Portfolio Companies: KOJO Worldwide Corporation; Naturade, Inc.; Ocean Pacific Apparel Corp.; and Tubetronics, Inc.

DRAPER FISHER JURVETSON

400 Seaport Court, Suite 250
Redwood City, CA 94063
650-599-9000   fax: 650-599-9726
www.dfj.com

Timothy C. Draper, General Partner
John H. N. Fisher, General Partner
Steve Jurvetson, General Partner
Warren Packard, Partner
Jennifer Scott Fonstad, Partner
Andreas Stavropoulos, Partner
Raj Atluru, Partner

total assets under management	*initial investment*	*year founded*
$2 Billion	$1–10 Million	1979

Draper Fisher Jurvetson is the leader in start-up venture capital, having invested in over 150 high-tech companies. In the majority of cases, it is the lead investor for a company's first round of financing. Draper focuses on information technology businesses with enormous market potential. Draper's role is to help entrepreneurs achieve their maximum potential through team building, partnerships, advice and support, as well as investments. By pursuing a people-focused approach to venture capital investing, Draper continues to fund entrepreneurs with the energy, vision, experience, and desire to build great companies.

DRESNER CAPITAL RESOURCES, INC.

29 South LaSalle Street, Suite 310
Chicago, IL 60603
312-726-3600   fax: 312-726-7448
www.dresnerco.com

Steven M. Dresner, President
Alan D. Bernstein, Vice President
John C. Riddle, Vice President

total assets under management	*initial investment*	*year founded*
$10 Million	$500,000–5 Million	1991

Dresner Capital Resources, Inc., is a private venture capital firm based out of Chicago, Illinois. Dresner Capital is a global investing company that has a geographic focus in the United States, Mexico, Latin America, and Western Europe. Dresner Capital has a lot of experience in the international arena and can help any company that deals with international trade. Dresner Capital wishes to invest in companies in one of the following stages: seed, start-up, first-stage, second-stage, mezzanine, bridge, acquisition, leveraged and management buy-outs, and recapitalization.

DYNAFUND VENTURES

21311 Hawthorne Blvd., Suite 300
Torrance, CA 90503
310-792-4929   fax: 310-543-8733
www.dynafundventures.com

Denny R. S. Ko, Ph.D., General Partner

Richard D. Whiting, Ph.D., General Partner

Tony Hung, General Partner

total assets under management	initial investment	year founded
$219 Million	$1–4 Million	1997

The majority of DynaFund Venture's investments are in early-stage companies. The Firm will reserve some of its capital for follow-on investments into its portfolio companies to provide critically needed financing at the growth stage. Later-stage opportunities will also be considered by the Firm if they fit within the overall strategy of DynaFund.

The primary investment focus is on emerging microelectronics, telecommunications, and information technology.

EARLYBIRD

525 University Avenue, Suite 410
Palo Alto, CA 94301
650-330-3633   fax: 650-330-3634
www.earlybird.com

Dr. Vera Kallmeyer, Partner

Roland Manger, Partner

total assets under management	initial investment	year founded
$350 Million	$3–5 Million	N/A

Earlybird's investment focus lies on information technology/Internet, life sciences/health care, and convergent technologies. Examples of its current focus includes enabling technologies, new business transaction models, communications/wireless, content-rich e-commerce, interactive entertainment, life sciences, health-care products/devices, convergent technologies, and e-health.

Earlybird's investment strategy is to be among the first venture investors in technology companies that seek to create new markets. It will enter a relationship in the early stages or the expansion phase, as long as the company is privately held. It often serves as the lead investor and joins the Board of Directors of companies in which it invests.

Portfolio Companies: abaXX Technology GmbH; AllAdvantage.com; Amaxa GmbH; Bernina Biosystems GmbH; bridgeCo; Calypso Medical; Conject AG; Cortologic AG; alloo AG; dooyoo.d AG; eCargo Service Inc.; ecomda GmbH; element 5 AG; Fact City Inc.; Gaudia.com; GMD GmbH; Graviton Inc.; Hemoteq GmbH; IDM GmbH Infrarot Sensoren; Interhyp AG; iXEC GmbH; Jamany GmbH; Kiwilogic.com AG; MIOCO GmbH; Music United.com AG; MuTek Solutions; NovaSonics; One Sheild; PNP Luftfedersysteme GmbH; Rauser Advertainmnet AG; Redeon Inc.; urbia.com AG; vitaGO AG; Wearix Software GmbH; and Wilex Biotechnology GmbH.

EDELSON TECHNOLOGY PARTNERS

300 Tice Boulevard
Woodcliff Lake, NJ 07677
201-930-9898   fax: 201-930-8899
www.dynafundventures.com

Harry Edelson, General Partner

total assets under management	*initial investment*	*year founded*
$125 Million	$300,000–1.5 Million	1984

In addition to the normal venture capital investment objectives of substantial long-term capital appreciation, Edelson Technology Partners (ETP) seeks to provide its corporate partners with a window on technology to complement its extensive in-house capabilities. The initial investment by ETP should be viewed as only the first of many continuing contributions made to the success of an emerging company. ETP frequently provides strategic and investment advice to its investee companies and often serves on their Boards to provide continuing guidance and counsel.

Other services include assistance in raising capital, introduction of merger candidates, and access to the ETP corporate partners for mutually beneficial relationships.

EDGEWATER FUNDS LP

428 Carnation Avenue
Corona Del Mar, CA 92625
949-675-9111   fax: 949-675-0911
www.edgewaterfunds.com

Robert G. Allison, Partner

Mark L. McManigal, Partner

total assets under management	*initial investment*	*year founded*
$300 Million	$1–20 Million	1992

Edgewater Funds is a private equity, middle- to later-stage development fund that is well diversified across a range of industries, including information services, health care, basic industries, and business services and equipment. The principals of the fund take active, Board-level roles in a number of the portfolio companies, assisting management with strategic planning and positioning, recruiting, operations, and financial organization. Edgewater Funds also has an office in Chicago, Illinois.

EL DORADO VENTURES

2884 Sand Hill Road, Suite 121
Menlo Park, CA 94025
650-854-1200   fax: 650-854-1202
www.eldoradoventures.com

Gary W. Kalbach, General Partner

Shanda Bahles, General Partner

Thomas H. Peterson, General Partner

Charles Beeler, General Partner

total assets under management	*initial investment*	*year founded*
$300 Million	$1–3 Million	1986

El Dorado Ventures invests primarily in early-stage, technology-based companies located on the West Coast, with a particular focus on information technologies.

THE ELVEY PARTNERSHIP

666 Fifth Avenue, 14th Floor
New York, NY 10103
212-977-1555   Fax: 212-582-3145
www.elvey.com

Malcolm Elvey, Principal Partner

Gavin Beekman, Partner

Stephen Bock, Partner

Matthew Elvey, Partner

Andrew Simon, Partner

Michael Griffin, Associate

total assets under management	*initial investment*	*year founded*
N/A	N/A	1999

The Elvey Partnership provides strategic solutions to early-stage companies that are involved in creating the content, infrastructure, and enabling technology for the future of e-business. Based in the heart of New York City, The Elvey Partnership draws on the vast experience of its Partners and on its extensive network to advise clients in the areas of strategy, structure, and finance.

The Elvey Partnership assists entrepreneurs with refining the product and/or service, developing a business plan, marketing and public relations strategies, fund-raising, and developing a management team.

Portfolio Companies: Argus; Bounty Systems; Cheetah Mail; Data Sphere; eBookers; eCal; ecuality; eLingo; eMergent; FastVoice; FultonStreet; Icras; Javelin; Looknbuy; MineTech; More.com; Odyssey Systems; Sessions.edu; SureSource; Taho Commerce; TravelByUs; VastVideo; Vencast; and WebPresence.

EMPIRE VENTURES

1020 S.W. Taylor Street, Suite 415	12707 High Bluff Drive, Suite 200
Portland, OR 97205	San Diego, CA 92130
503-222-1556	858-350-3980
fax: 503-222-1607	fax: 858-350-8724
www.empireventures.com	

Wade H. Bradley, Managing Director

Steven Brunk, Outside Advisory Member

Alan Rand, Senior Research Advisor

total assets under management	*initial investment*	*year founded*
$10 Million	$25,000–1 Million	N/A

Empire Ventures seeks out investments in software, Internet/Intranet, and new technologies located on the West Coast of the United States. Empire Ventures invests in seed-, early-, developmental mid- and late-stage companies.

Portfolio Companies: AuctioNet.com; AutoFusion; Consystant Design Technologies; Illumea Corporation; Klickback.com; Kurant Corporation; Learning.com; Net Conversions, Inc.; NONSTOP Solutions; NVST.com; Poundhouse.com; ServiceStop, Inc.; ShareThis, Inc.; SnapNames; SportChip.com; TriVium Systems; Upright Systems; WatchIT.com; and Zone Development.

ENCOMPASS VENTURES

777 108th Avenue NE, Suite 2300
Bellevue, WA 98004
425-468-3900   fax: 425-468-3901
www.encompassventures.com

Wayne C. Wager, Managing Director

Scot E. Land, Managing Director

Yasuki Matsumoto, Managing Director

Kiyoyuki Kubota, Managing Director

Andy Bose, Senior Technology Adviser

total assets under management	*initial investment*	*year founded*
$62 Million	$200,000–3 Million	1997

The goal at Encompass is to add value to an information technology company using unique skills and experience in the international markets. Encompass will make investments at any stage but prefers companies that are in the early or developmental stages. Encompass Ventures has focused its investments in the Western United States.

Portfolio Companies: ARTISTdirect; CNET; Cobalt; Confirma; emWare; Keystroke.com; LifeChart.com; Ticket Master Online-City Search; and Uproar.

ENDEAVOR CAPITAL MANAGEMENT

830 Post Road East
Westpoint, CT 06880
203-341-7788   fax: 203-341-7799

Anthony F. Buffa, General Partner

Nancy E. Hoar, General Partner

David Wisowaty, General Partner

Gene S. Solnihc, General Partner and CFO

Edward Jones, Venture Partner

David Miller, Venture Partner

total assets under management	*initial investment*	*year founded*
$50 Million	$100,000–2 Million	1988

Endeavor Capital Management invests primarily in early-stage growth companies. The General Partners use their extensive operating experience to build value by working closely with management teams on strategic and operating issues.

Companies do not have to be profitable; however, the company must have a completed product being sold to paying customers. Endeavor primarily invests in information technology, including telecom, software, and information services.

ENTERPRISE PARTNERS VENTURE CAPITAL

7979 Ivanhoe Avenue, Suite 550
La Jolla, CA 92037
858-454-8833   fax: 858-454-2489
www.epvc.com

Jim Berglund, General Partner

Tom Clancy, General Partner

Drew Senyei, General Partner

Bill Stensrud, General Partner

Ronald R. Taylor, General Partner

Carrie Stone, Venture Partner

total assets under management	*initial investment*	*year founded*
$745 Million	$500,000–10 Million	1985

Enterprise Partners is a venture capital firm investing in privately held early-stage and emerging companies. Enterprise Partners believes in tapping the track record of its own successful entrepreneurial experiences to help other entrepreneurs build lasting businesses. With particular strengths in information technology, communication, health care, as well as selected consumer products and services, Enterprise Partners has provided financing and has forged successful top-performing venture capital firms in the United States.

Portfolio Companies: Enterprise Partners is an early investor in Ligand Pharmaceuticals; Nanogen; Rhythms NetConnections; and Stamps.com; and more than 100 other companies.

EUCLIDSR PARTNERS

45 Rockefeller Plaza
New York, NY 10111
212-218-6880   fax: 212-218-6877
www.euclidsr.com

Milton Pappas, General Partner

Bliss McCrum, General Partner

Brenda Gavin, General Partner

Stephen Reidy, General Partner

Barbara Dalton, General Partner

Raymond Whitaker, General Partner

Graham Anderson, General Partner

John Braca, General Partner

Elaine Jones, General Partner

total assets under management	*initial investment*	*year founded*
$200 Million	$5–15 Million	2000

Prior to forming EuclidSR, (ESR) the General Partners were instrumental in the success of two other venture capital groups: Euclid Partners, founded in 1970, has managed four successful funds that invested in emerging information and health-care technologies; S. R. One Limited, founded in 1985 and generally regarded as the leading corporate life sciences venture fund, has provided both a window on health-care breakthroughs and significant investment returns to its corporate parent, Smith Kline Beecham.

ESR plans to divide its capital among the following sectors: health care, information technology, and e-health, or the convergence of two of these sectors. The partnership expects to invest in about 20 companies, with total investments of between $5 million and $15 million per company.

Portfolio Companies: Ironside Technologies; Innaphase; and I-Jet.

FIDELITY VENTURES

82 Devonshire Street, R27B
Boston, MA 02109-3614
617-392-1880   fax: 617-476-9023
www.fidelityventures.com

Robert C. Ketterson, Managing Director
Daniel H. Auerbach, Managing Director
Simon Clark, Managing Director

total assets under management	*initial investment*	*year founded*
N/A	N/A	1970

Fidelity Ventures is a venture capital firm interested in the Internet infrastructure, software, and business services industries. It invests in all stages of a company's development, from seed- and early-stage companies to later-stage companies. Fidelity Ventures offers business solutions and capital to companies worldwide. It has offices in Boston, London, Hong Kong, and Tokyo.

Portfolio Companies: Fidelity Ventures has over 70 portfolio companies, many of which have gone on to become or have been acquired by industry leaders, including COLT; Continental Cablevision; GeoTel; InterNAP Network Services; MCI; Nexabit Networks; Nextel; Nuance Communications; and ONI Systems.

FINANCIAL BROKER RELATIONS

179 Ruskin Drive East
Montgomery, TX 77356
936-597-7500 · fax: 936-597-7504
www.gopublic.com

Mike Fearnow, CEO

total assets under management	*initial investment*	*year founded*
N/A	N/A	1978

Financial Broker Relations specializes in working with smaller-growth companies that plan a public underwriting in 12 months. Financial Broker Relations does bridge loans, offers equity, and assists in the initial public offering and subsequent financings during the following one to three years. Financial Broker Relations invests in the Southwest, as well as in most places in the United States, if the prospect is attractive enough. Financial Broker Relations specializes in providing companies with first-stage, second-stage, acquisition, and leveraged and management buyout funding.

FINANCIAL RESOURCES CORPORATION

204 North Robinson, Suite 1400
Oklahoma City, OK 73102
405-235-5372   fax: 405-235-9372
www.finres.com

Jim Ratchford, President
Pam Meyers, Administrative Assistant

total assets under management	*initial investment*	*year founded*
N/A	$100,000–10 Million	1989

Financial Resources's mission is to help its clients achieve business success. It is a relationship-oriented investment banking and consulting firm. The Firm's strengths for its clients are strategic thinking, research, business planning, and financial resources.

FINANCIAL TECHNOLOGY VENTURES

601 California Street, 22nd Floor
San Francisco, CA 94108
415-229-3000   fax: 415-229-3005
www.ftventures.com

Richard Garman, General Partner
James C. Hale III, General Partner
Robert Huret, General Partner
Scott Wu, General Partner

total assets under management	*initial investment*	*year founded*
$200 Million	$5 Million	1998

Based in San Francisco, Financial Technology Ventures (FTV) is a $200 million fund that invests in companies that develop technologies that are transforming the financial services industry. Founded in 1998, it was the first venture capital fund in the United States to focus on this niche. It remains the primary go-to firm for technology companies that develop products and services applicable to financial services. FTV's limited partners include: U.S. Bancorp, BankAmerica Corp., Banque Nationale de Paris, National City Corp., Wells Fargo & Co., Deutsche

Bank, Credit Suisse Group, AIG, BANK ONE Financial, Key Corp, PNC Bank Corporation, Republic New York Corp., Royal Bank of Canada, Sallie Mae, Wachovia Corp., and Washington Mutual.

Portfolio Companies: 724 Solutions, Inc.; ClearCommerce, Inc.; Corillian Corporation; CrossLogix, Inc.; Cybersafe; Ecredit.com; E-Loan.com; Encirq; Financial Engines, Inc.; FreeDecision.com; PayMyBills.com; Servicesoft Technologies, Inc.; Synchrologic, Inc.; Valicert, Inc.; ValuBond.com; and Verbind Software.

FIRST AMERICAN CAPITAL FUNDING, INC.

10840 Warner Avenue, Suite 202
Fountain Valley, CA 92708-3847
714-965-7190   fax: 714-965-7193

Chuoc VoTa, President

total assets under management	*initial investment*	*year founded*
$4 Million	$25,000–50,000	1984

First American Capital Funding, Inc., is an SBIC that invests in small portions to a variety of different businesses. First American Capital Funding, Inc., specializes in small companies and wishes to provide mezzanine debt and senior debt as the main supply of capital. First American funds only start-up and second-stage companies. All of the companies First American invests in are located within California.

First American Capital Funding, Inc., invests in business services, medical health devices/services, and pharmaceutical companies.

FIRST ANALYSIS VENTURE CAPITAL

The Sears Tower
233 South Wacker Dr., Suite 9500
Chicago, IL 60606-6502
312-258-1400   fax: 312-258-0334
www.firstanalysisvc.com

F. Oliver Nicklin, President
Bret R. Maxwell, Managing General Partner
Mark Koulogeorge, Managing General Partner

total assets under management	*initial investment*	*year founded*
$600 Million	$250,000–5 Million	1985

First Analysis Venture Capital (FAVC) is a leading early-stage venture investor. FAVC has funded more than 150 successful companies, providing the infrastructure for an enhanced business-to-business environment. FAVC plays an active role in developing and scaling early-stage companies by providing entrepreneurs with assistance in strategy and corporate development, business development and alliances, as well as financing events. FAVC's investment professionals are located in Silicon Valley, Chicago, and New York.

FIRST CAPITAL GROUP

750 E. Mulberry, Suite 305
San Antonio, TX 78212
210-736-4233   fax: 210-736-5449
www.firstcaptx.com

Jeffrey P. Blanchard, Managing Partner

total assets under management	*initial investment*	*year founded*
N/A	N/A	1983

Companies that have the following characteristics will receive special consideration in First Capital Group's investment decisions: a management team with an outstanding performance record; a financial commitment to the company and unquestionable integrity; annual revenues exceeding $5 million with positive cash flow; multiple products and services with established distribution channels; competitive advantage resulting from proprietary products or market position; a large target market or an exceptionally profitable market niche with outstanding growth potential; the potential to achieve critical mass through internal growth or by acquisitions; significant barriers to market entry by prospective competitors; and expected return commensurate with risks.

The principals have invested in the following firms, which are representative of the types of companies in which First Capital Group prefers to invest: Bill Young Productions, Inc., audio and video productions; Communication Partners, Ltd., broadcasting and cable television; Contemporary Constructors, Inc., communication towers and fiber optics; Data Race, Inc., data communication equipment; Intelligent Technologies Corporation, fraud detection software; Microwave Networks, Inc., microwave radios; ProNet, Inc., radio common carrier; Rewind Holdings, Inc., multimedia productions; and U.S. Funds Express, Inc., telecommunication services.

FIRST MANHATTAN CAPITAL PARTNERS

One Village Green Circle
Charlottesville, VA 22903
804-296-5158   fax: 804-296-5159

Thomas W. Gilliam Jr., Managing Director
David J. Machlica, Managing Director

total assets under management	initial investment	year founded
N/A	$1–10 Million	1991

First Manhattan Capital Partners is a private investment banking and merchant banking organization with expertise and interest in a number of industries. Recent sectors of interest include videoconferencing, Internet, and telecommunications, where the company has provided or placed financing in the electronic publishing, cable/broadcasting, and energy areas. The company invests anywhere in the United States.

FLEMMING, LESSARD & SHIELDS, LLC

4225 Executive Square, Suite 1500
La Jolla, CA 92037-1487
858-642-2800   fax: 858-642-2830
www.flsllc.com

Gary L. Shields, Managing Director
Roy W. Lessard, Managing Director
B. Mason Flemming, Managing Director

total assets under management	initial investment	year founded
N/A	$3–5 Million	1990

Flemming, Lessard & Shields, LLC is an investment banking firm with offices in San Diego and San Francisco that provides financial consulting services to small- and mid-sized private companies. The Firm raises private equity (seed, expansion, and bridge financing) from venture capital firms, corporate partners, and private individuals in the following industries: computers, software, distribution, restaurants, consumer products and services, health care and telecommunications. The Firm also assists clients in areas of strategic planning, mergers, and acquisitions—

representing both buyers and sellers. The company's goal is to design and implement creative and effective solutions to meet the client's financial needs.

FLUKE VENTURE PARTNERS

11400 Southeast 6th Street, Suite 230
Bellevue, WA 98004-6423
425-453-4590   fax: 425-453-4675
www.flukecapital.com

Dennis P. Weston, Senior Managing Director

Kevin Gabelein, Managing Director

Kirsten Morbeck, Managing Director

total assets under management	*initial investment*	*year founded*
$100 Million	$500,000–2 Million	1976

Fluke Venture Partners (FVP), a leading venture capital firm, has invested in early- and later-stage high-growth companies in the Pacific Northwest for over 20 years. FVP recently received a new commitment of $50 million for new investments. With a primary focus on technology, FVP also has a strong interest in specialty retail and innovative service businesses and has assisted its portfolio management teams in all stages of company growth, from start-up through initial public offerings.

Portfolio Companies: Fluke Venture Partners has over 40 portfolio companies, including Aldus; Coinstar; Eagle Hardware & Garden; Edmark; ELF Technologies; Innova; Interlinq Software; Luxar Corporation; Media Passage; Panlabs International; Pet's Choice; Starbucks; Sur La Table; and Tegic Communications.

FORREST BINKLEY & BROWN

840 Newport Center Drive, Suite 480
Newport Beach, CA 92660
949-729-3222   fax: 949-729-3226

Nicholas B. Binkley, General Partner

Jeffrey J. Brown, General Partner

Gregory J. Forrest, General Partner

total assets under management	*initial investment*	*year founded*
$250 Million	$2–8 Million	1993

. Forrest Binkley & Brown (FBB) is a private equity partnership focused on investing in venture capital opportunities, leveraged buyouts, and growth buildups.
Since 1993, the Partners of FBB have generated consistently superior returns
from investments in over 200 privately held companies. FBB manages the investments of certain affiliated investment entities, including SBIC Partners, L.P., a
partnership formed and licensed in 1993 as a small business investment company
by the U.S. Small Business Administration.

   FBB is the managing general partner of SBIC Partners. Private funding to SBIC
Partners is provided by Sid R. and Lee M. Bass interests of Fort Worth, Texas.
FBB has completed investing the capital from SBIC Partners' first $135 million
fund and has raised a second $150 million fund in 1998.

FORWARD VENTURES

9255 Towne Centre Drive, Suite 300
San Diego, CA 92121
858-677-6077   fax: 858-452-8799
www.forwardventures.com

Standish Fleming, Partner

Ivor Royston, Partner

Jeffrey Sollender, Partner

Rose Ann Ignell, CFO

total assets under management	*initial investment*	*year founded*
$132 Million	$500,000–5 Million	1991

Forward Ventures pursues a mix of early-stage portfolio investments focused
in biotechnology and health care, with an emphasis on seed and start-up investments. The Firm pursues these early-stage investments in biotechnology
and health care, including therapeutics, diagnostics, devices, and services, primarily in Southern California, where it can remain in close contact with its investments.

   Portfolio Companies: ADIANA, Inc.; AGY Therapeutics, Inc.; AriZeke
Pharmaceuticals, Inc.; Avalon Pharmaceuticals; Camitro Corporation; Ciphergen
Biosystems, Inc.; CombiChem, Inc.; Coriz Corporation; Doctors Online Medical
Services; Dynavax Technologies Corp.; EndiCOR Medical, Inc.; Endonetics,
Inc.; GenQuest, Inc.; Genicon Sciences Corp.; Gryphon Sciences;
MedicineNet.com; MitoKor, Nereus Pharmaceuticals; Onyx Pharmaceuticals;

Sequana Therapeutics, Inc.; Tandem Medical, Inc.; Triangle Pharmaceuticals, Inc.; and Variagenics, Inc.

FOUNDATION CAPITAL

70 Willow Road, Suite 200
Menlo Park, CA 94025
650-614-0500   fax: 650-614-0505
www.foundationcapital.com

Jim Anderson, General Partner

Bill Elmore, General Partner

Kathryn Gould, General Partner

Paul Koontz, General Partner

Mark Saul, General Partner

Mike Schuh, General Partner

total assets under management	*initial investment*	*year founded*
$200 Million	$1–5 Million	1995

Foundation Capital is the only established venture firm with more years of operation experience than venture experience among the General Partners, so in many ways, the partners are entrepreneurs themselves. All of them worked as engineers before spending years in marketing, sales, and general management positions at companies like Cadence, HP, Oracle, and Silicon Graphics. Four partners have been vice presidents or CEOs at start-ups before entering the venture business.

They each left their successful operating careers to become venture capitalists because they believed they have a passion for working with entrepreneurs to build companies. They believe that a venture capital firm should be characterized by exceptional service to start-ups.

As lead investors, they're asked to take Board seats with almost all of their companies.

Foundation Capital's primary investment areas are enterprise and Internet software, communications and networking, technical software, and semiconductors.

Portfolio Companies: Foundation Capital has more than 25 portfolio companies.

FREEMAN SPOGLI & CO.

11100 Santa Monica Boulevard, Suite 1900
Los Angeles, CA 90025
310-444-1822
fax: 310-444-1870
www.freemanspogli.com

599 Lexington Avenue, 18th Floor
New York, NY 10022
212-758-2555
fax: 212-758-7499

Bradford M. Freeman, Co-Founder
Ronald P. Spogli, Co-Founder
Mark J. Doran, General Partner
Todd W. Halloran, General Partner
Jon D. Ralph, General Partner
John M. Roth, General Partner
Charles P. Rullman, General Partner
J. Frederick Simmons, General Partner
William M. Wardlaw, General Partner

total assets under management	*initial investment*	*year founded*
$11 Billion	$25–125 Million	1983

Freeman Spogli & Co. is a private equity investment firm with a focus on consumer-related companies, with an emphasis on retailing, distribution, direct marking, and service businesses. It is dedicated to working in partnership with management to help growing companies become successful businesses. Freeman Spogli & Co. is interested in companies with potential long-term earnings, as well as a need for capital to enable internal expansion or add-on acquisitions. Freeman Spogli & Co. will consider investments throughout the United States.

Portfolio Companies: Freeman Spogli & Co. has over 34 portfolio companies, including Advance Stores Company, Inc.; AFC Enterprises, Inc.; Asbury Automotive Group; AV Partnership; CB Richard Ellis Services, Inc.; Century Maintenance Supply, Inc.; Envirosource, Inc.; Galyan's Trading Company, Inc.; Greenlight.com; Hudson Respiratory Care Inc.; Medical Arts Press, Inc.; Micro Warehouse, Inc.; Miller Publishing Group, LLC; MVP.com; The Pantry, Inc.; PartsAmerica.com; Ross-Simons; Sur La Table, Inc.; and WebVision, Inc.

FREMONT VENTURES

50 Fremont Street, Suite 3500
San Francisco, CA 94105
415-284-8787   fax: 415-284-8102
www.fremontgroup.com

M. Hannah Sullivan, General Partner
Paul A. White, General Partner
Wm. Blake Winchell, General Partner

total assets under management	*initial investment*	*year founded*
N/A	$2–20 Million	1999

Fremont Ventures's mission is to build long-term partnerships with experienced managerial teams executing superior business models targeted at the seams of change within larger industries. Unlike "focus funds," which concentrate on a specific technology or investment strategy, Fremont Ventures is open to most investment opportunities and invests nationwide.

Portfolio Companies: Atairgin Technologies; CardioNow; DoveBid, Inc.; e-Appliance Corporation; Light Sand Communications; National Loan Exchange; RedMeteor.com; ServiceLane; Visfinity; and The Wedding List.

FRIEDMAN FLEISCHER & LOWE, LLC

One Maritime Plaza, Suite 1000
San Francisco, CA 94111
415-402-2100   fax: 415-402-2111
www.fflpartners.com

Tully M. Friedman, Chairman and CEO
Spencer C. Fleischer, Vice Chairman
David L. Lowe, Vice Chairman
Christopher Masto, Managing Director

total assets under management	*initial investment*	*year founded*
$350 Million	$25–75 Million	1998

Friedman Fleischer & Lowe, LLC, is a private equity investment firm targeting middle-market companies in a wide variety of industries. Friedman Fleischer & Lowe seeks various opportunities, such as recapitalizations, growth equity, consolidations, management buyouts, corporate joint ventures, and ownership restructuring in family-owned companies. It will consider investments throughout the United States.

Portfolio Companies: Friedman Fleischer & Lowe's principals have invested in over 40 companies over the past 15 years across many industry sectors. Current portfolio companies include Advanced Career Technologies, Inc.; Capital Source Holdings, LLC; and SteelPoint Technologies, Inc.

FULCRUM VENTURE CAPITAL CORPORATION

300 Corporate Point, Suite 380
Culver City, CA 90230
310-645-1271   fax: 310-645-1272
www.fulcrumventures.com

Brian E. Argett, President

Cedric J. Penix, Principal

total assets under management	*initial investment*	*year founded*
$12 Million	$250,000–500,000	1977

Fulcrum Venture Capital Corporation generally targets initial investment in amounts ranging from $250,000 to $500,000. Investments are typically structured with a minimum term of five years. Equity ownership by Fulcrum is usually less than 50 percent.

Fulcrum focuses its investment efforts on the extensive opportunities within Southern California. Within its market segment, the central investment strategy capitalizes on the market opportunity by providing acquisition/buyout capital and expansion capital to businesses with attractive cash-flow margins in large, fragmented, and rapidly consolidating industries.

Portfolio Companies: Art's Transportation, LLC; Chemrich Laboratories, Inc.; Metropolitan Teaching & Learning Company; Radio One, Inc.; and Si-Nor Incorporated.

FULL CIRCLE INVESTMENTS, INC.

1030 State Street
Erie, PA 16501
814-456-9963   fax: 814-456-9740

Kurt F. Buseck, President

total assets under management	*initial investment*	*year founded*
$100 Million	$2–10 Million	1992

Full Circle Investments, Inc., is focused on acquiring and then building mid-sized industrial companies in partnership with management. Full Circle invests mostly in acquisition, leveraged, and management buyouts, and recapitalization. Full Circle invests primarily in California, as well as in most parts of the United States and some parts of Western Europe and Mexico.

FUQUA VENTURES, LLC

1201 West Peachtree Street NW, Suite 5000
Atlanta, GA 30309
404-815-4500   fax: 404-815-4528
www.fuquaventures.com

J. Rex Fuqua, Managing Director

John J. Huntz Jr., Managing Director

David M. Guthrie, Partner

J. Scott Tapp, Principal

total assets under management	*initial investment*	*year founded*
N/A	$500,000–2 Million	N/A

As an active investor, Fuqua believes it can be most effective if the bulk of its investment activities are in the Southeast; however, it will consider any attractive opportunities that meet its criteria. Fuqua invests primarily in companies where insight, innovation, and achievement in technology are core components of the business strategy. When more than one venture capital organization is involved in a financing, Fuqua often acts as the lead investor; however, it is willing to join compatible syndicates when other active investors lead financing.

Private investments include Derivion Corporation, VerticalOne.com, Webforia, WebMD, Gatespace AB, and Manhattan Associates.

G. A. HERRERA & CO.

1502 Augusta, Suite 260
Houston, TX 77057
713-978-6590   fax: 713-978-6599
www.herrera-co.com

Gilbert A. Herrera, Principal

total assets under management	*initial investment*	*year founded*
$2.5 Million	$500,000–1 Million	1992

G. A. Herrera & Co. (GAH) is a private investment/merchant banking firm. It seeks equity interest in privately held, niche distribution entities. It will invest in acquisitions or management-led buyouts. GAH is a relatively small investment company, which allows close relationships and close personal attention between the Firm and its portfolio companies. GAH invests primarily in the Southwestern United States and Texas.

G-51 CAPITAL LLC

401 West 29th Street
Austin, TX 78706
512-476-5901   fax: 512-476-5666
www.g51.com
e-mail: info@g51.com

N. Rudy Garza, President

total assets under management	*initial investment*	*year founded*
N/A	$50,000–200,000	1996

G-51 Capital is pioneering the New World of the Gap Keeper for the Texas capital formation industry. Companies in its investment sector are exclusively in the software and Internet industries, primarily in the seed and early stages of their business life. G-51 invests nationwide.

Portfolio Companies: Digital Motorworks; eDocs.net; Hire.com; Sunset Direct; Terrace Mountain Systems; and T-Manage.

GE CAPITAL-EQUITY CAPITAL GROUP

120 Long Ridge Road	100 California Street, Suite 850
Stamford, CT 06927	San Francisco, CA 94111
203-357-3100	415-277-7400
fax: 203-357-3657	fax: 415-277-7501
www.equitycapital.com	

Joseph E. Parsons, President and CEO

Patrick Dowling, Managing Director

Michael S. Fisher, Managing Director

John L. Flannery, Managing Director

Paul A. Gelburd, Managing Director

John P. Malfettone, Managing Director

Jerome C. Marcus, Managing Director

Steven D. Smith, Managing Director

total assets under management	*initial investment*	*year founded*
$1.148 Billion	$5–50 Million	N/A

GE Capital is owned by General Electric's Pension Trust and by other limited partners. Its investment size ranges from $5 million to $50 million and typically involves minority holdings in established private companies but can also include selected investments in publicly traded companies. The portfolio is diversified over a wide range of industries, including financial services, transportation, logistics, information technology, telecommunication, health care, insurance, retail, consumer products, media/entertainment, and industrial products.

There are two major funds; fund I amounts to $210 million, while fund II, which was established in 1995, amounts to $938 million. GE Capital invests on a national and global basis. Some of GE Capital investments include Gemplus, IXL.com, Autobytel.com, iChat.com, and ACSi.com.

GEMINI INVESTORS LLC

20 William Street
Wellesley, MA 02481
781-237-7001   fax: 781-237-7233
www.gemini-investors.com

James J. Goodman, President
Jeffrey T. Newton, Managing Director
David F. Millet, Managing Director

total assets under management	*initial investment*	*year founded*
$300 Million	$2–8 Million	1993

Gemini Investors LLC invests in rapidly growing, established companies. Gemini invests throughout the United States in a wide range of industries. Areas of particular focus are information technology, business services, and consumer services.

Gemini will typically make minority equity investments of between $2 million and $8 million. The investment is usually in the form of preferred stock or subordinated debt. Typically, Gemini's investment horizon is five years from the date of investment.

Portfolio Companies: Act Teleconferencing; Adventure Entertainment; Art Technology Group; Appian Graphics; Aspen Dental; Benchmark; Buffalo Wild Wings; Eloquent, Inc.; gomembers.com; Hardware Corporation of America; Kitchen Etc.; Microcosm Technologies; MySeason.com; Mystic Transport Services; National Telemanagement Corporation; Novatel Wireless; Omni Facility Resources; Quail Piping Products; Sega Gaming Technology; TradeSouce; Tutor Time Learning Systems; Westsun International; and Wireless.

GENERAL ATLANTIC PARTNERS, LLC

Three Pickwick Plaza	650 Madison Avenue
Greenwich, CT 06830	New York, NY 10022
203-629-8600	212-759-5707
fax: 203-622-8818	fax: 212-759-5708
www.gapartners.com	

Steve Denning, Managing Partner

Peter Bloom, Partner

Mark Dzialga, Partner

Bill Ford, Partner

Bill Grabe, Partner

David Hodgson, Partner

Rene Kern, Partner

Matthew Nimetz, Partner

Cliff Robbins, Partner

Franchon Smithson, Partner

John Wong, Partner

total assets under management	*initial investment*	*year founded*
$10 Billion	$5–150 Million	1980

General Atlantic Partners, LLC, is a worldwide investment firm with a commitment toward creating market-leading IT, Internet, and Internet-enabled businesses. The Firm has approximately $10 billion in capital under management and $4 billion in capital available for investment. General Atlantic is unique in its global perspective on information technology, its worldwide presence, its long-term approach to investments, and its commitment to provide sustained strategic assistance aimed at creating maximum value for its portfolio companies.

Portfolio Companies: Abaxx Technology AG; Access Media; Apollis AG; ArsDigita; Atlantic Data Services; Belle Systems; BindView Development; Brigade Corporation; Brio Technology; Computer Learning Centers; Delirium Corporation; E*Offering; E*Trade Group; Eclipsys Corporation; efinanceworks; Entranet; Essentus; Exact Holding N.V.; EXE Technologies; Exult; Fandango; FirePond; GWI AG; Healthmarket; HEALTHvision; i-DNS, I-EMAIL; iFormation Group; Infogrames; InsightExpress; Internosis; InterPro Business Solutions; LifeCare; Macola Technologies; MAPICS; Meta4 N.V.; Mission Critical Linux; OptiMark Inc.; PlanetFeedback; Predictive Systems; Priceline.com; Priceline.com Europe; Prime Response; ProBusiness Services; Proxicom; Quintiles Transnational; Rebus Group plc; S.E.S.A. Software und Systeme AG; S1 Corporation; Screaming Media; SS&C Technologies; Staples.com; Synapse; Talus Solutions; TDS Informationstechnologie AG; Tickets.com; Upromise; Vindigo; Walker Digital; Xchanging; Zagat Survey; and Ztango.com.

GENERATION PARTNERS

One Maritime Plaza, Suite 1425
San Francisco, CA 94111
415-646-8620
fax: 415-646-8625
www.genpartners.com

551 Fifth Avenue, Suite 3100
New York, NY 10176
212-450-8500
fax: 212-450-8550

John A. Hawkins, Managing Partner
Mark E. Jennings, Managing Partner
Lloyd Mandell, Partner
Robert M. Pfieger, Partner

total assets under management	*initial investment*	*year founded*
$325 Million	$5–25 Million	1995

Generation Partners is a private investment firm with over $325 million of capital under management, focused on providing equity capital for technology-oriented growth companies. The Firm targets investments between $5 and $25 million, focused primarily on enabling technologies and infrastructure, communications, and Internet commerce. Offices are located in New York and San Francisco.

Portfolio Companies: Generation Partners's portfolio includes the following companies: Hotjobs.com (Nasdaq, HOTJ); iAsiaWorks (Nasdaq, IAWK); American Cellular Corporation; BarterTrust; DiscoverMusic.com; Driveway; e-STEEL; Explorador.net; Linguateq; National Transportation Exchange; New Wave Broadcasting; OrderFusion; Partminer; Promatory Communications; and Reliacast.

GENEVA VENTURE PARTNERS

Four Embarcadero Center, Suite 1400
San Francisco, CA 94111
415-732-5672   415-433-6635
www.genevaventurepartners.com

Igor Sill, General Partner
Robert Troy, General Partner

total assets under management	*initial investment*	*year founded*
$60 Million	$100,000–1 Million	1997

Founded in 1997, Geneva Venture Partners is a venture capital firm with interests in the following industries: Internet ASP/enterprise software, wireless communication software, and telecommunications software. The primary focus for Geneva Venture Partners is building superior Internet companies and receiving excellent returns on its investments. Its investments are focused on seed- and early-stage companies within the Northern California area. Geneva Venture Partners will consider investments outside California, including Europe.

Geneva Venture Partners is looking for founders and entrepreneurs who are passionate about business and determined to make their companies successful.

Portfolio Companies: BuzMe; Campsix; CollegeClub.com; CrossCommerce; ITS; iPIN; iWitness.com; Karna Technologies; Luxxon; OneMediaPlace; salesforce.com; and SoftCoin.

GENSTAR CAPITAL, LLC

555 California Street, Suite 4850
San Francisco, CA 94104
415-834-2350   fax: 415-834-2383
www.gencap.com

Jean-Pierre L. Conte, Managing Director

Richard F. Hoskins, Managing Director

Richard D. Paterson, Managing Director

total assets under management	*initial investment*	*year founded*
$350 Million	$5–25 Million	1988

Genstar Capital, LLC, is a private equity firm interested in making leveraged investments in quality companies. It pursues opportunities such as acquisitions of majority interests in public and private companies, management buyouts, leveraged recapitalizations, and significant minority investments. Its focus is on the life sciences, industrial technology, and information technology. Genstar Capital will consider investments located only in the United States.

Portfolio Companies: BioSource International, Inc.; Gentek Building Products, Inc.; NEN Life Science, Prestolite Electric Incorporated; Products, Inc.; Panolam Industriries International, Inc.; Stream International, Inc.; and Wolverine Tube, Inc.

GEOCAPITAL PARTNERS, LLC

2 Executive Drive, Suite 820
Fort Lee, NJ 07024
201-461-9292   fax: 201-461-7793
www.geocapital.com

Henry Allen, General Partner

Colin Amies, General Partner

Whitney Bower, General Partner

Dan Cahillane, General Partner

Stephen Clearman, General Partner

Kimberly Eads, General Partner

Nic Humphries, General Partner

Lawrence Lepard, General Partner

Richard Vines, General Partner

total assets under management	*initial investment*	*year founded*
$500 Million	$5–20 Million	1984

Geocapital Partners works with entrepreneurs and investors to build a select number of large, highly successful information services and technology companies in North America and Europe. Geocapital backs its funds with active and direct partner involvement, deep industry knowledge, and the extensive capabilities of a $500-million transatlantic venture capital firm.

Geocapital invests in rapidly growing software and information technology businesses in the Internet, communications, enterprise applications, and marketing services segments.

Geocapital Partners seeks a minority equity position as an adviser and partner and is not interested in running businesses or holding majority positions in companies.

Portfolio Companies: Geocapital Partners has over 50 portfolio companies.

GLYNN CAPITAL MANAGEMENT

3000 Sand Hill Road, Building 4, Suite 235
Menlo Park, CA 92045
650-854-2215   fax: 650-854-8083

John W. Glynn Jr., General Partner

Jacqueline Glynn, Associate

Steve Rosston, Associate

total assets under management	*initial investment*	*year founded*
N/A	$750,000	1983

Glynn Capital Management can assist with management advice and guidance in business planning, recruiting, and working with the financial community. Glynn Capital invests almost anywhere globally; however, the company is based in California. Start-up, first-stage, second-stage, mezzanine, bridge, acquisition, and management buyout are viable investments for Glynn Capital. The Firm invests in diversified industries that offer high-growth opportunities.

GRACE INTERNET CAPITAL

11 Newbury Street
Boston, MA 02116
617-351-0044   fax: 617-867-9089
www.graceinternetcapital.com

Gregory Grace, Manager and CEO

Christopher Grace, Chairman

total assets under management	*initial investment*	*year founded*
N/A	N/A	N/A

Grace Internet Capital is a private venture capital firm with a primary focus on investments in Internet companies. Since it specializes in assisting young companies, it is interested in making investments to seed companies or companies who are facing the first round of investment. Grace Internet Capital prefers to fund companies located in the Northeastern United States but will consider companies in all parts of the United States and worldwide.

Portfolio Companies: Beansprout Networks; Digi-Block; PharmasMarket.Com; Skila; and Unicast Communications.

GRANITE CAPITAL PARTNERS

10850 Wilshire Boulevard
Suite 826
Los Angeles, CA 90024
310-475-1990
fax: 310-475-9710
www.granitecp.com

251 Riverpark Drive, Suite 325
Provo, UT 84604
801-426-9292
fax: 801-426-9299

Richard C. Ehlert, Managing Director
Robb M. Taylor, Managing Director
Ed Moss, Director

total assets under management	*initial investment*	*year founded*
$30 Million	$2–10 Million	1999

Granite Capital Partners is a private equity investment firm with an interest in venture capital situations, emerging-growth companies, and management buyouts and recapitalizations. Granite Capital Partners has experience assisting management teams in many industries, including specialty retailing, distribution and wholesale, manufacturing, transportation, consumer goods, computer hardware and software, and health-care services. Most of its investments are in companies that are in the later stages of development, although Granite Capital Partners will consider investments in early-stage ventures with high growth potential. The company has an interest in investments throughout the United States.

GRANITE VENTURES

One Bush Street, 12th Floor
San Francisco, CA 94104
415-591-7700   fax: 415-591-7720
www.granitevc.com

Standish H. O'Grady, Senior Managing Director

Jackie Berterretche, CFO and Managing Director

Rupen Dolasia, Managing Director

Eugene Eidenberg, Managing Director

Tom Furlong, Managing Director

Chris Hollenbeck, Managing Director

Samuel D. Kingsland, Managing Director

Eric Zimits, Managing Director

total assets under management	*initial investment*	*year founded*
$600 Million	$2–6 Million	1998

Granite Ventures is an investment firm with an area of focus in emerging market opportunities. It tries to find the best people, technologies, and companies addressing these new markets. Its industry focus has been on software/networking services, communications/broadband connections, Internet, and media distribution.

Granite Ventures takes an investor's approach, rather than a manager's approach, to working with its portfolio companies. It assists portfolio companies with financial, recruiting, and strategic decisions; helps with introductions to potential partners and customers; and maintains one of the highest ratios of professionals to capital under management—maintaining a high level of support.

Portfolio Companies: 2WAY Corporation; Apogee Networks; AvantGo; Colorado MicroDisplay; Command Audio; Connected Corporation; Conscium; CopperCom; Covalent Technologies; Covia; CreativePro; Digimarc Corporation; Digital Fountain; DigitalThink; Direct Medical Knowledge; Electronic Submission; Evolve Software; Fractal Design Corporation; GigaNet; HAHT Software; iBiquity Digital; Impresse; InfoGear; InterNAP; LSSI; Lumedx; Luna Information Systems; Managing Editor; Media Bridge Technologies; NetBoost; NetClerk; Nexabit Networks; Paragon Networks; Peerless Systems Corporation; PictureIQ; Plumtree Software; Saros Corporation; Sendmail; Shutterfly.com; Siebel Systems; Sierra Wireless; Slamdunk Networks; SnapTrack; Speakeasy Networks; Top Layer Networks; Tumbleweed Software Corporation; Versata; Vignette Corporation; Virage; Virtualis; and XtremeSpectrum.

GRAYSON & ASSOCIATES, INC.

1200 17th Street, 16th Floor
Denver, CO 80202
303-628-3490   fax: 303-628-3440

Gerald Grayson, President

total assets under management	*initial investment*	*year founded*
$100 Million	$1 Million	1986

Grayson & Associates, Inc., provides investment banking and venture capital services on a national basis. It specializes in private placement for late-stage private and public companies and, as a corollary, identifying investment opportunities to potential investors. Grayson & Associates arranges affiliations of development-stage and emerging-growth companies with corporate partners and arranges corporate mergers, acquisitions, and divestitures of all parts of a business, leveraged buyouts, technology transfer, and licensing.

Grayson & Associates, Inc., is experienced in capital formation and transactional services required by entrepreneurial companies. The Firm employs a targeted approach based on personal business relationships, with an understanding of the interests of a broad range of capital sources.

GREAT HILL EQUITY PARTNERS

One Liberty Square
Boston, MA 02109
617-790-9400   fax: 617-790-9401
www.greathillpartners.com

Christopher S. Gaffney, Managing Partner

Stephen F. Gormley, Managing Partner

John G. Hayes, Managing Partner

Patrick D. Curran, Partner

Mark E. Evans, Partner

Matthew T. Vettel, Partner

total assets under management	*initial investment*	*year founded*
$1 Billion	$5–50 Million	1995

Great Hill Equity Partners is a private equity firm with over 20 years of experience investing in growth companies. The Firm is knowledgeable in fostering growth through acquisition.

Great Hill's industry focus is on media and information, telecommunications, and business and information technology services. It invests in start-up companies, as well as companies in various other stages of development. Preferably, the portfolio company should be located within the United States, have excellent senior management, and show either high customer retention or a significant level of revenue.

Portfolio Companies: American Broadband; AmStar Entertainment; Bloomington Broadcasting; CyberTech; Dame Broadcasting; Dental Economics; DURO Communications; Edge Connections; Haights Cross Communications; Adams Trade Press; High-Tech Institute; Horizon Telecom Int.; K-Solutions; LFI Worldwide; ManagedOPs.com; ManagedStorage International; Marks-Ferber Communications; Mergent; SmartMail; Sunburst Media; Teltrust; TriVin; and Voyager.net.

GREYLOCK

755 Page Mill Road, Suite A100
Palo Alto, CA 94304-1018
650-493-5525   fax: 650-493-5575
www.greylock.com

Aneel Bhusri, General Partner

Charles Chi, General Partner

Roger Evans, General Partner

David Sze, General Partner

Dave Strohm, General Partner

total assets under management	*initial investment*	*year founded*
$725 Million	N/A	1965

Greylock sponsors companies at various stages of development: start-ups, expansion stage, management buyout, and recapitalizations. It tends to focus on software, communications, and health care. Some of the companies it has worked with include American Management Systems, Amisys Managed Care, Copper Mountain Communications, Inc., Landacorp, Manugistics, Inc., Mentor Graphics Corporation, Pharmacopeia, Inc., SiTera, Sonix Communications Limited, Student Advantage, Inc., The Vincam Group, and Xircom, Inc.

   Portfolio Companies: Greylock has helped to build over 250 companies.

GRP

2121 Avenue of the Stars, Suite 1630
Los Angeles, CA 90067
310-785-5100   fax: 310-785-5111
www.grpvc.com

Steve Lebow, Partner

Yves Sisteron, Partner

Linda Fayne Levinson, Partner

Steven Dietz, Partner

Pierre Morin, Partner

total assets under management	*initial investment*	*year founded*
$650 Million	$5–25 Million	1996

GRP, based in Los Angeles, London, and Munich, makes private equity investments in start-up and early-stage companies in the United States and Europe. GRP has focused on investments in companies that leverage technology to deliver breakthrough models for the distribution of goods and services and that have the potential to become major players in the digital economy.

   Portfolio Companies: Asimba.com; CyberSource; Goto.com; iMotors; Protégé.

GTCR GOLDEN RAUNER, LLC

6100 Sears Tower
Chicago, IL 60606
312-382-2200   fax: 312-382-2201
www.gtcr.com

Bruce V. Rauner, Principal
Philip A. Canfield, Principal
David A. Donnini, Principal
Donald J. Edwards, Principal
Edgar D. Jannotta Jr., Principal
William C. Kessinger, Principal
Joseph P. Nolan, Principal

total assets under management	*initial investment*	*year founded*
$4 Billion	N/A	1980

GTCR has partnered with more than 150 management teams to build and grow successful companies. Industries have included health care, information technology, distribution, business services, marketing services, financial services and more.

GTCR manages more than $4 billion in capital, provided by pension funds, endowments, investment advisers, portfolio company executives, and GTCR principals. Equity funds and mezzanine funds allow the Firm to provide both debt and equity funding.

Portfolio Companies: GTCR Golden Rauner, LLC has over 65 portfolio companies.

GULFSTAR GROUP

700 Louisiana Street, Suite 3850
Houston, TX 77002
713-300-2020   fax: 713-300-2021
www.gulfstargroup.com

W. Clifford Atherton Jr., Managing Director
Stewart "Chip" Cureton, Managing Director
Thomas M. Hargrove, Managing Director
G. Kent Kahle, Managing Director
Edward H. Koehler Jr., Managing Director
Stephen A. Lasher, Managing Director
F. W. "Colt" Luedde, Managing Director
Daryl R. Swarts, Managing Director
Carrie Bowden, Manager

total assets under management	*initial investment*	*year founded*
N/A	$100,000–500,000	1990

GulfStar is an important resource for companies embarking on financial strategies that require timely advice and assistance in designing and executing major corporate transactions. GulfStar's clients are successful private companies that require sophisticated financial advice to assist in creating, preserving, or realizing shareholder value. The Firm specializes in assisting entrepreneurs to monetize their investment through a variety of corporate finance activities and also serves as a transaction sponsor in its merchant banking activities through privately financing growth and multiple acquisitions.

The Firm's eight principals have more than 150 years of combined investment banking experience with major Wall Street firms. This wealth of experience and large professional staff of professionals, together with the Firm's project selectivity and long relationships with financing sources, are responsible for GulfStar's high success rate on completing assignments.

Portfolio Companies: Allen-Stuart Equipment Co., Inc.; Associated Building Services; Barrett Kendall Publishing, Inc.; DR Acquisition Corp.; DuraTherm, Inc.; Gepirone Pharmaceutical Partners, L.P.; Goodman Manufacturing, Inc.; Hitox Corporation; Maintenance Engineering Corp.; Micro Carbide Tool Corporation; Modular Environmental Technologies; Operational Services, Inc.; Plassein Packaging Corp.; rePipe; Inc.Simple Communications LLC; Stellar Event & Presentation Resources, Inc.; Tide Air; Travis International, Inc.; and U.S. Parts, Inc.

HALPERN, DENNY & COMPANY

500 Boylston Street, Suite 1880
Boston, MA 02116
617-536-6602   fax: 617-536-8535
www.halperndenny.com

George Denny, Partner

John Halpern, Partner

Bill LaPoint, Partner

David Malm, Partner

Bill Nimmo, Partner

total assets under management	*initial investment*	*year founded*
$700 Million	$5–40 Million	1991

Halpern, Denny & Co. is a private venture capital firm that is actively seeking new deals. Halpern, Denny & Co. provides capital on a national basis and invests in companies ranging from early-stage to later stages of development.

Industries in which Halpern, Denny & Co. has substantial prior experience and will consider for investment include consumer products, media/publishing, retail, wholesale distribution, specialty manufacturing, restaurant/food concepts, and health care.

Portfolio Companies: ABRY Communications; All Seasons Services; Barneys New York; The Big Party!; Boston Common Press; Bridge Medical; EatZi's; Ecce Panis; Hollywood Digital/Todd-AO; Illuminations; Johnny Appleseed's; Johnny Rockets; Lids; MARS Music; PNV.net; Swifty Serve; Tealuxe; Total eMed; and Windward Petroleum.

HAMILTON TECHNOLOGY VENTURES

9645 Scranton Road, Suite 240
San Diego, CA 92121
858-552-3690   fax: 858-552-3695
www.hamiltonventures.com

Dr. Kerry Dance, Principal and CTO

Paul Bouchard, Principal

Richard Crosby, Principal

total assets under management	*initial investment*	*year founded*
$60 Million	$250,000–1 Million	1999

Hamilton Technology Ventures generally invests in seed- and early-stage companies. Its industry focus includes computer software, Internet and Intranet products (business-to-business), data communications hardware and software, telecommunications hardware and software, life sciences, bioinformatics, and medical devices.

Hamilton normally invests in the first round or second round of venture capital financing, often as the lead investor. For investments in hardware-oriented product companies, the Firm prefers to invest in companies that will create end-user solution products that combine hardware and software technologies. For software-oriented companies, the Firm prefers to invest in companies that will offer complete software solutions, including any necessary services. Niche opportunities that could result in the sale or licensing of technology are also of interest.

For stand-alone enterprises, the Firm would prefer to invest a total of $3 million to $5 million over two to three rounds. Hamilton requires completion of an initial screening document that it calls a "Preliminary Funding Request" in lieu of a business plan submittal.

HAMMOND, KENNEDY, WHITNEY & CO., INC.

230 Park Avenue, Suite 1616
New York, NY 10169
212-867-1010   fax: 212 867-1312

Forrest E. Crisman Jr., Partner

Andrew McNally IV, Partner

Glenn Scolnik, Partner

Ralph R. Whitney, Partner

Ward McNally, Managing Director

Matthew Hook, General Counsel

Maria Evangelista, Office Manager

total assets under management	*initial investment*	*year founded*
$20 Million	$2–5 Million	1903

Hammond, Kennedy, Whitney & Company, Inc. (HKW) is a private equity firm. HKW has the expertise to help companies grow, as well as having years of experience in later-stage financing. HKW invests globally, although most of its investments are within the continental United States.

HKW prefers to do later-stage financing, including acquisitions, buyouts, and special situations.

HARVEST PARTNERS INC.

280 Park Avenue, 33rd Floor
New York, NY 10017
212-599-6300   fax: 212-812-0100
www.hrvpart.com

Harvey P. Mallement, Managing General Partner

Harvey J. Wertheim, Managing General Partner

Thomas W. Arenz, General Partner

Stephen Eisenstein, General Partner

William J. Kane, General Partner

Ira D. Kleinman, General Partner

total assets under management	*initial investment*	*year founded*
$600 Million	$25–40 Million	1981

Harvest Partners is a private equity investment firm with a solid track record in creating successful businesses. It seeks to fund established mid-sized companies in the manufacturing, specialty services, and distribution industries. Harvest Partners is especially interested in structuring multinational buyouts. Harvest Partners will consider investments throughout the United States and Europe.

Portfolio Companies: Harvest Partners currently has 10 portfolio companies, including Community Distributors; Communication Dynamics; Global Energy Equipment Group, L.L.C.; Home Care Industries; Home Care Supply; IntelliRisk Management Corporation; Logisco; Lund International; priNexus; and TPS Holdings, Inc.

HEALTHCARE VENTURES LLC

44 Nassau Street   One Kendall Square, Suite 329
Princeton, NJ 08542   Cambridge, MA 02139
609-430-3900   617-252-4343
fax: 609-430-9525   fax: 617-252-4342
www.hcven.com

James H. Cavanaugh, General Partner

William W. Crouse, General Partner

Augustine Lawlor, General Partner

John W. Littlechild, General Partner

Christopher Mirabelli, General Partner

Harold R. Werner, General Partner

total assets under management	*initial investment*	*year founded*
$685 Million	$5–10 Million	1985

HealthCare Ventures LLC (HCV) is a venture capital firm with a commitment to building new biopharmaceutical companies. It works with early-stage companies in the biopharmaceutical industry, with an emphasis on genetic therapy, genomic sciences, drug discovery and delivery, neuroscience, cancer therapy, and organ and cellular transportation. HCV will consider investments located in the United States where its scientific, marketing, and business skills can convert a low-valuation investment into a high-valuation company.

Portfolio Companies: 3-Dimensional Pharmaceuticals, Inc.; Advanced Pharma, Inc.; Argonex Pharmaceuticals, Inc.; AVANT Immunotherapeutics; BioTransplant, Inc.; Delsys Pharmaceutical Corporation; Dendreon Corporation; Diacrin, Inc.; Diversa Corporation; Dyax Corporation; Integrity Pharmaceutical Corporation; Magainin Pharmaceuticals; MEMORY Pharmaceuticals Corporation; Millennium

Pharmaceuticals, Inc.; NitroMed, Inc.; Sensors for Medicine and Science, Inc.; Shire Pharmaceuticals Group plc; STC Technologies, Inc.; and Versicor, Inc.

HELLMAN & FRIEDMAN, LLC

One Maritime Plaza, 12th Floor
San Francisco, CA 94111
415-788-5111   fax: 415-788-0176
www.hf.com

F. Warren Hellman, Chairman

Matthew R. Barger, President

total assets under management	*initial investment*	*year founded*
$2.2 Billion	$100–300 Million	1984

Hellman & Friedman, LLC, is a private equity investment firm interested in companies with strong management teams, as well as a strong and defensible market position in growing markets. It typically invests in companies in the professional services, media and telecommunications, technology, and financial services industries. The Firm supports leveraged recapitalizations, acquisition financings, growth equity, traditional buyouts, and financial restructurings. It will consider investments on a nationwide level.

Portfolio Companies: Advanstar, Inc.; Blackbaud, Inc.; Brinson Partners, Inc.; Digitas Inc.; Eller Media Company, Inc.; Farallon Capital Management LLC; Formula One Motor Racing; Franklin Resources, Inc.; John Fairfax Holdings Limited; MidOcean Limited; Mitchell International; National Information Consortium, Inc.; National Radio Partners, L.P.; Oechsle International Advisors; Western Wireless Corporation/VoiceStream Wireless Corporation; and Young & Rubicam, Inc.

HICKORY VENTURE CAPITAL CORPORATION

301 Washington Street NW, Suite 301
Huntsville, AL 35801
256-539-1931   fax: 256-539-5130
www.hvcc.com

J. Thomas Noojin, President

total assets under management	*initial investment*	*year founded*
N/A	$1–2 Million	1984

Hickory Venture Capital seeks to back strong management teams imbued with entrepreneurial enthusiasm and the vision to build a highly successful company. It does not seek operating control and usually takes minority equity stakes. The Firm believes that the market potential must be large enough to allow the company to reach $50 million to $100 million or more in value over the next five to seven years.

Hickory Venture Capital focuses on investing in health-care services, information technology, and telecommunications. HVC invests in a mix of early- and later-stage companies, or companies ranging from an idea and a founder/partial management team to companies with revenue, profits, a complete team, and the need for expansion capital. HVC targets the Sunbelt (the Southwest and Southeast), the Mid-Atlantic and the Mid-West.

Portfolio Companies: Anivision; Cendex; Sprockets; and Talk.com.

HIGH STREET CAPITAL II, LLC

311 South Wacker Drive, Suite 4550
Chicago, IL 60606
312-697-4990   fax: 312-697-4994
www.highstr.com

Joseph R. Katcha, Principal

total assets under management	*initial investment*	*year founded*
$100 Million	$2–10 Million	1997

High Street Capital, LLC, is a private equity investment firm seeking to support experienced executives and managers in buying or expanding their businesses. The Firm prefers to fund middle-market companies that provide business-to-business services or are technology-related businesses. High Street Capital will consider investments located only within the United States.

Portfolio Companies: LaserExcel; MST Analytics; and The Store Room.

HIGHLAND CAPITAL PARTNERS

Two International Place   555 California Street, Suite 3100
22nd Floor   San Francisco, CA 94104
Boston, MA 02110   415-981-1230
617-531-1500   fax: 415-981-1229
fax: 617-531-1550
www.hcp.com

Robert F. Higgins, Managing General Partner
Paul A. Maeder, Managing General Partner
Wycliffe K. Grousbeck, General Partner
Daniel J. Nova, General Partner

total assets under management	*initial investment*	*year founded*
$1 Billion	$1–15 Million	1988

Highland Capital Partners is interested in equity investments in rapidly growing Internet/e-commerce, communications, software, and medical companies. All stages of investment are considered. Highland is actively investing in its newest fund, typically makes preferred equity investments, and actively assists in the strategic positioning and management of the portfolio company.

Portfolio Companies: Altign Networks; ANDA Networks; Ask Jeeves; Azanda Network Devices; Be Free; Beliefnet, Inc.; CardStore.com; Check Free; ClubMom; Coremetrics; Digital Commerce; Epylon; eToys; GemKey; GenVec; GuruNey Corporation; HotSocket; Lycos; MapQuest.com; Medscape; Navic Systems; New York Times Digital; NextCard; Ocular Networks; Plmarket; Spouse; Staples.com; telcobuy.com; Telica; and Wit Capital.

HLM MANAGEMENT COMPANY

222 Berkeley Street
Boston, MA 02116
617-266-0030   fax: 617-266-3619
www.hlmmanagement.com

Edward Cahill, Principal
Peter J. Grua, Principal
A. R. Haberkorn III, Principal
Ann B. Hutchings, Principal
Judith P. Lawrie, Principal
James J. Mahoney Jr., Principal

total assets under management	*initial investment*	*year founded*
$1 Billion	$20 Million	1983

HLM Management Company offers both public equity and private venture investment services in the technology, health-care, and business services industries. It has assisted its portfolio companies by: helping with the recruitment of a strong, experienced management team; offering business insight and advice regarding economic conditions, competitive challenges, emerging technologies, and target markets; providing networking opportunities within the industry and the investment community; and advising companies with regard to mergers and acquisitions and financing.

Portfolio Companies: Aspect Medical Systems, Inc.; Authoria, Inc.; HearMe; Spike Technologies; W3Health.

HOOK PARTNERS

One Lincoln Centre, Suite 1550
5400 LBJ Freeway
Dallas, TX 75240
972-991-5457   fax: 972-991-5458

David J. Hook, General Partner
George B. Chase, General Partner

total assets under management	*initial investment*	*year founded*
$103 Million	Under $2 Million	1978

Hook Partners is a private venture capital firm based out of Dallas, Texas. Hook Partners is an investment group that prefers to finance companies in their early stages and then continues to help them grow and expand. Hook Partners typically prefers to get into a financing situation in either the seed or start-up stage. Hook Partners funds companies located in the Southwest and West.

HOUSATONIC PARTNERS

88 Kearny Street, Suite 1610
San Francisco, CA 94108
415-955-9020
fax: 415-955-9053
www.housatonicpartners.com

11 Newbury Street, Suite 500
Boston, MA 02116
617-267-4545
fax: 617-267-5565

Barry D. Reynolds, Managing General Partner
William M. Thorndike Jr., Managing General Partner
Michael C. Jackson, General Partner

Brandson L. Nixon, General Partner

Eliot Wadsworth II, General Partner

Karen E. Liesching, Principal

H. Irving Grousbeck, Special Limited Partner

total assets under management	*initial investment*	*year founded*
$200 Million	$2–10 Million	1994

Housatonic Partners is a private equity investment partnership investing in later-stage companies in the business services, and in the media and communications industries. It seeks to invest in and build companies in cooperation with experienced and entrepreneurial managers. Its focus is to invest capital for long-term appreciation. Its portfolio companies exhibit favorable economic characteristics, including recurring revenues, moderate capital requirements, internal revenue growth, and the opportunity for follow-on investments.

Housatonic Partners maintains productive, ongoing relationships with its portfolio companies, typically serving on the Board of Directors.

Portfolio Companies: Housatonic Partners has over 35 portfolio companies.

HOWARD INDUSTRIES, INC.

136 Main Street
Westport, CT 06880
203-227-4900   fax: 203-227-3314
www.howardind.com

Peter H. Howard, Principal

total assets under management	*initial investment*	*year founded*
$1 Billion	$10–100 Million	1993

Howard Industries, Inc., is a private investment firm with an interest in middle-market companies. It works closely with management in a broad range of industries, such as metals processing and fabrication, electronics, telecommunications, plastic injection molding, textile, and assembly operations. Howard Industries seeks investment opportunities throughout the United States.

Portfolio Companies: Color Flex; Comair Rotron; and Engineered Data Products.

HUDSON VENTURES

660 Madison Avenue, 14th Floor
New York, NY 10021
212-644-9797   fax: 212-644-7430
www.hudsonventures.com

Jay Goldberg, General Partner

Lawrence Howard, M.D., General Partner

Doug Chertok, Managing Director

total assets under management	*initial investment*	*year founded*
$40 Million	$500,000–5 Million	1997

Hudson Ventures makes private equity investments in early-stage technology companies that need to diversify, revamp, or expand operations. Investment amounts range from $500,000 to $5 million, and often these investments are funded in stages. Hudson Ventures can also provide access to public and private markets for larger or subsequent sources of capital. Hudson Ventures is actively investing in the Internet, information technology, communications, and biotechnology industries.

   Portfolio Companies: Astata; Bla-Bla.com; CertifiedMail.com; ClientSoft; Comet Systems; i-Traffic; Mabool.com; Maxsol; Pathlight; PowerAdz.com; Query Object Systems; RocketBoard.com; Snickelways; The Square.com; and webMethods.

HUMANA VENTURES

500 West Main Street
Louisville, KY 40202
502-580-3922   fax: 502-580-2051
www.humanaventures.com

Thomas J. Listen, Senior Vice President

total assets under management	*initial investment*	*year founded*
$60 Million	$1–5 Million	N/A

Humana Ventures's main fields of interest are health-care services companies and health-care information technology companies, including e-health companies. The Firm focuses on companies ranging from early- to later-stage, whereby the investment size ranges from $1 to 5 million. Humana Ventures is actively seeking new deals on a national basis.

HUMMER WINBLAD VENTURE PARTNERS

Two South Park, 2nd Floor
San Francisco, CA 94107
415-979-9600   fax: 415-979-9601
www.humwin.com

John Hummer, Co-Founding Partner
Ann Winblad, Co-Founding Partner

total assets under management	*initial investment*	*year founded*
$900 Million	$500,000–20 Million	1989

Hummer Winblad Venture Partners is a venture capital firm with an exclusive focus on software. They seek entrepreneurs who have identified large, unmet market opportunities and have the determination and commitment to transform their ideas into market-leading businesses. Hummer Winblad Venture Partners will consider investments in the United States.

Portfolio Companies: Hummer Winblad Venture Partners has over 70 portfolio companies.

HUNTINGTON HOLDINGS, INC.

633 West 5th Street, Suite 6780
Los Angeles, CA 90071
213-617-1500   fax: 213-617-2325
www.hunthold.com

Jack B. Corwin, President
Bill Case, Associate

total assets under management	*initial investment*	*year founded*
N/A	N/A	1987

Huntington Holdings, Inc., is a merchant banking, merger and acquisition, and private LBO investment firm. Huntington Holdings advises, invests in, and acquires private middle-market companies located mostly in California. Huntington Holdings seeks companies with revenues in excess of $10 million and operating earnings in excess of $1.5 million.

Industry preferences include companies operating in the manufacturing, consumer product/services, aerospace and defense, and industrial products industries.

IDANTA PARTNERS, LTD.

4660 La Jolla Village Drive, Suite 850
San Diego, CA 92122
858-452-9690   fax: 858-452-2013
www.idanta.com

David Dunn, Managing Partner

Jonathan Huberman, General Partner

Mahesh Krishnamurthy, General Partner

Anita Colmie, CFO

total assets under management	initial investment	year founded
$400 Million	$1–10 Million	1971

Idanta Partners, Ltd., is an early-stage venture capital firm. The objective of the firm is to invest in young companies that have the potential to grow into substantial enterprises. The Firm invests on a national basis and as such does not have a particular geographic preference.

The Firm invests in all areas, including semiconductors, software, computer hardware, retailing, and medical technology.

IDG VENTURES

655 Montgomery Street, Suite 1900
San Francisco, CA 94111
415-439-4420   fax: 415-439-4428
www.idgventures.com

Pat McGovern, General Partner

Susan Cheng, General Partner

Kimberly Davis, General Partner

Pat Kenealy, Managing General Partner

total assets under management	initial investment	year founded
$160 Million	$500,000–4 Million	1996

IDG Ventures brings unique experience, perspective, and resources to its start-ups. IDG Ventures helps spread the information technology revolution by helping entrepreneurs grow innovative companies on a global basis.

Its industry focus is on PC and related hardware and software, client-server and related hardware and software, Internet and Intranet enabling hardware and software, advertiser and subscriber-supported new media content, and electronic commerce hardware, software, and systems.

Portfolio Companies: Andromedia; Aurigin; Baby Center; Digital Persona; F-5 Networks; FutureTense; Magmifi; Next Planet Over; Online Partners; Onova; PhotoAlley.com; Plansoft; Pronto; Sailnet; Service Merics; Spinner.com; Stagecast; Tavolo; VA Linux System; and Xuma.

iMINDS VENTURES

135 Main Street, Suite 1350
San Francisco, CA 94105
415-547-0000   fax: 415-547-0010
www.iminds.com

Randy Haykin, Managing Partner
Carl Nichols, Managing Partner

total assets under management	*initial investment*	*year founded*
$70 Million	$250,000–4 Million	1995

iMinds Ventures pursues seed- or early-stage investment opportunities within the Internet and information technology industries. Typical industry targets are Internet applications and services, electronic commerce, communications, and software applications. Geography is exclusive to companies based in the Western United States and primarily Silicon Valley and the San Francisco Bay Area.

Portfolio Companies: The Firm's "hands-on" approach to assisting start-ups has helped to launch companies such as America Onlines's Greenhouse; Delta Click Epicentric; NetChannel; and Yahoo!. iMinds has been the initial venture group involved in funding the launch of Buy Network; Goto.com; Impulse!; Kinecta; and Wit Capital.

IMPERIAL BANK

11512 El Camino Real, Suite 350
San Diego, CA 92130
858-509-2360   fax: 858-509-2365
www.imperialbank.com

Christopher Woolley, Managing Director

total assets under management	*initial investment*	*year founded*
$7 Billion	$30,000–3 Million	1963

Imperial Bank is a $7-billion Southern California–based business bank traded on the NYSE. Imperial Bank's Emerging Growth division provides loans and banking services exclusively to early-stage high-growth companies, primarily those with professional investor backing in the life sciences, Internet, software, and technology industries. The bank can also assist growth companies in identifying venture capital investors as well as other specialized providers in the legal and accounting fields.

Imperial Bank provides loans, deposit accounts, international banking, foreign exchange, electronic banking, investment management, factoring, leasing, and merchant card services. Specialized loan products include bridge loans for venture-backed companies, acquisition financing, and tenant improvement and equipment loans for building lab and production facilities.

Emerging Growth Division offices are located in the leading technology centers of the United States, including Los Angeles, Orange County, San Diego, Menlo Park, Palo Alto, and San Francisco, California.

INDOSUEZ VENTURES

2180 Sand Hill Road, Suite 450
Menlo Park, CA 94025
650-854-0587   fax: 650-323-5561

Nancy D. Burrus, General Partner
Guy H. Conger, General Partner
David E. Gold, General Partner

total assets under management	initial investment	year founded
$110 Million	$20,000–2 Million	1985

Indosuez Ventures is a Silicon Valley–based venture capital firm investing in technology-based, early-stage companies in the Western United States. The Firm focuses on computer and electronics, as well as health-care-related issues. An Indosuez Partner is always active on every one of its investments. The Partners bring many decades of experience in both operating and financial areas to their portfolio companies.

Portfolio Companies: Indosuez has over 35 portfolio companies in Internet, computer software and systems, telecommunications, semiconductor products and equipment, biotechnology, pharmaceuticals, and medical instrumentations.

INDUSTRIAL GROWTH PARTNERS

100 Spear Street, Suite 310
San Francisco, CA 94105
415-882-4550   fax: 415-882-4551
www.igpequity.com

Michael H. Beaumont, Principal
R. Patrick Forster, Principal
Gottfried P. Tittiger, Principal

total assets under management	*initial investment*	*year founded*
$150 Million	$7–30 Million	1997

Industrial Growth Partners (IGP), a private investment partnership, invests equity in a number of transactions involving changes in ownership, including management buyouts and buyins, recapitalizations, corporate divestitures, and industry build-ups. The Firm focuses exclusively on the manufacturing industry, particularly industrial components and equipment; electrical and electronic equipment; process instrumentation and controls; telecommunications equipment; specialty chemicals; fluid control, filtration, and pumps; analytical instruments and measuring devices; synthetic rubber, elastomers, and plastics; health-care and safety equipment; and energy services and equipment. IGP funds companies in the United States.

   Portfolio Companies: Airpax Corporation; Associated Chemists; Electronic Protection Products; Inc.; The Felters Group; Power Protection Products, Inc.; Thermal Sensing Products, Inc.; and WARCO.

INFINITY CAPITAL

100 Hamilton Avenue, Suite 400
Palo Alto, CA 94301
650-462-8400   fax: 650-462-8415
www.infinityllc.com

Lori Kulvin Crawford, Managing Director
John Hershey, Managing Director
Sam H. Lee, Managing Director
Virginia M. Turezyn, Managing Director

total assets under management	*initial investment*	*year founded*
$400 Million	N/A	N/A

Infinity Capital is an early-stage venture capital firm focused on cultivating an entrepreneur's ingenuity. Infinity Capital invests in the communication and Internet market sectors and has partnered with entrepreneurs to create dynamic companies developing leading-edge technology, growing into world-class enterprises.

Portfolio Companies: Allegro Networks; BeeLine Networks; Calmar Optcon; eAssist; I-Escrow; United Messaging; and White Amber.

ING FURMAN SELZ INVESTMENTS

55 East 22nd Street, 37th Floor
New York, NY 10055
212-409-6518   fax: 212-409-5874

Brian P. Friedman, President
James L. Luikart, Managing Director
Nicholas Daraviras, Associate
Seth E. Wilson, Associate
John M. Warner, Associate

total assets under management	*initial investment*	*year founded*
$300 Million	$5–30 Million	1994

ING Furman Selz Investments is a private equity firm with more than $300 million in funds under management. ING Furman Selz Investments focuses its investment activity on select industries in which their professionals have established expertise.

The industries in which ING Furman Selz Investments concentrates include: consumer leisure, education and training, financial services, health care, industrial, information technology, media and communications, and transportation. It invests in later-stage venture companies in management buyouts and in support of corporate expansion and industry consolidations.

INGLEWOOD VENTURES

12526 High Bluff Drive, Suite 300
San Diego, CA 92130
858-792-3579   fax: 858-792-3417

M. Blake Ingle, Ph.D., Partner

Daniel Wood, CFA, Partner

total assets under management	*initial investment*	*year founded*
$30 Million	$250,000–1.5 Million	1999

IngleWood Ventures invests primarily in biotechnology, medical devices, and medical products and services, including software and communications companies with a health-care focus. The Firm focuses on seed- and early-stage companies geographically located in San Diego County.

INNOCAL

600 Anton Boulevard, Suite 1270
Costa Mesa, CA 92626
714-850-6784   fax: 714-850-6798
www.innocal.com

James E. Houlihan III, Partner
H. D. Lamber, Partner
Daniel L. Bassett, Venture Partner

total assets under management	*initial investment*	*year founded*
$175 Million	$1 Million–5 Million	1993

InnoCal's investment focus is on early- and expansion-stage technology-based businesses that have the potential to be leaders within their respective industries. While the primary investment emphasis is on electronics, software, communications, and health care, high-growth businesses in other viable industries are also considered.

InnoCal prefers to focus on businesses located within California; however, other geographic locations are also considered. To support this effort, InnoCal has satellite offices in Saddle Brook, New Jersey, and San Diego, California, in addition to its headquarters in Costa Mesa, California.

INNOVEST VENTURE PARTNERS

2860 Zanker Road, Suite 207
San Jose, CA 95134
408-943-8413   fax: 408-943-1170
www.innovestventure.com

Chung Hsu, Partner

total assets under management	initial investment	year founded
$25 Million	Up to $1 Million	N/A

Innovest Venture Partners is a venture capital firm with a special emphasis on high-technology companies, particularly software, communications, semiconductor devices and equipment, and biotechnology. It will fund in all stages of a company's development, with a preference for start-up and early-stage phases. Innovest Venture Partners will consider funds located in Silicon Valley and greater China.

INSIGHT CAPITAL PARTNERS

680 Fifth Avenue, 8th Floor
New York, NY 10019
212-230-9200   fax: 212-230-9272
www.insightpartners.com

Jeff Horing, Co-Founder and Managing Director

Jerry Murdock, Co-Founder and Managing Director

Bill Doyle, Managing Director

Scott M. Maxwell, Managing Director

Roel Pieper, Managing Director

Peter Sobiloff, Managing Director

total assets under management	initial investment	year founded
$1.5 Billion	$10–20 Million	1996

Insight Capital Partners is a global private equity firm with an interest in business-to-business and related software infrastructure segments of the information technology markets. Its global approach enables it to understand key market dynamics and assist portfolio companies in execution across multiple geographic markets simultaneously. Insight Capital Partners strives to build lasting relationships with its portfolio companies and play an active role in: recruiting, board building, strategic positioning, financing, mergers and acquisitions, and strategic planning. With offices in New York and Amsterdam, Insight Capital Partners invests worldwide in companies and entrepreneurs who are seeking true value-added capital.

   Portfolio Companies: Agillion; Altitude Software (formerly Easyphone); AMS Services, Inc.; Apar Infotech Services; APP Group; Authorize.Net; Cadence

Network, Inc.; CarStation.com; C-Bridge Internet Solutions; CES International; Cleanwise.com; Click Commerce; ConnectCapital Holdings; Convergent Group; Customer Analytics; DownstreamEnergy; Eftia OSS Solutions; Eliance Corporation; Enermetrix.com; euSmart; Exchange Applications; FinLatin International, Inc.; Greenfield Online; Hologix, Inc.; HUON Corporation; IKANO Communications, Inc.; Illuminet; I-many, Inc.; iMedeon; IZOIC; LoanCity.com; MagCom; MarketMAX; mediapassage.com; Meta4, SA; NetPlane (formerly H & J); Nistevo; OneSwoop.com; Optum Software; paperX.com; Peace Software; Quest Software, Inc.; realink.com; RockPort Trade Systems; RxCentric, Inc.; SeeCommerce (formerly VIT); SLMsoft.com; SLP InfoWare; SeeBeyond Technology Corporation (formerly Software Technologies Corporation); Stonehenge Telecom N.V.; SynQuest, Inc.; Syntax Systems; TradingCars.com; USADATA.com; Webhelp.com; Xelus, Inc. (formerly LPA); XOIP; and YourNews.

INSTITUTIONAL VENTURE PARTNERS (IVP)

3000 Sand Hill Road
Building 2, Suite 290
Menlo Park, CA 94025
650-854-0132   fax: 650-854-5762
www.ivp.com

Norman A. Fogelsong, Partner

Todd C. Chaffee, Partner

Reid W. Dennis, Partner

Mary Jane Elmore, Partner

total assets under management	*initial investment*	*year founded*
$1.2 Billion	$500,000–4 Million	1980

Institutional Venture Partners (IVP), based in Menlo Park, California, manages over $1 billion in venture capital. IVP's goal is to invest in leading companies with advanced technology in the information technology field. IVP selectively invests in later-stage opportunities. Seventy-three IVP companies have gone public since 1980. These companies have revenues greater than $25 billion, employ more than 150,000 people, and have a combined market capitalization of over $75 billion.

IVP seeks to invest in high technology companies that can be leaders in their segments. Investment areas include communications, software, and the Internet and Intranet.

INTEGRA VENTURES

1114 21st Avenue East
Seattle, WA 98112
206-329-5009   fax: 206-329-5105
www.integraventures.net

Jospeh Piper, Managing Partner
Hans Lundin, Managing Partner

total assets under management	*initial investment*	*year founded*
$40 Million	$500,000–3 Million	1998

Integra Ventures seeks investments in seed- to later-stage life sciences companies. It considers business plans from experienced entrepreneurs passionately pursuing outsourcing products/services related to health-care software applications, bioinformatics, biotechnology tools, medical devices, and the Internet. Although Integra Ventures seeks opportunities across America, it focuses on innovative companies in the West and invests predominantly in companies requiring less than $5 million of initial capital. The Firm usually positions its investments as a part of a syndicate, partnering with firms that also have technical or market experience, capital depth, and/or strategic influence.

   Portfolio Companies: American WholeHealth; Amnis; Cara Vita; Finch Technologies; HealthHelp; National Healing; and Physicians' Edge.

INTEGRAL CAPITAL PARTNERS

2750 Sand Hill Road
Menlo Park, CA 94025
650-233-0360   fax: 650-233-0366
www.integralcapital.com

Roger McNamee, Co-Founder and Managing Director
John Powell, Co-Founder and Managing Director
Pamela Hagenah, Managing Director
Glen Kacher, Managing Director
Neil Stremingher, Managing Director
Robert McCormack Jr., Associate

total assets under management	*initial investment*	*year founded*
$1 Billion	$3–5 Million	1991

Integral Capital Partners, a venture capital firm, utilizes a network of investors, venture affiliates, and industry executives to assist its portfolio companies in reaching maximum potential. It will invest in all stages of a company's development beyond the start-up phase. Integral Capital Partners targets the information and life sciences industries located in the United States. Integral Capital Partners is also an active investor in public companies, making contributions with corporate strategy and business development opportunities.

Portfolio Companies: Integral Capital Partners has over 130 portfolio companies including: Agile Software; Centillium Communications; E.piphany; Extreme Networks; Flextronics; Interwoven; ONI Systems; PMC-Sierra; and Sycamore Networks.

International Capital Partners, Inc.

300 First Stamford Place
Stamford, CT 06902
203-961-8900   fax: 203-969-2212
www.intcapital.com

Ajit Huthessing, Managing Partner
Douglas L. Ayer, Managing Partner
Nicholas E. Sinacori, Managing Partner

total assets under management	*initial investment*	*year founded*
$250 Million	$100,000–8 Million	1990

International Capital Partners, Inc. (ICP), provides expansion capital in the form of equity and equity linked securities to smaller-growth companies. Generally, these companies are private and planning an IPO in the near future. ICP also invests primarily in public companies valued at under $150 million and, selectively, in Angel round investments. It is a condition of ICP investments that an ICP Managing Partner joins the Board of Directors of investee companies. Partners play a very active role in assisting the Firm's companies to grow rapidly.

Portfolio Companies: ICP has a record of successful investing in small companies, having invested over $100 million in more than 40 transactions with 27 companies.

Interprise Technology Partners, LP

1001 Brickell Avenue, 30th Floor
Miami, FL 33131
305-374-6808   fax: 305-374-3317
www.itpvc.com

Edmund Miller, Partner

David Parker, Managing Partner

J. C. Campuzano, Principal

Andrew Cohen, Principal

Carlos F. Mejia, Principal

total assets under management	*initial investment*	*year founded*
$110 Million	N/A	1999

ITP was founded in January 1999 to focus exclusively on Internet, IT companies, or businesses that strategically use the Internet and IT to significantly leverage their operations. Investments are made in expansion-stage private enterprises, that is, second- and third-round financing, as well as select early-stage situations.

A venture capital firm that focuses on Internet and IT companies or businesses that strategically use technology to significantly leverage their operations, ITP especially likes companies with a B2B e-commerce or logistics focus, as this takes advantage of the Firm's background and expertise.

Portfolio Companies: Cenetec, Inc.; Esauio, Inc.; International Parts; Luna Information Systems; Nexchange; VisualPlex Corp.; World Commerce Online, Inc.; and Yupi Internet, Inc.

INTERWEST PARTNERS VIII

3000 Sand Hill Road
Building 3, Suite 255
Menlo Park, CA 94025
650-854-8585   fax: 650-854-4706
www.interwest.com

Stephen C. Bowsher, Internet/E-Commerce

H. Barry Cash, Communications/Internet Infrastructure

Alan W. Crites, Internet/E-Commerce

Rodney A. Ferguson, Biopharmaceuticals and Medical Devices

Philip T. Glanos, Communications/Internet Infrastructure

W. Scott Hedrick, Internet/E-Commerce

W. Stephen Holmes, Administrative Partner

Dr. Gilbert H. Kliman, Health Care

Dr. Arnold L. Oronsky, Biopharmaceuticals and Medical Devices

Thomas L. Rosch, Communications/Internet Infrastructure and E-Commerce

total assets under management	*initial investment*	*year founded*
$1.6 Billion	$3–17.5 Million	1979

The InterWest Partners VIII's investment strategy will focus primarily on traditional venture capital investments in the information technology and medical technology sectors.

The focus of InterWest's information technology investments will continue to be the communications infrastructure and the e-commerce/Internet industries. Most of the investments will be in the early or expansion stages.

Investments in the medical technology sector will primarily be early- and expansion-stage in nature and will focus on the biopharmaceuticals and health-care devices industries.

Portfolio Companies: Airspan Networks; Arthrocare; Copper Mountain Networks; CIENA Corporation; Cor Therapeutics; Corixa; Coulter Pharmaceutical; and Xilinx.

ITU VENTURES

9250 Wilshire Boulevard, Suite 100
Beverly Hills, CA 90212
310-777-5900   fax: 310-777-5901
www.itu.com

Adam Winnick, Co-Founder, Managing Partner

Chad Brownstein, Co-Founder, Managing Partner

Jonah Schnel, Co-Founder, Managing Partner

total assets under management	*initial investment*	*year founded*
$6.6 Million	Up to $1 Million	2000

ITU Ventures is a leading venture capital firm that invests in and develops seed-stage technology businesses emerging from the nation's leading graduate schools. ITU has created a unique Peer-to-Peer Venture Finance strategy in which it employs a network of graduate students (Campus Partners) with exceptional professional experience to identify attractive investment opportunities on campus. ITU Ventures also provides operational support services for its portfolio companies, including accounting/cash management, business development, finance, human resources, PR/marketing, and technology. The company has a presence at the following universities: California Institute of Technology; Carnegie Mellon; Columbia University; Georgia Institute of Technology; Harvard University; Massachusetts Institute of Technology; Purdue University; Stanford University; University of California, Berkeley;

University of Michigan; University of Pennsylvania; and University of Texas at Austin.

   Portfolio Companies: Isovia, Inc.; OEwaves Corp.; Opient, Inc.; OnWafer Technologies, Inc.; and SkyFlow, Inc.

IVP (INSTITUTIONAL VENTURE PARTNERS)

3000 Sand Hill Road, Building 2, Suite 290
Menlo Park, CA 94025
650-854-0132   fax: 650-854-5762
www.ivp.com

Allen Beasley, Partner

Samuel D. Colella, Partner

Reid W. Dennis, Partner

R. Thomas Dyal, Partner

Mary Jane Elmore, Partner

Norman A. Fogelsong, Partner

Peter Gotecher, Partner

Timothy M. Haley, Partner

John M. McQuillan, Partner

Ruthann Quindlen, Partner

Rebecca B. Robertson, Partner

L. James Strand, Partner

William P. Tai, Partner

T. Peter Thomas, Partner

John K. Tillotson, Partner

Geoffrey Y. Yang, Partner

total assets under management	*initial investment*	*year founded*
$1 Billion	N/A	1974

IVP (Institutional Venture Partners) is a venture capital firm focusing on e-commerce, Internet media, communications, digital/personalized television, Web infrastructure and services, and medical devices. IVP targets companies in their later stages of development, such as divisional spinouts, buyouts, recapitalizations, industry consolidations, or a variety of other possible transactions in both private and public companies.

IVP believes it has the size, experience, and strategy to build partnerships with entrepreneurs and help them build successful companies. IVP invests in companies nationally.

Portfolio Companies: IVP has over 200 portfolio companies.

J. F. SHEA VENTURE CAPITAL

P.O. Box 489
Walnut, CA 91788-0489
909-594-9500   fax: 909-594-0935
www.jfshea.com/capital.htm

total assets under management	*initial investment*	*year founded*
N/A	N/A	1968

J. F. Shea Venture Capital is a division of J. F. Shea Co., Inc., and invests in the technology industry. It helps private start-up companies located in the United States, especially those located in Silicon Valley in California.

To date, the Firm has helped many start-ups go public, such as Altera Corporation; America West Airlines; Brocade Communications Systems; Compaq Computer Corporation; Excelan (which became Novell); Exodus Communications, Inc.; Genetech Inc.; Hambrecht & Quist Group, Inc.; Linear Technology Corporation; Rational Software Corp.; and The AES Corporation.

JAFCO VENTURES

505 Hamilton Avenue, Suite 310   One Boston Place, Suite 3320
Palo Alto, CA 94301   Boston, MA 02108
650-463-8800   617-367-3510
fax: 650-463-8801   fax: 617-367-3532
www.jafco.com

Barry Schiffman, President, Executive Managing Director, and CIO
Andy Goldfarb, Managing Director
Stephen Hill, Managing Director
Ullas Naik, Managing Director
Lynn Barringer, Vice President and CFO
Dave Fachetti, Vice President

David Polifko, Vice President

total assets under management	*initial investment*	*year founded*
$750 Million	N/A	1993

JAFCO Ventures invests in the information technology industry across various sectors. The Firm looks for experienced management teams with proven technical expertise and relevant industry knowledge. JAFCO implements a rigorous and thorough approach to evaluating and executing investments. It was listed as one of the most successful venture capital firms in 1999 by *Forbes* magazine and was fifth overall in terms of total return based on post-IPO performance in 1999.

Portfolio Companies: Digital Island; EnCommerce; The Lightspan Partnership; Net Perceptions; Silknet Software; AirGate PCS; Aptis Communications; Unisphere Solutions; Avanex Corporation; Moneterey Networks; Sentient Networks; Brocade Communications Systems; Creative Design Solutions; Obsidian, Inc.; Philsar Semiconductor; and Vixel Corporation.

JATOTECH VENTURES

301 Congress Avenue, Suite 2050
Austin, TX 78701
512-236-6950   fax: 512-236-6959
www.jatotech.com

Kari Hunt, Operations Director

Molly Pieroni, Partner

Walt Thirion, Partner

total assets under management	*initial investment*	*year founded*
$55 Million	$500,000–1.5 Million	1999

JatoTech Ventures typically invests in technology companies seeking to create new markets. The Firm focuses on early-stage investing and takes a labor-intensive, service-oriented approach in markets where it has direct experience.

JatoTech limits the number of companies it invests in, giving them an unusually high partner-to-capital ratio, and ensures that portfolio companies get the attention they deserve.

Portfolio Companies: Banderacom, Inc.; Cygnal; Loales Systems; Scenix; and Stream Machine.

JEFFERSON CAPITAL PARTNERS, LTD.
901 East Cary Street, 16th Floor
Richmond, VA 23219
804-643-0100   fax: 804-643-9140
www.jeffersoncapital.com

Palmer P. Garson, Managing Partner

R. Timothy O'Donnell, Managing Partner

Louis W. Moelchert III, Partner

Leslie M. Jackson, Associate

total assets under management	*initial investment*	*year founded*
$51 Million	$2–5 Million	1996

Jefferson Capital Partners, Ltd. (JCP), is a private equity firm seeking to invest in growth financings, management buyouts, and recapitalizations of well-managed, rapidly growing companies. Its primary focus is to identify investment opportunities within the consumer, health-care, and information services industries.

JCP will provide equity capital for any rapidly growing company meeting its investment criteria. Most candidates will have between $5 to $75 million of annual revenues. JCP will only pursue investments in which it believes it can develop true partnerships with management teams. JCP will act as the sole investor or will assemble syndicates of equity and/or debt. Although JCP is typically the lead institutional investor, it will also review opportunities to invest jointly with other private equity firms.

Portfolio Companies: Cornerstone Retail Solutions, Inc.; The Country Peddlers and Company of America; Global Trade Technologies, Inc.; Gold Coast Restaurants, Inc.; The Hobart West Group; iDolls; KaBloom, Ltd.; Kid Galaxy; MicroMass Communications, Inc.; NotifyMD; People's Pottery, Inc.; and Prestige Brands International, Inc.

JK & B CAPITAL
205 N. Michigan Avenue, Suite 808
Chicago, IL 60601
312-946-1200   fax: 312-946-1103
www.jkbcapital.com

Constance Capone, Executive Member

Al DaValie, Executive Member

Richard Finkelstein, Executive Member

Robert W. Humes, Executive Member

David Kronfeld, Chairman

Thomas M. Neustaetter, Executive Member

Nancy O'Leary, CFO

Tasha Seitz, Principal Member

Ali Shadman, Executive Member

Marc Sokol, Executive Member

total assets under management	*initial investment*	*year founded*
$600 Million	$5–20 Million	1996

JK & B Capital's primary investment focus is in telecommunications software and information technologies industries. Over time, JK & B seeks to invest between $10 and $30 million in any portfolio company. The Firm doesn't require a seat on the Board of Directors; however, it serves on the Board for the majority of its portfolio companies. JK & B works very closely with management in the development of the company's budgets and strategic plans. Its primary investment activity focuses on domestic businesses and companies with operations in the United States.

JOHNSTON ASSOCIATES INC.

181 Cherry Valley Road
Princeton, NJ 08540-7645
609-924-3131   fax: 609-683-7524

Robert F. Johnston, General Partner

Lynn D. Johnston, General Partner

total assets under management	*initial investment*	*year founded*
N/A	$250,000–2 Million	1968

Johnston Associates Inc. (JAI) invests its partners' private capital, as well as the capital of "friends of the Firm." JAI does not manage an investment fund. Accordingly, the Firm has no pre-set investment horizons, return objectives, investment limits, or size. Because of the time-consuming nature of start-ups, JAI typically invests in one enterprise every two years.

JAI's interests include therapeutics and delivery mechanisms, medical devices, diagnostics, separations and purification technologies, functional genomics, and databases for therapeutic discovery.

Since its foundation, JAI has launched several companies from the ground up, around unique and commercially promising technologies. The Firm also has financed established small companies with demonstrated growth potential.

Portfolio Companies: "A" Company Orthodontics; Biocyte; Bio Sepra; Cytogen; Ecogen; Envirogen; Immunicon; i-STAT; Praelux; Sepracor; and Sonomed.

JOSEPHBERG GROSZ & CO., INC.

633 Third Avenue
New York, NY 10017
212-974-9926   fax: 212-397-5832

Richard A. Josephberg, Chairman

total assets under management	*initial investment*	*year founded*
N/A	$2–20 Million	1986

Josephberg Grosz & Co., Inc., specializes in providing equity financing for emerging public and private companies. Josephberg Grosz & Co. invests in all stages of funding throughout the United States and other parts of the world. It has no industry restrictions.

KANSAS CITY EQUITY PARTNERS

233 West 47th Street
Kansas City, MO 64112
816-960-1771   fax: 816-960-1777
www.kcep.com

Thomas Palmer, Managing Director
William Reisler, Managing Director
David Schulte, Managing Director

total assets under management	*initial investment*	*year founded*
$75 Million	$1–3 Million	1993

Kansas City Equity Partners (KCEP) is a venture capital firm that takes part in a wide range of transactions, from early-stage to expansions to buyouts/consolidations. It has experience in the e-solutions, telecommunications, consumer retail, and industrial manufacturing industries. KCEP invests throughout the United States but focuses particularly on the Midwest.

KCEP believes it is more than just a funding source. The Firm offers help with strategic decisions, has a network of contacts and management sources, and assists with an array of issues that may face an entrepreneur in a growing business. Desirable traits for a portfolio include a qualified management team, well-defined product/service, competitive advantage, and a well-established marketplace demand.

Portfolio Companies: BeyondNow Technologies; Birch Telecom; Build-a-Bear Workshop; Energy Partners; freightpro; Itravel; Organized Living; PulseCard, Inc.; Three Dog Bakery; and Western CE.

KB PARTNERS, L.L.C.

1101 Skokie Boulevard, Suite 260
Northbrook, IL 60062
847-714-0444   fax: 847-714-0445
www.kbpartners.com

Keith Bank, Managing Partner

total assets under management	*initial investment*	*year founded*
$70 Million	N/A	1996

KB Partners desires to make investments in a diverse range of businesses that have the potential for substantial medium- and long-term capital appreciation. The Firm seeks to combine its expertise with that of existing management or to recruit the appropriate management team to maximize the potential of each company in which it invests. It seeks to make investments in the Midwestern United States.

KB Partners possesses broad-based experience in many areas and will consider investing in a variety of industries; however, the Firm can provide the greatest value-added investments in industries where the principals of KB Partners or associates have knowledge or previous experience. Some of these include: analytical instruments, computer hardware/software, engineering/technology, Internet services/products, information technology, and telecommunications.

KBL HEALTHCARE VENTURES

645 Madison Avenue, 14th Floor
New York, NY 10022
212-319-5555   fax: 212-319-5591
www.kblhealthcare.com

Marlene R. Krauss, M.D., Managing Director

Zachary C. Berk, O.D., Managing Director

Michael D. Kaswan, Vice President

Gauran Agganwal, Senior Associate

Theresa Fiorillo, Office Manager

total assets under management	*initial investment*	*year founded*
$100 Million	$1–4 Million	1991

KBL Healthcare Ventures (KBL) is a physician-run venture capital firm dedicated to discovering and developing innovative companies that create real, lasting value within the U.S. health-care system.

KBL makes venture capital investments in start-up, early-stage and emerging-growth companies that compete in the health-care industry. Targeted sectors within health care include medical devices, health-care Internet, health-care services, and niche pharmaceuticals.

Portfolio Companies: American Psych Systems, Inc.; Cambridge Heart, Inc.; Codman Group; Gynetics; iPhysician Net, Inc.; Lumenos, One Inc.; and Neuromedical Systems, Inc.

KECALP INC.

World Financial Center, South Tower
225 Liberty Street
New York, NY 10080-6123
212-236-7302   fax: 212-236-7364
www.kecalp.com

Matthias Boman, President and Chief Investment Officer

Edward J. Higgins, Managing Director

Margaret P. Monico, Chief Operating Officer

total assets under management	*initial investment*	*year founded*
$900 Million	$5–10 Million	1983

KECALP Inc., a wholly owned subsidiary of Merrill Lynch & Co., Inc., is the general partner of and investment adviser to limited partnerships formed exclusively for investment by employees of Merrill Lynch & Co., Inc., its subsidiaries, and affiliates. To date, KECALP Inc. has served as the general partner and investment adviser for nine partnerships.

The partnerships seek minority interest positions, primarily, in privately offered equity investments in both U.S. and non-U.S. issuers. Investments may include securities issued in conjunction with leveraged buyouts, financing of companies in an early stage of development, investments in growth equity situations, participation in real estate ventures, and transactions involving financial restructuring or reorganization.

Investments of $5 million to $10 million are preferred, although smaller investments in special situations will be considered.

KETTLE PARTNERS LP

350 West Hubbard, Suite 350
Chicago, IL 60610
312-329-9300   fax: 312-329-9310
www.kettlevc.com

David R. Semmel, General Partner

Lee Rosenberg, General Partner

Mark Achler, General Partner

Bruce Bearbower, CFO

Kevin Weinstein, Investment Associate

Susan Connor, Research Associate

total assets under management	*initial investment*	*year founded*
$75 Million	$1–5 Million	1998

Kettle Partners LP is a stage and geography independent, broadband focused venture capital fund. Kettle Partners is continuously looking for the best new companies, the brightest ideas, and the best entrepreneurs. The company focuses on early-stage companies seeking their first round of professional VC financing. Its investment size depends on the stage of the company and the total amount raised.

Portfolio Companies: MetaSolv Software; CopperCom; Diveo, Emperative; Novarra; Full Audio; Active.com; Ignite Sports Media; Egreetings; Concept Kitchen; and JuniorNet.

KEYSTONE VENTURE CAPITAL

1601 Market Street, Suite 2500
Philadelphia, PA 19103
215-241-1200   fax: 215-241-1211
www.keystonevc.com

Kerry J. Dale, General Partner

Peter E. Ligeti, General Partner

John R. Regan, General Partner

Robert Pace, Vice President

Atul Madatar, Vice President

total assets under management	*initial investment*	*year founded*
$150 Million	$3–5 Million	1982

Keystone Venture Capital focuses on equity investments in early- and expansion-stage companies in high-growth technology sectors. Targeted markets include Internet-enabling applications, telecom and wireless communications, and business-to-business and business-to-consumer e-commerce.

Portfolio Companies: CDNOW; DigiLens; eduction; i3Mobile; Imagicast Inc.; Infonautics; L90; NCT Delivery; Response Network; RSA Security Inc.; Solbright; VST Technologies, Inc.; Wisor Telecom; and Worldstor.

KLEINER PERKINS CAUFIELD & BYERS

2750 Sand Hill Road
Menlo Park, CA 94025
650-233-2750   fax: 650-233-0300
www.kpcb.com

Eugene Kleiner, Founding Partner

Tom Perkins, Founding Partner

total assets under management	*initial investment*	*year founded*
$1.2 Billion	N/A	1972

KPCB has raised over $1.2 billion in capital and has invested in companies whose total market value exceeds $80 billion. KPCB organizes its investment strategy around eight initiatives: the Internet, enterprise software, consumer media, communications, semiconductors, medical devices and diagnostics, drug discovery and therapeutics, and health-care services and informatics.

Portfolio Companies: AOL; Ascend Communications; AutoTrader.com; Corio, Excite.com; iVillage.com; LinuxCare; LSI Logic; Oblix; Optical Network; and Siara Systems.

KLINE HAWKES & COMPANY

11726 San Vicente Boulevard, Suite 300
Los Angeles, CA 90049
310-442-4700   fax: 310-442-4707

Frank R. Kline, Managing Partner

Jay Ferguson, Partner

total assets under management	*initial investment*	*year founded*
$275 Million	$5–15 Million	1995

Kline Hawkes & Co., through its funds Kline Hawkes California, L.P., and Kline Hawkes Pacific, L.P., provides investors with access to investment opportunities in emerging-growth and middle-market companies across the western half of the United States. The funds have up to $275 million of investment capital, mostly available from institutional investors such as CalPERS, LACERA, and ULLICO.

    The newest fund, Kline Hawkes Pacific, L.P., focuses on Internet infrastructure, software, telecommunications, health-care services, and business outsourcing. Individual investments, in mid- to late-stage companies, range from $5 to $15 million.

KLM CAPITAL GROUP

10 Almaden Boulevard	4516 Seton Center Parkway	1-13 D'Aguilar Street
Suite 988	Suite 170	Central, Hong Kong
10th Floor, Century Square	Austin, TX 78759	852-2537-3318
San Jose, CA 95113	512-338-9688	fax: 852-2537-3138
408-970-8888	fax: 512-338-9764	
fax: 408-970-8887		
www.klmtech.com		

Peter Mok, President and CEO

Donald W. Brooks, Chairman

Joel D. Kellman, Principal

Alfred Li, Principal

Jerald P. Shaevitz, Principal

Chay Kwong Soon, Vice Chairman

Rick Frasch, Principal

Godfrey Fong, Principal

total assets under management	*initial investment*	*year founded*
$200 Million	N/A	1996

KLM Capital Group's investment focus is on companies in semiconductors, information technology, and telecommunications. KLM Capital believes that these are lucrative fields for investment, and it has considerable expertise and networking in these fields through its principals and advisers.

Investments spread across four stages: seed, early-stage, mezzanine, and public investment. The actual mix of investments will be determined by the opportunities that become available.

KLM Capital seeks to add value to its portfolio companies by creating and facilitating cross-border transactions between North America and Asia. It is expected that U.S.-based early-stage technology companies will benefit from access to Asian manufacturing capabilities at competitive costs, as well as channels into high-growth markets in Asia, whereas established Asian enterprises and OEM manufacturers will benefit from proprietary technologies.

Portfolio Companies: Addvalue Technologies; Alacrity; Alaris; Amplify.net; Centillium Technology; CyberBills; Cyberplus Corporation; Cygnal Integrated Products, Inc.; Easent Communications, Inc.; Employchina.com, Inc.; Focused Semiconductor Group; House18.com; Icras, Inc.; Internet Corporation; JemPac International Corp.; MetroWave Communications, Inc.; nCommand, Inc.; Phone.com; Radiant Photonics., Inc.; ShareWave; Silicon Laboratories; Silicon Metrics Corp.; Syntricity; Talkway; Tmanage, Inc.; T.sqware; United Semiconductor; V-Bits, Inc. (acquired by Cisco); and YesVideo.com.

KOHLBERG & COMPANY, L.L.C.

258 High Street, Suite 100   111 Radio Circle
Palo Alto, CA 94301   Mt. Kisco, NY 10549
650-463-1480   914-241-7430
fax: 650-463-1481   fax: 914-241-7476
www.kohlberg.com

James A. Kohlberg, Founder and Managing Principal

Ranjis S. Bhonsle, Principal

Samuel P. Frieder, Principal

Christopher Lacovara, Principal

Evan Wildstein, Principal

total assets under management	*initial investment*	*year founded*
$300 Million	$15–75 Million	1987

Kohlberg & Company, L.L.C., is a private equity firm with an emphasis on middle-market investing. It is involved in a wide variety of industries, including retail, building products, health care, financial services, agricultural products, aerospace, and printing. Kohlberg & Company funds: traditional buyout opportunities, companies seeking to reduce excessive leverage, turnaround investments, family-run businesses in which owners desire near-term liquidity and continuous involvement, and divisions of larger companies seeking to enhance growth and profitability.

Kohlberg & Company strongly believes in working in partnership with the management of each portfolio company and typically gains voting control of each company in which it invests. It will consider investments throughout the United States.

Portfolio Companies: Airport Satellite Parking, L.L.C.; Allied Aerospace Industries, Inc.; American Homecare Supply, L.L.C.; BI Inc.; Camber Companies, L.L.C.; Color Spot Nurseries, Inc.; Holley Performance Products, Inc.; Innotek, Inc.; Katowah Capital; Northwestern Steel and Wire Company; Printing Arts America, Inc.; Radaelli Tacna; S.p.A.; Simplicity Manufacturing, Inc.; Southwest Supermarkets, L.L.C.; and United Signature Foods, L.L.C.

THE KRIEGSMAN GROUP

11726 San Vicente Boulevard, Suite 650
Los Angeles, CA 90049
310-826-5449   fax: 310-826-5529
www.kriegsmangroup.com

Steven A. Kriegsman, President

Ed Umali, Vice President

Al Talbot, Managing Director

total assets under management	*initial investment*	*year founded*
$50 Million	$1–4 Million	1989

The Kriegsman Group is a fast-growing investment banking firm in Southern California specializing in the development of alternative sources of equity capital for emerging-growth companies, both private and public.

The Kriegsman Group is currently working with private and institutional investors who have demonstrated a strong desire to bolster their asset base by acquiring large blocks of stock in American growth companies.

Unlike many major Wall Street firms, the Kriegsman Group is not governed by predetermined criteria but reviews each prospective client on an individual basis. Its mandate is to remain flexible and responsive to shifting market conditions, avoiding bureaucratic encumbrance whenever possible.

Clients of the Kriegsman Group benefit from an investment banking team with over 60 years of combined experience in venture capital, corporate finance, and investments. The principals of the Firm are personally involved in each transaction and have developed innovative approaches in raising equity capital to suit the individual needs of the client company. The Firm has a proven track record of effectiveness and is continually in search of qualified growth companies seeking additional capital.

Portfolio Companies: Advanced Tissue Sciences, Inc.; Algenix, Inc.; Calydon, Inc.; CapCo; Closure Medical Corporation; Comview Corporation; Efficient Marketing Services, Inc.; Ixion, Inc.; LifePoint, Inc.; Maxim Pharmaceuticals, Inc.; Medical Media Systems, Inc.; National Staff Network Holding, Inc.; Novoste Corporation; Profco, Inc.; ProtoSource Corporation; Saliva Diagnostic Systems, Inc.; Salus Media, Inc.; Wavephore, Inc.; and The Walking Company.

LABRADOR VENTURES

400 Seaport Court, Suite 250
Redwood City, CA 94063
650-366-6000   fax: 650-366-6430
www.labrador.com

Stuart Davidson, Managing Director
Larry Kubal, Managing Director
Sean Foote, Director

total assets under management	*initial investment*	*year founded*
$125 Million	$500,000–2 Million	1989

Labrador Ventures provides capital to seed- and early-stage businesses in the field of information technology. Over the last four years Labrador's investments have been largely related to the Internet. Of the 41 companies funded since the end of 1995, over 90 percent have been Internet-related. Labrador is ranked in the top quartile in performance of all venture funds.

Labrador is the first professional investor in its companies about 75 percent of the time. These first-round financings are either done solely by Labrador or in conjunction with either an Angel or VC partner, with the total financing typically ranging from $1 million to $5 million.

Labrador often invests in situations that, due to their current capital requirements, timing, or stage of development, fall below the interest levels or abilities of larger, traditional venture capital funds. Accordingly, Labrador fills the early-staged funding gap between undercapitalized Angel investors and large VCs who need to put $5 million or more to work in a single round. In filling this space, Labrador often works with both Angels and large VCs over the life of an investment.

Labrador invests throughout the United States and has offices in both the San Francisco Bay area and in New York.

LADENBURG, THALMANN & COMPANY, INC.

590 Madison Avenue, 35th Floor   11100 Santa Monica Boulevard, Suite 220
New York, NY 10022   Los Angeles, CA 90025
212-409-2000   310-444-9135
fax: 212-409-2169
www.ladenburg.com

Ward Blum, Chairman

Jon Groveman, President

Porter Bibb, Co-Director

Peter Graham, Co-Director

Herbert Hochberg, Co-Director

Lorne Caplan, Associate

total assets under management	*initial investment*	*year founded*
N/A	$500,000–2 Million	1876

Ladenburg, Thalmann & Company, Inc., is a private, middle-market investment bank specializing in media, communications, technology, medical/health, and consumer products. The Firm's client base is global and typical transactions range from $25 million to $250 million. The majority of funding goes to first-stage, second-stage, mezzanine, acquisition, and leveraged and management buy-outs.

LAKE SHORE CAPITAL PARTNERS, INC.

20 North Wacker Drive, Suite 2807
Chicago, IL 60606
312-803-3536   fax: 312-803-3534
www.lakeshorecapital.com

Carey D. Brunelli, Managing Director

Kipp M. Lykins, Managing Director

total assets under management	*initial investment*	*year founded*
N/A	$1–20 Million	1992

Lake Shore Capital Partners, Inc., is a private investment bank offering full service capabilities for private equity and debt financings and mergers and acquisitions. The Firm offers representation for sellers, buyers, issuers, or investors. Lake Shore is a global investor that specializes in the United States in most types of companies. Lake Shore invests in first-stage, second-stage, mezzanine, acquisition, leveraged and management buyouts, recapitalization, and special situations.

LAMBDA MANAGEMENT INC.

380 Lexington Avenue, 5th Floor
New York, NY 10168
212-682-3454   fax: 212-682-9231

Richard J. Dumler, Partner

Anthony M. Lamport, Partner

total assets under management	*initial investment*	*year founded*
$40 Million	$100,000–500,000	1979

Lambda Management Inc. likes to invest in niche companies and small buyouts (under $20 million). Investments are usually considered with later-stage prospects, such as second-stage, mezzanine, and leveraged and management buyouts. Geographically, Lambda Management invests in California, the Northeast, and the Mid-Atlantic across various industry sectors.

LAWRENCE FINANCIAL GROUP

11661 San Vicente Boulevard
Union Bank Tower #408
Los Angeles, CA 90049
310-826-1200   fax: 310-826-4424
www.lawrencefinancial.com

Larry Hurwitz, CEO

total assets under management	*initial investment*	*year founded*
$2 Billion	N/A	1990

Lawrence Financial Group is an investment banking firm based out of Southern California. Lawrence Financial Group invests in only second-stage financing. Lawrence Financial Group has many qualified personnel who are available to help individual companies grow and expand. Investments are only made in the Western United States, although investments in California are preferred.

LAZARD TECHNOLOGY PARTNERS

30 Rockefeller Plaza, 61st Floor
New York, NY 10020
212-632-6819
fax: 212-332-8677
www.lazardtp.com

5335 Wisconsin Avenue, N.W. Suite 410
Washington, D.C. 20015
202-895-1515
fax: 202-895-1501

Russell E. Planitzer, Managing Principal

Kevin J. Burns, Managing Principal

Gene Lowe, Principal

Tom Marler, Vice President

Gerry McClure, Vice President

Manu Rana, Vice President

total assets under management	*initial investment*	*year founded*
$100 Million	$250,000–5 Million	1998

Lazard Technology Partners (LTP) seeks to invest in technology companies that can be leaders in their segments. Investment areas include Internet/Intranet, software development, data communications, telephony, and technology services. LTP invests primarily in seed- and first-round financings in initial amounts of $250,000 to $5 million. It will invest in later-stage companies, selectively, if generating revenue.

LTP concentrates its efforts on sectors where its knowledge is deep. Its contributions extend well beyond financing to assist in strategy development and partnering.

Portfolio Companies: Bluestreak.com; ChannelWave Software, Inc.; Compatible Systems Corp.; Cyveillance; eAgents.com; eLink Communications; Essential Technologies, Inc.; Gillette Global Network, Inc.; infoShark; inshop.com; Intranets.com; MCK Communications; New River Investor Communications; NFR; Passkey.com; Quantum Bridge Communications, Inc.; SignalSoft; Sonoma Systems; telezoo.com; Terascape; Wizard World; 2Wrongs.com; and XSPEED-IUM.COM.

LEHMAN BROTHERS INCORPORATED

555 California Street	155 Linfield Drive	601 South Figueroa Street
San Francisco, CA 94104	Menlo Park, CA 94025	44th Floor
415-274-5200	650-289-6000	Los Angeles, CA 90017
fax: 415-274-5382		213-362-2500
www.lehman.com		

John Deal, Senior Vice President

Ted Breck, Head of West Coast Healthcare Group

total assets under management	*initial investment*	*year founded*
$5 Billion	N/A	1850

Lehman Brothers Investment Banking Division has 900 bankers worldwide, providing financing and advisory services to companies to investment-grade debt for established market leaders, as well as merger and acquisition advisory services to clients of all sizes. Lehman Brothers provides global, full-service relationship banking with the unique ability to engage in the life-cycle needs of its clients.

Lehman Brothers Global Technology Group has six offices worldwide with over 60 investment bankers and 18 research analysts. Over the past five years, the Group has raised more than $66 billion in financings for technology companies and announced $110 billion of mergers and acquisitions.

Lehman Brothers Global Healthcare Group has over 40 investment bankers and 14 research analysts in offices in New York, San Francisco, and London. Since 1978, the Group has completed more than 550 transactions valued at more than $120 billion for health-care companies.

LEONARD GREEN & PARTNERS, L.P.

11111 Santa Monica Boulevard, Suite 2000
Los Angeles, CA 90025
310-954-0444   fax: 310-954-0404
www.leonardgreen.com

Leonard I. Green, Founding Partner

total assets under management	*initial investment*	*year founded*
$1.8 Billion	$10 Million	1989

Leonard Green & Partners, L.P. (LGP), is a merchant and investment banking firm seeking investments in a broad range of industries. LGP invests primarily in the United States, along with select companies in Canada, Australia, and Europe. LGP will consider both private and public companies, as well as subsidiaries and divisions of a larger corporation.

Portfolio Companies: Acterna Corporation; Arrow Group Industries; Big 5 Corporation; Communications & Power Industries; Diamond Triumph Auto Glass; Dollar Financial Group; Gart Sports Company; Intercontinental Art; Leslie's Poolmart; Liberty Group Publishing; Petco Animal Supplies; Rite Aid Corporation; Twinlab Corporation; Veterinary Centers of America; and White Cap Industries.

LEONG VENTURES

146 Atherton Avenue
Atherton, CA 94025
650-327-1169   fax: 650-327-1169

George F. Leong

Stephanie A. Leong

total assets under management	*initial investment*	*year founded*
N/A	$100,000–1 Million	1976

Leong Ventures is a private venture capital firm that invests in early-stage companies. Preferable stages are seed, start-up, and first stage. Leong Ventures invests in companies located on the western portion of the United States, including California and the Northwestern States. Leong Ventures invests primarily in the life sciences arena.

LEVINE LEICHTMAN CAPITAL PARTNERS, INC.

335 North Maple Drive, Suite 240
Beverly Hills, CA 90210
310-275-5335   fax: 310-275-1441
www.llcp.com

Lauren B. Leichtman, CEO

Arthur E. Levine, President

Steven Hartman, Partner

Stephen Hogan, Partner

Mark Mickelson, Partner

Robert Poletti, Partner

Mark Sampson, Partner

Lewis Schoenwetter, Associate

total assets under management	*initial investment*	*year founded*
$450 Million	$5–40 Million	1984

Levine Leichtman Capital Partners invests in companies that require a substantial amount of money for later-stage projects. Levine Leichtman Capital Partners specializes in acquisitions, management buyouts, recapitalizations, and special situations. Levine Leichtman Capital Partners will invest throughout the Western region of the United States, principally California.

LIBERTY VENTURE PARTNERS

One Commerce Square
2005 Market Street, Suite 200
Philadelphia, PA 19103-7058
215-282-4484   fax: 215-282-4485
www.libertyvp.com

Karen Griffith Gryga, Co-Founder and Principal

Maria Hahn, CFO

Thomas R. Morse, Co-Founder and Principal

David J. Robkin, Co-Founder and Principal

total assets under management	*initial investment*	*year founded*
$150 Million	$1–2 Million	1996

Liberty Venture Partners' investment focus is on companies in the areas of wireless services and enabling technology, Internet technology and services, information technology, and health care. The Firm invests in entrepreneurs whose vision of a market opportunity is large and whose product or service will significantly affect its target customers. Liberty Venture Partners looks to work and partner with its investments over the long term and can act as a lead investor or as part of a venture-capital syndicate.

Portfolio Companies: kinkos.com; Lagos, Inc.; Mobilize; MEDecision, Inc.; Melard Technologies, Inc.; Outpost.com; Requisite Technology, Inc.; Shop4Cash.com; Tickets.com; USA.Net, Inc.; and U.S. Wireless Corporation.

LIBRA MEZZANINE PARTNERS, L.P.

11766 Wilshire Boulevard, Suite 850   44 Montogomery Street, Suite 1300
Los Angeles, CA 90025   San Francisco, CA 94104
310-996-9585   415-781-0886
fax: 310-996-9577   fax: 415-781-0887
www.libramezz.com

James B. Upchurch, President and CEO

Bailey S. Barnard, Managing Director

Michael A. Kane, Managing Director

Gregory J. Howorth, Principal

Alisa G. Frederick, Vice President

total assets under management	*initial investment*	*year founded*
$200 Million	$3–20 Million	1997

Libra Mezzanine Partners, L.P., funds growing mid-sized companies, providing capital for expansion, buyouts, acquisitions, and recapitalizations. Its industry focus is on manufacturing, distribution, retail, and service companies with a proven competitive advantage in niche markets. Libra Mezzanine Partners seeks a minority position in each of its portfolio companies, with no interest in gaining voting control. Libra Mezzanine Partners will fund companies located in the United States, with a geographical emphasis on the West.

Portfolio Companies: American Consolidated Media, Inc.; Campgroup, LLC; Centerprise Advisors, Inc.; Closet World, Inc.; Parking Company of America, LLC; Pritikin Enterprises, LLC; Quantic Industries, Inc.; QCI Offshore, LLC; Scientech, Inc.; Soff-Cut International, Inc.; and Wyle Laboratories, Inc.

LOMBARD INVESTMENTS INC.

600 Montgomery Street, 36th Floor
San Francisco, CA 94111
415-397-5900   fax: 415-397-5820
www.lombardinvestments.com

Joe Chulick, Founder

total assets under management	*initial investment*	*year founded*
$1 Billion	$5–25 Million	1985

With offices in San Francisco, Hong Kong, Sydney, and Taipei, Lombard Investments Inc. invests in a broad range of industries, with the exception of: real estate development, oil and gas exploration and development, alcoholic beverages, firearms, tobacco products, casinos, or gaming. Lombard Investments is interested in dynamic, expanding companies that need capital for corporate growth or acquisitions. Through a series of strategic partnerships, Lombard Investments can assist with management skills, market knowledge, contacts, relationships, and influence. The Firm will consider opportunities located in North America and Asia.

Portfolio Companies: Dakota, Minnesota & Eastern Railroad Corporation; Good Morning Securities; Harry London Candies; Indo Worth; Schmidt Group Practice Company Limited; and Thai Union Frozen Products Public Company Limited.

MACADAM CAPITAL PARTNERS

4800 Southwest Macadam Avenue, Suite 311
Portland, OR 97201
503-225-0889   fax: 503-225-0009
www.macadamcapital.com

David J. Alexander, Managing Director
Richard D. Durrett Jr., Managing Director

total assets under management	*initial investment*	*year founded*
N/A	N/A	1993

Macadam Capital Partners is an investment banking firm that focuses on established, private (or closely held public) companies in the Pacific Northwest. Primary activity is assistance in the development and execution of long-term strategic capital plans for growing (80 percent) and financially distressed (20 percent) companies, as well as mergers and acquisitions. For this reason, Macadam serves companies at least after the first-stage. Macadam's funding levels range from second-stage, mezzanine, bridge, acquisition, and leveraged and management buyouts to recapitalizations, special situations, consolidations, distressed debt, and privatization.

MADISON DEARBORN PARTNERS

Three First National Plaza, Suite 3800
Chicago, IL 60602
312-895-1000   fax: 312-895-1001
www.mdcp.com

John A. Canning Jr., President

total assets under management	*initial investment*	*year founded*
$7 Billion	$30–400 Million	1993

Madison Dearborn Partners (MDP), headquartered in Chicago, Illinois, is a leading private equity investment firm with more than $7 billion of capital under management. MDP focuses on management buyouts and growth equity transactions involving rapidly developing companies. MDP has significant investment experience in several specific industries, including communications, basic industries, financial services, consumer, and health care.

Portfolio Companies: Madison Dearborn Partners has over 80 portfolio companies.

MARQUETTE VENTURE PARTNERS

520 Lake Cook Road, Suite 450
Deerfield, IL 60015
847-940-1700   fax: 847-940-1724
www.marquetteventures.com

James F. Daverman, General Partner
Lloyd D. Ruth, General Partner

total assets under management	*initial investment*	*year founded*
$230 Million	$500,000–3 Million	1987

Marquette Venture Partners is a private venture capital firm founded in 1987 to invest in early-stage technology companies, growth-equity situations, and recapitalizations. Marquette is one of the leading venture capital firms between the East and West Coasts. While national in scope, its investment activities are focused in the Midwest. The major portion of its funds have been earmarked for early-stage and growth-equity investing in the health-care and information technology industries.

Portfolio Companies: Marquette Venture Partners has over 45 portfolio companies in the health-care, technology, Internet, and services industries.

MARWIT CAPITAL, LLC

180 Newport Center Drive, Suite 200
Newport Beach, CA 92660
949-640-6234   fax: 949-720-8077

Matthew L. Witte, Chairman/CEO

Chris L. Britt, President

Thomas W. Windsor, Associate

total assets under management	*initial investment*	*year founded*
$40 Million	$500,000–5 Million	1962

Marwit Capital, LLC, supplies subordinated debt and equity capital to established (8+ years) and profitable middle-market businesses. Its specialty is long-term mezzanine financing, with typically five to seven year subordinated loans with minority equity participation rights. Marwit prefers to work with expansion or acquisition of existing businesses, mergers, refinancing IPOs, and private placements. It is also an SBIC company.

MASON WELLS

770 N. Water Street
Milwaukee, WI 53202
414-765-7800   fax: 414-765-7850
www.masonwells.com

John Byrnes, Chairman and Managing Director

John Riley, Managing Director

Bill Krugler, Managing Director

Tom Smith, Director

Greg Myers, Director

Wendy Orthober, Director of Investor Relations

Jin Domach, CFO

Kevin Kenealey, Associate

Mathhew Lessard, Investment Analyst

total assets under management	*initial investment*	*year founded*
$350 Million	N/A	1982

Mason Wells is a private equity group in the Midwest. It provides premier financial services to entrepreneurs and management teams who need capital to acquire a business and support its growth. The Firm offers customized financial solutions, takes proprietary positions, facilitates access to a broad range of capital funding, and commits to the long-term prosperity of its investee companies.

Mason Wells's industry preferences include paper, packaging, printing, industrial products and materials, business services, and software.

Portfolio Companies: A. Sturm and Sons, Inc.; The Charlton Group; Converter Concepts; Creative Forming, Inc.; Duralam, Inc.; Electrotek Corporation; Encore Paper Company, Inc.; Framework Technologies Corp.; General American Corp.; General Automotive Manufacturing, LLC; HK Systems, Inc.; HyperEdge, Inc.; InterBay Technologies, LLC; KraftSeal Corporation; The Medalcraft Mint, Inc.; Predelivery Service Corporation; Premix, Inc.; Specialized Medical Services, Inc.; Third Wave Technologies, Inc.; WPC Brands, Inc.; and Wisconsin Porcelain Co.

MATRIX PARTNERS

2500 Sand Hill Road, Suite 113
Menlo Park, CA 94025
650-854-3131   fax: 650-854-3296
www.matrixpartners.com

Paul J. Ferri, Founding Partner

Andrew W. Verhalen, Founding Partner

Mark A. Vershel, Founding Partner

total assets under management	*initial investment*	*year founded*
N/A	$100,000–10 Million	1977

Matrix Partners is a venture capital firm that has been dedicated to helping exceptional entrepreneurs build successful companies. Matrix Partners focuses on creating new markets in software, networking equipment, semiconductors, computing, storage, and Internet business. It is an early-stage investment firm with an objective of playing an active role in building successful companies from ground zero.

Matrix Partners always serve on the Board of its portfolio companies, with a long-term commitment to build independent companies rather than acquisition targets. With offices on both coasts of the United States, Matrix Partners can offer a wide network of industry contacts.

Matrix Partners invests on a nationwide level.

Portfolio Companies: Matrix Partners has over 100 portfolio companies.

MAVERON, LLC

505 Fifth Avenue South, Suite 600
Seattle, WA 98104
206-447-1300   fax: 206-447-1334
www.maveron.com

Dan Levitan, Partner
Howard Schultz, Partner
Debra Somberg, Partner
Zack Herlick, Partner

total assets under management	*initial investment*	*year founded*
$415 Million	N/A	1998

Maveron, LLC, is a venture capital firm focused on the intersection of technology and the consumer. Its mission is to be the premier financial and strategic partner to the next generation of leading consumer businesses and companies that enable consumer businesses.

Portfolio Companies: Apex Learning; Brand Farm; DoughNET.com; Drugstore.com; eBay; eStyle; EXP.com; Flooz.com; Illuminations; Lucy.com; PeoplePC; Qsent; Quellos; ShopTalk; The Motley Fool; and Weave Innovations.

MDS VENTURE PACIFIC, INC.

555 West 8th Avenue, Suite 305
Vancouver, Canada V5Z-1C6
604-872-8464   fax: 604-872-2977

Darrell Elliott, President
Avtar Dhillon, M.D., Vice President

total assets under management	*initial investment*	*year founded*
$27 Million	$100,000–5 Million	1994

MDS Venture Pacific manages two Vancouver-domiciled venture funds. Through activity-managed investments, MDS Venture Pacific seeks to build successful life sciences companies. It provides financial and management support to outstanding managers of high-growth companies in health care, biopharmaceuticals, and medical devices, as well as medical-related information systems.

MDS Venture Pacific is a subsidiary of MDS Capital Corporation (MDSCC), Canada's largest venture capital company specializing exclusively in health care. MDSCC is owned by its partners, MDS Inc., and several of Canada's largest diversified, technology-based, health and life sciences companies.

MEDTECH VENTURES, INC.

655 Mariners Island Boulevard, Suite 303
San Mateo, CA 94404
650-286-2999   fax: 650-286-2992
www.medtechventures.com

Robert M. Curtis, President

total assets under management	*initial investment*	*year founded*
N/A	$500,000–3 Million	1989

MedTech Ventures, Inc., is a start-up enterprise accelerator with a mission to identify, evaluate, arrange funding for, and manage the early success of seed and start-up investment opportunities in the health-care arena.

MedTech Ventures combines the medical technology, market, investment, and company management experience of its president, Robert M. Curtis, with an advisory board made up of representatives from its four investment affiliates. The investment affiliate group is a powerful alliance of two respected and experienced early-stage venture capital funds, Vanguard Venture Partners and Bedrock Capital, and two major NYSE-traded corporations with an interest in health-care equity investing, Guidant Corporation and Tredegar Industries, via its Tredegar Investments affiliate.

MEDVENTURE ASSOCIATES

4 Orinda Way, Building D, Suite 150
Orinda, CA 94563
925-253-0155   fax: 925-253-0156

Annette Campbell-White, Managing General Partner
George Y. Choi, General Partner

total assets under management	*initial investment*	*year founded*
$120 Million	$100,000–1 Million	1986

Founded in 1986, MedVenture Associates (MVA) is a private venture capital firm specializing in early-stage financing of companies developing medical devices, medical information technology, e-health, health-care services, and pharmaceutical and biotechnology products.

MVA is dedicated to seeking out, then investing in, pre-seed, seed, and early-stage financing rounds of companies developing medical devices, medical information technology, e-health, health-care services, and pharmaceutical and biotechnology products. The Partners will also invest in later-stage health-care-related companies where they anticipate early investment liquidity.

The majority of the start-up companies in the Fund's portfolio originate in the Western United States, from San Diego up the coast to Seattle, from the Pacific Ocean to the state of Colorado. The Partners believe that to be an effective investor at the seed-capital stage, they must be readily available to consult with the on-site management team at a moment's notice. At all times, therefore, at least one Partner is a short two-hour plane ride away.

MELLON VENTURES, INC.

400 South Hope Street, 5th Floor
Los Angeles, CA 90071
213-553-9685   fax: 213-553-9690
www.mellon.com

Jeffrey H. Anderson, Managing Director

John S. Geer, Partner

Mark L. Patton, Associate

David E. Kantrovitz, Analyst

total assets under management	*initial investment*	*year founded*
$2.7 Trillion	$3–5 Million	N/A

Mellon Ventures's source of capital is Mellon Financial Corporation, one of the nation's largest investment management firms, with approximately $2.7 trillion in assets under management, administration, or custody. Mellon Ventures, Inc., sources, evaluates, and structures investments for Mellon Ventures, L.P., a partnership with a 50-year life.

Mellon Ventures invests at all stages of the growth cycle, from early-stage venture capital to later-stage growth financing and buyouts.

Mellon Ventures provides rapidly growing operating companies and superior management teams with access to unlimited capital to fuel their ambitious business plans. Mellon Ventures's portfolio companies also benefit from the resources of one of the nation's most successful financial services companies and the advice of an experienced and entrepreneurial investment team.

Portfolio Companies: AirNet Communications; ComputerJobs.com; Cooking.com; Digital Planet; eCredit.com; Essential.com; Exalt; FullTilt Solutions; in Power; Investor Force; IPNet Solutions; ixl; Kestrel Solutions; Lexar Media; Lifeminders; Multex.com; Novient; Paradigm wireless; Print Café; Velocom; and Yafo.

MENLO VENTURES

3000 Sand Hill Road
Bldg. 4, Suite 100
Menlo Park, CA 94025
650-854-8540   fax: 650-854-7059
www.menloventures.com

H. DuBose Montgomery, Managing Director

Thomas H. Bredt, Managing Director

Douglas C. Carlisle, Managing Director

John W. Jarve, Managing Director

Michael D. Laufer, Managing Director

Sonja L. Hoel, Managing Director

Mark A. Siegel, Managing Director

total assets under management	*initial investment*	*year founded*
$2.7 Billion	$10–15 Million	1976

Menlo Ventures is a private venture capital partnership providing long-term capital and management support to early-stage and emerging-growth companies. Menlo Ventures invests in the areas of communications, software, and Internet. Menlo Ventures's limited partners include corporate and public pension funds, university endowments, and insurance companies. Menlo Ventures invests nationwide.

Portfolio Companies: Agile Software; B2Bworks; BlueGill Technologies; Branders.com; Catena Technologies; Colo.com; Cyras Systems; Efficient Networks; Fireclick; FJ Networks; Hotmail; iBasis; Kinzan.com; and Optical Solutions.

MERITAGE PRIVATE EQUITY FUND, LP

1600 Wynkoop, Suite 300
Denver, CO 80202
303-352-2040   fax: 303-352-2050
www.meritage.net

G. Jackson Tankersley, Founder
Laura Beller, Principal
John Garrett, Principal
Tracy Kerr, Principal

total assets under management	*initial investment*	*year founded*
$340 Million	N/A	1999

Meritage Private Equity Fund, LP, is a private investment firm that invests exclusively in communications networks and communications services, businesses, and related consolidation opportunities. Meritage brings senior-level expertise to all steps of the investment process, with particular emphasis on providing proven value-creation capabilities to portfolio companies. With over $300 million in committed capital, Meritage intends to build an investment portfolio comprised of 12 to 14 high-growth companies, including companies founded by Meritage under its "fast start" program. Meritage invests substantial capital in a relatively small number of higher-quality opportunities that have the potential for significant return. It invests primarily in either early- or late-stage ventures, worldwide.

Portfolio Companies: CompleTel; Diginet Americas; Gabriel Communications Inc.; and inflow, Inc.

MERITECH CAPITAL PARTNERS

285 Hamilton Avenue, Suite 200
Palo Alto, CA 94301
650-475-2200   fax: 650-475-2222
www.meritechcapital.com

Mike Gordon, Managing Director

Paul Madera, Managing Director

Rob Ward, Vice President

Steve Simonian, CFO

Janet Heiss, Associate

total assets under management	*initial investment*	*year founded*
$1.1 Billion	$15–25 Million	1999

Meritech Capital is a late-stage venture capital fund that was co-founded and sponsored by five leading venture firms: Accel Partners, Brentwood Venture Capital, Oak Investment Partners, Redpoint Ventures, and Worldview Technology Partners.

Meritech seeks to lead investments in later-stage information technology companies. It pursues traditional-growth companies as well as co-investments in corporate buyouts and spinoffs of information technology companies alongside the sponsor funds. Investments are typically in companies with proven technology, market-tested business models, and seasoned management teams.

Meritech focuses on technology sectors, including optical systems and components, wireless and wireless communications equipment and services, as well as Internet enabling technologies and services.

Portfolio Companies: Meritech has over 50 portfolio companies in the communications, Internet, and software and services industries.

---

meVC

991 Folsom Street
San Francisco, California 94107
415-977-6150   fax: 415-977-6160
www.mevc.com

Peter S. Freudenthal, President, CEO, and Co-Founder
Andrew E. Singer, CFO and Co-Founder

total assets under management	*initial investment*	*year founded*
$316 Million	$1–15 Million	2000

meVC is a national venture capital investment management firm that allows all the individual investors to participate in private equity. It provides venture capital to entrepreneurs, as well as a national network of management services to support innovation and help build successful businesses.

Typically, venture capital has been limited to financial institutions, corporations, or high-worth individuals. meVC, however, offers individuals the opportunity to invest in private equity.

Portfolio Companies: Annuncio Software, Inc.; AuctionWatch.com; Endymion Systems, Inc.; eOnline, Inc.; EXP.com; eYak, Inc.; FOLIO*fn;* InfoImage, Inc.; *info*USA.com; IQdestination.com; Mediaprise; Pagoo; Personic, Inc.; and ShopEaze.com.

MEYER DUFFY VENTURES, LLC

780 Third Avenue, 15th Floor
New York, NY 10017
646-282-9260   fax: 646-282-9279
www.meyerduffy.com

Donald Duffy, Managing Partner
Eric Meyer, Managing Partner
John Mills, Partner

Thomas Hass, Vice President

Teddy Kaplan, Vice President

total assets under management	*initial investment*	*year founded*
$150 Million	$500,000–5 Million	1994

MDV's investment objective is to achieve long-term superior capital appreciation primarily through equity and equity-related investments in "best of breed" private technology companies.

MDV seeks investments in companies in earlier stages of development, where its General Partner's expertise is maximized for the greatest potential returns.

Portfolio Companies: Arc e-Consultancy; CCC Network Systems; Equinox Solutions, Inc.; Network Decisions; Paradigm 4; Predictive Systems; RiverSoft; and Solant.

MIDMARK ASSOCIATES, INC.

466 Southern Boulevard
Chatham, NY 07928
973-822-2999   fax: 973-822-8911
www.midmarkcapital.com

Wayne L. Clevenger, Managing Director

Denis Newman, Managing Director

Joseph R. Robinson, Managing Director

Matthew Finlay, Vice President

total assets under management	*initial investment*	*year founded*
$80 Million	$250,000–10 Million	1989

MidMark Associates, Inc., is both a small business investment company and a private MBO investment firm. MidMark Associates primarily invests in later-stage companies that need the following types of funding: acquisitions, management buyouts, and recapitalizations. It also provides minority equity growth capital. MidMark Associates will invest in most places in the United States if the companies fit the principals' investment criteria.

MILLENNIUM 3 VENTURE GROUP, LLC

6880 S. McCarran Boulevard, Suite A-11
Reno, NV 89509
775-954-2020   fax: 775-954-2023
www.m3vg.com

Robb S. Smith, Managing Principal

Christopher P. Howard, Managing Principal

total assets under management	*initial investment*	*year founded*
$30 Million	$500,000–2 Million	1999

Millennium 3 Venture Group (M3VG) is a venture capital firm looking to invest in companies with market-leading potential, preferably in the technology and services sector. M3VG offers not only additional capital to entrepreneurs but also sound strategic advice and other business resources necessary to build a substantial equity value.

   M3VG contributes to companies in two stages: early-stage companies that can benefit from M3VG's developing strategies and recruitment talent and later-stage companies that can benefit from M3VG's experience and resources when entering new markets and pursuing e-commerce opportunities. M3VG will also invest in companies that need working capital for expansions, acquisitions, leveraged and management buyouts/ins, and recapitalizations. M3VG invests primarily in Arizona, California, and Nevada.

MISSION VENTURES

11512 El Camino Real, Suite 215
San Diego, CA 92130
858-259-0100   fax: 858-259-0112
www.missionventures.com

Robert Kibble, Managing Partner

Dave Ryan, Managing Partner

Ted Alexander, General Partner

Jeffrey Starr, General Partner

Dave Holder, Venture Partner

total assets under management	*initial investment*	*year founded*
$63 Million	$750,000–2 Million	1997

Mission Ventures is a San Diego–based venture capital firm that invests primarily in information technology, health care, and service companies throughout Southern California. Mission Ventures focuses on high-quality leaders with innovative ideas and experience in markets that present significant growth opportunities. It has more than 50 years of experience in working with entrepreneurs to create highly successful companies and can offer not only personal insights but a valuable network of local and national business leaders and technologists.

Information Technology—Mission Ventures is interested in industries such as communications, software, Internet, and electronics.

Healthcare—The General Partners are particularly interested in ventures that leverage information technology within the medical industry, and they continue to examine deals regarding health-care services, devices, diagnostics, and instrumentation.

Services—Prospective investments related to the various macro-trends within the nation's economy, such as aging, growth of teen market, and changes in lifestyles, will be reviewed. Examples include outsourcing, senior care, and specialty retail opportunities.

Portfolio Companies: Accent Care; Alitum; BizRate.com; Cogent Healthcare; Complexions RX; e-rehab; Entropia; Eveo; iHome.com; KnowledgeLINK; MedicineNet.com; NowDocs; Sandpiper Networks; Sitematic/Net Objects; Stellcom; and TruCost Food Systems.

MITSUI & CO. (U.S.A.), INC.

200 Park Avenue, 36th Floor
New York, NY 10166-0130
212-878-4066   fax: 212-878-4070
www.mitsuipe.com

Yoichiro (Roger) Endo, General Manager

Richard E. See, Assistant General Manager

total assets under management	*initial investment*	*year founded*
$130 Million	$5 Million	1985

Mitsui & Co. is a private equity firm whose primary objective is to create substantial financial returns on its investments. The Firm targets the following industries: information technology, which includes software, data communication/telecommunications devices, Internet, e-commerce, and semiconductors; and health care, which includes medical devices, diagnostics, therapeutics, biopharmaceuticals, and medical services.

Mitsui & Co. is looking for opportunities in early-stage investments located in the United States.

Portfolio Companies: Array Biopharma, Inc.; Brightlink Networks; Broncus Technologies, Inc.; ChemConnect, Inc.; CommerX; Eclipse International Inc.; eCredit; e-STEEL; Graviton, Inc.; LuxN; Mahi Networks, Inc.; Mayan Networks, Inc.; Plumtree Software, Inc.; Promatory Communications, Inc.; Radix Wireless, Inc.; SURx, Inc.; and TradeCard.

MMC Capital C&I Fund

1166 Avenue of the Americas, 32nd Floor
New York, NY 10036
212-345-8222   fax: 212-345-8046
www.cifund.com

Charles A. Davis, Senior Principal

Stephen Friedman, Senior Principal

Robi Blumenstein, Principal

Robert Fox, Principal

John H. Coghlin, Associate

Charles Foster, Associate

Jenny Ho, Associate

Daniel S. Rosenthal, Associate

Agnes K. Tang, Associate

Tom Vander Schaaff, Associate

total assets under management	*initial investment*	*year founded*
N/A	$5–10 Million	2000

MMC Capital recently introduced the Communications and Information Fund. This fund operates out of New York City, Boston, Greenwich, and Washington, D.C. Its objective is to select early-stage companies in North America and Western Europe that are seeking additional capital and show promise for exceptional growth. Investments will span the entire value chain of the communications and information industry, including components, software, hardware, applications, services, and content.

   Portfolio Companies: GlobeRanger Corporation; PeopleStreet; Southampton Photonics, Inc.; and Xelus, Inc.

Mohr, Davidow Ventures

2775 Sand Hill Road, Suite 240
Menlo Park, CA 94025
650-854-7236   fax: 650-854-7365
www.mdv.com

Rob Chaplinsky, Partner

William H. Davidow, Partner

Bill Ericson, Partner

Jonathan D. Feiber, Partner

Debby Meredith, Partner

Geoffrey Moore, Partner

Donna Novitsky, Partner

Nancy J. Schoendorf, Partner

Michael Sheridan, Partner

Michael Solomon, Partner

Eric Straser, Partner

Randy Strahan, Partner

Mo Virani, Partner

George Zachery, Partner

total assets under management	*initial investment*	*year founded*
$390 Million	$250,000–20 Million	1983

Mohr, Davidow Ventures is a private venture capital firm that invests in early-stage technology companies. Preferred investment stages are R & D, seed, start-up, first-stage, and second-stage. Mohr, Davidow Ventures invests mainly in the West, in such areas as the Northwest, Southwest, California, and the Rocky Mountains.

Portfolio Companies: Mohr, Davidow Ventures has over 70 portfolio companies in the e-commerce, Internet infrastructure, Internet services, and semiconductor industries.

MONTGOMERY ASSOCIATES, INC.

P.O. Box 2230
San Francisco, CA 94126
415-421-4200   fax: 415-981-3601

Allen P. McKee, President

total assets under management	*initial investment*	*year founded*
$8 Million	$250,000–1 Million	1975

Montgomery Associates, Inc., is a small venture capital firm that provides close attention and personal advice. Montgomery Associates provides funding for start-up, first-stage, and second-stage companies. Montgomery Associates prefers to invest in California, although applicants from anywhere on the West Coast are acceptable.

MORGENTHALER

2730 Sand Hill Road, Suite 280
Menlo Park, CA 94025
650-388-7600   fax: 650-388-7601
www.morgenthaler.com

Robert C. Bellas Jr., General Partner
Gary R. Little, General Partner
Gary J. Morgenthaler, General Partner
Gary Shaffer, General Partner

total assets under management	initial investment	year founded
$1 Billion	$5–8 Million	1968

Morgenthaler has been an active firm and company builder since 1968, funding more than 150 companies, two-thirds of which have either become public companies or have been acquired by public companies, and have generated market valuations of billions of dollars. The Firm focuses on early-stage investments in information technology and health care, as well as management-led buyouts. Morgenthaler invests in entrepreneurial companies that have the potential to become leaders in their markets.

Industry preferences include communications, computer software, Internet and online services, health-care services, medical devices, and pharmaceuticals.

MULTIMEDIA BROADCAST INVESTMENT CORPORATION

3101 South Street, NW
Washington, D.C. 20007
202-293-1166   fax: 202-293-1181
www.mmbic.com

Walter L. Threadgill, President

total assets under management	initial investment	year founded
$200 Million	$100,000–1 Million	1979

Multimedia Broad Investment Corporation (MBIC) was established to provide a source of capital for minority, small-business, and other qualified entrepreneurs seeking ownership of broadcast properties. It is interested in a broad range of industries in the broadcasting sector, from broadcast-related technology to telecommunications. Its current investments take the form of either fixed-rate loans or equity, where the current loan policy covers electronic media facilities such as FM radio, cellular radio, multipoint distribution systems, pay telephones, and related wireless and telecommunications businesses. MBIC is seeking investment opportunities throughout the United States.

NATIONAL CORPORATE FINANCE, INC.

2082 Southeast Bristol, Suite 203
Newport Beach, CA 92660
949-756-2006   fax: 949-756-0611

Steven R. Rabago, President

Richard Way, Managing Director

total assets under management	*initial investment*	*year founded*
N/A	$7–50 Million	1983

National Corporate Finance, Inc., is an investment banking, consulting, and merger and acquisition firm. National Corporate Finance specializes in later-stage and special-situation funding. Acquisitions, leveraged and management buyouts, and recapitalizations are the usual types of funding National provides. National Corporate Finance invests in companies throughout the West Coast.

NEEDHAM ASSET MANAGEMENT

445 Park Avenue
New York, NY 10022
212-371-8300
fax: 212-751-1450

3000 Sand Hill Road
Menlo Park, CA 94025
650-854-9111

Chad W. Keck, General Partner

George A. Needham, General Partner

John C. Michaelson, General Partner

John J. Prior Jr., General Partner

Jack J. Iacovone, Vice President

Glen W. Albanese, CFO

total assets under management	initial investment	year founded
$200 Million	$1–4 Million	1986

Needham Asset Management focuses its investment activity on selected industries in which its professionals and those of its affiliate, Needham and Company Inc., have established expertise. The industry focus, together with its strategic and financial expertise, enables the Firm to add value beyond its invested capital and makes Needham Asset Management the ideal partner for entrepreneurs and business leaders.

The industries in which Needham Asset Management concentrates include: semiconductors, networking, electronics, industrial technology, outsourcing of manufacturing, health care, business services, and specialty retailing. It invests in private companies that it believes to be within one to two years of making an initial public offering. It is a mezzanine investor and looks for a company with a developed product in the market, products' revenues, and a management team in place.

NEOCARTA VENTURES

Two Embarcadero Center, Suite 460
San Francisco, CA 94111
415-277-0230   fax: 415-277-0240
www.neocarta.com

Karin Kissane, Managing Director
Tony J. Pantuso, Managing Director
Lee R. Pantuso, CFO

total assets under management	initial investment	year founded
$300 Million	$500,000–2.5 Million	1999

NeoCarta Ventures is a venture capital firm with an emphasis on start-up companies in the early and later stages of development. Its focus is on the Internet technology and the communications industries. In addition, NeoCarta Ventures places a strong emphasis on finding ways for its portfolio companies to work together in order to build a solid business network. The Firm believes in working in partnership with its portfolio companies, from first funding to IPO. NeoCarta Ventures seeks investment opportunities throughout the United States.

Portfolio Companies: NeoCarta Ventures has portfolio companies in the following categories:

—Data Everywhere: 3Ware; Actional; Data Synapse; and Nimble Technology.

—Industry Revolutionaries: Carstation; E-Markets; NexTdoor Networks; and Petroleum Place.
—Transaction Enablers: Actbig; etour; Promisant; and Stockback.
—Virtual Infrastructure: AppGenesus; Avienda; Perfect; and TrueSpectra.

NEW ENTERPRISE ASSOCIATES

2490 Sand Hill Road
Menlo Park, CA 94025
650-854-9499   fax: 650-854-9397
www.nea.com

Thomas C. McConnell, General Partner

total assets under management	*initial investment*	*year founded*
$2.5 Billion	$100,000–20 Million	1978

New Enterprise Associates (NEA) helps build companies of distinctive character and enduring value by providing significant resources, including equity capital, an experienced venture team, and a comprehensive business network to entrepreneurs and young companies. Its focus is on seed, early-, and expansion-stage companies. The NEA network of experienced venture professionals includes offices in Menlo Park, CA; Reston, VA; and Baltimore, MD. Through this network, NEA is committed to maintaining the high-quality standards that have made NEA a national leader in the venture capital industry.

NEW WORLD VENTURES

1603 Orrington Avenue, Suite 1070
Evanston, IL 60201
847-328-0300   fax: 847-328-8297
www.newworldvc.com

Lisa Flashner, Managing Director
Chris Girgenti, Managing Director
J. B. Pritzker, Managing Director

total assets under management	*initial investment*	*year founded*
$100 Million	$2–4 Million	N/A

New World Ventures and William Blair Capital Partners have partnered to create a fund focusing on start-up, early-stage, and emerging innovative high-technology

U.S.-based firms. Software, Internet, networking, and telecommunications industries are its primary target. Its expertise, resources, and contacts provide the entrepreneur with the resources critical for growth. A "virtual" incubator allows portfolio companies to seek management advice, legal services, accounting, public relations, recruiting, and technical development at low cost.

Portfolio Companies: Active.com; Aircell; Away.com; BULKMarkets.com; eCollege.com; Eppraisals.com; Egreetings.com; Ignite Sports Media; iLink Global; JobsOnline.com; JuniorNet; and Tavve Software.

NEW YORK PARTNERS, LLC

One Union Square West, #803
New York, NY 10003
888-975-4321   fax: 212-202-5329
www.newyorkpartners.com

John Chambers, Partner

Robert Lopez, Partner

total assets under management	*initial investment*	*year founded*
N/A	$500,000–4 Million	2000

New York Partners, LLC, is a financial and consulting service organization that uses both new technologies and traditional sources to assist clients in creating Internet-based solutions. The Firm acts as an Internet accelerator for portfolio companies that need assistance with the development of Internet projects, including early-stage and mezzanine funding, marketing, consulting, hiring, and implementation. Its industry focus is on: e-commerce, new-media content, Web-enabling technology, network infrastructure, and Internet service. New York Partners will invest in companies throughout the United States, with an emphasis on the Northeast.

NEWBURY VENTURES

535 Pacific Avenue, 2nd Floor
San Francisco, CA 94133
415-296-7408   fax: 415-296-7416
www.newburyven.com

Bruce J. Bauer, General Partner
Ossama R. Hassanein, General Partner
Jay B. Morrison, General Partner

Colleen E. Young, General Partner

total assets under management	*initial investment*	*year founded*
$70 Million	$250,000–1 Million	1992

Newbury Ventures is a private venture capital partnership focusing on investments in communications and health-care technology companies throughout the world. It specializes in identifying opportunities for significant capital appreciation, by investing in promising entrepreneurial companies at early stages of their corporate development.

The General Partners of Newbury seek to invest in and work with highly motivated and talented entrepreneurs with whom they can enjoy a close collaborative partnership in building global enterprises. The Newbury Partners draw upon a board range of skills, strengths, and industry experiences in helping young companies effectively manage the challenges of early development. They provide assistance with business strategy, corporate development, and recruitment of key managers, as well as assistance with subsequent financing. Through the international experience of their partners and their Global Venture Alliance, Newbury Ventures is in a favorable position to create and finance companies that are structured with bi-national operations.

Portfolio Companies: Newbury has over 30 portfolio companies, including Fundtech Ltd.; Guardian Health Group; Paradigm Geophysical Ltd.; and Summit Design, Inc.

NEWTEK VENTURES

500 Washington Street, Suite 720
San Francisco, CA 94111
415-986-5711   fax: 415-986-4618

John E. Hall, General Partner
Peter J. Wardle, General Partner

total assets under management	*initial investment*	*year founded*
$55 Million	$250,000–1 Million	1983

Newtek Ventures was founded in 1983 for the purpose of making equity investments in emerging high-technology companies. Newtek, privately held, is structured as a limited partnership and manages over $50 million.

Investors include U.S.- and foreign-based pension funds, insurance companies, corporations, individuals, and college endowment funds. The General Partners have a combined history of venture investing that exceeds 40 years. In general, Newtek makes investments in the Rocky Mountains, California, and the Southwest. Newtek funds seed, start-up, first-stage, second-stage, mezzanine, recapitalization, and special-situation projects.

NEWVISTA CAPITAL

540 Cooper Street, Suite 200
Palo Alto, CA 94301
650-329-9333   fax: 650-328-9434
www.nvcap.com

Roger Barry, General Partner
Frank S. Greens, General Partner

total assets under management	*initial investment*	*year founded*
$50 Million	$500,000–1 Million	1997

The NewVista Capital Fund is a $50-million venture capital fund investing in early-stage information technology companies. The primary fund investment focus is on women and minority entrepreneurs able to operate, grow, and succeed at Internet speed.

NewVista Capital offers assistance with business strategy, recruitment of key personnel, formation of strategic relationships, development of distribution channels, and raising later-stage financing.

Portfolio Companies: Beyond Software, Inc.; eCircles, Inc.; Epicentric, Inc.; HyNet, Inc.; Skytron Corporation; Uniteq Application Systems, Inc.; and ZNYX Corporation.

NIF VENTURES USA, INC.

5 Palo Alto Square, 9th Floor
Palo Alto, CA 94306
650-461-5000   fax: 650-858-0534
www.nif.co.jp

Yuzuru Miyamoto, President
Jim Timmins, Partner

total assets under management	*initial investment*	*year founded*
$2.7 Billion	N/A	1996

NIF Ventures USA, Inc., is a subsidiary of NIF Ventures, Co., Ltd., one of the leading venture capital funds in Japan. NIF Ventures is looking to invest in small- and medium-sized companies in all stages of development for the primary objective of high-growth potential and an attractive return. The focus of investments is in the following industries: communications, e-commerce, electronics, security, and software. The current geographical focus is on Asia, North America, Europe, and Israel.

NIF Ventures is a global player, with a portfolio of companies from 35 different countries and local offices in Singapore, Taipei, and California. Due to its global presence and a network of affiliations, the Firm is able to offer a very broad spectrum of services to both entrepreneurs and investors.

Portfolio Companies: NIF Ventures has over 350 portfolio companies from 35 countries around the world.

NOKIA VENTURES

545 Middlefield Road, Suite 210
Menlo Park, CA 94025
650-462-7250   fax: 650-462-7252
www. nokiaventures.com

W. Peter Buhl, Partner

John Gardner, Partner

Antti Kokkinen, Partner

Martti Malka, Partner

John Malloy, Partner

Thomas Kenney, Principal

total assets under management	*initial investment*	*year founded*
$150 Million	$1–5 Million	1998

Nokia Ventures is a U.S. $150-million venture capital fund formed in 1998 to invest in early-stage, high-growth information technology companies. The fund's sole Limited Partner, Nokia Corporation, has invested in the fund with the express intent to gain exposure to and learn about new markets, business models, and technologies beyond the reach of Nokia's current business unit strategies. Nokia invests globally.

Portfolio Companies: @Hand Corporation; 12 Snap; AVS Technologies; Caly Networks; Categoric Software; eCal; eVoice; FreedomPaly.com; FusionOne; HotPaper.com; Informative; IntelliSeek Inc.; Main Sail Networks; Mongo Music;

NetSanity; PhoneSpan; Pogo.com; RIOT Entertainment; Sinia; Soft Coin; X.com; and ZebraPass.

NORTH HILL VENTURES, LP

Ten Office Square, 11th Floor
Boston, MA 02109
617-788-2150   fax: 617-788-2152
www.northhillventures.com

Shamez A. Kanji, Managing Director
Brett J. Rome, Managing Director
George M. Overholser, Senior Vice President
Benjamin H. Malka, Senior Associate
Polly Ross Ribatt, Senior Associate

total assets under management	*initial investment*	*year founded*
N/A	$2–5 Million	1999

North Hill Ventures seeks to invest in financial services, Internet, telecommunications, and direct-to-consumer marketing businesses that require capital to continue or accelerate their growth.

North Hill Ventures invests $2–5 million in middle- to late-stage companies seeking expansion capital, reserving additional funds for follow-on investments. North Hill Ventures can arrange larger financing through syndication with other investment partnerships. North Hill Ventures acts as both a lead investor and as a co-investor alongside other venture firms and strategic investors. North Hill Ventures invests nationwide.

Portfolio Companies: eVite.com; Forfield, Inc.; MarketSwitch; OpenPages, Inc.; and Veridiem.

NORTHWOOD VENTURES LLC

485 Underhill Blvd., Suite 205
Syosset, NY 11791-3419
516-364-5544   fax: 516-364-0879
www.northwoodventures.com

Henry T. Wilson, Managing Director
Peter G. Schiff, President
Paul R. Homer, Associate

total assets under management	*initial investment*	*year founded*
$200 Million	$500,000–5 Million	1983

Northwood Ventures LLC and Northwood Capital Partners LLC is a private venture capital firm that invests in first-stage, second-stage, acquisition, management buyouts, and consolidations.

Norwest Venture Partners

245 Lytton Avenue, Suite 250
Palo Alto, CA 94301
650-321-8000   fax: 650-321-8010
www.norwestvp.com

Promod Haque, Managing Partner
George J. Still Jr., Managing Partner
Blair P. Whitaker, Partner
Vab Goel, Venture Partner
James R. Lussier, Venture Partner
Robert B. Abbott, Principal
Matthew D. Howard, Principal

total assets under management	*initial investment*	*year founded*
N/A	$10–15 Million	1961

The investment focus of Norwest Venture Partners, broadly defined as information technology, includes enterprise software, communications systems, and communication services.

Its enterprise software interests include client-server, Internet, and e-commerce technology. In communication systems, the Firm invests in data communications, telecommunications, and semiconductor chip companies. In communications services, it is interested in subscriber-based businesses: for example, wireless carriers, Internet service providers, competitive local exchange carriers, or other service providers.

Novak Biddle Venture Partners

1750 Tysons Blvd., Suite 1190
McLean, Virginia 22102
703-847-3770   fax: 703-847-3771
www.novakbiddle.com

E. Rogers Novak Jr., Founder and General Partner

A. G. W. Biddle III, General Partner

Stephen M. Fredrick, Partner

total assets under management	*initial investment*	*year founded*
$85 Million	$100,000–5 Million	1997

NBVP was established in 1997 to provide equity financing and assistance to the management of young information technology companies. While NBVP focuses on information technology companies in the very early stage through the first round, NBVP will consider financing later-stage opportunities and spinouts where NBVP can add significant value. NBVP also has the ability to syndicate larger, later-stage rounds through its limited partners and other venture firms in the venture community.

    Portfolio Companies: Answer Logic; Blackboard Inc.; DiamondBack; Engenia Software, Inc.; Entevo Corporation; Giga Information Group; LifeMinders.com, Inc.; NEW Customer Service Companies, Inc.; Para-Protect Services, Inc.; Paratek Microwave, Inc.; Princeton Optronics, Inc.; Simplexity.com; Tantivy Communications, Inc.; Telogy Networks, Inc.; Torrent Systems; Vision, Inc.; Woodwind Communications Services, Inc.; and Xtreme Spectrum, Inc.

NOVELTEK CAPITAL CORPORATION

521 Fifth Avenue, Suite 1700
New York, NY 10175
212-286-1963   fax: 212-661-7606

Gabor Baumann, President

total assets under management	*initial investment*	*year founded*
N/A	$1–10 Million	1983

Noveltek Capital Corporation invests in first-stage, second-stage, mezzanine, bridge, acquisition, management buyouts, special-situation, and fast-track IPO-type companies. Noveltek emphasizes a close link between the prospects to obtain the best financing and the company's strategy plan. Noveltek seeks high-growth situations in vibrant industry segments, where a fast-track exit is possible. Savvy, innovative management is a must. See Noveltek's President's book: *Poised for Growth—Taking Your Business to the Next Level,* published by McGraw-Hill, 1997. Noveltek will invest anywhere in the United States, Canada, and Western Europe, in companies that fit well.

NOVUS VENTURES, LP

20111 Stevens Creek Blvd., Suite 130
Cupertino, CA 95014
408-252-3900   fax: 408-252-1713
www.novusventures.com

Shirley Cerrudo, General Partner

Randy Hawks, General Partner

Greg Lahann, General Partner

Daniel D. Tompkins, General Partner

Elaine Bailey, Venture Partner

total assets under management	initial investment	year founded
$120 Million	$500,000–2 Million	1994

Novus Ventures, LP is a venture capital firm, located in Silicon Valley specializing in early-stage investments in Internet, software, and wireless-enablement companies.

Daniel Tompkins and Shirley Cerrudo founded the firm in 1994. Novus currently has $120 million of capital under management and prefers to invest in early-stage companies, including seed, start-up, and first-stage, with a primary concentration on companies located in Silicon Valley. An SBIC company, Novus is also an active participant in most of the companies in which it invests.

Portfolio Companies: The fund has invested in over 24 companies and is active in a number of different software and Internet businesses.

NTH POWER TECHNOLOGIES

100 Spear Street, Suite 1450
San Francisco, CA 94105
415-974-1668   fax: 415-974-0608
www.nthfund.com
e-mail: david@nthfund.com

Nancy C. Floyd, Managing Director

Maurice E. P. Gunderson, Managing Director

Tim Woodward, Managing Director

total assets under management	initial investment	year founded
$200 Million	$500,000–2 Million	1993

Nth Power Technologies is a venture capital firm focused on high-growth invest-ment opportunities arising from the restructuring of the global energy utility mar-ketplace. The fundamental changes taking place in the $300 billion global energy utility industry have given rise to many venture capital investment opportunities, and Nth Power has emerged as a leading source of venture capital for this sector. Nth Power invests globally.

Portfolio Companies: Inari; NanoGram; Capstone; Mettallic Power; Evergreen Solar; Semi Power; Main Street Network; and Water Management Services.

NU CAPITAL ACCESS GROUP, LTD.

7677 Oakport Street, Suite 105
Oakland, CA 94621
510-635-7345   fax: 510-635-1068
www.nucapital.com

Rodney M. White, Managing Director
Will P. Stevens Jr., Managing Director

total assets under management	*initial investment*	*year founded*
N/A	$250,000–1 Million	1993

NU Capital Access Group, Ltd., is a private venture capital firm. NU Capital Access Group invests in various industries that are in need of later-stage funding. The later stages preferred are second-stage, mezzanine, leveraged buyout, and special situations. NU Capital Access Group likes to get involved with compa-nies as they grow and expand.

OAK INVESTMENT PARTNERS

525 University Avenue, Suite 1300
Palo Alto, CA 94301
650-614-3700   fax: 650-328-6345
www.oakinv.com

Bandel L. Carano, General Partner
Fredric W. Harman, General Partner

total assets under management	*initial investment*	*year founded*
$2.6 Billion	$1–5 Million	1978

Oak Investment Partners (OIP) is a private venture capital firm investing its own capital. OIP deals in seed-, start-up, first-stage, leveraged buyouts, and special situations.

OIP's investment history matches the different waves of innovation that have swept through the economy over the last 20 years. OIP started investing during the integrated circuit and office automation booms. These triggered the explosive growth of networking and enterprise software. The 1980s added waves of innovation in health care and retail. OIP now focuses on financing the Internet economy. OIP is active in scaling the Net, bridging the last mile, servicing portals and e-businesses, driving commerce to the Net, and Web enabling the enterprise.

Portfolio Companies: OIP has over 75 portfolio companies.

ODEON CAPITAL PARTNERS, LP

One State Street Plaza, 29th Floor
New York, NY 10004
212-785-1300   fax: 212-785-3159
www.odeoncapital.com

Jeffrey E. Finkle, Managing Partner
Matthew A. Smith, Managing Partner
Ira Machefsky, Partner
Marc D. Aronstein, Principal

total assets under management	*initial investment*	*year founded*
$115 Million	$3–5 Million	1998

Odeon Capital Partners, LP, is a private equity limited partnership with the objective of offering capital and talent to companies that share a common vision for creating markets and wealth in the networked economy. It seeks emerging start-up companies in the information technology field, especially those dealing with software and services, e-commerce, and consulting and implementation services. Odeon Capital Partners will consider investment opportunities throughout the United States.

Portfolio Companies: AsiaNet Corp. Ltd.; The Avicon Group; Bowstreet Software; CarDay; CyberSites; Dealtime.com; EB2X; e-MaiMai.com; Electron Economy; FreeRide.com; GoShip; IntendChange; iProperty.com; Media Market Maker; Opus360; ServiceChannel.com; ShareMax.com; ShipLogix, Inc.; ShockMarket; Spree.com; and VoiceMate.

OLYMPIC VENTURE PARTNERS

2420 Carillon Point   340 Oswego Pointe Drive, Suite 200
Kirkland, WA 98033   Lake Oswego, OR 97034
425-889-9192   503-697-8766
fax: 212-661-7606   fax: 503-697-8863
www.ovp.com

George H. Clute, General Partner

Gerald H. Langler, General Partner

William D. Miller, General Partner

David Y. Chen, Venture Partner

Charles P. Waite Jr., General Partner

Linda Hoban, Executive Assistant

Bill Funcannon, Administrative Partner

Morgan Reichman, Research Associate

Kristin Doyle, Executive Assistant

total assets under management	*initial investment*	*year founded*
$317 Million	$100,000–1 Million	1982

Olympic Venture Partners makes equity investments in early-stage technology-based companies located in the western third of North America, focusing on the Pacific Northwest. Specific emphasis is on firms in the software, life sciences, communications, health-care, and Internet sectors. Olympic Venture Partners is a venture capital limited partnership formed to invest in emerging companies with rapid growth potential. The General Partners are interested in investment opportunities with unique value-added product offerings, selling into large, rapidly growing markets and managed by a team of aggressive, experienced, and ethical professionals.

ONELIBERTY VENTURES

150 Cambridge Park Drive
Cambridge, MA 02140
617-492-7280   fax: 617-492-7290
www.oneliberty.com

Edwin M. Kania Jr., Managing General Partner

Duncan C. McCallum, General Partner

Stephen J. Ricci, General Partner

total assets under management	*initial investment*	*year founded*
$400 Million	$100,000–8 Million	1995

OneLiberty Ventures is a venture capital firm that believes strongly in the importance of the entrepreneur and the management team. For this reason, OneLiberty Ventures typically invests only in early-stage companies, usually in their concept or product development phase. The Firm also participates in all rounds of financing prior to IPO or sale and maintains close involvement with the company during the entire period.

OneLiberty Ventures focuses on the information technology, medical technology, and telecommunications industries. It seeks investments located in the United States.

Portfolio Companies: OneLiberty Ventures has over 50 portfolio companies.

ONSET VENTURES

2400 Sand Hill Road, Suite 150
Menlo Park, CA 94025
650-529-0700   fax: 650-529-0777
www.onset.com

Darlene K. Mann, Partner
Robert F. Kuhling, General Partner
Terry L. Opdendyk, General Partner
Tom Winter, General Partner
Leslie Bottorff, Venture Investor
Susan A. Mason, Venture Investor

total assets under management	*initial investment*	*year founded*
$200 Million	$250,000–1 Million	1984

ONSET Ventures is a venture capital firm specializing in seed- and early-stage information and medical technology-based companies, primarily in Northern California and Austin, Texas. In addition to direct funding, the partners at ONSET Ventures often provide hands-on assistance in company development through a unique incubation program that increases the success of start-up companies.

OPPORTUNITY CAPITAL PARTNERS

2201 Walnut Avenue, Suite 210
Fremont, CA 94538
510-795-7000   fax: 510-494-5439
www.opportunitycapital.com

J. Peter Thompson, Managing Partner

Lewis E. Byrd, Partner

Anita P. Stephens, Principal

total assets under management	*initial investment*	*year founded*
$35 Million	$1–2.5 Million	1970

Opportunity Capital Partners provides equity and equity-related financing capital to minority-controlled businesses. Preferred investment areas are the manufacturing, communications, and health-care industries.

ORION PARTNERS, L.P.

20 William Street, Suite 145
Wellesley, MA 02481
781-235-1904   fax: 781-235-8822
www.orionlp.com

Steven A. Kandarian, Managing Director

Jeffrey R. Ackerman, Vice President

Mark Manzo, Associate

Bong-Seok Choi, Associate

total assets under management	*initial investment*	*year founded*
$51 Million	$2–10 Million	1993

Orion Partners, L.P., specializes in acquisitions of established mid-sized companies.

Orion seeks to earn superior returns by acquiring companies with the potential to appreciate significantly in value over five to seven years. Orion typically acts as lead investor in change-of-control situations, including management buyouts, corporate divestitures, and private company sales or recapitalization. Orion is prepared to make investment commitments anywhere in the United States or Canada, and is quickly backed by its private equity fund.

OVATION CAPITAL PARTNERS

120 Bloomingdale Road
White Plains, NY 10605
914-285-0011   fax: 914-684-0848
www.ovationcapital.com

Greg Frank, Managing General Partner

Alan Clingman, General Partner

Henry Schachar, General Partner

Kevin Arenson, General Partner

Steven Blend, General Partner

Todd Squilanti, Partner

Adam Rosenberg, Principal

total assets under management	*initial investment*	*year founded*
$27 Million	$500,000–5 Million	2000

Ovation Capital Partners typically invests in early-stage companies introduced by the company's strong network of limited partners and industry contacts, although Ovation Capital will review unsolicited submissions. The company's target investment focus revolves around three key industry sectors, which are directly related to the background of the company's professionals: Internet services, including ASPs and software-based models; Internet infrastructure and Web enablement, including networking, hardware, and wireless technologies; and e-commerce, primarily focusing on business-to-business models and wireless applications.

Portfolio Companies: Copera; The EC Company; Federation; RentPort.com; TradeOut.com; and Ultimate Bid.

OXFORD BIOSCIENCE PARTNERS

650 Town Center Drive
Suite 810
Costa Mesa, CA 92626
714-754-5719
fax: 714-754-6802
www.oxbio.com

31 St. James Avenue
Suite 905
Boston, MA 02116
617-357-7474
fax: 617-357-7476

315 Post Road West
Westport, CT 06880
203-341-3300
fax: 203-341-3309

Jeffrey T. Barnes, General Partner

Michael J. Brennan, M.D., Ph.D., General Partner

Jonathan J. Fleming, General Partner

Edmond M. Oliver, General Partner

Cornelius T. Ryan, General Partner

Dr. Alan G. Walton, General Partner

total assets under management	*initial investment*	*year founded*
$400 Million	$250,000–3 Million	1991

Oxford Bioscience Partners (OBP) is a life sciences venture capital firm that provides equity financing and management assistance to start-up and early-stage, entrepreneurial-driven companies in the bioscience and health-care industries. The General Partners of OBP currently manage venture funds with combined committed capital of more than $400 million.

Portfolio Companies: Oxford Bioscience Partners has over 65 portfolio companies, including Gene Logiz; Geron Corporation; and Materni Care.

Pacesetter Growth Fund, L.P.

2435 North Central Express Way, Suite 200
Richardson, TX 75080
972-991-1597   fax: 972-991-4770
www.mvhc.com

Thomas G. Gerron, Managing Director

Divakar R. Kamath, Managing Director

Donald R. Lawhorne, Managing Director

total assets under management	initial investment	year founded
N/A	$500,000–5 Million	1970

Pacesetter Growth Fund, L.P. (Pacesetter), is a private equity partnership that provides growth capital to expand, acquire, or modernize companies. Pacesetter's industry preferences include general manufacturing, electronics, broadcasting, telecommunications, and food processing.

Portfolio Companies: BioGenex; BroadLink Communications; City Cableworks; Genaissance Pharmaceuticals; Metropolitan TLC Holding, Inc.; Netcom Solutions International, Inc.; Perpetua, Inc.; QVS, Inc.; Radio One, Inc.; SFI, Inc.; Tele-Media Communications Holding, LLC; and Vista.

Pacific Corporate Group, Inc.

1200 Prospect Street, Suite 200
La Jolla, CA 92037
858-456-6000   fax: 858-456-6018
www.pcgfunds.com

Christopher J. Bower, CEO

Kelly DePonte, Executive Operating President

Philip Poster, CFO

total assets under management	*initial investment*	*year founded*
$13.5 Billion	$5–500 Million	1979

Pacific Corporate Group (PCG) has been a leader in private equity investments for more than 20 years. PCG categorizes alternative investments as indirect investments in limited partnerships and direct investments. PCG has extensive experience in providing a full range of services, including sourcing, evaluating, structuring, negotiating, and monitoring. PCG's clientele includes some of the largest and most sophisticated institutional investors in the world, including the California Public Employees' Retirement System, Fire and Police Pension Association of Colorado, New York City Employees' Retirement System, and Oregon Public Employees' Retirement Fund. In addition, PCG serves hundreds of individual investors through its diversified private equity fund vehicles.

PACIFIC HORIZON VENTURES

1001 Fourth Avenue Plaza, Suite 4105
Seattle, WA 98154
206-682-1181   fax: 206-682-8077
www.pacifichorizon.com

Richard Carone, General Partner
Donald J. Elmer, General Partner
Bruce Jackson, General Partner

total assets under management	*initial investment*	*year founded*
$15 Million	$500,000–2 Million	1993

Pacific Horizon Ventures is a Seattle-based venture capital firm, with national presence, focused on the life sciences and health-care industries. With a successful track record of over seven years, as demonstrated by its first two funds, the Firm invests in early-, expansion-, and late-stage private companies across North America.

Pacific Horizon Ventures applies in-depth knowledge of the life sciences and health care to identify the best private investment opportunities.

Portfolio Companies: AtheroGenics, Inc.; Carewise, Inc.; Cell Pathways, Inc.; Coral Systems, Inc.; Creative Multimedia; Diametrics Medical, Inc.; Edmark Corporation; Focal, Inc.; Inhibitex, Inc.; Innova Corporation; NeoPath, Inc.; Norian Corporation; Novocell, Inc.; Orquest, Inc.; Proxim, Inc.; RTIME, Inc.; Sapient Health Network, Inc.; Selective Genetics; SleepMed, Inc.; Therion Biologics Corporation; Transmolecular, Inc.; Trimeris, Inc.; and VitaGen, Inc.

Pacific Mezzanine Fund

2200 Powell Street, Suite 1250
Emeryville, CA 94608
510-595-9800   fax: 510-595-9801
www.pacmezz.com

Nathan W. Bell, General Partner
Andrew B. Dumke, General Partner
David C. Woodward, General Partner

total assets under management	*initial investment*	*year founded*
$82 Million	$1–5 Million	1994

Pacific Mezzanine Fund invests $2–5 million in the form of debt with warrants, primarily in support of expansion and acquisition financings. A current cash yield is mandatory.

Pacific Northwest Partners SBIC, L.P.

305 108th Avenue NE, 2nd Floor
Bellevue, WA 98004-5706
425-455-9967   fax: 425-455-9404
www.pnwp.com

Theodore M. Wight, General Partner
Nancy Y. Isely-Fletcher, Vice President of the General Partner

total assets under management	*initial investment*	*year founded*
$14 Million	$500,000–2 Million	1994

Pacific Northwest Partners SBIC, L.P. (PNP), deals in seed- and first-stage funding. PNP focuses on Pacific Northwest companies, located in Washington, Oregon, and Idaho. PNP expects companies to perform at $20–30 million in revenues in three to five years.

Pacific Venture Group

16830 Ventura Boulevard, Suite 244
Encino, CA 91436
818-990-4141   fax: 818-990-6556
www.pacven.com

Annette M. Bianchi, Managing Director

Layton R. Crouch, Managing Director

Eve M. Kurtin, Managing Director

Ralph C. Sabin, Managing Director

total assets under management	*initial investment*	*year founded*
$100 Million	$1–5 Million	1995

Pacific Venture Group's focus is investment opportunities in health care, and related information systems and services across a broad range of financing stages, from start-up and early-stage situations to buyouts, recapitalizations, and consolidations.

Pacific Venture Group is a highly differentiated venture capital fund due to the strength and capabilities of its team of managing directors and its unique combination of major health-care corporations, leading institutions' investors, and experienced individuals that comprise the limited partners of the partnership. The Managing Director Team embodies strong track records in a number of areas relevant to the venture capital process, giving its members particular insight into the perspectives of both investors and entrepreneurs. Their experience includes venture fund management, transaction structuring, and turnaround management. The Managing Directors' experience is heavily oriented toward health-care services and finance, largely gained in the progressive and innovative Southern California health-care market. The Managing Directors have highly developed abilities in recognizing, developing, and marketing promising health-care services business opportunities.

PALOMAR VENTURES

100 Wilshire Blvd., Suite 1620
Santa Monica, CA 90401
310-260-6050   fax: 310-656-4150
www.palomarventures.com

Jim Gauer, General Partner

Randall Lunn, General Partner

Rick Smith, General Partner

total assets under management	*initial investment*	*year founded*
$80 Million	$2–5 Million	1999

Palomar Ventures invests in start-up and early-stage information technology companies. On occasion, Palomar Ventures also participates in seed funding. Current areas of strategic focus for investment include datacom/telecom/broadband communications, infrastructure software for e-business, and business-to-business/business-to-consumer e-commerce. Palomar invests mainly in Southern California.

Portfolio Companies: AdExchange; AristaSoft; Clarity Communications; Continuous Computing; Dorado.com; Efficient Networks; gotajob.com; RightStart.com; Syntricity; ViaSource/TeleCore; and YellowShirt.

PARADIGM CAPITAL PARTNERS, LLC
6410 Poplar Avenue, Suite 395
Memphis, TN 38119
901-682-6060   fax: 901-328-3047
www.paradigmcp.com

Robert B. Blow, Senior Managing Director

Frank A. McGrew IV, Managing Director

Bill Razzouk, Venture Partner

Warner B. Rodda, General Counsel

Kathy Williams, CFO

Wallace Madewell, Chief Administrative Officer

Alexander J. Sadusky, Vice President

Andrew Seamons, Vice President

Craig Nadel, Associate

Pravin J. Thakkar Jr., Financial Analyst

total assets under management	initial investment	year founded
N/A	$1–5 Million	1999

Paradigm Capital Partners was formed in 1999 to serve the capital and advisory needs of emerging-growth companies.

Paradigm provides its portfolio companies with business model assessment, recruiting, sales and marketing strategy, and first-hand knowledge in developing new products, negotiating strategic partnerships, raising capital, managing growth, and evaluating the appropriate "exit" strategy, whether through a strategic alternative, such as a merger or acquisition, or through a public offering of equity. Paradigm believes that personalized attention and extensive involvement between its team and each portfolio company is essential.

Paradigm's deep expertise and experience come from a wide variety of industries and situations, including: advertising, aviation, basic manufacturing, cable television, health care, information technology, investment management, media, recreation and leisure, real estate, and telecommunications.

Portfolio Companies: 3Re.com; Carrot's Ink Cartridges; Control Top; dotLogix; espins; Firstdoor.com; fob.com; Mediacentrix; more.com; Nueweb Interactive; OpenAir.com; and Vention.

PARTECH INTERNATIONAL

50 California Street, Suite 3200
San Francisco, CA 94111
415-788-2929   fax: 415-788-6763
www.partechintl.com

Thomas G. McKinley, Managing Partner

Vincent Worms, Managing Partner

Philippe Cases, General Partner

Nicolas El Base, General Partner

Glenn Solomon, General Partner

Dave Welsh, General Partner

Scott J. Matson, General Partner

total assets under management	*initial investment*	*year founded*
$500 Million	N/A	1981

Partech International is one of the leading international venture capital firms. Its primary mission is to continue to provide superior long-term returns to its limited partners by identifying the product and service leaders of tomorrow, assisting in the development of their business models, and the execution of their growth plans. For almost two decades the team of dedicated partners in San Francisco, Paris, and Tokyo has helped U.S. and Western European entrepreneurs build world-class companies, from the seed-stage to IPO.

Partech typically invests in ideas that it expects will have an international market. In addition to the resources provided by traditional U.S. venture firms, it offers a unique "cross-border" assistance. Employing as necessary the assistance of its network of contacts in the United States, Europe, or Asia, it helps companies gain access to foreign markets quicker and easier.

Portfolio Companies: Partech has over 65 portfolio companies in the information technology, life sciences, and business services industries.

PETRA CAPITAL PARTNERS, LLC

172 Second Avenue North, Suite 112
Nashville, TN 37201
615-313-5999   fax: 615-313-5990
www.petracapital.com

Mike Blackburn, Partner

Joe O'Brien, Partner

Rob Smith, Vice President

total assets under management	*initial investment*	*year founded*
$150 Million	$2–5 Million	1998

Petra Capital Partners, LLC, is a private investment management firm engaged in providing expansion capital for high-growth, private companies. It prefers to invest in companies that are in the later stages of development. Petra Capital Partners is interested in a wide range of industries, such as telecommunications, information technology, the Internet, health care, consumer services, and business services.

Petra Capital Partners seek investments primarily in the Southeast but will also invest on the West Coast.

Portfolio Companies: Petra Capital Partners has over 30 portfolio companies.

PINECREEK CAPITAL MANAGEMENT, L.P.

24 Corporate Plaza, Suite 160
Newport Beach, CA 92660
949-720-4620   fax: 949-720-4629
www.pinecreekcap.com

Randall F. Zurbach, President

John C. Wilbur Jr., Executive Vice President

total assets under management	*initial investment*	*year founded*
$48 Million	$500,000–2.5 Million	1996

Located in Newport Beach, California, Pinecreek Capital Partners, L.P., is a licensed small business investment company engaged in providing mezzanine financing for middle-market companies. Investments will normally be in the form of subordinated debentures ranging in size from $500,000 to $2.5 million. These debentures will typically be issued with detachable equity rights or warrants. The maturity of these loans will range from five to seven years. Pinecreek's industry focus includes distribution, manufacturing, service, software, and transportation. Pinecreek's primary objective is to provide growth financing, but it will also consider recapitalizations, management buyouts, and leveraged buyouts. Potential portfolio companies must have quantifiable historical cash flow and a proven management team.

POINT WEST VENTURES

1700 Montgomery Street, Suite 250
San Francisco, CA 94111
415-394-1201
www.pointwestventures.com

Bradley N. Rotter, Co-Founder

Chris P. Rodskog, Senior Vice President

Michael Reeves, Analyst

total assets under management	*initial investment*	*year founded*
N/A	$500,000–1 Million	N/A

Point West Ventures is a venture capital firm committed to providing financial and strategic guidance to emerging small companies. It seeks long-term partnerships with the management teams of its portfolio companies and is committed to transforming small companies into market leaders in the telecommunications and information technology industries. It funds middle and later-stage companies located within the United States.

   Portfolio Companies: Acteva; Circadence; Actuality Systems; CornerHardware.com; Cresenda Wireless; Enikia; EoSports; Ez2get.com; FlashNet; Homeseekers.com; Mind Arrow; N2H2; Nomadix; Telenisus; and Tradius.

POLARIS VENTURES PARTNERS

1000 Winter Street	701 5th Avenue	804 Las Cimas Parkway
Suite 3350	Suite 6850	Suite 140
Waltham, MA 02451-1215	Seattle, WA 98104	Austin, TX 78746
781-290-0770	206-652-4555	512-225-5400
fax: 781-290-0880	fax: 206-652-4666	fax: 512-225-5444
www.polarisventures.com		

Alan Spoon, Managing General Partner

Stephen D. Arnold, General Partner

James Earl Brown III, General Partner

Brian Chee, General Partner

Jonathan A. Flint, General Partner

Thomas A. Herring, General Partner

Michael Hirschland, General Partner

Terrance G. McGuire, General Partner

John Gannon, CFO and Partner

Dave Barrett, Venture Partner

George H. Conrades, Venture Partner

Zack Thompson, Associate

total assets under management	*initial investment*	*year founded*
N/A	$250,000–15 Million	1996

Polaris Ventures Partners, founded in 1996, is a venture capital firm that targets the information technology, life sciences, and medical technology industries for its investments. The Firm is interested in Internet software, Internet commerce, network hardware, network software, computer systems, medical devices, pharmaceuticals, genomics, and health-care services.

Polaris Ventures Partners tends to invest mostly in companies at the early stages of development, from seed stage to companies that are generating initial revenue.

Portfolio Companies: Polaris Ventures Partners has over 50 portfolio companies, including AIR; Akamai; Alive.com; Allaire; Avici Systems, Inc.; Aspect Medical; Centra Software; Classified 2000; Kestrel Solutions; MarketXT; Paradigm Genetics; and Solid Works.

PREMIER MEDICAL PARTNER FUND L.P.

12225 El Camino Real
San Diego, CA 92130
858-509-6402   fax: 858-509-8919
www.premiernc.com

Richard Kuntz, Senior Managing Director

Palmer Ford, Managing Director

Doug Lee, Managing Director

total assets under management	*initial investment*	*year founded*
$116 Million	$1–5 Million	1995

Premier Medical Partner Fund (PMPF) is a private venture capital fund that was founded in 1995. Investment is focused on companies in the life sciences, medical devices, and health-care industries. PMPF considers investment opportunities on a national basis. Investments range from early- to later-stage deals.

PRIMEDIA VENTURES

745 Fifth Avenue, 21st Floor
New York, NY 10151
212-745-1203   fax: 212-610-9422
www.primediaventures.com

Larry Phillips, Managing Director

Andy Thompson, Managing Director

Jason Chervakas, Venture Partner

Jim Carlisle, Entrepreneur in Residence

total assets under management	*initial investment*	*year founded*
N/A	$1–3 Million	1998

Primedia Ventures invests in early-stage Internet software and services companies. At present, Primedia is particularly interested in the following areas: business-to-business industrial exchanges and related services enabling software and services for business-to-business and business-to-consumer e-commerce, distance learning/selling software, streaming media applications and content, community-oriented services for consumers, Web-based business services, other vertically focused enterprise software applications, advertising and direct marketing services, and software.

   Portfolio Companies: CarsDirect; fourthchannel; Internet Gift Registries; Military.com; MobileSpring; MyPoints; Netpodium Inc.; NextVenue; perfect.com; SocialNet; StickyNetworks; Utility.com; and ZZSoft.

PRIMUS VENTURE PARTNERS, INC.

5900 Landbrook Drive, Suite 200
Cleveland, Ohio 44124
440-684-7300   fax: 440-684-7342
www.primusventure.com

James T. Bartlett, Managing Director

Jonathan E. Dick, Managing Director

William C. Mulligan, Managing Director
Steve Rothman, Managing Director
Loyal W. Wilson, Managing Director

total assets under management	*initial investment*	*year founded*
$500 Million	$3–10 Million	1983

Founded in 1983, Primus Venture Partners is a private equity investment firm with a single and straightforward goal: to invest in enterprises with exceptional potential for capital appreciation. The Primus team has 90 combined years of industry experience and manages over $500 million of private equity capital.

While Primus prefers investments that range from $5–10 million, it will invest in seed- or developmental-stage companies that demonstrate "industry leader" characteristics. It funds companies at all stages of development in a variety of industries, with a focus in Internet/e-commerce, telecommunications, business/education services, and health care.

Primus does not limit itself by geography or industry. It is most interested in partnering with outstanding managers of companies with dynamic growth potential.

Portfolio Companies: Access Global; Athersys; Bioanalytical Systems; Captivate Network; Carrier 1; CBG; Complient.com; Cyberian Outpost; DecorateToday.com; Golf Galaxy; iWon; LCI International; Mail.com; Marlin Leasing; MedHost; and Nextec Applications.

PRISM VENTURE PARTNERS

100 Lowder Brook Drive, Suite 2500
Westwood, MA 02090
781-302-4000   fax: 781-302-4040
www.prismventure.com

Robert C. Fleming, General Partner
Duane R. Mason, General Partner
Laurie J. Thomsen, General Partner
John L. Brooks III, General Partner
William M. Seifert, General Partner
David William Baum, General Partner
Daniel C. Wright, CFO

total assets under management	*initial investment*	*year founded*
$560 Million	$2–10 Million	1996

Prism Venture Partners is a leading venture capital firm providing equity investments in early-stage and growth companies in the communications, Internet, and health-care industries. Prism has successfully combined the venture capital expertise, operational entrepreneurial expertise, and strategic relationships of its General Partners to build significant value for its investors.

Portfolio Companies: Prism Venture Partners has over 45 portfolio companies in the telecommunications and information systems, health-care, and Internet industries.

PUTNAM LOVELL CAPITAL PARTNERS INC.

Los Angeles Office:
501 Deep Valley Drive, Suite 300
Rolling Hills Estates, CA 90274
310-750-3600   fax: 310-265-1920
www.putnamlovellcapital.com

Jeffrey D. Lovell, Chairman and CEO
Jennings J. Newcom, General Counsel
James E. Minnick, President
Cameron L. Miller, Principal

total assets under management	*initial investment*	*year founded*
$142.5 Million	$5–25 Million	1988

Putnam Lovell Capital Partners Inc. is the private capital affiliate of Putnam Lovell Securities Inc. and was formed to provide growth capital to developing companies in the financial services industry. Within the financial services industry, it focuses on asset management, financial planning, and e-finance. Putnam Lovell Capital Partners participates in management buyouts, leveraged recapitalizations, and consolidations.

With offices located in Los Angeles, New York, and San Francisco, Putnam Lovell Capital Partners seeks investments throughout the United States.

Portfolio Companies: Arrowstreet Capital; AssetMark Investment Services; Codexa; Centurion Capital Group; Direct Capital Markets; HedgeWorld; StoneRidge Investment Partners, LLC; and Van Deventer & Hoch.

RADER REINFRANK & CO., LLC

9465 Wilshire Boulevard, Suite 950
Beverly Hills, CA 90212-2617
310-246-2977   fax: 310-246-2988
www.rrco.com

Steve Rader, Founding Partner

Rudy Reinfrank, Founding Partner

Josh Gutfreund, Partner

total assets under management	*initial investment*	*year founded*
$100 Million	$5–20 Million	1997

Rader Reinfrank & Co., LLC (RRCO), manages a $100-million Los Angeles–based private equity fund. It provides long-term capital, management support, and financial expertise to emerging-growth companies in the communications, telecommunications, media, and electronic-commerce industries. The Firm focuses on identifying emerging technology and industry trends that will help drive future growth. It seeks strong entrepreneurial management teams that it can actively partner with to achieve long-term capital appreciation and maximum enterprise value.

Portfolio Companies: CoSine Communications; Cyras systems, Inc.; eMind.com; Iwin.com, Inc.; Multex.com, Inc.; One Tel Ltd.; OneSoft Corporation; Optical Capital Group; Rotor Communications; TelePacific Communications; Trillium Digital Systems; and xSides Corporation.

RAVENSWOOD CAPITAL VENTURE FUND

225 West Washington Street, Suite 1650
Chicago, IL 60606
312-443-5243   fax: 312-368-9015
www.ravenswoodcapital.com

David Abraham, Partner

Dan Kanter, Partner

total assets under management	*initial investment*	*year founded*
N/A	$1–5 Million	1998

Ravenswood Capital Venture's mission is to help build early-stage Internet companies into long-term industry leaders through investment and ongoing support. Ravenswood makes venture capital investments in several target markets: business-to-business, business-to-consumer, direct marketing, and educational services.

Ravenswood targets investments in companies pursuing rapid-growth strategies. This growth may be generated from new product development, geographic expansion, or acquisitions.

Portfolio Companies: AnnuityScout.com; Carparts.com; Education Networks of America; FastWeb; JusticeLink; and U-Access.

REDLEAF GROUP, INC.

Pacific Headquarters
14395 Saratoga Avenue, Suite 130
Saratoga, CA 95070
408-868-0800
fax: 408-868-0810
www.redleaf.com

Atlantic Headquarters
100 First Avenue, Suite 950
Pittsburgh, PA 15222
412-201-5600
fax: 412-201-5650

John Kohler, Co-CEO

C. Lloyd Mahaffey, Co-CEO

total assets under management	*initial investment*	*year founded*
N/A	N/A	1999

Redleaf Group is a technology operating company that leverages a powerful, digital GRID (Global Resource for Internet Development) to provide services and capital for seed-stage Internet technology companies and communities. Redleaf provides its partner companies with market access, strategic counsel, and operational support from a team of seasoned professional managers whose specialties include finance, engineering, product development, systems integration, marketing, and human capital management. These capabilities are offered today to partner companies, through Redleaf Group's GRID, in offices throughout the United States, Europe, and soon in Asia.

Portfolio Companies: Bitlocker, Inc.; edFood.com, Inc.; Edgewood Creek, Inc.; Furndex, Inc.; Inceutica.com, Inc.; Ipeer, Networks Inc.; Lightningcast, Inc.; LumiCyte, Inc.; Medebiz, Inc.; MediaFlex.com, Inc.; Moai Technologies, Inc.; QuickDog, Inc.; and RedCreek Communications, Inc.; Stars and Stripes Omnimedia, Inc.; Startups.com, Inc.; Telicor, Inc.; ThreadExchange.com, Inc.; and Webversa.

REDPOINT VENTURES

11150 Santa Monica Boulevard
Suite 1200
Los Angeles, CA 90025
310-477-7678
fax: 310-312-1868
www.redpoint.com

3000 Sand Hill Road
Building 2, Suite 290
Menlo Park, CA 94025
650-926-5600
fax: 650-854-5762

Allen Beasley, Partner

Jeff Brody, Partner

Rom Dyal, Partner

Peter Gotcher, Venture Partner

Tim Haley, Partner

Brad Jones, Partner

John McQuillan, Venture Partner

John Walecka, Partner

Geoff Yang, Partner

total assets under management	*initial investment*	*year founded*
N/A	$100,000–20 Million	1999

Redpoint Ventures is a venture capital firm focused on next-generation Internet and broadband companies, with an emphasis on enabling infrastructure, service and application providers, business-to-business platforms and services, business-to-consumer platforms and services, and dot-com spinoffs. Redpoint Ventures is interested in investing at the earlier stages of a company's development, usually in the first round. It also selectively invests at the seed stage and in the second round. Redpoint Ventures seeks investment opportunities in the United States.

Portfolio Companies: Big Band Networks; BizBuyer.com; Calix Networks; D-STAR Technologies, Inc.; eNet; ePeople; Fandom; Fusient Media Ventures; Longitude Systems; Multilink Technology Corporation; Nexgenix; Octopus; Panthera Networks; and Reflect.com.

RED ROCK VENTURES

180 Lytton Avenue
Palo Alto, CA 94301
650-325-3111   fax: 650-853-7044
www.redrockventures.com

Bob Todd, General Partner

Kip Myers, General Partner

Bob Marsh, General Partner

Peter Dumanian, General Partner

Laura Brege, General Partner

total assets under management	*initial investment*	*year founded*
$130 Million	$1–3 Million	1997

Red Rock Ventures is a Palo Alto, California–based venture capital investment partnership specializing in seed- and early-stage information technology investments.

Red Rock Ventures invests in seed- or first-round equity investment opportunities for companies that focus on business-to-business Internet software or commerce.

Portfolio Companies: Active Research; All Bases Covered; Crosslogix; Digital Market; Disappearing, Inc.; Ejasent; Freeworks; Gazooba; Harmony; HiFive Networks; Iescrow; Imparto; Live Capital; Mondo Media; My Contracts; Ncommand; Open Shelf.com; Plum Tree; RWT Corp.; Silicon Energy; Simpata; Softcoin; Supplybase; Tivix; Vivity; and Zantaz.

RICHLAND VENTURES

200 31st Avenue North, Suite 200
Nashville, TN 37203
615-383-8030   fax: 615-269-0463
www.richlandventures.com

Jack Tyrrell, Managing Partner
Pat Ortale, Managing Partner
John Chadwick, General Partner

total assets under management	*initial investment*	*year founded*
$456 Million	$5–15 Million	1994

Richland Ventures has extensive experience in helping entrepreneurs grow their companies into large, successful enterprises.

Richland provides expansion capital to service companies operating in the health-care, communications, media, and information services industries with a proven business model and a large target market. Richland companies are primarily headquartered in the Southeast and Southwest, although the Firm will consider investments in other regions of the country.

Richland's stage of investment is early-stage and late-stage.

Portfolio Companies: @plan; Aperture; Appriss; Axolotl Corporation; ClearVision Laser Centers; Darwin Networks; The Delta Group; First Insight; Genus.net; halftheplanet.com; Harmony Health Plan; Iform DX; Mainbancorp; Manorhouse Retirement Centers; Mattress Giant; Media1st.com; MindLeaders.com; Network One; PeopleFirst.com; PRIMIS; Swell.com; Symbion; Synhrgy; Televox; TORCH Health Care; TriVergent Communications; U.S. Healthworks; and Z-Tel.

RIDGE VENTURES

1860 El Camino Real, Suite 200
Burlingame, CA 94010
650-652-1500   fax: 650-652-1504
www.ridgeventures.com

Eric Hautemont, Managing Director

John Stockholm, Managing Director

total assets under management	*initial investment*	*year founded*
$20 Million	$500,000	1998

Ridge Ventures is a $20-million venture capital partnership focused on making seed investments in Silicon Valley–based high-tech companies. Through its unique Base Camp incubation program, Ridge Ventures offers portfolio companies extensive access to hands-on operational expertise and management.

Ridge Ventures does seed- and very early-stage financing. Ridge Ventures likes to be the first investor in a company and usually takes a leadership position in the initial round of financing. Ridge will invest side-by-side with business Angels or with the company's founders at start-up/business plan time when appropriate.

Portfolio Companies: ExOffice; Light Logic; LuckySurf.com; Signio; Weave Innovation; and Xenote.

RIDGESTONE CORPORATION

10877 Wilshire Boulevard, Suite 2000
Los Angeles, CA 90024
310-209-5300   fax: 310-209-0040
www.ridgestonecorp.com

Abbott L. Brown, Chairman

D. Stephen Antion, President

Christopher S. Kiper, Senior Associate

total assets under management	*initial investment*	*year founded*
$100 Million	$1–5 Million	1997

Ridgestone Corporation, based in Los Angeles, is a private equity firm focusing on investments in established operating companies in telecom, technology, manufacturing, media, finance, and consumer products. Ridgestone has available capital in excess of $100 million. Ridgestone's early major focus was an investment in the predecessor company to Global Crossing Ltd., an international provider of telecommunications services. In addition, Ridgestone has invested in a variety of other businesses. The principals of Ridgestone have a broad array of business skills, which, when needed, are used to introduce strategic partners, realign strategies, strengthen management, and raise capital. Ridgestone has extensive experience in business management, finance, and acquisitions. As a result, Ridgestone seeks investments where the skills and contacts of its principals can add value and where active involvement is beneficial.

Portfolio Companies: e-mind.com; Global Crossing; Oingo Inc; and TheBrain.

RIORDAN, LEWIS & HADEN

300 South Grand Avenue, 29th Floor
Los Angeles, CA 90071
213-229-8500   fax: 213-229-8597

Patrick C. Haden, General Partner

J. Christopher Lewis, General Partner

Richard J. Riordan, General Partner

Murray E. Rudin, General Partner

total assets under management	*initial investment*	*year founded*
N/A	$5 Million	1974

Riordan, Lewis & Haden (RLH) is an investment firm that invests its own capital and focuses on acquiring companies with significant growth opportunities, that have sales of $20 to $200 million, and that are located in California. RLH specializes in later-stage funding, such as acquisition and leveraged and management buyouts, and deals with special situations.

RIVER ASSOCIATES LLC

633 Chestnut Street, Suite 1640
Chattanooga, TN 37450
423-755-0888   fax: 423-755-0870
www.riverassociatesllc.com

J. Mark Jones, Principal

total assets under management	*initial investment*	*year founded*
$60 Million	$1–7 Million	1989

River Associates LLC is aggressively seeking acquisition and recapitalization candidates that exhibit strong potential for growth in sales and operating income. The Firm seeks to invest with management and provide assistance to grow portfolio companies through acquisition and market penetration. River Associates currently has investments in industries such as adhesives, furniture, carpet, specialty tooling, environmental remediation, and household cleaning products. The ideal acquisition candidate is a low-to-medium technology manufacturer or distributor that exhibits the following characteristics: a historical and defensible cash flow, a strong and competitive niche in its market, a talented and committed management team that will participate with River Associates in its investment, and a total transaction size between $5 million and $50 million. River Associates strives to be honest and responsive and welcomes inquiries from potential acquisition candidates and intermediaries alike. River Associates's principals have substantial operational and financial experience and will gladly provide multiple references.

ROCKET VENTURES

3000 Sand Hill Road, Building 1, Suite 170
Menlo Park, CA 94025
650-566-1565   fax: 650-561-9183
www.rocketventures.com

David Adams, Managing Partner

Jeff Allen, Managing Partner

Nigel Backwith, Managing Partner

total assets under management	*initial investment*	*year founded*
$75 Million	$100,000–5 Million	1998

Rocket Ventures is a seed- and early-stage venture capital firm investing in high-growth information technology companies, particularly e-business, e-commerce, and communication infrastructure companies.

Rocket Ventures believes that the greatest growth opportunities lie in companies that help large enterprises increase revenues, strengthen supplier and customer relationships, and improve the communications capabilities of the Internet.

Portfolio Companies: Abovenet; AneuRx; CombiChem; Cyberbills; Digi System; eHealthInsurance.com; Financial Interactive; Flyte Comm; Harmony Software; Hipbone; NeoMagic; Network Appliance; Nvidia; One Day Free; Peerless System; Positive Communication; Pharmacyclic; Sequana Therapeutics; and Women.com.

ROCKY MOUNTAIN CAPITAL PARTNERS, LLP

1125 17th Avenue, Suite 2260
Denver, CO 80202
303-297-1701   fax: 303-297-1702
www.rockycapital.com

Edward C. Brown, Managing Partner

Paul A. Lyons Jr., Partner

Stephen N. Sangalis, Partner

D. Michael Everage, Associate

total assets under management	*initial investment*	*year founded*
$180 Million	$2–6 Million	1994

Rocky Mountain Capital Partners, LLP is the General Partner of the Rocky Mountain Mezzanine Fund II, LP, and the Hanifen Imhoff Mezzanine Fund, LP, which provide long-term, subordinated debt and equity-related capital for management buyouts, recapitalizations, and expansion financing.

Prospective investment companies must be generating revenues of at least $10 million, with a profit of at least $1 million. Preferred investments are in the Rocky Mountain, Midwest, and Southwest regions of the United States.

ROYALTY CAPITAL MANAGEMENT, INC.

5 Downing Road
Lexington, MA 02421-6918
781-861-8490   fax: 781-674-2363

Arthur Fox, President

total assets under management	*initial investment*	*year founded*
$2.9 Million	$100,000–300,000	1994

Royalty Capital Management, Inc. (RCM), manages two unique royalty-based funds: Royalty Capital Fund and Royalty Capital Fund Limited Partnership I. RCM uses a unique royalty-based investment methodology that enables businesses to obtain growth capital by providing investors with a royalty stream derived from gross revenue. This investment structure enables the business owner/entrepreneur to limit dilation of his or her equity position.

RCM's first objective is to have the royalty stream return the initial invested capital within 18 months from the time the investment was made. RCM focuses on businesses that need capital to launch or expand the market for a new product/service. The product/service must be ready to market, and the marketplace must be ready to enthusiastically receive the product/service.

RCM focuses on businesses that have high gross profit margins. Companies that market proprietary products to niche markets are normally the best match for royalty financing. RCM will not fund companies' products that rely on aesthetics or style for their sales appeal.

RRE VENTURES

126 East 56th Street
New York, NY 10022
212-418-5116   fax: 212-418-5123
www.rre.com

Stuart J. Ellman, General Partner
James D. Robinson III, General Partner
James D. Robinson IV, General Partner

total assets under management	*initial investment*	*year founded*
$350 Million	$5–7 Million	1994

RRE Ventures is a venture capital firm that invests nationally in information technology companies. It focuses on creating market leaders in the software, communications, Internet, and related technology industries. RRE Ventures seeks young companies that are completing product development and beginning to offer products/services in a large and well-defined market.

Portfolio Companies: RRE Ventures has over 60 portfolio companies.

RWI GROUP

835 Page Mill Road
Palo Alto, CA 94304-1011
650-251-1800
www.rwigroup.com

William R. Baumel, General Partner
Donald A. Lucas, Managing General Partner

total assets under management	*initial investment*	*year founded*
$14 Million	$1 Million	1995

RWI Group is a privately held venture capital firm with a single goal: to invest in high-quality start-up companies and help turn them into market leaders. RWI Group focuses on information technology companies poised for rapid growth, with a focus on communications, software, semiconductor, and Internet companies. RWI invests primarily in Silicon Valley but will invest globally.

Portfolio Companies: Fujant, Inc.; GoDigital Networks Corp.; Integral Access, Inc.; Kestrel Solutions, Inc.; Lightspeed International, Inc.; Luminous Networks, Inc.; LongBoard, Inc.; Novalux, Inc.; Pluris, Inc.; RangeStar Wireless Corporation; WhereNet, Inc.; Cephren, Inc.; Conduct, Ltd.; CrossLogix, Inc.; Cybrant Corp.; Extricity, Inc.; Intraspect Software, Inc.; KhiMetrics, Inc.; nQuire Software, Inc.; Preview Systems, Inc.; Prodea Software; Proxinet, Inc.; slp InfoWare; Tsola, Inc.; VPNX.com, Inc.; WorkingWomanNetwork, Inc.; Xporta, Inc.; Intensys Corporation; iReady Corporation; Microcosm Technologies, Inc.; PDF Solutions, Inc.; Aksys Ltd.; Coulter Pharmaceutical, Inc.; Intuitive Surgical, Inc.; and Pinnacle Composite Solutions, Inc.

SALIX VENTURES

350 Townsend Street, Suite 405	30 Burton Hills Boulevard, Suite 370
San Francisco, CA 94107	Nashville, TN 37215
415-369-9626	615-665-1409
fax: 415-369-9624	fax: 615-665-2912
www.salixventures.com	

Mark Donovan, Principal

Marty Felsenthal, General Partner

Christopher Grant Jr., General Partner

David Ward, General Partner

total assets under management	*initial investment*	*year founded*
$175 Million	$3–7 Million	1998

Salix Ventures is unique among health-care venture capital firms. Its partners are former health-care entrepreneurs with more than 25 years of operating experience, managing successful venture-backed health-care services companies. The Firm has created and built outpatient-oriented, physician-driven entrepreneurial companies, so it understands what is necessary to develop an idea into a successful enterprise. This experience allows the Salix partners to assist entrepreneurs with developing a strategy, a management team, and financial resources.

Salix Ventures invests primarily in early-stage health-care service and health-care information technology companies raising their first or second round of institutional venture capital funding. The Firm does not provide seed capital. It typically invests $5 million into its portfolio companies and devotes a great deal of time to them. Salix Ventures prefers to bring in at least one other venture firm. It prefers to take a seat on the Board of Directors.

Portfolio Companies: AccentCare; Confer; Domain; Dr Goodwell.com; food buy.com; ican, Inc.; Intellicare; MedContrax; ParkStone; Pathology Partners; PayerPath.com; Point Share; Radiant Research; SemperCare; The Collaborative Group; Vivius; and W3 Health.

SAND HILL CAPITAL

3000 Sand Hill Road, Building 2, Suite 110
Menlo Park, CA 94025
650-234-0410   fax: 650-234-0414
www.sandhillcapital.com

William Del Biaggio III, President and CEO

Daniel Corry, General Partner

Ian Schnider, General Partner

total assets under management	*initial investment*	*year founded*
$100 Million	$5 Million	1996

Founded in 1996, Sand Hill Capital is named after Menlo Park, California's renowned Sand Hill Road—the worldwide center of venture capital. The company is led by Founder, President, and Chief Executive Officer William "Boots" Del Biaggio, one of Silicon Valley's most successful young entrepreneurs. The Sand Hill team, which is comprised of veterans from the technology-finance industry, has more than 200 years of combined experience.

In addition to its Menlo Park headquarters, Sand Hill Capital operates regional offices in Boston, Seattle, and Los Angeles. To date, the company has completed more than 100 loan and equity transactions and manages more than $100 million in assets.

Portfolio Companies: 2Bridge Software; AIM Technologies; Boxerjam; Certicom; Clarus; Confer Software; Co Via Technologies; Geocast; Haht Commerce; Holocom Networks; IQ.com; Looksmart; NBCi; Net Schools; Opticom; Snowball.com; Team On; ThinkLink; UpShot.com; Video Networks; Vitessa; and Visto.

SANDERLING VENTURES

2730 Sand Hill Road, Suite 200
Menlo Park, CA 94025-7067
650-854-9855   fax: 650-854-3648
www.sanderling.com

Fred Middleton, General Partner

Robert McNeil, Ph.D., General Partner

Tim Mills, Ph.D., General Partner

total assets under management	*initial investment*	*year founded*
$150 Million	$100,000–3 Million	1979

Sanderling Ventures's fields of interest center around seed- and early-stage investments in new biomedical market opportunities. Investments are focused in biotechnology, pharmaceuticals, drug delivery, medical devices, imaging and diagnostics, health-care services and information systems, and e-medicine.

SANDLOT CAPITAL, LLC

600 South Cherry Street, Suite 525
Denver, CO 80246
303-893-3400   fax: 303-893-3403
www.sandlotcapital.com

Alden Brewster, Partner, New York

Michael Bugdanowitz, Partner, Denver

Paul Mockapetris, Ph.D., Partner, Los Altos

total assets under management	*initial investment*	*year founded*
N/A	$500,000–2 Million	1998

Sandlot Capital, LLC is a venture capital firm that invests in early-stage opportunities, primarily in the United States, in the information technology arena, which Sandlot broadly defines to include computer and communication hardware, software, services, content, and commerce. Sandlot prefers scaleable investments with compelling revenue models that enable networking, improve enterprise performance, or bring about new markets.

Sandlot's objective for portfolio companies is to set and achieve critical milestones within a six- to eight-month period, which will enable the company to obtain next-round financing at a valuation that is a significant multiple of that established by the Sandlot round.

Portfolio Companies: Aegis Analytical; Authentor Systems; Bazar.net; and realLegal.com.

SANTA BARBARA TECHNOLOGY INCUBATOR

320 Nopal Street
Santa Barbara, CA 93103
805-564-8005   fax: 805-564-7188
www.sbtechnology.com

Dennis J. Cagan, Chairman and CEO

Larry Green, CTO

Ron Macleod, Senior Vice President, Business Development and Marketing

Jason Spievak, Senior Vice President, Investments

total assets under management	*initial investment*	*year founded*
N/A	N/A	2000

Santa Barbara Technology Incubator (SBTi) targets high-technology companies in the Internet services and software, computer software and devices, and communications industries. As an incubator, the Firm nurtures early-stage Santa Barbara start-ups so that they may become successful businesses, guiding the start-up toward its first round of venture financing. SBTi helps entrepreneurs achieve this financing as quickly as possible, with strategic investors and at the highest possible valuation. SBTi provides everything from seed capital and office space to management resources and communications infrastructure.

SCHRODER VENTURES LIFE SCIENCES

60 State Street, Suite 3650
Boston, MA 02109
617-367-8100   fax: 617-367-1590
www.svlifesciences.com

Jim Garvey, CEO and Managing Partner

Jonathan Gertler, M.D., Venture Partner

Hengge Hsu, M.D., Partner

Eugene Hill, Partner

Charles Warden, Partner
Jeffery Ferrel, Principal
Don Nelson, CFO

total assets under management	*initial investment*	*year founded*
$410 Million	$3–15 Million	1983

Schroder Ventures Life Sciences Advisers (UK) Limited and Schroder Ventures Life Science Advisers, Inc. (together SVLS), advise international funds that offer private equity finance and long-term development assistance exclusively to companies in the life sciences sector. SVLS's transatlantic team advises two funds with capital totaling over $410 million.

Investments are typically made in the following areas of the life-sciences sector: biotechnology, pharmaceuticals, e-health, clinical diagnostics, medical devices and instruments, medical electronics, health-care services, outsourcing services, hospital products and equipment, health-care information technology, and environmental biotechnology.

Portfolio Companies: SVLS has over 80 portfolio companies within health-care buyouts and services, instrumentation/diagnostics, medical devices, e-health, and therapeutics.

SCRIPPS VENTURES

200 Madison Avenue
New York, NY 10016
212-293-8700   fax: 212-293-8717
www.scrippsventures.com

Douglas Stern, President, CEO, and Co-Founder
Benjamin Burditt, Senior Vice President and Co-Founder

total assets under management	*initial investment*	*year founded*
$150 Million	$1–5 Million	1996

Scripps Ventures is a venture fund that was created by the E. W. Scripps Company. It primarily finances early-stage Internet companies in well-defined consumer and business-to-business segments. Scripps Ventures takes pride in working side-by-side with entrepreneurs to refine market strategies, build exceptional management teams, and facilitate alliances that can be essential to a young company's growth.

Scripps Ventures would like to collaborate with companies located in North America.

Portfolio Companies: Centra Software; Citizen r; Cityfeet.com; Comet Systems; Digital Theater Systems; Educational Structures; eHow.com; eTang.com; Family Network; Family Point Inc.; garden.com; homeportfolio.com; Impromtu Gourmet; ingredients.com; iSyndicate; JobDirect.com; MakeTheMove.com; MediaSeek Technologies; Mondera.com; Novica.com; Palladium Interactive; Structured Web; Tavolo, Inc.; VideoShare; VIPdesk.com; and WorldRes.

SeaPoint Ventures

777 108th Avenue, NE, Suite 1895
Bellevue, WA 98004
425-455-0879   fax: 425-455-1093
www.seapointventures.com

Thomas S. Huseby, Managing Partner

Susan P. Sigi, General Partner

Mellisa Widner, General Partner

total assets under management	*initial investment*	*year founded*
$35 Million	$1–3 Million	1997

SeaPoint's partners have seen the world through entrepreneur's eyes. As founders of technology start-ups, SeaPoint partners have earned the financial rewards and personal satisfaction of growing successful companies.

SeaPoint focuses specifically on wireless infrastructure, Internet communications infrastructure, and Internet transaction infrastructure. Continued success will result from the pursuit of the company's investment objectives: initial seed-stage investments in start-up companies that will become attractive later-stage investments for the company's sponsors, first- and later-stage co-investments.

Portfolio Companies: Airspan Communications Corp.; Appliant; Bridgewave Communications; Entomo, Inc.; HubSpan, Inc.; LizardTech, Inc.; Qpass Inc.; Symmetry Communications Systems; Talisma Corporation; Viathan Corporation; and Zydeco.com.

Selby Venture Partners, LP

2460 Sand Hill Road, Suite 200
Menlo Park, CA 94025
650-854-7399   fax: 650-854-7039
www.selbyventures.com

Doug Barry, General Partner

Bob Marshall, General Partner

Jim Marshall, General Partner

total assets under management	*initial investment*	*year founded*
$130 Million	$500,000–3 Million	1998

Selby Venture Partners, LP, is a venture capital firm employing a hands-on approach to provide assistance to early-stage companies. It funds seed- and early-stage technology and Internet companies located in Silicon Valley, California.

Selby Venture Partners's primary objective is to narrow the gap between the incubation phase of start-ups and the traditional, first-round venture financing.

Portfolio Companies: 3ware; 4charity; Bay Microsystems; Blue Pumpkin Software; Colbartcard; Consumer Review; Coremetrics; FilmsOn.com; ForRetail; HotRail; IBT Financial; OneChannel.Net; Pagoo; Panopticon; PowerMarket.com; Pulsent; QuickSilver Technology; Silicon Planet; Smart Calendar; and Urbanite.

SENTINEL CAPITAL PARTNERS

777 Third Avenue, 32nd Floor
New York, NY 10017
212-688-3100   fax: 212-688-6513
www.sentinelpartners.com

David Lobel, Founder and Managing Partner

John McCormack, Co-Founder and Senior Partner

total assets under management	*initial investment*	*year founded*
$200 Million	Up to $30 Million	1995

Sentinel Capital Partners is a private equity investment firm that specializes in building and buying middle-market companies in various industries, including consumer-driven businesses, business-to-business services, and outsourced manufacturing and services. Sentinel focuses on leveraged buyouts and recapitalizations, corporate divestitures, growth financings, industry consolidations, and restructuring.

With investments throughout the United States, Sentinal Capital Partners prides itself in its high partner-to-portfolio company ratio, which enables the Firm to be attentive to its companies' needs.

Portfolio Companies: Border Foods, Inc.; Buffets, Inc.; Cottman Transmission Systems, Inc.; Digital Commerce Corporation; Computer Centers, Inc.; Falcon Holdings, LLC; Floral Plant Growers LLC; Frame-n-Lens Optical, Inc.; Growing Family, Inc.; hiho.com; International Financial Network; iSalvage.com; Met

Merchandising Concepts; NorSun Food Group; Office Depot, Inc.; Rocky Mountain Savings Bank; and Roma Restaurant Holdings, Inc.

SEQUOIA CAPITAL

3000 Sand Hill Road, Building 4, Suite 280
Menlo Park, CA 94025
650-854-3927   fax: 650-854-2977
www.sequoiacap.com

Mark Stevens, General Partner

total assets under management	*initial investment*	*year founded*
$2 Billion	$2–15 Million	1972

Sequoia Capital focuses on seed-, early-, and later-stage financing in the industries of semiconductors, computers, communications, software, and health-care software and services. The Firm has invested in over 350 companies and has completed over 125 IPOs and successful acquisitions.

Portfolio Companies: AMCC; Amylin; Apple; Cisco Systems; Combichem; CommQuest; Forward Ventures; LSI Logic; Medibuy.com; MP3.com; Vitease Semiconductor; and Yahoo!.

SEVEN HILLS PARTNERS, LLC

930 Montgomery Street, Suite 301
San Francisco, CA 94133
415-273-7160   fax: 415-273-7171
www.sevenhillspartners.com

Cabot Brown, Managing Director
Ellen Koskinas, Managing Director
Aseem Giri, Associate

total assets under management	*initial investment*	*year founded*
$75 Million	$3–7 Million	1996

Seven Hills Partners, LLC, founded in 1996, is a private equity firm that sponsors venture capital investments and structured equity transactions involving highly promising entrepreneurial enterprises, primarily in the areas of health care and internet software and services. In each of these areas, the Firm seeks to affiliate with entrepreneurs who are taking advantage of shifts in demographic, technological, and competitive forces to build innovative and fast-growing businesses that have the potential to dominate their industries.

Seven Hills operates as a "stage-independent" investor. Its goal is to invest in great companies regardless of their stage of development. If circumstances warrant, the Firm will provide seed capital, late-stage funding, or buyout financing. It has helped found three of its portfolio companies and has led buyouts of two others.

SEVIN ROSEN FUNDS

169 University Avenue	13455 Noel Road, Suite 1670
Palo Alto, CA 94301	Dallas, TX 75240
650-326-0550	972-702-1100
fax: 650-326-0707	fax: 972-702-1103
www.srfunds.com	

Jon Bayless, General Partner

Steve Domenik, General Partner

Steve Dow, General Partner

Jackie Kimzey, General Partner

Charles Phipps, General Partner

Jennifer Gill Roberts, General Partner

Dave Shrigley, General Partner

total assets under management	*initial investment*	*year founded*
$1 Billion	$250,000–5 Million	1981

Sevin Rosen is a leading venture capital firm that focuses on early-stage investment in technology and biomedical companies. The Firm has an established reputation in helping build companies. Many of Sevin Rosen's portfolio companies have gone public, including Citrix, Ciena, Compaq, and Lotus.

Portfolio Companies: Sevin Rosen has over 95 portfolio companies.

SHAW VENTURE PARTNERS

400 Southwest 6th Avenue, Suite 1100
Portland, OR 97204-1636
503-228-4884   fax: 503-227-2471
www.shawventures.com

Ralph R. Shaw, General Partner

total assets under management	*initial investment*	*year founded*
$80 Million	$250,000–3 Million	1982

Underlying Shaw Venture Partners's investment philosophy is a basic tenet to provide not only the essential infusion of capital but also the benefits of broad and relevant experience acquired by its partners and associates in the business world. Generally, it is not expected that the emerging company would initially possess all the skills necessary to successfully direct a business. Much of this experience will eventually be acquired as the company grows and prospers.

Shaw Venture Partners focuses on the communications, biotechnology, wholesale, information technology, and life sciences industries.

Portfolio Companies: Actel; Costco Wholesale; Protocol Systems; Sequent Computer Systems; and Telestream.

Sienna Holdings

2330 Marinship Way, Suite 220
Sausalito, CA 94965
415-339-2800   fax: 415-339-2805
www.siennaholdings.com

Daniel L. Skaff, Managing Partner

Robert J. Conrads, Operating Partner

Mark S. Balbanian, Principal

Nancy A. Roset, Principal

total assets under management	*initial investment*	*year founded*
$195 Million	$3–5 Million	1990

Sienna Holdings is a privately held growth-capital firm with an emphasis in the following industries: communications, networking, the Internet, and information technology. It invests in companies with significant growth potential that are in the early stages of development. In addition to providing financial assistance, Sienna Holdings encourages supportive working relationships and provides an extensive network of capital and organizational resources.

Sienna Holdings invests in the United States.

Portfolio Companies: @Motion; AdFlight; Atomic Tangerine; autobytel.com; CampSix; Embark.com; IdeaEdge; KnowledgeFirst; MyEvents.com; Phone.com; Ranch Networks; ThirdAge Media Protocol; and Widcomm.

SIERRA VENTURES

3000 Sand Hill Road, Building 4, Suite 210
Menlo Park, CA 94025
650-854-1000   fax: 650-854-5593
www.sierraven.com

Jeffrey M. Drazan, General Partner
David C. Schwab, General Partner
Peter C. Wendell, General Partner
Steven P. Williams, General Partner

total assets under management	*initial investment*	*year founded*
$1.1 Billion	N/A	1982

Sierra Ventures is a private venture capital firm made up of a collaboration of eight venture capital partnerships. It focuses its investments on early and pre-public communications, software and Internet-related content, and infrastructure companies within the United States.

Sierra Ventures takes an active role as an investor and strives to build new companies into successful businesses. Typically, the General Partners of Sierra Ventures serve on the Board of Directors of their portfolio companies to assist entrepreneurs and management teams even further.

Portfolio Companies: 3F Therapeutics; Adflight; Advanced Medicine; Again Technologies; Bridge Medical; Candescent Technologies; ClickRadio; CrossLogix; Edgeflow; Endovasix; ePhysician; Evolve; Fairmarket; FatBrain; GenVec; GotAjob; Healtheon; Heartport; iAM.com; iMarket; Interact Commerce Corporation; Intuitive Surgical Devices; Kanisa; Knowledgenet; Lancast; MyEvents; NovaMed; OneMedia; PGI; Redknife; RightStart.com; Rocketcash; SeeCommerce; Solus Micro Technologies; StarQuest; Symphonix; TherOx; VenPro; Vertel; and Vina.

SIGMA PARTNERS

1600 El Camino Real, Suite 280
Menlo Park, CA 94025
650-853-1700   fax: 650-853-1717
www.sigmapartners.com

Wade Woodson, Managing Director, Menlo Park
John R. Mandile, Managing Director, Boston

total assets under management	*initial investment*	*year founded*
$700 Million	$5 Million	1985

Sigma Partners is a venture capital firm with an emphasis on high technology. Due to its extensive knowledge and experience in computers, electronics, software, and communications, Sigma Partners offers a wide range of services to its portfolio companies.

Sigma Partners invests in companies in the early stages of development in the high-technology field. The Firm invests primarily in the United States.

Portfolio Companies: Sigma Partners has over 40 portfolio companies.

SIGNAL EQUITY PARTNERS

10 East 53rd Street, 32nd Floor
New York, NY 10022
212-872-1180   fax: 212-872-1192
www.signal-equity.com

Timothy P. Bradley, Managing Partner and Co-Founder

total assets under management	*initial investment*	*year founded*
$100 Million	$3–6 Million	1998

Signal Equity Partners makes equity or equity-linked investments in the communications and information technology industries. The Firm is looking for businesses with a solid management team, a sustainable competitive advantage, and an established revenue base. Signal Equity Partners has experience funding early-stage and growth capital to acquisition and buyout transactions and seeks investment opportunities within the United States.

Portfolio Companies: Centennial; Datazen; Evoke Software; FiberNet; Infotrieve; Spike; Step 9; TeleCommunications Systems Inc.; and Trinagy.

SIGNATURE CAPITAL, LLC

565 Sheridan Road
Winnetka, IL 60093
847-501-5105   fax: 847-501-5108
www.signaturecapital.com

William N. Sick, Co-Manager and Founder
William J. Turner, Co-Manager and Founder

total assets under management	initial investment	year founded
N/A	N/A	1997

Signature Capital, LLC, is a results-oriented venture capital firm with a focused and disciplined investment approach. It works primarily with early-stage growth companies that have innovative product solutions in proven markets, with IPO potential in two to three years. Signature Capital invests in high-technology firms, with an emphasis on software, computers, telecommunications, Internet, electronics, and the medical field.

Signature Capital will consider investments within the United States.

Portfolio Companies: Acoustic Technologies; Additech; Netnumber.com; and VIRxSys.

SILICON VALLEY BANK

5414 Oberlin Drive, Suite 230
San Diego, CA 92121
858-558-3808   fax: 858-535-1611
www.svb.com

Susan L. Batchen, Senior Vice President

Linda S. LeBeau, Senior Vice President

John W. Otterson, Senior Vice President

Clifford White, Senior Vice President

Jeff M. Huhn, Vice President

Raquel B. Sidlo, Vice President

total assets under management	initial investment	year founded
$5.1 Billion	N/A	1983

The founders of Silicon Valley Bank set out in 1983 to capture a growing market that until that time had been greatly underserved by commercial banks— emerging life sciences and technology companies. Many companies in this unique market were just getting started and had yet to realize a profit; some simply were not yet considered "credit-worthy" by local community or regional banks.

Since that time, Silicon Valley Bank has established a national reputation for excellence in the banking industry, based on a high level of expertise in a number of technology niches, including life sciences, software, communications, computers and peripherals, and the Pacific Rim. With a solid understanding of the true risks and rewards of early-stage companies, the Bank is widely recognized for its ability to develop innovative approaches to meet clients' lending challenges. Building on its successful experience in Northern California, the Bank has expanded to additional major life sciences and technology centers around the country.

The Bank provides a full array of specialized products and services, which are tailored to meet its clients' changing needs as they progress through their business life cycles. These services include senior credit facilities, working capital lines of credit, equipment loans, asset acquisition loans, real estate loans, commercial finance, international services, cash management services, deposit services, investment services, executive banking services, and factoring services.

SILVER CREEK TECHNOLOGY INVESTORS

730 17th Street, Suite 690
Denver, CO 80202
303-573-3720
fax: 303-573-3740
www.silvercreekfund.com

5949 Sherry Lane, Suite 1450
Dallas, TX 75225
214-265-2026

Mark C. Masur, General Partner

Michael T. Segrest, General Partner

William D. Stanfill, General Partner

Stephen M. Hamilton, CFO

total assets under management	*initial investment*	*year founded*
$60 Million	$3–5 Million	1989

Silver Creek Technology Investors is a venture capital firm with a proven investment strategy to help entrepreneurs build market-leading companies in the high-technology industry. In particular, Silver Creek Technology Investors is interested in telecommunications, data networking, and information technology. It funds companies in all stages of development and located anywhere in the United States.

Portfolio Companies: Alteon WebSystems, Inc.; Ateq, Inc.; Centennial Communications; Chromatic Research, Inc.; Corsair Communications; Credence Systems Corp.; Crystal Semiconductor; Diamond Lane Communications Corp.; MetroPCS, Inc.; OpenConnect Systems, Inc.; Optical Data Systems, Inc.; ONI Systems Corp.; ProNet, Inc.; Shomiti Systems, Inc.; STARTech; VertiCom, Inc.; WaferScale Integration, Inc.; and Xilinx, Inc.

SOFTBANK VENTURE CAPITAL

200 West Evelyn Avenue, Suite 200
Mountain View, CA 94041
650-962-2000   fax: 650-962-2020
www.sbvc.com

Bill Burnham, General Partner

Bradley Feld, General Partner

Greg Galanos, General Partner

D. Rex Golding, General Partner

Greg Prow, General Partner

Gary Rieschel, General Partner

Heidi Roizen, General Partner

Carl Rosendahl, General Partner

total assets under management	initial investment	year founded
$2 Billion	N/A	1981

SOFTBANK Technology Ventures is an SBIC ventures capital fund. The family of funds includes seven funds that invest in early-stage companies.

SOFTBANK Technology Ventures, founded in 1981, makes privately negotiated equity and equity-related investments in companies attempting to capitalize on opportunities in digital information technology, including Internet communications, commerce, and content.

SOFTBANK Technology Ventures is affiliated with SOFTBANK Holdings, Inc., a subsidiary of SOFTBANK Corporation. Its headquarters are located in Japan, but SOFTBANK has rapidly expanded its global presence through acquisitions in the United States and elsewhere.

Portfolio Companies: Cybercash; E*Trade; Intervista; Pointcast; USWeb; Vxtreme; and Yahoo!.

SORRENTO ASSOCIATES, INC.

4370 La Jolla Village Drive, Suite 1040
San Diego, CA 92122
858-452-3100   fax: 858-452-7607
www.sorrentoventures.com

Robert Jaffe, President
Vincent Burgess, Vice President

Caroline Barberio, Vice President of Finance

total assets under management	*initial investment*	*year founded*
$115 Million	$1–7 Million	1985

Sorrento Associates, Inc. (the General Partner family of Sorrento Ventures funds), is a San Diego–based venture capital firm focused on promising emerging-growth companies in San Diego and Southern California. The Firm focuses on health-care (biotechnology, medical devices, drug discovery, and drug delivery), communications, computer hardware and software, electronics, and consumer-related industries. The Firm's limited partners consist of over 85 San Diego business executives and community leaders, as well as the San Diego Gas & Electric company Pension Plan and the San Diego County Employees Retirement Association.

SOUTHWEST MERCHANT GROUP

3422 Binkley
Dallas, TX 75205

Steven J. Cook, Managing Director

total assets under management	*initial investment*	*year founded*
$18 Million	$1–5 Million	1989

Southwest Merchant Group is a merchant-banking firm that manages investments for its own accounts and its clients, using equity capital, mezzanine debt, and senior debt. Southwest Merchant Group offers $1 million to $5 million in financing to second-stage, mezzanine, bridge, acquisition, leveraged and management buyouts, recapitalization, and special situations. Southwest Merchant Group focuses on the Southwest region.

SPACEVEST

One Fountain Square
11911 Freedom Drive, Suite 500
Reston, VA 20190
703-904-9800   fax: 703-904-0571
www.spacevest.com

John B. Higginbotham, Founder and Chairman

Richard L. Harris, Vice President

total assets under management	*initial investment*	*year founded*
$200 Million	$100,000–10 Million	1991

SpaceVest is a leading private equity investor for emerging industries. The Firm brings a focused, value-added investment approach to growth companies applying advanced capabilities and technologies to major market opportunities. SpaceVest is defined by its innovative portfolio companies, which are primarily in the space industry, next generation, and network industries.

Portfolio Companies: Analytical Graphics, Inc.; ArcSecond, Inc.; Assuresat, Inc.; Astron Antenna Co.; Astrovision International, Inc.; atyourbusiness.com; CodeStream Technologies Company; Computer I/O Corporation; Constellation Communications, Inc.; Cronos Integrated Microsystems, Inc.; Currie Technologies, Inc.; Digital 5, Inc.; Enginia Software, Inc.; GER Holdings Corporation; GlobalCom International, Inc.; Global-Net, Inc.; MDLinx.com; MIDAS Vision, Inc.; Mesa Systems Guild, Inc.; MSI Software, Inc.; SPACE.com; Vbrick Systems, Inc.; Visual and Audio Surveillance Technologies, Ltd.; and Woodwind Communications.

SPENCER TRASK SECURITIES INC.

535 Madison Avenue, 18th Floor
New York, NY 10022
212-326-9200   fax: 212-751-3362
www.spencertrask.com

Bill Dioguardi, President

total assets under management	*initial investment*	*year founded*
$500 Million	$250,000–15 Million	1991

Spencer Trask Securities Inc. seeks investment opportunities in which the portfolio companies are willing to sell a stake in their company in return for the financing they need. The Firm invests primarily in early-stage companies that have the following characteristics: a value-creating mission, proprietary technology or service, talented and experienced management, a large and growing market, and a significant amount of potential. Spencer Trask will fund companies located throughout the United States.

Sports Capital Partners

65 E. 55th Street, 18th Floor
New York, NY 10022
212-634-3304   fax: 212-634-3374
www.sportscapital.com

David S. Moross, Managing Partner
Paul J. Behrman, Principal
Charles T. Leon, Principal

total assets under management	*initial investment*	*year founded*
$200 Million	$5–40 Million	1998

Sports Capital Partners is a private equity investment firm with an interest in sports-related industries, such as broadcasting, publishing, Internet/e-commerce, consumer goods and apparel, teams and leagues, facilities, and services such as camps, trade shows, ticketing, and event supply companies. Sports Capital's objective is to capitalize on its exclusive affiliation with IMG, the world's largest sports management and marketing company, to achieve above-average rates of return on private equity investments. Sports Capital provides assistance with sales and marketing, brand development, international expansion, and business relationships. Sports Capital will consider investment opportunities worldwide.

Portfolio Companies: The Golf Warehouse; Skip Barber Racing School; SmallWorld Media; Sports.com; SportsYA!; and Tickets.com.

Spray Venture Partners

One Walnut Street, 4th Floor
Boston, MA 02108
617-305-4140   fax: 617-305-4144
e-mail: spray@sprayfund.com

Dan Cole, General Partner
Kevin Connors, General Partner
Dan Sachs, Managing Director

total assets under management	*initial investment*	*year founded*
$50 Million	$1,000,000–2 Million	1996

Spray Venture Partners is a venture capital firm that invests in seed- and early-stage health-care companies. Spray's mission is to achieve superior returns for its limited partners by helping entrepreneurs and clinicians build successful health-care companies. The Spray team includes individuals who have founded and grown emerging medical technology companies, and who have served as senior executives in Fortune 500 corporations. Spray has a successful track record working in partnership with entrepreneurs, clinicians, technical founders, research organizations, and other funding sources to form and build leading health-care companies. It is supportive at all levels of the business-development process, from strategy development and management team building to corporate partnerships and liquidity events.

The health-care industry is under significant pressures that are driving structural changes in the delivery of health care. It is Spray's belief that superior financial returns can be obtained by appropriately applying technology to reduce treatment costs and improve patient outcomes. Spray's focus is on medical technology, cell therapy, drug discovery and delivery, and health-care information systems.

Sprout Group

277 Park Avenue, 42nd Fl.   3000 Sand Hill Road   200 West Madison, 5th Fl.
New York, NY 10172   Building 3, Suite 170 Chicago, IL 60606
212-892-3600   Menlo Park, CA 94025   312-345-8275
fax: 212-892-3444   650-234-2700   fax: 312-345-8276
www.sproutgroup.com   fax: 650-234-2779

Keith B. Geeslin, Managing Partner

Patrick J. Boroian, General Partner

Philippe O. Chambon, M.D., General Partner

Robert E. Curry, General Partner

Stephen M. Diamond, General Partner

Robert Finzi, General Partner

Janet A. Hickey, General Partner

Kathleen LaPorte, General Partner

Alexander Rosen, General Partner

Rakesh Sood, General Partner

total assets under management	*initial investment*	*year founded*
$2 Billion	$5–25 Million	1969

The Sprout Group is one of the oldest and largest sources of private equity capital for growth companies. Established in 1969 as a venture capital subsidiary of

Donaldson Lufkin & Jenrette (DLJ), Sprout has managed 12 major investment partnerships totaling nearly $2 billion in commercial capital. Twenty-seven professionals manage Sprout's most recent investment partnerships—Sprout VIII, an $860 million fund that makes early-stage, growth, mezzanine, and buyout investments primarily in technology and telecom, e-commerce, services, and health industries. Sprout is one of very few venture firms in the country affiliated with a leading investment bank—a unique relationship that provides access to a broad spectrum of resources and complements Sprout's activities as a venture capital investor.

St. Paul Venture Capital

Three Lagoon Drive
Redwood City, CA 94065
650-596-5630   fax: 650-596-5711
www.stpaulvc.com

Patrick A. Hopf, Managing General Partner and Founder
Brian Jacobs, General Partner

total assets under management	*initial investment*	*year founded*
$3 Billion	$1–15 Million	1988

St. Paul Venture Capital (SPVC) is a venture capital firm with offices in California, Massachusetts, and Minnesota. The source of its capital is the St. Paul Fire and Marine Insurance Company, which enables SPVC to have the security and the freedom to invest with a long-term perspective. SPVC is interested in the following industries: communications, business Internet, consumer technology, and health care.

St. Paul Venture Capital primarily focuses on very early-stage investing, although the Firm devotes 20 percent of its resources to later-stage companies. SPVC invests throughout the United States.

Portfolio Companies: St. Paul Venture Capital has over 80 portfolio companies.

Staenberg Private Capital, LLC

2000 1st Ave, #1001
Seattle, WA 98121
206-374-0234   fax: 708-575-1324
www.staenberg.com

Jon Staenberg, Managing Partner

total assets under management	*initial investment*	*year founded*
$80 Million	$100,000–3 Million	1998

Staenberg Private Capital, LLC, is a venture capital fund with a primary focus in the high-technology arena. It funds companies located in the Pacific Northwest and Silicon Valley in the Internet and telecommunications fields. Staenberg Private Capital is interested in companies of all stages of development, from early stage to later stage.

The partners of Staenberg Private Capital assist companies through sourcing, researching, or financing deals or by acting as venture catalysts and mentors.

Portfolio Companies: Staenberg Private Capital has over 70 portfolio companies.

STONECREEK CAPITAL, INC.

840 Newport Center Drive
Newport Beach, CA 92660
949-759-5585   fax: 949-759-7628

Michael S. Gordon, Co-Chairman

John H. Morris, Co-Chairman

Bruce N. Lipian, Managing Director

Drew H. Adams, Managing Director

Frank Edelstein, Vice President

total assets under management	*initial investment*	*year founded*
$61 Million	$2–15 Million	1992

StoneCreek Capital, Inc. (SCC), manages a $61 million private equity fund, focusing on middle-market acquisitions ($20 million to 100 million purchase price) in selected industries through the formation of a working partnership with the managers of the operating company. SCC pursues investments throughout the United States, with an emphasis on West Coast companies. The principles of SCC (formerly the Gordon & Morris Group) previously constituted the West Coast office of Kelso & Company. During the past eight years, the principals of SCC have acquired 25 companies, averaging about $70 million in purchase price per transaction. Such acquisitions have included International House of Pancakes, Arkansas Best Freight, Wickes Furniture, Aerosol Services, and Steel Horse Automotive.

Summer Street Capital Partners, LLC

11 Summer Street
Buffalo, NY 14209
716-882-2929
fax: 716-883-1510
www.summerstreetcapital.com

171 Dwight Road, Suite 310
Longmeadow, MA 01106
413-567-3366
fax: 413-567-6556

Michael P. McQueeney, Managing Partner

Richard B. Steele, Managing Partner

total assets under management	*initial investment*	*year founded*
$60–100 Million	$2–8 Million	1999

Summer Street Capital Partners, LLC (SSCP), operates an SBIC fund, investing in mature, profitable businesses with revenues exceeding $10 million. SSCP invests alongside management, either participating as a minority investor or leading a transaction.

Summit Partners

499 Hamilton Avenue, Suite 200
Palo Alto, CA 94301
650-321-1166   fax: 650-321-1188
www.summitpartners.com

James D. Atwell, General Partner

Gregory M. Avis, Managing Partner

Walter G. Kortschak, Managing Partner

Peter Y. Chung, General Partner

Christopher W. Sheeline, General Partner

total assets under management	*initial investment*	*year founded*
$4 Billion	$5–200 Million	1984

Summit Partners is an investment firm that provides exceptional strategic assistance, analytical resources, and financial support to help companies become successful businesses. It invests primarily in later-stage companies in the following industries: software, communications, electronics, Internet solutions, health care, information technology services, and business services.

With offices located in Boston and Palo Alto, California, Summit Partners will consider investments throughout the United States and Europe.

Portfolio Companies: Summit Partners has over 200 portfolio companies.

SUTTER HILL VENTURES

755 Page Mill Road, Suite A-200
Palo Alto, CA 94304
650-493-5600   fax: 650-858-1854

David L. Anderson, Managing Director
G. Leonard Baker Jr., Managing Director
Tench Coxe, Managing Director
James C. Gaither, Managing Director
Greg P. Sands, Managing Director
William H. Younger, Managing Director

total assets under management	*initial investment*	*year founded*
$300 Million	$100,000–10 Million	1962

Sutter Hill Ventures has been a leader in financing technology-based companies for more than 35 years. Sutter Hill Ventures wishes to make investments in companies in the following stages: seed, start-up, first-stage, and management buy-outs. Sutter Hill invests in companies throughout the United States.

SVOBODA, COLLINS LLC

30 N. LaSalle Street, Suite 3520
Chicago, IL 60602
312-759-7850   fax: 312-759-7855
www.svoco.com

Michelle L. Collins, Founder
John A. Svoboda, Founder

total assets under management	*initial investment*	*year founded*
$160 Million	$2–10 Million	1998

Svoboda, Collins LLC (SC) is an investment firm seeking to fund small- to medium-sized growth companies. SC will consider the following investments: early-stage financings of innovative businesses; financings of established companies for growth or liquidity purposes; or management buyouts and recapitalizations of larger companies.

SC will generally require an ownership of at least 20 percent in each of its investments. The Firm will consider value-added distributors, industry consolidators, information and business services companies, and health-care service and distribution companies located within the United States.

Portfolio Companies: Entertainment Marketing Inc.; Epotec; Four Wheel Drive Hardware; In the Swim Discount Pool Supplies; MilesTek; Orbit Commerce; Parts Now; Peisers; SPS Commerce; Webmiles.com; Wilmar; and World Data Products.

TA ASSOCIATES

125 High Street, Suite 2500
Boston, MA 02110
617-574-6700
fax: 617-574-6728
www.ta.com

70 Willow Road, Suite 100
Menlo Park, CA 94025
650-328-1210
fax: 650-326-4933

C. Kevin Landry, Managing Director and CEO

Thomas P. Alber, Principal and CFO

total assets under management	*initial investment*	*year founded*
$5 Billion	$15–200 Million	1968

TA Associates is a leading private equity investment firm with offices located in Boston, Menlo Park, and Pittsburgh. It seeks investment opportunities in growing private companies in all stages of development and will provide capital for management-led buyouts of growth companies. TA Associates specializes in: technology, including Internet infrastructure and services, communications, software, semiconductors, and e-services; business services; consumer products and services; financial services; and health care.

TA Associates will fund companies located in the United States.

Portfolio Companies: TA Associates has over 320 portfolio companies.

TAT CAPITAL PARTNERS LTD.

P.O. Box 23326
San Jose, CA 95153-3326
408-270-9200   fax: 408-270-4140
www.tat.ch

Dr. Thomas Egolf, Switzerland—Managing Director, Partner

Rolf Haegler, Switzerland—Managing Director, Partner

Mark Putney, Silicon Valley—Managing Director, Partner

Johan Ekman, Sweden—Managing Director, Partner

total assets under management	*initial investment*	*year founded*
$100 Million	$1–5 Million	1997

TAT Capital Partners Ltd. is a transatlantic venture firm with offices in the United States, Sweden, and Switzerland. Due to its global presence, TAT Capital Partners offers a wide range of knowledge and support to early-stage and established companies in the technology and medical-devices industries. TAT Capital Partners looks for companies located in Scandinavia, Europe, or the United States.

TAT Capital Partners seeks to fund companies that have the potential to be major market leaders in the technology industry in the United States, Europe, and Japan.

Portfolio Companies: BOS Systemhaus Ltd.; Card Guard Inc.; Diamedica AG; Nextek Inc.; ndd Medizinaltechnik AG; nLine Systems Corp.; SciVac, Inc.; Sunlight Ltd.; Surface Interface Inc.; Unitive Electronics, Inc., Xemics AD; and ZF MicroSystems Inc.

TD iCapital

31 West 52nd Street, 20th Floor
New York, NY 10019
212-827-7760   fax: 212-827-7236
www.td-icapital.com

Paul Ciriello, Managing Director

David J. Grossman, Vice President

Joshua Crane, Associate

Adam B. Fisher, Associate

total assets under management	*initial investment*	*year founded*
$100 Million	$2–15 Million	2000

TD iCapital was launched by TD Capital and TD Bank affiliate TD Waterhouse. TD iCapital is a venture capital firm targeting online-oriented financial services investments. It focuses on many facets of financial services, from content services to enabling technologies. It will fund companies in the seed, mid-, and later-stages of development and typically plays a major role in its portfolio companies' business. The Firm will consider investment opportunities throughout the United States.

Portfolio Companies: BondDesk; Decade System; eCal; epicRealm; Epoch Partners; ePolicy; Financeware; MetaMarkets; Validea; Worldly Information Network; and XpenseWise.

TECHNOLOGY CROSSOVER VENTURES

575 High Street, Suite 400
Palo Alto, CA 94301
650-614-8200   fax: 650-614-8222
www.tcv.com

Jay Hoag, General Partner

Rick Kimball, General Partner

Chris Nawn, General Partner

Tom Newby, General Partner

Jake Reynolds, General Partner

Mike Linnert, General Partner

Carla Newell, General Partner

Brooke Seawell, General Partner

Robert Bensky, General Partner

total assets under management	*initial investment*	*year founded*
$2.5 Billion	N/A	1995

Technology Crossover Ventures is a stage-independent Internet-focused venture capital firm partnering with premier Internet companies throughout their rapid growth phase. The Firm focuses on investments primarily in five sectors of the Internet: Internet infrastructure, e-business applications, Internet services, business-to-consumer, and business-to-business. Its goal is to find great companies in industries it knows well, regardless of the stage of development, and to invest with integrated private and public investing crossover.

Portfolio Companies: Just a few of the many companies in TCV's portfolio are: Alteon WebSystems, Inc.; Copper Mountain; Actuate; Firepond; ONYX Software; eLoyalty; Inventa; Viant; C|NET; Homestore.com; iVillage.com; Ariba; Intraware; and Mortgage.com.

TECHNOLOGY FUNDING, INC.

2000 Alameda de las Pulgas, Suite 250
San Mateo, CA 94403
650-345-2200   fax: 650-345-1797
www.technologyfunding.com

Charles R. Kokesh, Managing General Partner

Gregory T. George, Partner

total assets under management	*initial investment*	*year founded*
$315 Million	$750,000–2.5 Million	1979

Technology Funding invests primarily in seed-stage, first-round, second-round, and mezzanine-level financing. Some of the industries that Technology Funding considers include information technology, medical technology, and industrial technology.

TECHNOLOGY INVESTMENTS

P.O. Box 704
Los Altos, CA 94023
650-948-1561   fax: 650-948-3003
www.carsten.com

Jack C. Carsten, General Manager

total assets under management	*initial investment*	*year founded*
N/A	$50,000–250,000	1990

Technology Investments is a Northern California seed-stage investment firm owned and operated by Jack C. Carsten. Typical investments range from $50,000 to $250,000 and are usually made at the inception of the firm. Potential investments are selected from information technology in Northern California. The Firm usually takes an active role and has had Board of Director participation in a majority of investments.

Portfolio Companies: Harmonics; Photon Dynamics, Inc.; Resound Inc.; and Socket Communications, Inc.

TECHNOLOGY PARTNERS

550 University Avenue
Palo Alto, CA 94201
650-289-9000   fax: 650-289-9001
www.technologypartners.com

Ted Ardell, Partner

Lisa Buyer, Partner

Ira Ehrenpreis, Partner

Bill Hart, Partner

Roger Quy, Partner

Sheila Mutter, Partner

Jason Yotopoulos, Partner

total assets under management	*initial investment*	*year founded*
$400 Million+	$1–20 Million	1980

Technology Partners invests in technology-based ventures in information processing, communications, and health care. Emerging markets in which the firm has enjoyed early success include e-commerce, wireless communications, enterprise software, interactive multimedia, and preventive health care. Most often, Technology Partners initially invests at the seed or first stages of ventures. Later-stage investments are considered in areas of strategic interest.

Portfolio Companies: Some of the portfolio companies that are now trading publicly are as follows: American Mobile Satellite; CellNet Data Systems; E-LOAN; ImageX.com; Silicon Gaming; Spectrum Holobyte; The 3DO Co.; Trimble Navigation; Calypte; Cell Pathways; Cholestech; Iridex; and Medwave.

TECHNO-VENTURE

2465 East Bayshore Road, Suite 348
Palo Alto, CA 94303
650-565-8297   fax: 650-565-8295
www.techno-venture.com

Mike Kaneyoshi, Adviser

Jonathan J. MacQuitty, Ph.D., Chairman, U.S. Ventures

total assets under management	*initial investment*	*year founded*
N/A	N/A	1989

Techo-Venture is an experienced venture capital firm with nine funds—primarily in Japan and the United States. Techno-Venture selects companies for investment that have exhibited the qualities necessary for their development into leading producers in their respective fields. Technology-based companies are the Firm's main focus; however, it has invested in the printing, communications, medical, semiconductor, and a variety of service industries.

Techno-Venture has Japanese staff, which strengthens the U.S. access to Japanese firms and import/export.

Portfolio Companies: Argonaut Technologies, Inc.; Dotcast, Inc.; Extensity, Inc.; Greenlight.com; Lightspan Partnership, Inc.; Nanogen, Inc.; NanoGram Corporation; Offrond Capital, Inc.; Symyx Technologies, Inc.; and Zing Network, Inc.

TECHSPACE XCHANGE

41 East 11th Street, 11th Floor
New York, NY 10003
212-331-1100   fax: 212-331-1248
www.techspace.com

2500 18th Street
San Francisco, CA 94110

Stephen Nordahl, Managing Director

Caryn Kaplansky, Associate

total assets under management	*initial investment*	*year founded*
N/A	$250,000–2.5 Million	2000

TechSpace Xchange, LLC (TSX) is a venture capital fund formed by TechSpace, LLC (TechSpace), a provider of technologically advanced office environments and premier start-up services to early- and expansion-stage technology companies, and Safeguard Scientifics, Inc., a leader in identifying, developing, and operating technology companies in the Internet infrastructure market. The significant value that TechSpace Xchange provides its investments is increased exponentially through leveraging its partnerships with TechSpace and Safeguard Scientifics.

TSX focuses its investments in the Internet-enabling service and technology space. Unlike traditional venture capital funds, TSX is uniquely positioned to seize the best investment opportunities in the locations where TSX and TechSpace have offices (New York, Boston, Toronto, San Francisco, Miami, and Austin).

Portfolio Companies: Buystream; FreeSamples.com; iSyndicate; MagicbeanStalk; Onepage; Venture Architects; and Vividence.

TELECOMMUNICATIONS DEVELOPMENT FUND

2020 K Street, NW, Suite 375
Washington, D.C. 20006
202-293-8840   fax: 202-293-8850
www.tdfund.com

Ginger Ehn Lew, CEO

Darrel A. Williams, CIO

Charles E. Ross, Principal

total assets under management	*initial investment*	*year founded*
$25 Million	$370,000–1 Million	1998

Telecommunications Development Fund is a private corporation based in Washington, D.C., that finances early-stage growth telecommunications companies in the United States. The Firm typically invests in wireless voice data communications and broadcast, cable, satellite, and Internet casting. Investments usually last from three to six years. TDF brings its background in these industries to benefit its portfolio companies.

Portfolio Companies: invertix; Kobalt Interactive; Synovial; and Wisor Telecom.

TeleSoft Partners

1450 Fashion Island Blvd., Suite 610
San Mateo, CA 94404
650-358-2500   fax: 650-358-2501

Arjun Gupta, Founder and CEO
Victor Liao, Senior Associate

total assets under management	*initial investment*	*year founded*
$162 Million	$200,000–10 Million	1997

TeleSoft Partners is a venture capital firm focused on next-generation communication companies, which include telecom, datacom, and the Internet. TeleSoft will consider all stages of investments from seed to pre-IPO. The Firm is currently raising a second fund.

Telos Venture Partners

2350 Mission College Blvd., Suite 1070
Santa Clara, CA 95054
408-982-5800   fax: 408-982-5880
www.telosvp.com

Paul Asel, General Partner
Bruce R. Bourbon, General Partner
Athanasios Kalekos, General Partner

total assets under management	*initial investment*	*year founded*
$100 Million	$1–4 Million	1996

Telos Venture Partners is a leading venture capital firm located in the Silicon Valley. Telos provides industry contacts, business guidance, and executive staff mentoring, using the considerable high-tech senior management experience of Telos partners. To best leverage industry experience, Telos concentrates its investments in the information industry, with a focus on software, Internet, semiconductor, and communications market segments. It generally invests in early-stage companies in first or second post-seed financing that are completing the development of a new product or building initial sales momentum.

   Portfolio Companies: Alchemy Semiconductor; CareThere, Inc.; Cephren, Inc.; Extricity Software, Inc.; Integrated Memory Logic, Inc.; Intensys Corporation; Intraspect Software; iReady Corporation; KhiMetrics, Inc.; Microcosm

Technologies, Inc.; Microtune, Inc.; nQuire Software, Inc.; PDF Solutions, Inc.; Preview Systems; Softface, Inc.; Tsola, Inc.; VPNX.com, Inc.; and Working Woman Network, Inc.

THIRD EYE VENTURES, LLC

533 Anacapa Terrace
Sunnyvale, CA 94085
408-733-6933   fax: 408-514-6680
www.thirdeyeventures.net

Debjyoti Das, Co-Founder and Managing Partner, Technology

Hadi Taheri, Co-Founder and Managing Partner, Finance

Felix Litman, Co-Founder and Managing Partner, Marketing

Mukesh Advani, Co-Founder and Adviser, Legal

total assets under management	*initial investment*	*year founded*
$10 Million	$100,000–2 Million	N/A

Third Eye Ventures, LLC, is primarily focused on investing in early-stage Internet infrastructure start-ups. Thus, the focus areas cover the realms of broadband communications, wireless infrastructure, P2P (peer-to-peer) applications, and infrastructure and optical networking.

The Firm takes pride in being "strategic investors," providing emerging companies with intensive, strategic support in engineering, business design, financials, operations, marketing, partnership development, and strategic funding. It also incubates a number of emerging companies with extraordinary value propositions and innovative offerings.

THOMA CRESSEY EQUITY PARTNERS

233 South Wacker Drive
92nd Floor
Chicago, IL 60606
312-777-4444
fax: 312-777-4445
www.thomacressey.com

4050 Republic Plaza
370 Seventeenth Street
Denver, CO 80202
303-592-4888
fax: 303-592-4845

One Embarcadero Center
Suite 2930
San Francisco, CA 94111
415-263-3660
fax: 415-392-6480

Bryan C. Cressey, Partner

Robert J. Manning Jr., Partner

William W. Liebeck, Partner

Carl D. Thoma, Partner

Orlando Bravo, Partner

Lee M. Mitchell, Partner

David J. Mayer, Partner

total assets under management	*initial investment*	*year founded*
$1.2 Billion	$30–70 Million	1998

Thoma Cressey Equity Partners (TCEP) is a private equity firm focused on creating and growing market-leading businesses through acquisitions and internal expansion. TCEP provides equity to companies with exceptional management teams to assist with acquisitions and expansion, complete buyouts, recapitalizations, or going-private transactions. It focuses particularly on business services, information technology/Internet services, health-care services, and local consumer services industries. TCEP invests in the United States.

   Portfolio Companies: American-Amicable Holding, Inc.; Assistive Technology Group, Inc.; ConnecTech, Inc.; Eclipse Networks, Inc.; Essent Healthcare, Inc.; Folio Exhibits, Inc.; FutureSource Communications, Inc.; Global DocuGraphiX, Inc.; Meridian Mortuary Group, Inc.; MSP Holdings, Inc.; NerveWire, Inc.; Select Medical Corporation; Vista Travel Ventures, Inc.; and Voice Integrators, Inc.

THOMPSON CLIVE, INC.

3000 Sand Hill Road
Building 1, Suite 185
Menlo Park, CA 94025
650-854-0314   fax: 650-854-0670

Robert E. Patterson, Principal

Gregory Ennis, Principal

Michelle Stecklein, Principal

total assets under management	*initial investment*	*year founded*
$200 Million	$1–3 Million	1977

Thompson Clive, Inc., provides a balance of management and financial expertise designed to assist growing companies. Thompson Clive likes to work in partnership with portfolio companies, often providing a complementary range of strategic and financial skills to those of operating management, although the Firm is prepared to take on direct management responsibility when appropriate.

Thompson Clive, with offices in London, Paris, and Menlo Park, California, is uniquely positioned to assist its portfolio companies with their international expansion. Thompson Clive's ultimate aim, and the yardstick by which the Firm wishes to be judged, is to assist and participate in the growth of such companies and to achieve an above-average return on investment.

THORNER VENTURES

P.O. Box 830
Larkspur, CA 94977-0830
415-925-9304   fax: 415-461-5855

Tom Thorner, Managing General Partner
Oscar Winnipeg Fuddy, Special Partner

total assets under management	*initial investment*	*year founded*
$10 Million	$200,000–600,000	1982

Thorner Ventures is a small virtual venture capital firm based in the San Francisco Bay Area. It is highly selective and invests in only two or three new companies per year. Thorner Ventures invests in California companies.

THREE ARCH PARTNERS

2800 Sand Hill Road, Suite 270
Menlo Park, CA 94025
650-854-5550   fax: 650-854-9890

Thomas J. Fogarty, M.D., General Partner
Wilfred E. Jaeger, General Partner
Mark A. Wan, General Partner
Jeffrey Bird, Partner
Michael Kaplan, Partner
Richard Lin, Partner
Barclay Nicholson, Director of Finance and Administration

total assets under management	*initial investment*	*year founded*
$300 Million	$1–5 Million	1994

Three Arch Partners is a venture capital firm that invests solely in the health-care industry. The Firm participates in seed- or first-round equity financings.

TIMBERLINE VENTURE PARTNERS

P.O. Box 2159
Vancouver, WA 98668
360-882-9577   fax: 360-882-9590
www.timberlinevc.com

Bill Kallman, Managing Partner

total assets under management	*initial investment*	*year founded*
$60 Million	$500,000–4 Million	1996

Timberline Venture Partners is focused on early-stage start-ups and corporate spin-offs in the Pacific Northwest, Southern California, and surrounding areas. It is interested in lead deals that fit the team's specialized talents for superior returns on info-tech companies. The info-tech emphasis is on information technology, computers, communications, electronics, networks, and software. The Firm will also consider other opportunities based on advances in materials, applied and life sciences, businesses, and nontechnology-based opportunities benefiting from Northwest corporate advantages and their role in Pacific Rim trade.

TL VENTURES

The Annex Building
3110 Main Street
Santa Monica, CA 90405
310-450-1800   fax: 310-450-1806
www.tlventures.com

Massoud Entekhabi, Managing Director
Robert N. Verratti, Managing Director
Sujit Banerjee, Principal
R. Neil Malik, Principal

total assets under management	*initial investment*	*year founded*
$750 Million	N/A	1988

TL Ventures is a national venture capital firm with a deep commitment to working in partnership with its portfolio companies. The Firm seeks early-stage companies in the following arenas: the Internet, software, information technology, communications, and life sciences. Most of its investments have been in California, the Northeast, and Texas, where the Firm assisted companies with business and product strategy, recruiting, technology partnerships, business and channel development, and financing.

Portfolio Companies: TL Ventures has over 100 active portfolio companies.

TONDU CORPORATION

2700 Post Oak Boulevard, Suite 1050
Houston, TX 77056
713-961-4222   fax: 713-961-1405
www.tonducorp.com

R. J. Tondu, President
Beverly Z. Baker, Managing Partner

total assets under management	*initial investment*	*year founded*
N/A	$100,000–1 Million	1978

Tondu Corporation is an investment and business-development firm with the objective of helping its portfolio companies succeed in the marketplace. It focuses on capitalizing on high-return emerging businesses in the energy industries, including oil, gas, electricity, and natural resources. The Firm funds seed and early-stage companies and seeks to work with entrepreneurs with strong business ideas. Tondu Corporation also supports project development in companies that need substantial amounts of debt financing. Tondu Corporation seeks investment opportunities worldwide in politically stable countries.

TOUCAN CAPITAL CORP.

3 Bethesda Metro Center, Suite 700
Bethesda, MD 20814
301-961-1970   fax: 301-961-1969
www.toucancapital.com

Robert F. Hemphill Jr., Managing Director
Linda F. Powers, Managing Director

total assets under management	*initial investment*	*year founded*
$60 Million	$100,000–5 Million	1998

Toucan Capital Corp. is a venture firm specializing in seed- and first-round financing, primarily for information technology start-up companies. Typical investments have been with telecom and Internet infrastructure, business systems and applications, intelligent search technologies, security and privacy technologies, bioinformatics, and life sciences products and services.

Toucan Capital Corp. is focused entirely on the business-to-business sector and does not fund any consumer-oriented companies. It invests in the United States and Canada.

Portfolio Companies: Business Forward; eMedia Club; Foundry Film Partners; The Grosvenor Fund; Mednav.com; OptiGlobe, Inc.; StarRemote.com; Trident Capital Partners IV; Venturehouse Group; and WomenAngels.net.

TRANS COSMOS USA, INC.

777 108th Avenue NE	555 Twin Dolphin Drive	21205 Yacht Club Drive
Suite 2300	Suite 570	Suite 280
Bellevue, WA 98004	Redwood City, CA 94065	Aventura, FL 33180-4052
425-468-3900	650-631-0051	305-933-0085
fax: 425-468-3901	fax: 650-631-0053	fax: 305-933-6881
www.transcosmos.com		

Shozo Okuda, Chairman

Yasuki Matsumoto, President and CEO

James J. Geddes Jr., Senior Managing Director

total assets under management	*initial investment*	*year founded*
$750 Million	$500,000–20 Million	1966

Trans Cosmos USA, Inc., is the United States branch of Trans Cosmos, a leading outsourced customer service and information technology support solutions provider in Japan. The firm is dedicated to helping leading-edge companies from America and Europe expand into the Japanese marketplace. Trans Cosmos USA focuses on new media, e-commerce, customer care, and marketing services companies with an international outlook. It funds companies in the United States and Europe.

Portfolio Companies: 2ROAM; Acadio Corp.; Access Markets International Partners, Inc.; ArtistOne; AsiaContent.com; AtomFilms; AudioBase, Inc.; Autobytel.com; BeVocal; Blue Pumpkin; Brand3; ccRewards.com; Click2Learn.com; Data Critical Corp.; DataChannel; DoubleClick Inc.; eIndia.com; Equator Technologies; Etinuum; Everest e-Commerce; F5 Networks; FatPipe; Fresher; HongKong.com; iJapan.com Inc.; InterWorld Corp.; Junglee; kana; KOZ.com; Liquid Audio; Listen.com; Live Inc.; LuckySurf.com; Lutris Technologies, Inc.; Mail.com, Inc.; MediaRing.com Ltd.; MixxOnline; Mjuice.com;

Mobilee; mySimon Inc.; Net Perceptions Inc.; NetRatings Inc.; Noel Co. KK.; Nuance Communications; PayPlace.com; PlaceWare Inc.; Pop2it.com; Presenter.com; Preview Systems; Primus Knowledge Solutions Inc.; Pulse Entertainment; RealNetworks Inc.; Riffage.com Inc.; RightSpring.com Inc.; RPK; Savvion; Sendmail Inc.; Sequel Technology Corporation; Simplexity.com; SiteROCK; Snapfish.com Corporation; Sprider Technologies; Spinner.com; Thinque Systems; TicketMaster Online; Total Sports; Tranz-Send Broadcasting Networks; Uproar; Veon; Vicinity Corp.; The Voice Works Inc.; Wit Capital Corp.; and Yack.com.

TRELLIS PARTNERS

2600 Via Fortuna
The Terrace, Building One, Suite 150
Austin, TX 78746
512-330-9200   fax: 512-330-9400
www.trellispartners.com

John L. Long Jr., Co-Founding Partner

H. Leland Murphy, Co-Founding Partner

Alexander C. Broeker, Partner

Sonja J. Eagle, Partner

total assets under management	*initial investment*	*year founded*
$67 Million	N/A	1997

Trellis Partners is a team of Texas-based venture capital professionals whose focus is on helping build leading technology companies through early-stage investment. The Firm's strategy is investing with a smaller, more exclusive list of companies, while applying similar parameters to the amount of capital managed. This enables the Partners to work more closely and collaboratively with each company, providing assistance, support, sponsorship, and handcrafted investor groups with specific co-investment firms.

Portfolio Companies: Covasoft; Extreme Devices; General Bandwidth; Novoforum; Questlink; Wayport; and Works.com.

TRIDENT CAPITAL

505 Hamilton Avenue, Suite 200
Palo Alto, CA 94301
650-289-4400   fax: 650-289-4444
www.tridentcap.com

Steve Beitler, Managing Director

Donald Dixon, Managing Director

Bonnie Kennedy, Managing Director and CFO

Venetia Kontogouris, Managing Director

Christopher Marshall, Managing Director

John Moragne, Managing Director

Robert McCormack, Managing Director

Peter Meekin, Managing Director

Rockwell Schnabel, Managing Director

Todd Springer, Managing Director

total assets under management	*initial investment*	*year founded*
$610 Million	$5–20 Million	1993

Trident Capital invests exclusively in information and business services companies. Trident Capital makes private equity investments in growth companies and management-led buyouts. Typical investments range from $5 million to $20 million and generally permit the Firm to be the lead investor. Trident invests in early-stage companies with proprietary products and services in rapidly growing markets, closely held companies that desire private equity to expand operations or accelerate growth, companies formed by experienced management teams that plan to build a large company through acquisitions or consolidation, or management-led buyouts.

Trident brings significant value to its portfolio companies by taking an active role in building strong management teams, developing business strategies, and assisting management in acquiring complementary product lines or businesses. Trident's offices are located in Palo Alto, California; Los Angeles; Lake Forest, Illinois; and Westport, Connecticut.

TRINITY VENTURES

3000 Sand Hill Road, Building 4, Suite 160
Menlo Park, CA 94025
650-854-9500   fax: 650-854-9501
www.trinityventures.com

Larry Orr, Managing General Partner

Noel Fenton, General Partner

Tod Francis, General Partner

Tim McAdam, General Partner

Jamie Shennan, General Partner

Gus Tai, General Partner

Fred Wang, General Partner

total assets under management	*initial investment*	*year founded*
$1 Billion	$5–15 Million	1986

Trinity Ventures is a venture capital firm with a focused approach to help entrepreneurs build successful businesses. It is interested in software, communications, and e-commerce companies offering Internet infrastructure and services. Trinity Ventures funds early-stage technology companies located within the United States. In addition, Trinity Ventures offers a wide network of industry leaders and recruiting, marketing, legal, and accounting services.

Portfolio Companies: Trinity Ventures has over 70 portfolio companies, including: 24/7 Media; Extreme Networks; KIVA Software; Network Alchemy; NextCard; and SciQuest.

TRITON VENTURES

6801 North Capital of Texas Highway
Building 2, Suite 225
Austin, TX 78731
512-795-5820   fax: 512-795-5828
www.tritonventures.com

Scott Collier, Managing Director

Laura Kilcrease, Managing Director

total assets under management	*initial investment*	*year founded*
$40 Million	$500,000–4 Million	1999

Triton Ventures is a venture capital firm with a special interest in spin-out opportunities. It targets companies in business software and infrastructure; business-to-business Internet-based companies; communications technology; and technology-enabled services. Triton Ventures funds companies in the United States.

Portfolio Companies: Applied Science Fiction; BPA Systems; Charitygift; Exterprise; GalleryWatch.com; Greenmountain; Hart Information Services; and Mindflow Technologies.

TSG Equity Partners LLC

636 Great Road
Stow, MA 01775
978-461-9900   fax: 978-461-9909
www.tsgequity.com

Thomas R. Shepherd, Chairman
T. Nathanael Shepherd, President

total assets under management	*initial investment*	*year founded*
$25 Million	$500,000–2 Million	1997

TSG Equity Partners LLC is a private equity investment firm providing early-stage, growth, and acquisition financing to venture and middle-market companies. The Firm focuses on companies with high-growth potential, a defensible competitive advantage, and unique market-ready products and services. TSG Equity Partners LLC prefers to make investments in companies that have completed the initial conceptual stage of their development and are either collecting revenue from their product or service or are on the cusp of taking the product or service to market. In addition, the Firm seeks investments in later-stage special situations and smaller leveraged acquisitions. While not limited to any one industry or geographic area, TSG Equity Partners does give first priority to companies located in New England engaged in businesses focused on communications, consumer products, Internet commerce and media, traditional media, niche manufacturing, software, and technology.

Portfolio Companies: 4R Systems, Inc.; aMedia, Inc.; Andover.Net, Inc.; Berkshire Wireless, Inc.; Community Resource Systems, Inc.; EnvisioNet Computer Services, Inc.; Houston Street Exchange.com, Inc.; myutility.com, Inc.; Pro-Safe Fire Training Systems, Inc.; Protocol Technologies Incorporated; Katahdin Industries, Inc.; Shoplink.com, Inc.; SpeedMerchant, Inc.; Tower Ventures, LLC; and The Vermont Teddy Bear Co., Inc.

Tullis Dickerson & Co., Inc.

Southwest Regional Office
150 Washington Avenue, Suite 201
Santa Fe, NM 87501
505-982-7007   fax: 505-982-7008
www.tullisdickerson.com

Jim Tullis, Principal

Tom Dickerson, Principal

Michael Schafer, Resident Principal, Santa Fe

total assets under management	*initial investment*	*year founded*
$37.5 Million	$250,000–5 Million	1998

Tullis Dickerson & Co. has formed a Southwest fund (TD Origen) for early- and expansion-stage companies in the areas of biotech/life sciences; health-care information technology/Internet; health-care services/managed care; medical devices; and medical distribution. These investors are based in Santa Fe, New Mexico, and are looking for companies west of this area that have a unique and proprietary technology and experienced management team and demonstrate a product need.

Portfolio Companies: AmericasDoctor.com, Inc.; BioQ.com; Integrated Biosystems, Inc.; Phase-1 Molecular Toxicology, Inc.; Quorex Pharmaceutical, Inc.; Scimagix, Inc.; SupplyPro, Inc.; and Transmolecular, Inc.

TVM TECHNO VENTURE MANAGEMENT

101 Arch Street, Suite 1950
Boston, MA 02110
617-345-9320   fax: 617-345-9377
www.tvmvc.com

Friedrich Bornikoel, Managing Partner—Information and Communications Technology

Dr. Helmut Schühsler, Managing Partner—Life Sciences

Dr. Alexandra Goll, Partner

Christian Claussen, Partner

Dr. Peter L. Levin, Partner

Dr. Gert Caspritz, Partner

John J. DiBello, Partner

Bernd Seibel, Partner

total assets under management	*initial investment*	*year founded*
$650 Million	N/A	1984

TVM Techno Venture Management (TVM) is a European-U.S. venture capital firm with an intent to capitalize on transatlantic opportunities. Its investment focus is the information and communications technology industry and the life sciences industry. Within the information and communications technology field, the Firm concentrates on photonics, mobile communications, design automation, software technologies, and applications for large companies. In the life sciences industry, TVM focuses on genomics and chemistry, drug concepts derived from traditional natural medicine, drug-delivery technology, tissue engineering, replacement medicine, and medical devices.

TVM funds early-stage to later-stage companies located in Europe and the United States.

Portfolio Companies: Techno Venture Management has over 60 active portfolio companies.

U.S. VENTURE PARTNERS

2180 Sand Hill Road, Suite 300
Menlo Park, CA 94025
650-854-9080   fax: 650-854-3018
www.usvp.com

Wiliam K. Bowes Jr., Founding Partner

Irwin Federman, General Partner

Winston S. Fu, General Partner

Jason E. Green, General Partner

Steven M. Krausz, General Partner

Lucio L. Lanza, General Partner

David Liddle, General Partner

Jonathan D. Root, M.D., General Partner

Philip M. Young, General Partner

total assets under management	*initial investment*	*year founded*
$600 Million	$500,000–8 Million	1981

U.S. Venture Partners (USVP) is a Silicon Valley–based firm with principal interest in early-stage investments on the West Coast in the information technology and medical technology industry sectors and, to a lesser degree, in consumer product/retail businesses. Within the information technology industry sector, USVP has particular interest in software (design tools and enterprise software), Internet and Intranet (infrastructure and electronic commerce–related) businesses, network/data communications hardware and software, and semiconductors. In the medical technology sector, the Firm has particular interest in medical devices and biopharmaceutical-related businesses.

USVP typically prefers to make equity investments in seed-, start-up, and pre-revenue development stage companies, but it also invests in expansion rounds and in leveraged buyouts when such situations are sufficiently attractive.

Portfolio Companies: USVP has over 100 portfolio companies.

UNION ATLANTIC CAPITAL, L.C.

6600 North Andrews Avenue
Suite 304B
Fort Lauderdale, FL 33309
954-229-3290
fax: 954-229-3289
www.ualc.com

1215 Hightower, Suite B220
Atlanta, GA 30350
770-992-6900
fax: 770-992-6800

Dan Cruz-DePaula, Managing Partner
Paul T. Mannion, Managing Director
Andrew S. Reckles, Managing Director

total assets under management	*initial investment*	*year founded*
N/A	$500,000–10 Million	2000

Union Atlantic Capital, L.C., a NASD member firm, is a wholly owned subsidiary of vFinance.com. Union Atlantic Capital, L.C., is a full service investment banking firm with offices in Ft. Lauderdale, Florida, and Atlanta, Georgia, specializing in mergers and acquisitions and private placements in public companies (PIPEs).

Portfolio Companies: America Champion Entertainment; Detourtv; Famous Fixins; Pan Interconnect; Speedcom Wireless; Singlepoint Systems; Stupid PC; vFinance.com; Webcat Online; and Zapworld.com.

UV PARTNERS

423 Wakara Way, Suite 206
Salt Lake City, UT 84108
801-583-5922
fax: 801-583-4105
www.uven.com

720 31st Street
Manhattan Beach,
CA 90266
310-546-2777
fax: 310-546-6757

7400 SW Barnes Road
Suite 332
Portland, OR 97225
503-574-4125
fax: 503-574-4213

Alan Dishlip, General Partner
Jim Dreyfous, General Partner

Allan Wolfe, General Partner

Steve Borst, Partner

total assets under management	*initial investment*	*year founded*
N/A	N/A	1984

Utah Ventures is committed to meeting the needs of seed- and early-stage information technology and health-care companies located west of the Rocky Mountains. These companies include: software and tools, telecommunications, networking and Internet-based companies, biotechnology, medical devices, health-care services, and information systems. UV Partners invests in people who have developed a track record of related accomplishments. The Firm has offices in Salt Lake City, Portland, and Los Angeles.

   Portfolio Companies: Axent Technologies, Inc.; eHealthDirect, Inc.; IOMED, Inc.; Knowlix Corporation; Orbit Commerce, Inc.; Pointshare Corporation; Premisys Communications, Inc.; Red Gorilla; Salus Therapeutics; Sonic Innovations, Inc.; Sonus Pharmaceuticals; Spreeride; Supplybase, Inc.; and WebMiles.com Corporation.

VALLEY VENTURES, L.P.

6720 North Scottsdale Road, Suite 280
Scottsdale, AZ 85253
408-661-6600   fax: 408-661-6262

Michael A. Collins, M.D., General Partner

John M. Holliman III, General Partner

total assets under management	*initial investment*	*year founded*
$30 Million	$250,000–2 Million	1984

Valley Ventures, L.P., is a private venture capital firm that invests in early- and late-stage companies. The Firm will invest in a broad range of industries, excluding real estate, natural resources, and consumer retail, with a particular expertise in the medical industry. Valley Ventures focuses on the Southwestern U.S., from Southern California to Texas.

VANGUARD VENTURE PARTNERS

525 University Avenue, Suite 600
Palo Alto, CA 94301
650-321-2900   fax: 650-321-2902
www.vanguardventures.com

David L. Eilers, General Partner

Jack M. Gill, Ph.D., General Partner

Robert D. Ulrich, Ph.D., General Partner

Donald F. Wood, General Partner

Paul A. Slakey, Partner

total assets under management	*initial investment*	*year founded*
N/A	N/A	1981

Vanguard Venture Partners is a venture capital firm specializing in seed- and early-stage investments and has offices in Palo Alto, California, and Houston, Texas. Vanguard's focus is in three areas: telecommunications, Internet infrastructure and software, and life sciences. These companies should need both equity capital and management assistance and would preferably allow Vanguard to be a lead investor with potential to own 20 to 30 percent of the company.

Portfolio Companies: Advanced Fibre Communications; Aldus (acquired by Adobe); Blaze; Ciena; Cobalt; Cooking.com; CSFluids; FlyPaper; Luminous; Network Appliance; Novalux; Percadia; Sylantro; TissueLink; Tut Systems; Digital Island; and Zip Realty.com.

VECTOR FUND MANAGEMENT

1751 Lake Cook Road, Suite 350
Deerfield, IL 60015
847-374-3947   fax: 847-374-3899
www.vectorfund.com

Barclay A. Phillips, Managing Director

Douglas Reed, M.D., Managing Director

total assets under management	*initial investment*	*year founded*
$240 Million	$5–15 Million	N/A

Vector Fund Management seeks superior long-term capital appreciation through negotiated equity investments in later-stage private and public companies in the life sciences and health-care industries. Vector Fund Management combines industry expertise with a proven investment strategy to generate value for its portfolio companies and limited partners. The firm seeks companies managed by seasoned life sciences and health-care industry professionals and companies poised to move from development stage to commercially viable operating entities in a relatively short time. Areas of investment activity have included biotechnology, pharmaceuticals, medical devices, diagnostics, plant and animal sciences, health-care services, health-care information technology, and consumer applications of emerging health-care technologies.

Portfolio Companies: Acorda Therapeutics, Inc.; Acist Medical Systems; Align Technology, Inc.; Assistive Technology, Inc.; Avocet Medical, Inc.; Axya Medical, Inc.; Cambridge Antibody Technology Ltd.; Cell Therapeutics, Inc.; Cellomics, Inc.; Codman Group; Datamedic; Decibel Instrument, Inc.; Digirad Corporation; Guilford Pharmaceuticals, Inc.; IBAH Inc.; Infocure Corporation; Insmed, Inc.; Intermune Pharmaceuticals, Inc.; Laser Diagnostic Technologies, Inc.; LifeCell Corporation; Magainin Pharmaceuticals Inc.; Martek Biosciences Corporation; MaterniCare, Inc.; Matrix Pharmaceutical, Inc.; Novacept; Perigon Medical Distribution Corp.; Pharmacopeia, Inc.; Pozen Inc.; SciQuest.com, Inc.; Spinal Concepts, Inc.; StressGen Biotechnologies Corp.; Triangle Pharmaceutical; and Xcyte Therapies, Inc.

VENCON MANAGEMENT, INC.

301 West 53rd Street
New York, NY 10019
212-581-8787   fax: 212-397-4126
www.venconinc.com

Irvin Barash, President

total assets under management	*initial investment*	*year founded*
N/A	$1 Million	1972

Vencon Management, Inc., is a venture capital firm also providing advisory services. VMI is a principal in buyouts, including those with management.

VMI considers investments in seed, start-up, and expansion categories. Industry criteria include environmental, nutrition, medical, biotech/chemicals, and semiconductors. The Firm considers deals on a national basis. Vencon's role is the identification and, often, the creation of unique venture situations in various technology sectors. VMI takes an active role with new ventures in the post-closing, transition stage of unsettlement.

VMI's established relationships, over 25 years with major American and foreign companies, provide the Firm with a direct route to spinoffs, management buyouts, and strategic alliances for its venture deals.

VENTANA

8880 Rio San Diego Drive, Suite 500
San Diego, CA 92108
619-291-2757   fax: 619-295-0189
www.ventanaglobal.com
e-mail: ventana@ventanaglobal.com

Thomas O. Gephart, Founder and Managing Partner

F. Duwaine Townsen, Co-Founder and Managing Partner

total assets under management	*initial investment*	*year founded*
$230 million	$2 million	1974

Ventana is located in the Southern California technology corridors of Orange and San Diego Counties. This corridor is supported by its local, but world-class, research universities; established global technology-oriented companies; and business leaders. San Diego's technology-based companies have benefited from alliances with research institutions such as Scripps Institute, Salk Institute, Burnham Institute, and San Diego State University, with the University of California at San Diego leading the way. In addition, private industry has spawned significant players in the semiconductor, computer, and telecommunications industries.

Ventana's Gateway concept has been developed to augment opportunities available in California by creating a platform through which its Investor Partners are exposed to cutting-edge technologies. In addition, Investor Partners are given the opportunity to make strategic or financial investments directly into portfolio companies. Many of Ventana's Investor Partners have taken advantage of such opportunities to create strategic alliances with individual portfolio companies, leading to various marketing, distribution, research, and development arrangements. Ventana's proactive investment style provides its portfolio companies with access to a global network of strategic and financial Investor Partners, resulting in significant opportunities for growth, technology transfers, and product development.

Portfolio Companies: Agouron Pharmaceuticals, Inc; Advanced Tissue Sciences, Inc.; La Jolla Pharmaceutical Company; Hyperion, Inc.; and PolyPharm Corporation.

VENTURE FUNDING, LIMITED

321 Fisher Building
3011 West Grand Boulevard
Detroit, MI 48202
313-871-3606   fax: 313-873-4935

Monis Schuster, President

total assets under management	*initial investment*	*year founded*
N/A	$250,000–5 Million	1983

Venture Funding, Limited, is a private venture capital and consulting firm that invests in most regions within the United States. Venture Funding invests in R&D,

seed, start-up, mezzanine, leveraged and management buyouts, and special-situation stage companies. Venture Funding invests in a variety of industries.

Venture Growth Associates

2479 E. Bayshore, Suite 710
Palo Alto, CA 94303
650-855-9100   fax: 650-855-9104

James R. Berdell, Managing Partner
Robert Ledoux, Managing Partner

total assets under management	*initial investment*	*year founded*
$200 Million	$1–2.5 Million	1982

Venture Growth Associates is based in Palo Alto, California, and is a serious competitor with other private venture capital firms in the Silicon Valley. Venture Growth Associates supplies financing for first-stage, second-stage, mezzanine, acquisition, and leveraged and management buyouts in a variety of industries. Venture Growth Associates is particular to investing in the West, preferring to invest in California.

Venture Management Associates

1104 Camino Del Mar, Suite 7
Del Mar, CA 92014-2606
858-350-3910   fax: 650-329-6889
www.vmapartners.com

Richard E. Amen, Partner
Scott F. Wilson, Partner

total assets under management	*initial investment*	*year founded*
N/A	$1–$10 Million	1987

Venture Management Associates is interested in most stages of investing. The different levels of funding include: first-stage, second-stage, mezzanine, acquisition, leveraged and management buyouts, recapitalizations, and special situations. Venture Management Associates invests in the United States in general; however, there is a special interest in the Pacific Rim, Rocky Mountains, and California. Venture Management Associates specializes in high-tech and high-growth industries.

VENTURE STRATEGY PARTNERS

655 Third Street
San Francisco, CA 94107
415-558-8600   fax: 415-558-8686
www.venturestrategy.com

Joanna Rees Gallanter, Founder and Managing Partner

Anthony Conrad, Partner

Matt Crisp, Partner

David Likins, Partner

total assets under management	*initial investment*	*year founded*
$225 Million	$200,000 and up	1996

Venture Strategy Partners is a San Francisco–based venture capital firm that accelerates the growth of emerging businesses at the nexus of technology and brand. Venture Strategy Partners invests in technology-focused companies that recognize the strategic importance of brand, backing leading companies in the enabling technology, broadband, and wireless sectors. Venture Strategy Partners defines "brand" as a business system that permeates an entire organization and believes that a well-defined brand is essential to an emerging technology company's success. The Venture Strategy Partners team delivers domain knowledge and hands-on operational experience to build hallmark technology companies.

Portfolio Companies: Post Communications; Flooz.com; Millenia Vision; AllBusiness.com; eSyle; QuinStreet; Nexgenix; and iVast.

VENTUREPLEX

Symphony Towers
750 B Street, Suite 1200
San Diego, CA 92101
858-335-5138
www.ventureplex.com

Dante Fichera, Managing Director

Dave LaFrenz, Managing Director

total assets under management	*initial investment*	*year founded*
N/A	$15,000–50,000	2000

Ventureplex is a technology and life sciences incubator located in the heart of San Diego, just minutes away from the airport. Ventureplex provides infrastructure, technical support, business development support, and networking to promising early- and mid-stage companies. Services are provided in exchange for fees and/or equity. Ventureplex has mentoring programs and innovative strategies to expedite the funding process with potential investors. Ventureplex's services greatly enhance the percentage of young companies that succeed while reducing the time to market.

The directors and advisory board are some of the most reputable and experienced business persons in San Diego and are dedicated to assisting incubatees in reaching their full potential. Ventureplex is also involved with the community and the local universities; it has come up with mutually supportive programs to benefit incubatees, students, and community organizations.

VERSANT VENTURES

3000 Sand Hill Road, Building 1, Suite 260
Menlo Park, CA 94025
650-233-7877   fax: 650-854-9513
www.versantventures.com

Sam Colella, Managing Director

Don Milder, Managing Director

Ross Jaffe, M.D., Managing Director

Barbara Lubash, Managing Director

Brian Atwood, Managing Director

Beckie Robertson, Managing Director

Bill Link, Managing Director

total assets under management	*initial investment*	*year founded*
$250 Million	$2–10 Million	1999

Versant Ventures is a team of experienced health-care investors from three of the best-performing diversified venture capital funds of the 1990s: Brentwood Venture Capital, Crosspoint Venture Partners, and Institutional Venture Partners (IVP). Versant offers early-stage companies both significant capital and a venture capital team with substantial operating experience and a domain expertise in health care. The Versant team partners with entrepreneurs to surmount the challenges facing young medical-device, biopharmaceutical, health-care service, and e-health companies.

Portfolio Companies: Tensys Medical, Inc.; Cogent Healthcare; Pharmion; Syrrx; Flaca.com; and eHealthcontracts.com.

VERTEX MANAGEMENT, INC.

3 Lagoon Drive, Suite 220
Redwood City, CA 94065
650-591-9300   fax: 650-591-5926
www.vertexmgt.com

Joo Hock Chua, Senior Vice President

total assets under management	*initial investment*	*year founded*
$800 Million	$1–5 Million	1988

Vertex Management, Inc., is a venture capital fund manager. It is part of the Vertex Group of companies, which manages more than $800 million through global offices in Singapore, the United States, London, Savyon (Israel), Taipei, and Beijing. Investment focus is on early-stage technology companies with the potential to grow into large entities serving huge markets. The Firm has made many such investments in the United States, Europe, Israel, Taiwan, Singapore, and China.

Portfolio Companies: Accrue Software; ActivCard; Aurum Software; Brokar; Centillium; Chordiant; Com21; Creative Technology; Embark.com; Enba; Fogdog Sports; Gemplus; GRIC; Hitron; Hyperchip; InnoMedia; MediaRing; MoreCom; Optimight; PlanetWeb; Portran; Premisys Communications; Ramp Network; SCM Microsystem; SeedNet; Silknet Software; and Transmedia.

VISION CAPITAL

3000 Sand Hill Road
Building 4, Suite 230
Menlo Park, CA 94025
650-854-8070   fax: 650-854-4961
www.visioncapital.com

Dag Tellefsen, Managing Partner

total assets under management	*initial investment*	*year founded*
$100 Million	$250,000–5 Million	1982

Vision Capital can provide introductions and assistance in establishing a company internationally. The Firm invests in most stages of funding, particularly: first-stage, second-stage, acquisition, leveraged and management buyouts, recapitalization, and special situations. Its geographic investment range includes California and Western Europe, and its focus is on information technology sectors.

VIVENTURES

66 Bovet Road, Suite 318
San Mateo, CA 94402
650-356-1071   fax: 650-356-1074
www.viventures.com

Jean-Pascal Tranié, Managing General Partner

Edward Colby, General Partner

Benoist Grossmann, General Partner

Slim Shekar, General Partner

total assets under management	*initial investment*	*year founded*
$700 Million	$3–9 Million	1998

Viventures is a venture capital firm with a presence in the United States and Europe. The Firm was established to provide capital for innovative telecommunications and Internet businesses in the start-up or expanding stages. Viventures typically takes minority ownership stakes in businesses that show promising innovative strategies designed to develop new applications, new uses for their products and services, or new production methods.

Portfolio Companies: Some of the U.S. portfolio companies are: OneMediaPlace; Campsix; Centerpoint; Cyras; DirectHit; E-Sync; HiFive!; Lightlogic; Luxxon Corporation; NetBrowser; Netonomy; MediaQ; Redcart; UGO Networks; and Xpedion.

W. B. McKee Securities

7702 East Doubletree Ranch Road, Suite 230
Scottsdale, AZ 85258
480-368-0333   fax: 480-607-7446

William B. McKee, Chairman

Jan Koontz, Vice President/Investment Banking

Chris Nicholson, Corporate Finance Associate

Marck Jazwin, Analyst/Corporate Finance

Ed Nicholson, Information Technology

total assets under management	*initial investment*	*year founded*
$190 Million	$1–15 Million	1987

McKee & Company is a full-service investment banking firm. McKee & Company invests in second-stage, mezzanine, bridge, acquisition, and leveraged/management buyouts. Geographic locations must be in the United States, although the Northwest, Southwest, Rocky Mountains, and California are preferred. McKee & Company provides expertise and experience to all of its clients and has experience with all types of venture capital projects.

WALDEN CAPITAL PARTNERS L.P.

708 Third Avenue, 21st Floor
New York, NY 10017
212-355-0090   fax: 212-755-8894
www.waldencapital.com

Martin B. Boorstein, Principal

John R. Costantino, Principal

Allen Greenberg, Principal

total assets under management	*initial investment*	*year founded*
$60 Million	$1–4 Million	1996

Walden Capital Partners L.P. is a licensed small-business investment company (SBIC) with an interest in companies in need of growth capital for expansion. It focuses on a variety of industries, including manufacturing, distribution, Internet, software, hardware, and health-care and medical-related companies. The partners at Walden have experience with a wide range of transaction structures, such as expansion-stage private financings, management buyouts, leveraged buyouts, PIPEs, ESOPs, recapitalizations, and roll-ups. Walden Capital Partners invests primarily in the Northeast and Mid-Atlantic and co-invests in other areas of the United States.

Portfolio Companies: Ameriscape Inc.; Bemiss-Jason Corporation; CA Technology, Inc.; Clayton Acquisition Corporation; eShare Technologies, Inc.; IriScan Inc.; Jemtech Solutions, Inc.; OMNA Medical Partners, Inc.; Outlast Technologies, Inc.; Plymouth Inc.; Prototype Acquisition Corporation; RemoteReality, Inc.; Snickelways Interactive, Inc.; SpectraCell Laboratories, Inc.; Window Products LLC; and Vox Radio Group LLC.

WALDEN VC

750 Battery Street, 7th Floor
San Francisco, CA 94111
415-391-7225   fax: 415-391-7262
www.waldenvc.com

Arthur Berliner, General Partner

George Sarlo, Partner

Steve Eskenazi, General Partner

Philip Sanderson, General Partner

Rich LeFurgy, General Partner

Alex Gove, Vice President

total assets under management	*initial investment*	*year founded*
$500 Million	$1–7 million	1974

Walden VC is a San Francisco–based venture capital firm that specializes in investments in early-stage Internet and new media companies. Focus areas include advertising, e-commerce, education, enhanced TV, and entertainment. Walden VC manages funds in excess of $500 million. Corporate investors include Apollo Group (APOL); Electronic Arts (ERTS); GartnerGroup (IT); New Line Cinema, a division of Time Warner (tWX); Times Mirror (TmC); *Washington Post* (WPO); and Kaplan, a division of the *Washington Post.* Some of Walden VC's representative investments include AdKnowledge; iPIX (IPIX)/bamboo.com; DigitalThink (DTHK); Snowball.com (SNOW); AllAdvantage.com; Moai Technologies; ICSA.net; and WorldRes.com.

WASATCH VENTURE FUNDS

1 South Main Street, Suite 1400
Salt Lake City, UT 84133
801-524-8939   fax: 801-524-8941
www.wasatchvc.com

Todd J. Stevens, Managing Partner

Kent Madsen, Managing Partner

Nick Efstratis, Managing Partner

total assets under management	*initial investment*	*year founded*
$100 Million	$250,000–1 Million	1994

Wasatch Venture Funds was funded by Zions Bank, Utah Technology Equity Foundation, and other institutions for the purpose of providing equity capital to small business. Its objective is to finance businesses with extraordinary management that have developed proprietary products that are capable of creating exceptional growth in sales and profits. Wasatch will pursue a people-biased, back-to-basics, early-stage (first-stage, second-stage, and mezzanine) approach to venture capital investing.

Wasatch invests in information, communication, Internet/Intranet, software, and medical product companies based in Utah, California, Arizona, Nevada, and other Western states.

Portfolio Companies: Advanced Software; Alta Technologies; Ancestry.com; CFM Technologies; Comspec; and Digital Entertainment.

WASSERSTEIN ADELSON VENTURES, L.P.

31 West 52nd Street
New York, NY 10019
212-969-2700   fax: 212-702-5635
www.wassersteinperella.com

Townsend Ziebold, Managing Director

Sam Gupts, Managing Director

Dera Akbarian, Principal

George Leuro, Principal

Thomas Muang, Associate

total assets under management	*initial investment*	*year founded*
$135 Million	$2–9 Million	1988

Wasserstein Adelson Ventures is a small-business investment company, venture capital subsidiary, and private equity subsidiary that invests in mid-stage to later-stage financings. Wasserstein Adelson targets equity investments of $2 million to $9 million. There is no geographic restriction, as long as it is within the United States. Investments vary across many industries, including digital media technologies, wireless applications, Internet infrastructure, and selected B2B areas.

WEBVESTORS EQUITY PARTNERS, LP

SunTrust Center, Suite 1850
200 S. Orange Avenue
Orlando, FL 32801
407-835-7900   fax: 407-835-7901
www.webvestors.com

Edward P. Grace III, Managing Director

Steven A. Collins, Partner

Michael S. Heller, Partner

total assets under management	*initial investment*	*year founded*
N/A	$250,000–3 Million	1999

WebVestors Equity Partners, LP, invests in information technology companies participating in rapidly evolving industries such as wireless and broadband infrastructure, telecommunications, networking equipment and services, and software/information services, with emphasis on commercialization of military technology in all of these fields. The Firm typically invests in seed and early-stage ventures; however, it will invest opportunistically in mezzanine rounds. WebVestors looks to support entrepreneurial teams with assistance in team building and recruiting, operational guidance and support, brand-building and marketing, additional financing, and developing strategic relationships.

  Portfolio Companies: Bungo; CoolSavings; Mantra Communications; MeshNetworks, Inc.; MILCOM Technologies, Inc.; SkyCross; StructuredWeb; and Theseus Logic.

WELSH, CARSON, ANDERSON & STOWE

320 Park Avenue, Suite 2500
New York, NY 10022-6815
212-893-9500   fax: 212-893-9575
www.welshcarson.com

Bruce K. Anderson, General Partner

Russell L. Carson, General Partner

Anthony J. DeNicola, General Partner

Thomas E. McInerney, General Partner

Robert A. Minicucci, General Partner

Andrew M. Paul, General Partner

Johnathan M. Rather, General Partner

Rudolph E. Rupest, General Partner

Paul B. Queally, General Partner

Lawrence Sorrel, General Partner

Patrick Welsh, General Partner

total assets under management	*initial investment*	*year founded*
$7.6 Billion	$100–500 Million	1979

Welsh, Carson, Anderson & Stowe (WCA&S) is a private investment firm, specializing in leveraged and management buyouts. WCA&S has the size, power, and specialization to provide impeccable service to its portfolio companies. WCA&S invests primarily in companies based in the United States. WCA&S has chosen to concentrate exclusively on the health-care and information technology services industries. The Firm invests throughout the United States.

Portfolio Companies: Welsh, Carson, Anderson & Stowe has over 30 portfolio companies in the information services, telecommunications, and health-care industries.

WESTERN STATES INVESTMENT GROUP

9191 Towne Centre Drive, Suite 310
San Diego, CA 92122
858-678-0800   fax: 858-678-0900
www.wsig.com

Scott Pancoast, Executive Vice President
William Patch, Vice President

total assets under management	*initial investment*	*year founded*
$40 Million	$1–5 Million	1976

Western States Investment Group invests in a broad range of businesses, including medical products, telecommunications, software, and electronics. The Group is currently seeking investment opportunities ranging from start-up ventures to management-led buyouts. Western States Investment Group approaches every investment as a long-term partnership. It assists management in the development of a proper foundation of a business strategy that maximizes long-term value.

WESTERN TECHNOLOGY INVESTMENT

2010 North First Street, Suite 300
San Jose, CA 95131
408-436-8577   fax: 408-436-8625

Salvador O. Gutierrez, General Partner
Ronald W. Swenson, General Partner

total assets under management	*initial investment*	*year founded*
$300 Million	$500,000–10 Million	1980

Western Technology Investment specializes in providing asset-based financing for start-up and emerging-growth companies that want to preserve their equity capital by financing capital equipment and working capital needs. Western Technology Investment acquires companies into its portfolio that are in the following stages: R&D, seed, start-up, first-stage, second-stage, mezzanine, leveraged buyouts, and special situations. Western Technology will invest in the United States or anywhere in the world.

WESTON PRESIDIO CAPITAL

343 Sansome Street, Suite 1210
San Francisco, CA 94104-1316
415-398-0770   fax: 415-398-0990
www.westonpresidio.com

Michael F. Cronin, Managing Partner
Michael P. Lazarus, Managing Partner
James B. McElwee, General Partner
Carlo A. von Schroeter, General Partner
Philip W. Halperin, General Partner
Mark L. Bono, General Partner
Thomas A. Patterson, General Partner
Kevin M. Hayes, General Partner
Alan L. Stein, Venture Partner

total assets under management	*initial investment*	*year founded*
$2.2 Billion	$5–100 Million	1991

Weston Presidio Capital's investments are based on management teams rather than on industry or geography. Weston Presidio's strategy is to originate investment opportunities in a diverse set of industries and companies operated by management teams with proven records of success. The Firm's focus is on growth companies; recapitalizations and buyouts; and companies that are closely held, family-controlled, or initially financed by institutional investors. Over 130 years of private equity investment experience gives Weston Presidio investors the ability to advise and counsel; negotiate and raise debt or equity financing; recruit additional management; assist with strategic planning; negotiate and advise on acquisitions, sales, or mergers; assess partners; and develop compensation and incentive programs.

Portfolio Companies: Over 65 companies inclusive of Internet, telephony, specialty retailing, service businesses, manufacturing, health care, technology, restaurants, and consumer goods.

WHITNEY & CO.

177 Broad Street
Stamford, CT 06901
203-973-1400
fax: 203-973-1422
www.jhwhitney.com

580 California Street, 20th Floor
San Francisco, CA 94104
415-229-4000
fax: 415-229-4001

Julian A. L. Allen, Managing Director, San Francisco

Peter M. Castleman, Chairman and CEO, Connecticut

William Laverack Jr., Vice Chairman and Chief Investment Officer,
  Connecticut

Michael R. Stone, President and COO, Connecticut

total assets under management	*initial investment*	*year founded*
$5 Billion	$5–10 Million	1946

Whitney & Co., one of the pioneers of the venture capital business, is a leading global manager of alternative assets. Whitney's private equity investments are focused on the communications, financial services, information technology, health-care, and "transforming" industries. The Firm seeks out exceptional entrepreneurs who have clear strategic and operating plans to capitalize on attractive market opportunities and achieve long-term growth. Whitney & Co. invests worldwide in both private and public equity. In addition, it manages several funds that invest in mezzanine debt, high-yield debt, bank loans, and a variety of special situations.

   Portfolio Companies: Whitney & Co. has over 150 portfolio investments.

WI HARPER GROUP

50 California Street, Suite 2920
San Francisco, CA 94111
415-397-6200   fax: 415-397-6280
www.wiharper.com

Peter Liu, Chairman

Thomas Tsao, Managing Director, Hong Kong

total assets under management	*initial investment*	*year founded*
$175 Million	N/A	1989

WI Harper Group is one of the first San Francisco–based high technology venture capital firms focused exclusively on creating a bridge between Silicon Valley and the Greater China Region (Hong Kong, China, and Taiwan). It has created a unique network combining entrepreneurial energy, superior technical know-how, manufacturing capabilities, human resources, capital, and market channels on both sides of the Pacific Rim. The Firm focuses particularly on investment opportunities in the high-technology sector in the aforementioned regions and in the sectors such as e-commerce, digital media, wireless applications, broadband, optical networking equipment, and biotechnology. It invests 40 percent in seed, 40 percent in expansion, and 20 percent in mezzanine stages. WI Harper currently has two combined funds called INC Funds, a third called the Beijing Technology Development Fund, and another joint Singapore fund called Springboard-Harper.

Portfolio Companies: WI Harper Group has over 80 high-technology portfolio companies in the Pacific, the U.S. West, and the Greater China regions.

WINDAMERE VENTURE PARTNERS, LLC

12230 El Camino Real, Suite 300
San Diego, CA 92130
858-350-7950   fax: 858-350-7951

John F. Burd, General Partner
Kenneth J. Widder, General Partner
Scott L. Glenn, Managing Partner

total assets under management	*initial investment*	*year founded*
$68 Million	$100,000–5 Million	1999

Windamere Venture Partners, LLC invests in early-stage companies that are operating in the health-care industry. Windamere has invested in such companies as Santarus and Optimize.

WINSTON PARTNERS

1750 Tysons Boulevard, Suite 200
McLean, VA 22102
703-905-9555   fax: 703-905-9019
www.winstonpartners.com

Scott Andrews, Managing Partner/Co-Founder

Marvin Bush, Managing Partner/Co-Founder

total assets under management	*initial investment*	*year founded*
$300 Million	N/A	1993

Winston Partners has a private equity fund seeking long-term capital appreciation through private equity investments in carefully selected developing and middle-market companies with enterprise values ranging from $5 to $100 million, principally in the United States. The firm invests in a range of industries, including IT and telecom services, outsourced business services, manufacturing, and direct marketing businesses. Winston Partners believes that smaller private companies offer significantly enhanced opportunities for growth.

Portfolio Companies: Winston/Thayer Partners Fund: Applied Predictive Technologies; The Hobart West Group; Impressa; Renaissance Interactive Holding Corporation; Riveon Corporation; National Waste Services. Winston Capital Funds: Amsec International; Axolotl Corporation; Capital Transportation; Learning Byte International; Logotel; MetroPCS; and TechnoBrands.

WINWARD VENTURES

12680 High Bluff Drive, Suite 200
San Diego, CA 92130
858-259-4590   fax: 858-259-4541
www.windwardventures.com

David Titus, General Partner

Jim Cole, General Partner

total assets under management	*initial investment*	*year founded*
$80 Million	$1–2 Million	1997

Windward Ventures invests in early-stage technology and health-care companies in Southern California. Preferred industries are communications, software, business Internet applications, and medical devices.

WOODSIDE FUND

350 Marine Parkway, Suite 300
Redwood Shores, CA 94065
650-610-8050   fax: 650-610-8051
www.woodsidefund.com

Vincent M. Occhipinti, Managing Director

Robert E. Larson, Managing Director

Charles E. Greb, Managing Director

Daniel H. Ahn, Principal

John C. Occhipinti, Principal

Matthew J. Bolton, Analyst

Angelos M. Kottas, Analyst

total assets under management	*initial investment*	*year founded*
$200 Million	$250,000–10 Million	1983

Woodside Fund focuses on technology companies that are still early in their development. Internet and electronic commerce, computer software, and telecommunications and networking are the primary industry targets. The Firm is looking for companies with a large market potential and proprietary technology or specialized expertise. As partners, Woodside Fund helps to refine business plans, strengthen management, and identify new markets, products, customers, partnerships, and funding.

   Portfolio Companies: Alis Technologies; APX; Brightware; Digital Microwave; Enterprise Link; Evans & Sutherland; HotRail; Infinitec; Intertrust; New Era of Networks; Novell; Quintiles; Sharing Technologies; SS8 Networks; Street Fusion; Trivida; and US Build.com

---

WORLDVIEW TECHNOLOGY PARTNERS

435 Tasso Street, Suite 120
Palo Alto, CA 94301
650-322-3800   fax: 650-322-3880
www.worldview.com

James Wei, General Partner and Co-Founder

Michael Orsak, General Partner and Co-Founder

John Boyle, General Partner

Ajit Shah, General Partner

Colin R. Savage, General Partner

total assets under management	*initial investment*	*year founded*
$750 Million	N/A	1996

Worldview Technology Partners helps build leading U.S. information technology companies and assist these businesses with international expansion. Investments are focused toward telecom equipment, telecom services, Internet software infrastructure, and Internet service companies, in all stages of business development. Worldview can assist with assessing market opportunities, developing an international business strategy, defining product specifications, initiating technology partnerships, establishing manufacturing and distribution partnerships, identifying and introducing customers, securing funding for subsidiaries, forming subsidiaries, and recruiting local executives.

Portfolio Companies: Assured Access; ClickService; Cogent; Corvis; Cosine; Mirapoint; NVIDIA; Redstone; Tensilica; and Triton.

WRF Capital

2815 Eastlake Ave. E., Suite 300
Seattle, WA 98102
206-336-5600   fax: 206-336-5615
www.wrfcapital.org

Ronald S. Howell, President
Loretta Little, Managing Director
John Reagh, Managing Director

total assets under management	*initial investment*	*year founded*
$30 Million	$100,000–2 Million	1981

WRF Capital manages the Washington Research Foundation's seed venture fund by creating and investing primarily in technology-based start-up companies that have strong ties to the University of Washington and other nonprofit research institutions in Washington.

WRF Capital looks for companies with definable products, having a strategic advantage in a large potential market. The company should have a strong proprietary position with a potential high-investment return within two to seven years.

Portfolio Companies: Amnis Corp.; Confirma, Inc.; Consystant Design Technologies, Inc.; EKOS Corporation; Koronis Pharmaceuticals, Inc.; Micronics, Inc.; Numinous Technologies Inc.; Point of CareWare; and Therus Corp.

Zone Ventures

241 S. Figueroa, Suite 340
Los Angeles, CA 90012
213-628-2400   fax: 213-628-2433
www.zonevc.com

David L. Cremin, Partner

total assets under management	*initial investment*	*year founded*
$135 Million	$500,000–2 Million	1998

Based in Southern California, Zone Ventures is a venture capital firm investing in early-stage information and Internet technologies. Zone Ventures provides more to its portfolio companies than capital. A start-up venture capitalist should become a company's financial strategist, headhunter, investment banker, and corporate "therapist," providing support and confidence to a fledgling management team. The investment advisers and strategic investors who make up Zone Ventures can assist management in solving problems that may face a small company.

Zone Ventures is a partnership funded by institutions for the purpose of providing equity capital to young companies. Its objective is to finance capable people whose ideas and talents can lead to exceptional growth in sales and profits. Zone Ventures will work closely with its investors to fund new businesses largely in the Southern California region.

Portfolio Companies: estyle, Inc.; gowarehouse, Inc.; Hiwire, Inc.; showbiz-data.com; and Zkey.com.

PART TWO

Insider Secrets and Tools You Can Use

The 10 Things a Company Needs to Do to Get Venture Capital Funding

BILL STENSRUD AND DAVID LEE

There was once a time when every waiter in Hollywood seemed to have a movie script for sale. These days, the same waiter is also a would-be New Economy entrepreneur who has a business plan in the trunk of his car. The New Economy has brought out the entrepreneurial spirit in nearly everyone.

However, of late the bull market in venture capital has certainly cooled. Venture capital firms are more selective than ever in picking start-ups they choose to fund. As the oldest venture capital firm in Southern California, Enterprise Partners has heard and read thousands of business plans and proposals. While some plans have promise, most fail because the entrepreneur does not understand what venture capitalists (VCs) look for. And these aren't necessarily things you'll find in an MBA textbook on how to write business proposals. What type of entrepreneurs do we like and what exactly do we look for in proposals?

We like entrepreneurs who have researched what they need besides money. Venture capital money is essentially a commodity. Money from one VC is basically the same as that from another VC. The difference between VCs rests on what, in addition to the money, a particular VC can bring to the table. We like proposals that reflect what the entrepreneur already knows he wants from the VC.

In this day and age of trendy venture capital, there is some confusion about what type of funding would be truly useful to the entrepreneur. Because of the high returns on investments among venture capital firms during the past few years, VCs of every type and size are popping up everywhere. Stereotypes and misconceptions abound regarding the definition of venture capital. Many entrepreneurs do not realize that there are actually different kinds of VC firms, from Angel to institutional to corporate VC firms. In general, if your firm is just getting started, Angels investing sums of less than $1 million are ideal. If your company is already off the ground but needs long-term strategic help and successful former entrepreneurs who can bring knowledge and experience to your venture, then go find an early-stage institutional venture capital firm. Some firms, however, such as Enterprise Partners, will also fund early-stage ventures that fundamentally change or create industries.

VCs prefer business plans that have been referred or filtered by a known professional. We therefore like entrepreneurs who have consulted with their local professional service providers (lawyers, accountants, public relations agencies, etc.) who deal regularly with the VC community. Competent professionals in these fields know which VC firm might work well with the entrepreneur. In particular, they know which VC firm would be the best fit, personality-wise, with the entrepreneur. We work with entrepreneurs for two to three years to build foundations for long-lasting businesses, so it's critical that a good chemistry exists between the entrepreneur and VC.

Once you have done your homework, how do you get VCs excited about your business proposition? Here are our top 10 suggestions.

First, the fundamentals:

Define your business in terms of *precisely who is going to buy and precisely why.* Who are your customers? Why will they buy your product or service? This is so fundamental that it is surprising how often corporations, big and small, get it wrong. Cool products and great technologies don't create great businesses. Innovative solutions create great businesses when they solve real problems facing real people.

Target a *rapidly growing market.* Market growth creates an ecology where it is much easier for a well-run and focused business to thrive. Real examples of customer opportunities and specific needs are much more interesting than a consultant's projections of market size.

Offer a *compelling differentiation* to your customer. Why is your product or service significantly better than other solutions and competitors? The noise level is very high and you have to be able to rise above it. Be able to explain this compelling difference simply and in very few words.

Possess a *sustainable advantage.* It is hard to innovate and easy to emulate. Why is your business hard to copy? Great business models are sticky with the customer, making switching costs high. They also build barriers to competitors with technology that is strongly patented or with products or businesses that are hard to build and therefore copy.

Commit to *management excellence.* Great people create great businesses. Start-ups are not the place to learn a new job. Are you, the founder, the right CEO? If not, are you anxious to relinquish the CEO position to someone who has the skills and experience to help you build a great business? Are you committed to work with your investors to build the best possible team to make the business successful? Either way, make it clear so that there are no misunderstandings.

Do something you love. Many people are stuck in businesses they feel no passion for. Others are doing it just for the money. Smart VCs look for entrepreneurs who are committed to their vision, will plow through the obstacles, and get it done. VCs can sense entrepreneurs' passion and excitement. These are the entrepreneurs who will succeed and these are the people VCs want to partner with.

Build to last. The "build a business and sell it" model will not be funded by a quality venture firm. If it doesn't sell, you have nothing. The company's business model must stand on its own. If you build a great company, it may get acquired, but it will be your choice, on your terms, and at a much higher price.

Second, the tactics:

Perfect the *elevator pitch* (the executive summary). Imagine you find yourself in an elevator with your prospective investor and you have 10 floors to capture attention. Can you create a compelling summary of your business opportunity within 60 seconds or in less than one page? And do it without using the words *leading* and *premier?* Dump the jargon. Don't explain that the Internet is growing, that more people are conducting business on the Net, or that communication speeds are increasing (you simultaneously waste your prospective investor's time and insult his or her intelligence). Get to the point!

Target your investors. Money is available, but an investor should bring more than that. Acquire and show knowledge of the targeted VC firm, its successes, and its specialties. How can the targeted VCs bring their expertise and entrepreneurial experience into play? Why is your opportunity a good fit for them? Why can they help you succeed?

Cultivate high-profile affiliations. Get Cindy Crawford on your board (I actually got a plan with this claim. I read it!). All kidding aside, eStyle got a lot of media attention when it signed Cindy as its spokesperson last year. Celebrities can bring visibility, good advice, and introductions to important partnership opportunities. In addition, few business plans get funded unless referred by someone known and respected by the VC firm.

There is no magic formula for getting a business funded. If you have a great business opportunity, solid people, and an indomitable will, you will succeed. Remember, VCs are as interested in the person bringing in the business as they are in the business itself. Both parties need to know that each will adjust to a virtually guaranteed shift in the industry and will have the resolve and resources to see the entire venture through. For entrepreneurs, it means being able to bank on VCs who have enough funds and previous successful experience, and to depend on them when things are not going well. For VCs, it means backing seasoned veterans and passionate, determined founders. Good VCs, however, recognize that every successful entrepreneur needs to be a first-time entrepreneur at some time, and these firms will back high-energy individuals with compelling visions on a selective basis.

One outcome worse than not getting funded is getting funded when you shouldn't. Spending three or four years of your life working 100 hours a week on a poorly conceived business that ultimately fails is a great learning experience, but it isn't much fun. A good venture partner will not only provide money. He is a good test of the quality of your business opportunity and, when you get funded, your investors should be great partners in helping you succeed.

In the end, with all that's happening in the market, entrepreneurs should be looking to create long-term value through cutting-edge, proprietary technology or a uniquely compelling business model. To do justice to your business idea, it is important to have the commitment to seek a VC partner for more than just the "event" of funding.

BILL STENSRUD
General Partner
Enterprise Partners Venture Capital
As an individual investor, prior to joining Enterprise Partners in January 1997, Bill Stensrud served as an adviser to a number of venture and LBO investment firms and made two significant personal investments into what became three multi-billion dollar companies: Juniper Networks (NASDAQ: JNPR), Paradyne Corporation (NASDAQ: PDYN), and GlobeSpan Corporation (NASDAQ: GSPN).

Since joining Enterprise Partners less than three years ago as a General Partner, two of Bill's portfolio companies have gone public, including Rhythms NetConnections (NASDAQ: RTHM), which he founded, and Packeteer (NASDAQ: PKTR). These companies have a combined market capitalization of over $4 billion.

DAVID LEE
Senior Associate
Enterprise Partners Venture Capital
David Lee joined Enterprise from McKinsey & Co. and the Leo Burnett Company, where he spent over six years developing and implementing strategic plans and marketing programs for start-ups. Mr. Lee holds a bachelor of arts degree from Harvard University and a master's in business administration from the University of Chicago's Graduate School of Business.

Angels on Earth
Seeking Venture Capital from Private Investors

JOE SULLIVAN

Every entrepreneurial company requires cash. With most businesses, the faster the growth, the greater the need for funds to build infrastructure, fuel a sales force, and finance inventory and receivables. A typical technology start-up may go through five stages of raising equity capital:

1. *Personal cash and credit* from the founders' own pockets. In most cases, this is only enough to pull together a team of volunteer helpers, test a concept, and write a business plan.
2. *Friends and family* are the next source of capital, after the entrepreneur has maxed out personal credit and turns for help from close personal contacts.
3. *Angel investors* are experienced, sophisticated individuals who invest in early-stage companies. Some will invest as early as "two people with a dog and a plan." Others want a proven concept and the beginnings of a management team. Angel money is employed to complete product development, fill out the management team, and begin market introduction.
4. *Venture capital funds* are professionally managed partnerships that invest institutional risk capital. Professional venture firms are most likely to invest after a company has proven a market need, demonstrated its product or service performance, and built a management team.
5. *Initial public offering* is when capital is raised on the public markets. Few companies reach this stage. Unsuccessful companies fall by the wayside. Successful companies are more likely to be acquired than go public.

ANGELS IN AMERICA

At the end of the 20th century, the boom in venture financing was remarkable. Research firm Venture One reports that venture capital firms invested $37 billion into 3,153 companies in 1999. In the first six months of 2000, venture firms invested another $35 billion in 2,138 companies.

Less recognized or documented is the amount of money invested in start-up companies by private Angel investors. Professor Jeffrey Sohl, Director of the University of New Hampshire's Center for Venture Research, estimates that 2 million Angels are in the United States, of whom 400,000 are active in a given year. Together, they invest $30 to $40 billion into more than 50,000 start-ups each year. In other words, Angel investors fund at least 10 times the number of companies funded by professional venture firms.

The typical Angel is a successful business owner or entrepreneur who has built substantial wealth. He is motivated by wanting to stay current with new concepts or technology, a desire to help others succeed, and the opportunity to be on the ground floor of an exciting new venture. The Angel is probably very experienced in a particular field and regards himself as a sophisticated investor. This person may limit his start-up investments to a particular area of expertise.

Angel investors must usually be "accredited" within the meaning of the securities laws. An "accredited investor" must have an annual income of at least $200,000 or a net worth of at least $1,000,000. This "accreditation" is self-declared. That is, at the time of the investment the investor will be asked to certify his eligibility to the company.

Angel money does not travel. Experienced Angels know that time follows money. Entrepreneurs will require time for advice, counsel, and oversight. Since venture investing is a side activity, the Angel doesn't have the time to travel to stay in touch with his investments. So your Angel prospects are likely to be local.

WHEN TO LOOK FOR AN ANGEL

Outside investment in your company is appropriate when:

- You plan to build a substantial business entity with the objective of creating liquid wealth for yourself, your management team, your employees, and your investors.
- You need cash to develop the business.
- Your company is not ready or suitable for institutional venture financing.

- You have tapped out your own resources, as well as those of your family and your friends.
- You have an "elevator pitch," a business plan, an executive summary, and an investor presentation.
- You have planned at least six months to find this new funding.

How Is an Angel Different from Friends and Family?

Friends and family who invest in you do so to support your effort. They probably do so without making an independent judgment about the risks. Their assessment of your entrepreneurial skills is not likely to be objective. They may expect to be very involved in your business, for better or worse. They may be willing to remain indefinitely as a minority shareholder and will probably not be sophisticated enough to think about potential exit strategies.

An Angel investor will likely make a more independent assessment of your business's potential and of whether your management team has the requisite background and skills to exploit the opportunity. The Angel investor needs to see a likely exit strategy and/or a liquidity event such as an acquisition or public offering that will return the investment 100-fold.

How Is an Angel Different from a Professional Venture Capitalist?

Venture capital funds are formed with the specific purpose of investing other people's money in entrepreneurial companies, often with a specific industry focus. Venture firms see myriad business plans from which to pick and choose. Professional analysts and managers work full time evaluating these opportunities, conducting due diligence, and making investment decisions in concert with their partners.

The Angel decision to invest is very personal. The Angel is investing personal discretionary funds that could otherwise be used to take a cruise, buy a car, or speculate in the stock market. Angels are investing funds that can be lost without jeopardizing their kids' college education.

Individual investors do not have a wide range of opportunities or the time and resources to conduct thorough due diligence. Angels tend to invest in groups, along with friends or associates whom they trust. They plan to spend time with the company, so they invest in local opportunities. Angels like to be involved in the venture in some way, as a Board Member or adviser, for example. They are looking for psychological and emotional rewards, as well as the financial return of being involved with a winner.

THE ANGEL'S APPETITE: SIZE OF INVESTMENTS

An entrepreneur who needs $250,000 to $1 million to achieve significant milestones in the development of his business is a likely prospect for Angel financing.

There are occasional "Archangels" who invest $1 million or more in individual companies. Sometimes small investors may invest $10,000 or so. However, the common size of an individual check is $25,000 to $50,000. A $1 million round may be "led" by an individual providing $250,000 to $500,000, with the balance being made up by smaller investors.

It is extremely difficult and time-consuming to raise more than $1 million from individual Angels unless you already have an extraordinary track record and a gold Rolodex. If your plan calls for more than $1 million in initial outside equity, you should consider breaking your development into phases, where the first significant milestone can be achieved with less money.

DRIVING THE INVESTMENT DECISION

Angels invest in things they understand. The most likely investors in your new business are people who are already familiar with your industry. For example, a hotel reservation service raised over $1,000,000 from hotel owners. A health records organization raised significant equity from independent insurance agents. A company developing software for the printing industry found its seed capital from print shop owners.

As with venture investors, Angels will evaluate your business concept, the size of the market opportunity, the management team, the probability of finding continued financing, and the likely exit strategy. At this stage the investor does not expect you to have all the answers. She will probe, however, to see if you have asked yourself the appropriate questions.

Venture capitalists are often quoted as saying that they would "rather invest in an A team with a B idea than a B team with an A idea." They know that the original business concept will change with time. The management team needs to be smart and experienced enough to respond quickly to changing conditions.

Angel investors, on the other hand, are likely to put more weight on the concept and less on the management team. In screening an opportunity, I ask myself:

- Do I understand the problem you are addressing?
- Would I buy your proposed solution?
- Do I believe you can make it work?
- Am I convinced you have a profitable business model?
- Do I feel that I understand the competitive environment?

- Do I think the founding group has a chance of pulling this off?
- Can I foresee likely sources of follow-on funding?
- If successful, can I foresee a liquidity event? Is this a company that is a likely IPO candidate? Can likely acquirers be identified?

RETURN ON INVESTMENT

The Angel investor is already making a fair return on other investments in the stock market, in real estate, or in her own business. Angels' participation in start-ups is high risk and should be high reward. The investor often doesn't rigorously analyze rates of return since she knows that any financial projections are a gamble. She is looking for the potential "big hit," the "home run," the "jackpot" that brings not only a high financial return but also significant bragging rights.

Your Angel does not want to be a long-term minority investor in a privately held company. You must have a plan to create liquidity through sale of the company or an IPO at an appropriate early date. If you cannot show the potential for a return of 10 times the investment in less than five years, you are probably not in a strong position to attract outside investors.

ADDED VALUE OF ANGELS

The sophisticated Angel will evaluate the resources required, in management and money, to get the company ready for the next round of financing. Along with money, the investor can help the company fill any holes. For example, the right investor can help recruit team members; refer customers, suppliers, or professional service firms; and introduce follow-on investors. In an ideal situation, the entrepreneur should look to the lead Angel investor as a trusted adviser and coach.

PREPARING YOUR INVESTOR PRESENTATION

Before seeking outside investors, you should prepare the following material:

1. *Your "elevator pitch."* This is a provocative and concise concept description that can be delivered in less than a minute over the phone, on the golf course, or as the lead sentence in an e-mail. An example might be: "I am a former marketing executive for Big Pet Food Company. Did you know that owners spend $6 billion a year on food for their pets? In my new company I have partnered with a veterinary nutritionist to sell a proprietary line of weight-loss products for dog and cats. We are seeking $500,000 in equity to complete product development and finalize a distribution contract with Petsmart."

The purpose of the elevator pitch is simply to generate further discussion.

2. *A business plan and executive summary.* The executive summary should include a detailed schedule for use of the Angel funds and a timeline with a list of benchmarks to be achieved.

3. *A computer graphic presentation* (such as PowerPoint) to lead prospective investors through the main points of your plan. This presentation should take no more than 20 minutes.

4. *A term sheet,* prepared with the help of your attorney, that will cover the main points of the valuation and terms you seek. It is not necessary to prepare complete deal documentation until you have an agreed-on term sheet with a live investor.

How Do I Find Prospective Investors?

Not all of us know people who have the wealth and interest to be Angel investors. However, we all know people who *know* these people. This is a synergistic situation. You need introductions to suitable investors. By the same token, these investors are likely to consider your opportunity only when it has been referred by a trusted source.

A rich source of referrals will be people with whom you have worked. They know your level of skill and enthusiasm. They may already know something about your business concept. Organize a campaign to tell all of your contacts about your new business and your need for capital. Ask them directly for introductions to likely investors.

Your attorney and accountant should be able to introduce you to prospective investors. If not, it is time to get a different attorney and accountant. Well-developed informal networks of entrepreneurially oriented attorneys, accountants, bankers, and other service providers are active not only in Silicon Valley but in mid-size technology centers such as San Diego, Portland, Austin, and Charlotte. In less-urbanized areas, these informal networks revolve around service clubs (such as Rotary, Kiwanis, and Lions) and even country clubs. It takes just one successful contact to penetrate these networks.

Don't overlook investors who have turned you down. After thanking them for their time and interest, ask if they know of anyone else who might want to see your opportunity.

What About Nondisclosure Agreements?

The search for money is an almost endless round of meetings and presentations. The entrepreneur often worries that disclosing the business idea will make it vulnerable to theft. This concern is sometimes addressed by asking a potential investor to sign a nondisclosure agreement (NDA).

Sophisticated investors will not sign NDAs early in an evaluation process. It is not reasonable to expect the person with the money to take on some vague liability for the privilege of meeting with you and considering an investment in your company. Only a naive entrepreneur sees value in an idea. The experienced investor realizes that value is created in the execution.

It is appropriate to ask for an NDA when a serious investor needs a detailed briefing on your proprietary technology or business practices.

How Long Does the Process Take?

Raising Angel capital is time-consuming, pick-and-shovel prospecting work. There is no good substitute for face-to-face meetings between the entrepreneur and the prospective investor. The objective of the first meeting is to get the second meeting, the second meeting to get a third, and so on, and on to close.

I have known entrepreneurs who reached their funding goals in four weeks, and others who are still looking after 12 months.

A prudent entrepreneur will plan for this process to take an average of 20 hours a week over the course of six months, from the completion of the business plan to the close of funding.

What Does a Typical Angel Deal Look Like?

The primary objective of the entrepreneur and the investor, when negotiating legal terms, should be to facilitate the later sale of equity to new and larger investors.

In technology companies, the standard instrument for an Angel financing is usually a "Series A Convertible Preferred." This preferred stock is converted to common stock on a 1:1 basis at the time of a future venture financing, a sale of the company, or a public offering. The stock will have a liquidation preference over the founders' common stock. It may accrue dividends, which are not paid in cash but are included when converted to common.

An alternative that has become popular in the last few years is a convertible debt instrument. This debt converts to equity at the time of a future venture financing, with the debt holder receiving a discounted conversion price or warrant coverage to recognize the risk of the earlier investment. Neither side expects the principal to be repaid—the company will either find additional funding that causes the note to convert or will fold without assets to cover the debt.

For a variety of reasons, convertible debt is less attractive than straight equity to the sophisticated investor.

VALUATION

Valuation refers to the imputed total value of all of the company's outstanding stock. Valuation determines the percentage of the company you must sell to bring in a given amount of investment. It is calculated by the percentage of equity you sell to an investor and the amount the investor pays for the equity. The value is set by negotiation between a willing seller (the entrepreneur) and a willing buyer (the Angel investor). While there may be rules of thumb on start-up valuations, it would be misleading to publish any guidelines because transactions will vary with the characteristics of a particular opportunity, the geographic location of the company, the environment on Wall Street, and the whims of investor fashion.

Valuation is usually discussed as "pre-money" or "post-money." The algebra involved is circular but simple. For example, if an investor agrees to invest $200,000 for 20 percent of the issued equity, then the total post-money valuation of the business equals $200,000/.20 = $1,000,000. The pre-money valuation, then, was the total post-money valuation ($1,000,000) minus the new money ($200,000) = $800,000. The per-share price for the new investor is calculated by dividing the total post-money valuation by the total number of shares outstanding after the financing. Continuing the previous example, if there were 800,000 shares issued to the founders before the investment, and the new investor received 200,000 shares, then the total number of shares outstanding would be 1,000,000 and the per-share price would be $1.

The price agreed on in a term sheet is usually reached by negotiating the pre-money valuation and the amount of new money to be raised. The actual calculation of shares issued and share price can be determined in the preparation of final deal documents.

In ideal circumstances you will find a "lead" Angel—one who is enthusiastic about your company and able to fund a major portion of the money being raised. You hope to avoid negotiating with several parties by agreeing to price and terms with that lead Angel. That is then presented to following investors as the agreed-on term sheet.

While it is theoretically possible for an entrepreneur to negotiate valuation with competing investors, I have never seen that work in practice. For one reason, it is the fortunate entrepreneur who has even one enthusiastic prospect. For another, your prospective investors will want to talk to each other during the due diligence process.

HOW WILL THE INVESTOR BE INVOLVED IN MY BUSINESS?

A good Angel brings more than money to your business. She can bring valuable advice, important contacts, and friendly support. To avoid misunderstandings, you should try to be clear on your mutual expectations early in your relationship.

When you have taken other people's money, it is time to organize a formal Board of Directors. Individual investors or groups of investors may expect a Board seat. This should be negotiated before closing the transaction.

It may be advantageous to organize an informal Board of Advisers. These are investors and other individuals who do not have the fiduciary responsibilities of Directors but who agree to make themselves available to help when appropriate.

At the very least, the CEO should plan to send monthly progress updates and quarterly financial reports to all investors.

ANGEL AT YOUR TABLE

In summary, Angel investors are local, wealthy individuals who might be induced to invest money, time, and advice in your start-up business. Finding and wooing potential investors involves a serious marketing campaign that should be undertaken with forethought and preparation. Preparation includes seeking counsel from an experienced attorney and a qualified accountant.

An Angel investor can become an important resource as the management team wends its way through the ups and downs of building a successful business. The proper Angel will patiently continue to support your drive toward success. Even after a liquidity event, in which investors may cash out, the Angel will continue to be with the company in spirit.

JOE SULLIVAN
Founder of Flextronics
Angel Investor

Joe Sullivan was a Founder of Flextronics (NASDAQ: FLEXF), a manufacturing services company headquartered in Silicon Valley that serves the computer, telecommunications, and medical device industries. Since his retirement in 1993, he has been active in the Southern California entrepreneurial community as a private investor and adviser to early-stage technology companies. He has recently organized the Aztec Venture Network (LLC), a group of Angels that invests in start-up opportunities.

Sullivan is a noted speaker and Founding Director of the Entrepreneurial Management Center at San Diego State University. He is a graduate of San Diego State University and the Harvard Business School.

From Seed Round to "C" Round

The Early-Stage Build-Out

WADE H. BRADLEY

Creating a start-up company is one of the most exciting events in an entrepreneur's life, although selling it for millions is just a bit better. The key in getting a start-up from A to Z is in building the foundation and guiding principles that will launch your enterprise. The following sections illustrate several of the key areas that our entrepreneurs have most benefited from while creating their start-ups.

CORPORATE STRUCTURE

One of the first important decisions an entrepreneur needs to make when forming a start-up is whether to incorporate. Generally, the most viable location is Delaware, for several reasons. First, Delaware corporate law is very favorable for growing companies and for companies wanting to go public. This market attractiveness has led multitudes of U.S. companies to incorporate in Delaware, while headquartered elsewhere.

In addition, in the course of due diligence, most Angel investors and venture capital firms (VCs) hire top-tier law firms, the vast majority of which are familiar with Delaware corporate law. Furthermore, registering as a Delaware firm has the added advantage of reducing the amount of resources used to research corporate laws in other states. Generally, it is more difficult, time-consuming, and expensive to ascertain the corporate laws of each individual state in the nation for a West or East Coast Angel or VC.

When incorporating, always file as a standard "C" corporation. It is never a good idea to incorporate as a limited partnership, limited liability company, S-Corp, and so on. These flow-through corporate entities were primarily designed to take advantage of large capital losses that would occur during very long periods of research and development prior to a company being able to have a liquidity event. Companies today, though, have dramatically different abilities, in which start-ups have the ability to merge, be acquired, or go public at unprecedented speeds, all while operating with very substantial losses.

Avoiding these pitfalls will reduce time and other resources wasted in restructuring and unnecessary resources spent on due diligence. Furthermore, such structuring will expedite the potential of investors coming on board and can shorten your start-up's time frame for a liquidity event to occur.

DILUTION AND GROWTH

Before beginning your capital formation, you should take several steps to eliminate any surprises regarding dilution. You can eliminate time wasted down the road, and worrying if you will have as much equity at the end of the day as you had wished, by initially structuring funding milestones that will feed your corporate milestones and vice versa.

It is important to design a funding model that takes into account an average of 30 percent dilution at each funding round, including seed, A, B, and C, or mezzanine. The initial capitalization table should be laid out so that the founder's equity and the employee stock option pool (generally 20 to 30 percent) are set aside. The stock option pool should have budget room for potential nonfounding CEO, CFO, and CTO personnel (approximately 5 to 7 percent, 3 to 5 percent, and 3 to 5 percent, respectively). In addition, advisory board members each generally receive option equity of 0.5 to 1 percent, with actual board members receiving 1 to 2 percent of the equity. All of this equity should be delivered under vesting agreements that stretch out over 24- to 36-month time frames.

After making these advised provisions, the founders will be in a better position to decide whether their start-up is actually ahead or behind the curve in their corporate and funding milestones and will have a clearer picture of the estimated retained equity at different stages of liquidity events. An important note to remember: As long as you're taking in sufficient capital to be able to increase your start-up's value by a greater percentage than that of the dilution caused by selling more equity, you are not necessarily causing dilution. Always question, do you want 100 percent of nothing or 10 percent of a $1-billion company?

VALUATIONS

When a company is funding its seed and early rounds with Angel investors, the process of valuing the enterprise can be quite difficult. First, many Angels, while they may be experienced entrepreneurs or seasoned industry leaders, are not experienced in valuing privately held seed- and early-stage start-ups. The simplest and oftentimes best approach is to have your investors fund your seed and even your "A" round via a convertible promissory note. Convertible notes speed the funding process along and reduce much of the investors' and entrepreneurs' anxiety by allowing the valuation to occur when the next round is funded, generally by the venture capitalists.

A convertible note is generally laid out with the following format: It should have the basic covenants for anti-dilution, right of participation (follow-on rights), liquidation preferences, optional and automatic conversions, voting rights, registration rights, and several protective provisions. As well, a convertible note usually carries a discount to the next round in the form of additional shares (i.e., at a lower price) or in the form of warrant coverage, with either option usually equaling 20 to 30 percent of the investment. Both of these scenarios take into account that the start-up is assumed to have another round of funding in a short to medium time frame (five to nine months).

Generally, the convertible note holder should also have some protection to be able to be priced into your equity at a reasonable level, in case your company is merged or sold out of the gate. Nobody wants to have a great liquidity event occur on an early success, only to have all of the Angel investors upset because they were priced at only a 30 percent discount to the sale price. Angels are not investing in start-up companies to realize 30 percent returns on successful corporate mergers and acquisitions. They generally look for a minimum of 10 to 100 times return on their investments.

Always work these basic rights into your convertible notes in case the business progresses faster than anyone had initially anticipated or the markets embrace your product or service more quickly and it becomes a hot sector, thus an additional round of capital will not be not needed. Also, your Angel investors are quicker to come onboard and to refer you to their friends if they believe that you are being fair and looking out for their best interests. When you have an initial idea, it is yours alone. However, when you sell equity in a company, your idea is owned by all of the employees and shareholders as one team. Treating your investors and employees as part of one team creates a winning start-up with great long-term potential.

EXPERIENCED LAW FIRMS

When looking for a law firm to represent your company, remember that you are both on parade. The firm wants to bring on a client company with a well-thought-out plan and an entrepreneurial team that will be able to raise the funds necessary to execute their plan. As long as you are executing and raising funds, the firm's account is being paid, and the equity you will probably give it to come on board is increasing in value.

As an entrepreneur, you need a firm with venture experience and you need a champion, preferably a partner in whom you will receive at least part-time attention and high-level document review. Services received from a partner should also include a developing and referring investor, a senior-level management team, and strategic partner introductions.

The present and future climate for technology is very strong within the United States. As such, entrepreneurs must be wary of law firms and attorneys that are trying to get in on the technology wave. Look for firms that already represent the local leaders and the hot up-and-comers in your community. If no firms fit the bill, then look to the Silicon Valley or San Francisco firms, or your nearest major city, and so on.

The worst thing an entrepreneur can do is to hire an attorney who is not up-to-speed on how Angel and venture capital transactions are formed and consummated. When you have only six months to be first to the market and need to complete two or three funding rounds in that time frame, you will find that there is absolutely no substitute for qualified and experienced legal counsel. In addition, investors are generally more comfortable working with experienced attorneys with whom they are familiar or have existing relationships.

AGGRESSIVE NETWORKING

Aggressive networking is one of the best ways you can build a viable start-up quickly. To begin networking, contact your local or regional technology organizations and get a list of their special interest groups (SIGs), finding those that you can gain benefit from. Start attending their meetings and attend often, while continuing to look for other SIGs that can deliver even more benefits. Many entrepreneurs find that attending these groups' meetings allows them not only to increase the amount of new entrepreneurs or engineers in their network but also to build out a wider circle of people to help problem-solve and brainstorm. In addition, it is a good idea to attend local business seminars and special Angel and VC events that tend to attract technical talent, entrepreneurs, and even Angel or venture capitalist investors. It is as important to build these networks as it is to build your business. Always look for the A-team players at every event, and when you find them, continually keep in touch. And most of all, remember this when networking: The more value you provide to your network, the more value your network can provide to you. It is definitely a two-way street.

VALUE-ADDED INVESTMENT PARTNERS

Smart money, not easy money, needs to be the entrepreneur's mantra. Everybody loves to close a round of funding, but more important, it is crucial to close a round of funding with at least several strong value-added partners. Value-added partners are successful entrepreneurs; key strategic advisers in marketing, finance, legal, sales, or operations; and if possible, strategic industry partners.

These value-added partners can bring a critical eye to a start-up enterprise that is generally hard to find within the entrepreneur's immediate inner circle, and this makes the value-added partner's worth much greater than his capital investment. Value-added partners have a "been there, done that" knowledge that can assist in propelling start-ups forward by avoiding common and not-so-common mistakes and by capitalizing on their already developed, comprehensive distribution and sales channels and moving new businesses at Internet speed.

Value-added partners also increase a start-up's credibility with co-investors, future investors, and venture capitalists. Each group wants to see this value-added partner in place and involved, as much as the start-up needs him or her. Having local entrepreneur heroes, respected consultants, and business leaders to draw knowledge from will create greater opportunities for success. Value-added partners will also lend much-needed respectability to a start-up, as local community members see that these individuals' belief is so strong that they are committing capital, time, and, more important, their names and successful reputations to helping the start-up.

DEVELOPING AN ADVISORY BOARD

An advisory board is as important to a start-up as its business plan. During the seed stages of a start-up, building a strong, viable board of advisers should be the focus. Choosing an advisory board is much the same as enlisting value-added investors, though some of the advisory board members may not actually invest until possibly later in the venture. As well, each advisory board member should receive an equal amount of equity in the venture. Generally, members receive 0.5 to 1 percent equity interest, and again, this should be vested over a 24- to 36-month period. The vesting of the equity makes it easier for the entrepreneur to ask for and get the most out of advisers and to push them to work on needed issues. Advisers who have connections with potential customers and partners, plus have entrepreneurial experience to help shape the company and its offerings and assist in the overall focus and direction of the company, can be absolutely invaluable.

BUILDING THE "A" TEAM

When building teams, it is crucial to hire only A-team players. The A team will cost more initially but should deliver far better results much more quickly by eliminating costly mistakes that experience often prevents. To find these players, once again, value-added investors and advisory board members should be utilized. In addition, your aggressive networking and your company's legal and accounting firms should also be used as resources. An A-team mentality should extend throughout the company's technical, sales and marketing, and management teams. One tremendous benefit of garnering an A-team is that many of the local and regional Angels and venture capitalists either already know that these individuals are of A-team caliber, or it will come out during due diligence. Literally, hiring these exceptionally qualified individuals who cost more, but deliver better service more quickly and build enterprises in Internet-time with the least amount of roads traveled twice, will also increase the potential of your start-up to raise additional capital faster. This will save a tremendous amount of time during your early rounds.

MONEY RAISERS

Hiring a firm that claims to raise money for entrepreneurs is generally not a good idea. One of the best tests of an entrepreneur is being able to close the first $1-million round from either Angels or venture capitalists. Either group of investors will lend confidence to the next round of investors, so that the entrepreneur will be able to close the next round as well. The more your investors are convinced that their round will close, the more likely they are to lend their backing, which increases your start-up's credibility and makes your funding cycle a self-fulfilling prophecy.

When raising capital for a small business, though it is definitely not recommended, entrepreneurs often find themselves in discussions with persons or groups that claim to raise money. Firms that charge up-front fees should be avoided. Successful investment banks and brokerage firms charge fees based upon the legal limits allowed by the SEC, generally 12 percent, and this should always be based upon the funds raised (performance-based). Remember that private groups or individuals wanting retainers or monthly service fees to raise capital are not the groups with whom you want to work. Most firms that operate with up-front fees and retainers are extremely unlikely to ever perform on your behalf, and they can waste a tremendous amount of your time. Firms that are professional and upstanding will take their fees on the back end in the form of commissions raised. Finally, make certain that any firm you consider for contracting is registered with State Securities offices and/or the National Association of Securities Dealers (NASD). There are no shortcuts to funding.

Every minute of every day an entrepreneur is born. If you take the time to walk a bit before you run, you will develop the endurance needed to potentially carry your team all the way to the finish line—if not the first time, then the next.

WADE H. BRADLEY
Founder and Managing Partner
EmpireVentures

Wade H. Bradley is a Founder and Managing Partner for EmpireVentures. Headquartered in Portland, Oregon, Empire Ventures provides seed-, early- and mid-stage investments and acceleration services to business-to-business software, Internet, and wireless infrastructure companies. Under his guidance, the EmpireVentures IT Fund I has completed 23 equity investments in the software, Internet, and wireless industries.

Mr. Bradley has more than 15 years experience in venture capital and investment banking and analyzing, as well as in directing equity investments in hardware, software, Internet, and wireless ventures. He serves on the Boards of several private companies. Mr. Bradley attended the University of Minnesota.

An Early-Stage Venture Capitalist's Perspective on Risk Management

Larry Kubal

From the first reading of a business plan through the sale or IPO of a portfolio company, a venture capitalist strives to recognize and understand the risks that may threaten the life of an investment. In pursuit of significant capital gains, significant risks are inherent in the types of companies in which a venture capitalist invests. The challenge for any VC is to identify and isolate the most significant risks in a portfolio company and mitigate those risks. In much the same way, an entrepreneur must understand and constantly assess the risks facing her company. The risk management framework outlined further on provides guideposts to navigate the risks inherent in building a business in our new, dynamic economy.

My thoughts on risk management are from the perspective of an investor in early-stage technology companies. I have been involved closely with the entrepreneurial process for the last 11 years as a founding partner of Labrador Ventures, a leader in start-up financings in the gap between undercapitalized Angel investors and the mega venture funds. These years of experience with early-stage management teams have placed me squarely in the entrepreneurial process in the lives of dozens of companies. The insights on risk management garnered from these experiences are applicable to both the investor and entrepreneur alike.

UNDERSTANDING RISK

The etymology of the word *risk* comes from French and Spanish origins for a "steep rock" and was probably first used in context among sailors. Risk is seen as something dangerous, something to be avoided lest one's ship be lost. In further reflection, I asked my 12-year-old daughter, whose concept of risk turned out to be the danger of getting caught doing something wrong! (Perhaps not so distant from a VC's when explaining to his partners why an investment floundered.) Finally, I remember an investment course that Professor Jack McDonald and Mr. Bob Kirby co-taught at Stanford University's Graduate School of Business in the early 1980s. These two gentlemen taught a concept of risk that spanned the spectrum from the rational/academic to the gut level/experiential— from complex calculations in the Capital Asset Pricing Model to racing Porsches on the European circuit.

In my experience, the concept of risk for an entrepreneur in a technology start-up tends to fall closer to the gut level/experiential end of the spectrum. The analogy of both the speed and the adrenaline rush of auto racing matches an entrepreneur's experience. The entrepreneur, like an investor, is reacting in real time and making decisions along the way to formulate an ultimate strategy. Experienced entrepreneurs and VCs are better sailors in these waters simply because they have been through similar waters before. They have internalized guidelines from past experiences to draw upon in their current situations. This is an invaluable context on which to base gut-level risk decisions. Absent direct experience, learning from others' experience is the best substitute.

I share Labrador's organizing principals on risk management, in the hope that they will serve as guideposts in the everyday entrepreneurial decision-making process. Labrador's risk-management framework and process have contributed to our success, helping us to consistently rank in the top quartile of performance of all venture funds. May what follows help you succeed and become a better sailor while successfully navigating the steep rocks of the entrepreneurial process.

DIVERSIFICATION

The cornerstone of reducing risk in any investment portfolio is adequate diversification among the individual components of the portfolio. This is the single instance where the VC's and entrepreneur's perspectives are divergent. While the VC builds a portfolio of companies, the entrepreneur is driven to build one. The single-minded focus and passion for growing a business into a major enterprise defines the entrepreneur. This concentration of risk for entrepreneurs places them in an inherently higher risk/reward situation than the VC.

Over the last 40 years, venture capital returns have averaged better than 18 percent annually, outpacing stocks, bonds, and real estate, according to Morgan Stanley. Over the past 10-, 5-, and 3-year periods, these returns have averaged greater than 25 percent, 46 percent, and 53 percent, respectively, according to *Venture Economics*. Even when the performance of the 25 percent worst-performing venture funds is analyzed, their portfolios do better than break even on average and return more than their limited partners' invested capital. The power of diversification achieved by investing in 15 to 25 companies has a significant impact on mitigating the risk associated with investing in a single company.

Much of the risk reduction derived from diversification is undone if the portfolio is too concentrated in a single company. While it is a venture capital truism to "feed your winners," undisciplined feeding can create the potential for disaster. Discipline is required because it is another venture truism that "today's winner can quickly become tomorrow's loser." Labrador Ventures has established an internal guideline that sets 10 percent of committed capital as the maximum investment in any one company.

Similarly, my partners and I diversify among types of companies and business models. In Labrador's 11 years we have seen great fluctuations among "hot" investment areas. As a result, we avoid concentrating a portfolio in B- to C-branded ventures, in advertising-based revenue models, or even in current favorites like wireless applications or optical networking components. We have certainly had investments in each of these, but our internal guideline is to avoid concentration.

DEAL FLOW

In order to achieve diversification across types of businesses and business models, deal flow itself must be both voluminous and varied. The quantity and quality of an investment partnership's deal flow are critical to its ultimate success. The capabilities of a VC in selecting investments and nurturing them after the investment has been made are a necessary, but not sufficient, requirement for a successful venture fund. A venture fund can invest only in those opportunities to which it is exposed. Accordingly, it is appropriate to consider the venture fund's deal flow prior to examining its strategies and tactics for making and managing its investments.

To give a little perspective, more than 3,000 investment proposals come through Labrador Ventures's offices alone on an annual basis. Over the last two years this flow has doubled annually. Not all of these deals match our selection criteria. The highest-quality portion of the deal flow comes from referrals made by other venture capitalists, other entrepreneurs, and service professionals in the venture business, such as lawyers, accountants, and incubators. In fact, almost 60 percent of our deal flow comes through these connections. From this deal flow, at least 1,500 of the business plans match Labrador's objectives well enough to receive a detailed review by one or more of the directors. Those that appear to be promising candidates for investment are invited to present their business plans to me or to one of my partners.

Figure 1 is a funnel diagram based on our past experience and represents the winnowing process employed by Labrador from receipt of business plans through commitment to invest. Out of the 1,500 qualified plans that get a serious reading, we expect to make 10 to 15 new investments per year.

As our deal flow, its quality, the intensity of the time-compressed technology market, and the number of investment professionals all increase, the number of new investments made per year also grows.

Before moving to the investment evaluation and selection process, it is important to consider those factors that increase the likelihood of strong, quality deal flow. Deal flow is correlated to the reach of the venture fund's network—both from the contacts of its partners and its base of value-added limited partners. Strong relationships with other venture capitalists generate a plethora of investment opportunities. In addition, building a portfolio of name-brand investments both heightens awareness of a venture fund within the venture capital community and attracts entrepreneurs who want to work with VCs associated with winning companies. Finally, Labrador has an Industry Partner Program composed of well-known and highly regarded management veterans with deep domain knowledge. Through their experience and networks, they increase Labrador's deal flow, expand the due diligence network, and assist with the business development of portfolio companies.

INVESTMENT AND RISK EVALUATION

The selection of an individual investment to include in the portfolio is a multi-stage process. The obvious goal of the process is to select the investment that

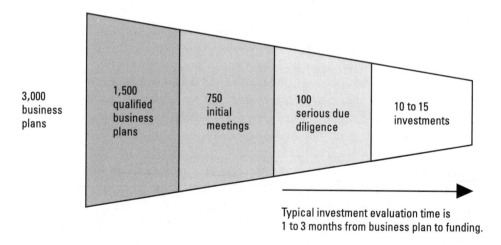

Figure 1 The VC Process

meets our investment criteria and objectives. The subcontext of the process is to understand and evaluate the risks of the prospective venture.

Every venture capitalist has an investment-screening process by which he reviews each and every deal. Following is a list of Labrador's investment-screening criteria:

While the management team does not need to be complete, the founders need to be committed, outstanding, creative, and resourceful individuals who are driven to build a major enterprise.

It is important that they can work together as a team and that they have clearly delineated areas of responsibility. Each member of the founding team must have a demonstrated ability to prioritize and a will to win. Personal characteristics of intelligence, integrity, and a strong work ethic are also necessary characteristics.

MARKET	The size and growth rate of the market are often crucial to a company's success and certainly have a major impact on the ultimate size of that success. As discussed earlier, a few outstanding investments will determine the degree of financial success of the fund. Accordingly, market size and growth characteristics are very important in the partnership's evaluation of an investment opportunity. Markets requiring regulatory approval are avoided.
PRODUCT/SERVICE	The product or service must be unique and serve a genuine need, cost-effectively, without requiring a significant behavioral change on the part of the purchaser or end user.
	The stage of development of the product or service is generally six months prior to revenues to one year after sales begin. Projects with a high inherent development risk are avoided.
	Service businesses that are personnel-intensive are not favored.
BUSINESS MODEL	The economics of the business must be such that (1) it is not capital-intensive and (2) it provides for high, sustainable gross margins. The combination of these two elements allows for a high,

BUSINESS MODEL
(continued)

internally sustainable growth rate, thereby reducing or eliminating the need for significant follow-on financing. These characteristics are also highly valued in the public markets or by potential acquirers.

Gross margins need to be at least 50 percent and in most cases should be greater than 60 percent. Their sustainability implies barriers to entry and a defensible advantage over competition.

For first-round investments, there must exist a reasonable business scenario for a return multiple of 25 within five years.

The business should ultimately be an attractive IPO or acquisition candidate. These should also be the desired outcomes of the founding team.

RISK FACTORS

The various risk factors confronting a start-up are very important to understand, whether from the perspective of a VC or as a member of the management team. VCs must understand these risks to assess which opportunities to pursue and then to effectively manage those opportunities once an investment has been made. Similarly, entrepreneurs need to be aware of the sharp rocks that stand between them and success. A keen and realistic understanding of a venture's risks also facilitates the fundraising process and serves to impress potential investors.

The structure of Labrador's risk evaluation is based on reasons start-up companies commonly fail. In this structure, the probability of one or more of these factors occurring constitutes the risk of the company's failing (i.e., the risk to the VC's investment). These risk factors or reasons for failure are categorized in Table 1.

Financial Risk

Financial risk arises after a VC has made an investment. Most early-stage companies fail because their expenses consume the cash invested and they are unsuccessful in attempts to raise additional capital. This often occurs because one or more of the previous risk factors has come to fruition. For example, the marketing risk: customers do not buy and revenues do not grow as quickly as anticipated. The company runs short of cash and cannot conclude a financing. Being out of money equates to being out of business and a loss of the venture

RISK FACTOR	DESCRIPTION	RISK MANAGEMENT: VENTURE CAPITALIST	RISK MANAGEMENT: ENTREPRENEUR
DEVELOPMENT RISK	Company unable to execute prototype with capabilities envisioned, on schedule, or within budget.	Development projects generally not funded—working prototype required.	Large company funded development, such as a spinout. Recruit an experienced and proven development team.
MANUFACTURING RISK	Quality, cost, or supply problems in quantity production.	Early production subcontracted to experienced manufacturer with similar products.	Same as VC. Recruit experienced manufacturing person as part of team.
SCALABILITY RISK	Architecture of service offering does not scale—latency, reliability, and security issues occur with volume.	Due diligence on technology assessment. Independent third-party simulation testing is important.	Same as VC. Ensure that CTO/System Architect has experience in constructing scalable solutions.
COMPETITIVE RISK	Well funded, more advanced, or larger competitor.	Due diligence interviews with competitors and their customers. Understanding of key differentiators.	Extensive competitive intelligence survey to gain understanding of competitors' economics, technology, and direction.
MARKETING RISK	Customers do not buy ("the dogs do not eat the dog food"). Market fails to grow or develop as anticipated. Revenues lag plan.	Due diligence interviews with beta users or customers. Analysis of analogous markets. Ventures that require user behavioral change to succeed are generally not funded.	Address a true customer need and focus on mission–critical applications—not merely enhancements. Design product or service from a user's perspective.
BUSINESS MODEL RISK	Business model does not work. Margins are insufficient: cost or price assumptions faulty. Costs too much to get customer, support customer, renew customer. Does not build enough value to meet return objectives.	Detailed analysis of the business plan assumptions as part of due diligence. Only ventures that are neither capital nor labor intensive and have high, sustainable gross margins are considered for funding.	Same as VC. Perform sensitivity analysis on assumptions and make conservative assumptions.
MANAGEMENT RISK	Founders not competent to build business. Cannot work as a team. Cannot delegate, inflexible, loss of drive. Goals different from investors.	Extensive contact with management team prior to funding. Analyze past experience. Check references. Structure deal to align objectives of management and investors.	Use extreme care in assembling the management team. Competence, flexibility, work ethic, and chemistry are all critical components. It is essential to spend time together prior to committing.
NETWORKING/ CONNECTEDNESS RISK	Founders not well connected in their business segment and, as a result, difficulties arise in recruiting and partnering.	Favor teams with domain expertise. Assess the network of the founding team. Labrador's Industry Partner Program.	Network, recruit domain expertise, choose VC and service providers with strong, relevant networks.

Table 1 Risk Factors

fund's investment. Because the management of financial risk is so crucial, venture firms take a number of specific actions to mitigate it.

Financial Risk Management

- Companies must have a business model that drives to revenues and shows a clear path to profitability. Therefore, the company's growth expenses are offset by revenues relatively early in its life.
- Cash must be ruthlessly managed. Most companies miss the projections and assumptions in their business plans. Usually, if revenues are slow to

materialize, the expense ramp must be similarly reduced. In most first-round investments, Labrador Ventures takes a Board seat and formally reviews the company's cash position, financial situation, and progress at monthly Board meetings.

- Often, venture funds will partner with another fund in the first round to spread the financial risk and to enlist other resources for follow-on financing.
- Funding contingency plans are always in place. When venture funds make an investment, an amount is typically reserved for follow-on financing.
- A VC must keep other potential venture investors informed of a company's progress to facilitate their inclusion in the financing syndicate of later rounds.
- Discipline is imposed against overpaying as a financing is structured. In a conscious and disciplined way, a fund will not overpay for its first-round investment. A VC's overall IRR (Internal Rate of Return) is very sensitive to first-round investment pricing. Partners have a very good sense of the marketplace, based on the number of deals they see.
- Typical terms in the structure of the VC's financings include many protections for an investment, including preferred stock with associated investor-friendly rights.

Clearly, many of these same ways of mitigating financial risk are equally applicable to entrepreneurs. In addition, entrepreneurs can take steps to assemble a team of solid financial investors. For example, a group of Angel investors may offer a high seed-round valuation but lack the financial stamina of a VC in later-round financings. In this case and others, company valuation is often at odds with the reduction of financial risk. The rule of thumb for the entrepreneur is very simple here: Always take the money and, when a choice is available, choose the strongest investors possible.

ACTIVE INVOLVEMENT WITH PORTFOLIO COMPANIES

Investments, especially early-stage investments, require nurturing. A VC must stay close to the development of portfolio companies, especially during the first few years, both to sound an early alarm should the enterprise get off course and to facilitate the company's growth. This close association commonly takes the form of a director functioning as an active board member.

Labrador's partners bring many years of business experience and, specifically, many years of working with small, high-growth technology companies, to their portfolio companies. We believe that we add considerable value and reduce risk through our guidance and assistance in policy-level decisions. VC's leverage their network of contacts to help a company with high-level introductions that are necessary for its success in business development, recruiting, and marketing. While a venture capitalist does not seek control of management, we regard management as our business partner in growing the enterprise. We strive to avoid involvement in daily operations. In addition, we endeavor to assemble the management team that can take the company to the next level. Finally, a venture capitalist actively assists in any successive financing required, often as both a participant and a link to additional investors.

From an entrepreneurial standpoint, founders must effectively leverage their investors for value-added assistance beyond capital. While founders are always actively involved in their start-ups, it is incumbent upon them to engage their investors in a productive partnership that reduces the risk of the venture for all.

LOOKING FORWARD

We live in a time of entrepreneurial excellence and energy. There is more capital available for technology start-ups than at any other time in history. Business opportunities to build major life-changing enterprises based on fundamental shifts in technology abound. While both venture capitalism and entrepreneurship are fraught with considerable risk, those who understand the inherent risks and can make good decisions under such pressure will have the greatest chances of building strong, profitable companies and of reaping the rewards at the end of their entrepreneurial journey.

LARRY KUBAL
Founder and Managing Director
Labrador Ventures
Larry Kubal is a Founder of Labrador Ventures and serves as a Managing Director of Labrador Venture I, II, III, and IV. Mr. Kubal has invested in early-stage technology companies for the last 10 years.

In addition to his investment experience, Mr. Kubal was a management consultant with Booz, Allen & Hamilton in its corporate strategy practice. He has also held an executive position with a venture-backed PC software company. He received his undergraduate degree from Duke University, *cum laude* with departmental distinction, and his master's degree in business administration from Stanford's Graduate School of Business.

How to Fund That Compelling Business Idea

ROBERT F. KIBBLE

It is said that venture capitalists (VCs) only invest in 1 or 2 percent of the plans that cross their desks. Given these long odds, the entrepreneur knows that the major challenge is to get the business plan opened, read, and seriously considered. From my experience, few plans are read from cover to cover, and fewer still are scrutinized in detail by the venture capitalist. This frustrates the earnest entrepreneur because the passion and effort that have been put into taking this major step toward entrepreneurship are rewarded in many cases with only a cursory read—and sometimes with scant acknowledgment.

WHAT YOUR PLAN SHOULD INCLUDE

So how do you get your plan more than just seen, but read? Here are a few pointers from my 20 years in the venture capital profession. Fortunately, these tips are not brain surgery; they are rooted in plain old common sense.

In writing your business plan, remember to act as a marketer. View the potential investor as your customer. Plenty of books and articles will tell you what to include in the plan and how to title the different sections. Here are some of the important elements and themes that you need to get across.

Executive Summary

Make sure there is an executive summary at the beginning of your business plan. Your VC is terribly busy (imagine that she is in a constant rush to catch the next plane) and is far more likely to spend time on deals that appear immediately appealing. Make your plan easy to understand. Draw attention to it with a pithy narrative summarizing its salient points. Here is an example of the points you want to get across in the executive summary. You might want to think of using subparagraph headings to make everything stand out:

- Describe, in one or two sentences, the vision and business proposition for the company—the so-called "elevator speech."
- Indicate the amount of money that you seek to raise and how long it is expected to last.
- Describe the product or service in a simple way that is understandable, while drawing attention to its uniqueness or proprietariness. Indicate the stage of development and the timing of when you expect to deliver it to the customer.
- Indicate the "value proposition" that you are delivering to the customer, and try to illustrate the magnitude of the economic benefit.
- Summarize the market size and scale of the opportunity, with a reference to competition.
- Management team: One- or two-line bios on the key founders and management are critically important. You must convince the investors that your team is uniquely qualified to deliver on the vision.

Mark Twain said that he would have written a shorter letter if only he had the time. For this reason, you must spend much time agonizing over each sentence in this executive summary. It represents the expression of your business vision and economic proposition. You might want to construct this after writing the rest of the business plan, even though it comes at the beginning.

Value Proposition

State right up front your value proposition. Lots of business ideas are clever, elegant, interesting, and useful but nevertheless are sure money losers. A new company has a lot of overhead to cover and probably competition to fend off. The selling proposition of the product or service must be compelling, by an order of magnitude over what exists today in the market—at least half the price or double the productivity of existing solutions is a good rule of thumb to use. Imagine what your salesperson would actually say in pitching the business proposition to the intended customer. Always start with the customer when imagining what the value you create will mean to the market. Is it compelling? If it isn't, save yourself the time (cost), and don't write another sentence.

Management

Some venture capitalists look no further than the executive summary and the section on management to decide whether to read the rest of the plan or visit the company. Put yourself in your client's shoes—that is, the venture capitalist's.

Would you want to back a group of people that does not have the relevant experience for the business proposition? Play "make believe" and ask yourself where you would find the best possible people for the business plan you propose.

If your own management team is not close to the "dream team" for the task envisioned, you can probably bet that your VC will reach that conclusion, too. Your team does not have to be complete; just a lone but brilliant engineer or an impassioned and articulate visionary will do.

In addition, you must be persuasive. You must be convinced you can attract the right people, even if you need the lure of the VC's money to get you there.

Finally, when it comes to management, a sense of passion and conviction about the business opportunity must be communicated in a compelling way, along with the team's ability to execute the plan effectively.

Market Dynamics

Venture capitalists generally prefer new, emerging markets for products and services—markets that are not large today but will be tomorrow. Aside from the obvious growth potential, emerging markets are attractive to VCs because a leader in a rapidly expanding market can often cover a lot of mistakes in execution. Be realistic, however, about market size, and make sure you understand the difference between potential and available market.

Competitive Barriers

Articulate how competitive barriers will be created and sustained. Devote serious time and effort to identifying actual and potential competitors. I have noticed that one failure entrepreneurs make is to compare their product or service of tomorrow with their competitor's product of today. Remember, usually your actual or potential competitors are not sleeping while you are developing.

In the United States there exists a plethora of talent across a wide range of industries. For many wishing to enter this culture, the journey from a novel idea to a coherent, compelling business plan can feel like a marathon. By taking into account the five tips outlined previously, you are one step closer to creating a business plan that not only gets read but that also maybe gets financed.

In the end, it is not so much the business plan that gets the company funded but the entrepreneur's ability to effectively communicate how he has the right team of people to capitalize on a rapidly emerging market opportunity. The business plan is only a tool that you will use to convince your funding source that you have thought through the issues.

WHERE TO GO FOR FUNDING

How does one decide where to go for funding? There are a number of options:

Self

Even that credit card can help in the boot-strapping process. The venture capitalist will be impressed if the entrepreneur invests an appropriate amount of his own capital.

Relatives and Friends

These are best avoided unless you are absolutely sure that later on you will attract the bulk of the money needed from other sources. Friends and relatives might forgive you for failure, but they might not feel so good if it is subsequently proven that you could not attract any less biased capital to the venture.

Angel Investors (Angels)

They will supply smaller amounts of money than perhaps venture capitalists would like to commit. So raising money through them might reduce the risk and enable the major money to be raised some time in the future at a substantial mark-up. The value of Angels varies according to who is involved—how committed, how well connected, and how helpful can they be? You want to be careful of the "fair-weather" friend investor, because even the best investments encounter a few squalls along the way. Unfortunately, it is not unusual to see a company financed by Angels at an excessively high valuation. While this can work out if the company is extraordinarily successful with the funds it raises, more normally it will pose a significant obstacle to future funding. If in a subsequent financing round, the venture investors can only do so in a "down" round of financing, this is a negative for the company. It can cause angst with the Angels who suffer the dilution, and it can be demoralizing to management. These two results might inhibit the venture capital investors from even choosing to get involved.

Corporate Investors

These are great for that strategic round. They can lend credibility and provide marketing channels and connections. Furthermore, they may be less valuation-sensitive because they are investing very often for reasons other than financial return. However, usually you cannot expect them to play a major role in helping to recruit management, and sometimes you cannot count on their participation in the subsequent rounds of financing. Some can be ideal candidates to buy your firm at a later stage of development, while others will have no future interest other than to be kept abreast of your latest technological advancements. You will want to have your hands relatively untied, allowing yourself the flexibility to sell the company to whomever in the future. So, it's best to bring these investors into that round when your product advantage is clear and you want to develop market momentum from your competitive advantage.

Venture Capitalists

We are the professionals in this field—we do nothing else except invest and help grow promising companies. We are used to the problems encountered by growing companies, and we want to support the investments so long as the business proposition is still achievable. Before you go to any one venture capital firm, check out its reputation, look at the investments it has historically made, and when you get really serious with the firm, check out references from other management groups funded by the venture fund.

Choosing a funding source should be approached with as much care and thought as choosing an individual to join the team. You will want to invite somebody to invest in your company who can provide the counsel and contacts that can help your company grow. It should not just be the money but a truly "value-added" investor whom you want. You have a long road to ride and the more help your investors can provide, the better. Invest the time in due diligence on your investors to make sure they are the right fit. Some considerations that you might want to keep in mind in approaching sources of capital are the following:

The Individuals Involved

Do these individuals maintain the values and character that are in line with yours? Are they people you trust, like, and respect, and with whom you want to build an enduring working relationship?

Track Record

What are their past investment successes? What companies and industries do they have experience in, and what public companies have they had in their portfolio?

Local Presence

Are they a local firm that can provide immediate value and attention as needed, with regional ties and resources? This can be essential if you want the investor to truly service a start-up and add value on a continual basis.

Focus

Does your company clearly fit the profile of the funding source's area of expertise? Is it also at the right stage? Some sources of capital clearly focus on later-stage funding, while others clearly desire to be the first institutional investor in the deal. Do you want a passive investor or an active lead investor, who will add considerable benefits besides money?

Network of Industry Resources

Are the investors able to leverage a strong network of technologists, CEOs, and business leaders to help you build your company? Can they assist in building the team, filling in gaps in the management, and finding key leadership? Can they sustain this commitment over the long term? If a future round of financing is needed, will they be able to contribute? Can they help provide deal leadership in bringing in new investors in the next round of financing?

One of the key issues to identify right at the start is, who will be your lead investor? The lead investor is the one who will commit to the largest participation in the financing. This person, or entity, will negotiate the term sheet with you and, once agreed upon, will help you sell that term sheet to other participants who might be needed to round out the investment syndicate. I have observed that one of the most frustrating situations for an entrepreneur is to spend countless hours with a potential investor, only to have that prospect finally say, "Well, I am interested. Let me know when somebody else commits, and, by the way, I am interested in a $500,000 piece." If you had been looking for a $5 million total investment, there is no way that a $500,000 contingency commitment will do very much for you until you find the lead. So the key is to find out from the outset how much your potential investors might be able to invest and if they can be a "lead." You need to focus all your efforts on the potential leads.

MATCHING THE FUNDING SOURCE AGAINST THE MILESTONES

First, as an entrepreneur, you must ask yourself before approaching one of these sources of capital: "How much money do I really need and when will I need it?"

By laying out a clear set of milestones that represents various stages of risk reduction, an entrepreneur can use these milestones as benchmarks to establish a premise for an effective financing plan. Simply put, one needs to identify how much in the way of equity funds will be needed before a "financable event" is reached. A financable event is that stage in a company's evolution by which sufficient progress has been made that substantial risk has been eliminated from the project. When this is achieved, you can raise additional equity funds by approaching new investors to fund the next phase of your plan—and, in all likelihood, at a higher valuation than the previous round. Examples of milestones that might constitute a financable event are:

- You have created a working prototype.
- You have rounded out the management with some stellar players.
- You have gotten the market to pay attention to your idea and you are now in beta test with initial customers.
- You have signed a major and meaningful strategic relationship with a major corporation.
- You have started shipping product and the backlog is building rapidly.

Once these milestones have been identified and the financing plan has been established, you can decide who is the best source of capital to help you reach the particular set of milestones identified. The best source of funds from those listed previously will probably be relatively obvious once you have identified the amount of money that will required to meet the milestone identified. Bear in mind that you should allow three to six months to raise the money, from the time you start the fund-raising process to when the money is in the bank. Your existing investors might bridge the company, but a bridge loan could put undue pressure on management, might make your investors nervous, and might weaken your negotiating position with new investors.

FIND A GREAT INTRODUCTION

Business plans that get financed are rarely those that just come in over the transom. "It's not what you know, but who you know" rings very true in the venture capital industry. I would encourage you to find a powerful introduction to a VC from a credible source. This will give you a "leg up" on all those other plans. Seek out strong recommendations from industry experts and technologists to support your plan. I am likely to be much more impressed if a well-known executive or technologist has committed to invest in your company, even if it is contingent on a venture capitalist putting in the "serious" dollars. The best such source is a highly respected person from the industry in which you intend to operate, somebody who believes in you and your business proposition.

ROBERT F. KIBBLE
Managing Partner
Mission Ventures
Robert F. Kibble is a founding Managing Partner of Mission Ventures, a San Diego–based early-stage venture capital fund with $280 million under management. Mission Ventures invests in

information technology, Internet, and business service companies throughout Southern California. Mr. Kibble was for 17 years a Founding Partner of a San Francisco Bay Area venture capital firm, Paragon Venture Partners, and prior to that he was Vice President of Citicorp Ventures Capital. Prior to Citicorp, he was an investment banker on Wall Street.

Mr. Kibble is a Director for a number of private companies and holds a master of arts degree from Oxford University and a master's degree in business administration from the Darden School, University of Virginia.

The Capital-Raising Process

Benjamin E. N. Blumenthal

In today's economy, an entrepreneur seeking capital must confront the daunting task of raising it from venture capital sources. Venture capital firms are inundated with business plans, some receiving up to 50 proposals a day. As a result, venture capitalists (VCs) will often review only business plans that have been referred to them by an existing client, a close banking relationship, or another accredited source. Direct and unsolicited submissions are often never read. Entrepreneurs who believe that forwarding their company's business plan directly to a group of venture capital funds will result in an investment are truly misguided.

THE NEED FOR A FINANCIAL ADVISER

For entrepreneurs seeking capital in today's market, there is a growing need to work with qualified financial advisers who are registered with the Securities and Exchange Commission (SEC). These advisers can act as a placement agent for private or public companies and leverage their existing relationships with venture capital funds to make personalized introductions on behalf of the company seeking capital. The advisers are charged with the tasks of ensuring that the documentation for submission is enticing and comprehensive; of making introductions to venture funds; of penetrating the intense screening process; of engaging in the rapid exchange of critical information; and of securing a meeting with management. At later stages, the financial adviser will assist in negotiating the company's valuation and will facilitate the due diligence process and related documentation.

SELECTING THE RIGHT FINANCIAL ADVISER

It is critical that an entrepreneur be certain that his financial adviser is experienced, well connected, and registered with the SEC as a National Association of Securities Dealers (NASD) broker-dealer, since raising capital is the result of selling securities. Companies encounter difficulties in the initial public offering (IPO) process as a result of security law violations in the early financing.

An entrepreneur should always look for an NASD broker-dealer who is confident of successfully raising the capital and is therefore willing to work on a success-fee basis without up-front fees. Typically, the terms of such an arrangement are a cash fee of 5 to 10 percent of the amount of money raised, warrants equal to 5 to 10 percent of the number of shares sold, plus the reimbursement of expenses.

There will usually be a specified "offering period" during which time an agent working on a success-fee basis will retain exclusivity over all investors in the financing, ensuring a monetary reward for his work. However, the company seeking capital will typically generate an exclusion list of investors with whom a dialog has already been established prior to the engagement of the adviser. If the investors on the company's exclusion list invest, the agent might receive a modified success fee, as his involvement was not instrumental in the raise. In all other instances, the agent will receive his full fee.

DOCUMENTATION

Prior to contacting any venture fund, a company must generate proper documentation. The typical business plan is not enough, nor is a slide show, nor is a company brochure. Venture investors must be able to quickly access specific information without having to filter through the ramblings of an entrepreneur, no matter how ingenious, articulate, or well inspired the business pitch sounds. The simple facts are that these venture investors receive hundreds of plans a week and, therefore, the business plan must be very concise yet complete.

A good broker-dealer will transform your business plan into a formal information memorandum or private placement memorandum, documents standard in the industry. Depending on the quality of your plan, your lawyer or your investment banker can rewrite and organize it fairly easily to conform to the standard documentation expected by the venture investor.

Typically, a four-page executive summary will summarize the memorandum. The executive summary will contain the following sections: company overview, description of product or service, market overview, competitive advantages, business strategy, investment considerations, management, summary of financial information, and proposed financing.

Finally, a comprehensive due diligence package must be compiled. An interested investor will ask for a complete history and background check of the company. This package must include all signed contracts, including employment, partnership, consulting, options, and warrant contracts, as well as fee agreements and all shareholder agreements.

THE PROCESS

Once the agent and the company approve the documentation, the process of raising the capital will begin. The agent's first step is the development of the prospective investor list. In order to avoid wasting time or money, the agent must be familiar with the investment focus and strategy of the venture funds. For example, a venture fund may have previously invested in early-stage technology companies, but after the decline in the Internet sector, the fund may have shifted its mandate to later-stage companies. A knowledgeable agent will be familiar with these nuances and can generate a highly targeted and focused list of qualified investors.

After the list of investors has been generated, the agent will send out an executive summary to all of them and will follow up with each potential investor. The list may be anywhere from 50 to 500 individuals and/or institutions, depending on the industry and developmental stage of the company, as well as the deal structure. The agent must penetrate the VC's screening process and ensure that the executive summary is seen and interest is accessed.

Once the agent contacts the venture investor, there is a rapid exchange of critical information. In this part of the process, the agent adds significant value to the company. Entrepreneurs are typically very emotional and passionate about the company and try to sell it, as they should. However, an experienced agent knows precisely what questions will be asked and how best to respond to them, not wasting any time.

For example, a VC might ask, "What does this company do again? I haven't looked at the deal. I'm swamped." An entrepreneur will begin to explain the company, the market, the competition, the opportunity, the projections, the management, the business strategy. A good agent will respond concisely to the question asked, knowing that the next five minutes will contain 10 more questions, all highly focused with the purpose of extracting only the critical information. At the end of those 10 questions and five minutes, the VC will have his answers and can make a decision if he wants to receive the memorandum, knowing that it will be structured in the same orderly and concise manner, delivering specific and targeted pieces of information. At that point, he may also choose to take a face-to-face meeting or set up a conference call. By contrast, after five minutes on the phone with an entrepreneur, the VC will still have many questions unanswered and may be out of time or patience. Remember, it is easier to say "no" and pass on the opportunity when the venture investor is flooded with financing requests.

Once a conference call is established or a face-to-face meeting is set up, the presence of an experienced agent is important. While management will give the investor presentation and answer all questions about the company, the agent can respond to questions regarding the financing. When the time comes to ask for $5 million dollars, entrepreneurs usually fumble that part. Professional agents do not. It's a matter of experience and practice.

Similarly, experienced agents know how to broach the subject of valuation. Calling upon comparable companies, influential factors in the industry, and similar recent financing in the market are all valuable tools that a good agent will use in the negotiation of a company's valuation. If the agent agreement stipulates compensation in warrants at a set price below the offering price, the company will have provided the agent with a strong incentive to negotiate the highest possible valuation, yielding the least dilution to the company's shareholders.

TIMING

Entrepreneurs usually want their money yesterday. However, realistic expectations are important for a successful financing. There is no set time period that a financing should take. If the market conditions are just right and the VC has just raised a new fund and the deal fits perfectly within the fund's mandate and all other factors fall into place magically, the deal should take four to six weeks to close. Typically, venture deals, especially early-stage deals, take three to five months to close, from the time that the first executive summary is sent to the closing. This does not include the time for development of the necessary documentation.

IN SUMMARY

By delegating the responsibility of raising the capital to an experienced agent, an entrepreneur can focus on business development and furthering strategic alliances in the industry, creating the essential pieces of good news to sweeten the deal once it is submitted to the VCs. Management will attend the meetings and should be prepared to reiterate all the recent good news and developments since the documentation was submitted. Management should also maintain steady communication with the agent, providing regular updates that are attractive to potential investors.

BENJAMIN E. N. BLUMENTHAL
Vice President
Bristol Investment Group, Inc.

Benjamin Blumenthal is the Vice President of Bristol Investment Group, Inc., responsible chiefly for analyzing new investment opportunities. Bristol Investment Group, Inc., is a private investment firm focused on investing in and assisting high-growth and special-situation companies in industries that include telecommunications, Internet, and new media. In addition to investing growth capital in both public and private companies, Bristol also provides strategic planning and merger and acquisition advice.

In 1997, Mr. Blumenthal founded Capital Guidance Systems, one of the first online venture capital forums dedicated to educating entrepreneurs in business plan development, identification of online market, and securing funds through venture capital groups and private investors.

Mr. Blumenthal studied at Oxford University in England and has a bachelor's degree from Emory University, with advanced studies in marketing.

The Venture Valuation Process
Arriving at a Value for Your Business

STANDISH M. FLEMING

When your innovative idea or high-potential business cannot grow without professional money, expertise, and guidance, then it's time to consider a partnership with the right venture capital firm. An initial round is usually one of the only times in the financing cycle when the entrepreneur must deal directly and often alone with a venture capitalist. In later rounds you can expect that your current venture backers will hold your hand in negotiations with other venture groups.

If you have an idea or an existing business for which you wish to pursue venture capital financing, this chapter is designed to provide you with an idea of what to expect from the valuation and partnering process. We address what kind of entrepreneurs and businesses are best suited to partner with a venture capital company and how to make the deal work.

GETTING STARTED

What can you and the venture firm expect from the valuation process? What are the basic rules of thumb that allow both sides to evaluate progress?

The process of establishing a valuation and concluding a financing should produce more than cash; it should bring the expertise and resources you need to grow your business in competitive markets. This expertise is bundled with cash from the VC community. The entrepreneur can make the job easier by understanding how and why venture firms make investments. As in any profitable partnership, the quest is to combine skills and strengths in true relationship building with a venture capital partner—not just to secure money—based on short-term valuations and expected cash flow.

What Is a Venture Capital Valuation?

A venture valuation is not a banker's fixed appraisal of your idea or company or an abstraction reflecting abstruse and intense calculations by a disinterested third party.

Venture valuation is an evolving process. It starts with the first meeting, culminates with the agreed-upon term sheet in the first round of financing, and then starts all over again when new financing is due. The serious valuation, arrived at in the context of "doing a deal," looks at potential value based on predicting growth, costs, milestones, and investment payoff. That's why judgment and industry experience are so important.

Evolving over the entire due-diligence review process, this "big-picture" valuation reflects the whole spectrum of opportunities, problems, and solutions. For its part, the venture firm will focus on assessing real-world risks and the potential rewards that benefit its shareholders.

If the process is successful, you and the venture capitalist will arrive at a valuation, the basis of which results in the VC acquiring a portion of your company stock. Exchanging stock for cash and essential resources is not the end but the beginning of a working partnership and a personal relationship, even a lifelong friendship. Properly shared, equity is a wonderful tool for aligning disparate interests and transforming otherwise separate parties into a coherent business team.

A warning is in order: Taking venture capitalists into your company (and life!) means you must now share ownership, management, and control. Your decisions, your time at work, and your company will never again be wholly your own. If you get the price and the partnership right so that the value received surpasses what you give up, then success and wealth come to you in perhaps 5, maybe 10 years upon a profitable exit.

If the deal is not properly done, the valuation can cause an entrepreneur huge disappointments and conflict with the venture firm and its partner.

Do You Need a Venture Capital Partner?

Whether venture capital fits your needs and situation depends on:

- How great your need is for high-level advice and financial expertise (especially professional management).
- What your long-term business goals are.

Do you still expect to control everything in 15 years, or are you looking forward to an IPO, strategic partnership, merger, or outright sale? If you don't need sizable amounts of money, expertise, networking, or help in exit strategies, you are better off without all the obligations and entailments that venture capital brings.

If you don't require more than $2 million over the life of the company, consider "boot strapping" with friends and family, mentors, industry sources, or Angels (private investors). Furthermore, if you want to leave the business to the kids or have the luxury of building a company over 10 or 20 years, venture capital is probably not for you.

WHAT BENEFITS DOES VENTURE CAPITAL BRING?

Although the previously listed sources are usually less expensive than venture money, they don't deliver the "value-added" benefits of a professional investment firm. There is only one reason to take venture capital: You'll make more money with it than without it. Venture money is very expensive unless it brings other critical resources, namely:

- Industry experience: to help clarify your vision, goals, and objectives.
- Networking: to access business services and support.
- Management consulting: to find personnel and provide capital, an IPO, or a buyout.
- Catalyst for growth: to enhance your overall ability to make things happen.

Of course, if the company fails, venture capital is a bargain, because you don't have to pay it back. Barring that scenario, the multiple, "value-added" benefits that you get with venture capital make it worthwhile. A good early-stage venture investor brings more than money to the table. Advice based on her experience with similar companies is the most valuable asset that an early-stage venture capitalist brings to portfolio companies.

Because many of the best venture opportunities arise from developing truly novel businesses, it may be difficult to find firms experienced in your specific technology. But good, early-stage venture groups are experts at doing what has never been done: creating new opportunities in new fields.

A core set of skills is required for all start-ups. If you can find a group with a track record in your industry, you should give these investment sources careful consideration. There is no substitute for hands-on experience, and reinventing the wheel can be expensive and time-consuming.

Second, venture capitalists should bring extensive networks that link an emerging company to essential services and support from all business sectors. When the company's resources are most constrained, its need for accurate and effective work by providers, such as attorneys, accountants, and technical and business consultants, is highest. The systems, the agreements, the relationships that are put in place in a business's first year of life set the pattern for all that follows. Major mistakes at this stage jeopardize survival.

Past and present portfolio companies and an endless flow of resumes provide venture capitalists with access to all kinds of experienced operating personnel to help propel a start-up. These can range form laboratory technicians and secretaries to department mangers and even CEO candidates.

Another important contribution from your venture partner involves access to additional financing sources to meet your company's ongoing capital needs. Above all, a venture capitalist regularly assesses a company's need for financial support and positions it to make the most efficient use of all the available resources in both private and public markets. Many venture capitalists are well connected within key industry segments and can provide access to important corporate resources. Few entrepreneurs can match venture capitalists' experience in negotiating corporate sales, partnerships, or buyouts.

In sum, an early-stage venture capitalist can accelerate development of a company to the point at which he and other private investors can realize liquidity through a buyout or an initial public offering (IPO). Because being first to commercial and financial markets provides a substantial premium for technology companies, time is the most valuable benefit you purchase with venture equity. As one well-known venture group summed up its strategy: "We want to invest in companies that can be first and dominant in a field."

Your venture partner will play a major role in achieving both of those goals.

SEED-STAGE VERSUS LATER INVESTORS

At this point it is useful to distinguish seed and start-up venture capitalists from later- and mezzanine-stage players. The differences involve the roles played, the kinds of contributions made, the risks taken, and the payoff expected. The seed-stage investor gets a project off the ground; the second group wants to gets on board after a business has been established with a credible management team.

The principal difference lies in how the venture groups invest their human capital. Both will conduct an extensive due diligence review, but the seed-stage investor uses that knowledge as the basis to make a significant investment of personal human capital.

Generally, as an active investor, Board Member, or even in a temporary operating role, the seed-stage investor contributes knowledge, skills, and time directly into your business to create value for all shareholders.

The later-stage investor may make a contribution through a Board seat or may provide informal advice and support, but the bulk of this person's human capital goes to personal education as an investor and not directly into the company. From another perspective, an early-stage investor takes a higher risk (greater uncertainty) for compensation in the form of a favorable (low) price. This investor also commits personal resources, or human capital, to reduce that risk for all shareholders.

STAGES AND RANGES OF VENTURE INVESTMENT

In seeking a venture partner, you should keep in mind the match between the funding required to complete your development plan and the appetite of different venture funds that make early-stage investments. The preferred level of overall investment generally correlates with the size of the venture fund. Though all but dedicated mezzanine funds do start-ups, focused seed- and early-stage funds tend to be smaller. They generally have less than $100 million in assets, with some under $30 million. These firms may commit up to 10 percent of the total fund value into a single investment, usually over two or three rounds of financing.

A typical initial investment format would be:

- $50,000–500,000 for a proof-of-concept investment.
- $500,000–1.5 million for a seed investment.
- $1–3 million for a start-up investment.

A company could move through these stages in succession or start at any of the three, depending upon the level of development of its idea. Total investment in the second round can range from $3 million to $15 million; third and mezzanine rounds could be from $10 million to $20 million.

Overall, an efficient biopharmaceutical company can require up to $30 million or more of private equity, plus a similar amount of corporate partnership money. Device and diagnostic opportunities require half that amount or less. Service companies such as physician practice management companies or contract research organizations require considerably less and generate corresponding revenues and profits at lower risk than technology development.

The only firm rule in every situation and through each stage is that the amount of money raised cannot be more than is justified by the expected payoff.

Choose the firm that suits your needs and style and shares your dreams. Finding the right match involves much more than taking the highest price per share. Try to secure balance in terms of size, industry knowledge, and business expertise from your investment partners.

DOES YOUR VENTURE CAPITAL PARTNER NEED YOU?

A venture capitalist's first question is, "Can your opportunity/business grow large enough to provide the returns I want?" Venture investors price their participation to achieve a target multiple of their money within their investment horizon. But the real aim is a "grand slam"—what one veteran calls a "ten bagger." This investment appreciates tenfold or more in value after the IPO, justifying all the work and all the risk in the entire portfolio.

Second, before putting any money in, a venture capitalist must know how to get it out. Whether it's a public offering, a merger, or a buyout that turns share value into publicly traded stocks or cash, no investor comes in the front door without anticipating a profitable way out. Using industry experience, market studies, and evaluation of the overall business strategy, top venture firms assess at the beginning both the upside potential and all exit opportunities.

A key purpose of due diligence is to determine how receptive you will be to the venture process. Will you make a good partner? Do you share a common vision? Will you embrace and advance your investors/Partners' agenda?

If you aren't willing to share authority and problem solving, if you are not forthcoming about all the details of your business, a venture capitalist will find someone who is. Life is too short to invest in a fistfight.

Venture Expectations

As the venture firm pursues its due diligence review, not only is the valuation likely to change, but the methodology evolves over time. The entrepreneur advances business and personal interests by understanding the venture agenda and what success means to both sides. In this light, consider the venture capitalist as a first customer, not for your product, but for your whole business.

What you are selling, first and foremost, must satisfy the investor's needs, or you will not make the sale. In the simplest case, the venture capitalist asks what percentage of your business must be acquired to make a targeted portfolio return. Table 2 displays an idea of venture expectation in the health-care industry.

These "expectations" include an allowance for the "reality" that most portfolio companies take longer and return less. A venture capitalist must aim with hopes of hitting the target. One principal cause for friction between entrepreneurs and venture capitalists is the innate optimism of the former group, which makes them less sensitive at the outset to the difficulties that a start-up inevitably faces.

A seed- and early-stage investor who invests $1.5 million in a start-up company wants to receive a value of $15 million at an initial public offering within a three- to five-year period. If the up-front work is done right, the investor can expect a valuation for the company at the IPO of $100 million or more. This means owning 15 percent of the company at the IPO for this $1.5 million investment. To arrive at the proper, early-round ownership percentage, a venture capitalist anticipates dilution from later private rounds.

Another way of putting it is that the seed stock that cost $1 a share should be worth $10 a share at the IPO. The next-round shareholder should expect to pay $2 a share; the mezzanine investor can pay up to $5 share. Thus, the bigger the

STAGE OF INVESTMENT	SIZE OF INVESTMENT	DESIRED RETURN	TIME OF LIQUIDITY
Seed and Early Stage	$500,000–2 million	10x	3–5 Years
First, Second Round	$2–10 million	5x	2–4 Years
Mezzanine	$10–20 million	2x	1–3 Years

INDUSTRY SECTOR	VALUE OF IPO	ROUNDS OF IPO	TOTAL PRIVATE EQUITY	MONEY RAISED AT IPO
Biopharmaceuticals	$100–200 million	3	$20–40 million	$20–50 million
Devices	$50–200 million	2–3	$3–15 million	$15–30 million
Services	$100–200 million	2–3	$10–50 million	$15–30 million

Table 2 Venture Expectations

perceived opportunity, the smaller the piece the venture capitalist needs to own to "make numbers."

A professional investor also wants significant upside potential. A $200 million IPO valuation means a 20-times return on an investment! Other venture groups have different formulas. Some say that they must own a certain percentage of the company (e.g., 30 percent) at an IPO and will invest accordingly.

VALUATION IS A PROCESS, NOT AN END POINT

No one number is sufficient to establish a valuation. A venture capitalist will triangulate on an opportunity to make sure that several different valuation methodologies yield similar results. Three important considerations include:

1. Direct comparisons or precedents from similar companies.
2. The price expected from later-round investors.
3. Fairness in future dealings.

One question always on the investor's mind is, "What are similar companies going for?" In real estate this is known as "comparables."

Few entrepreneurs readily know current private market values because few non-venture people do more than one or two such deals in a lifetime. Attorneys and other service providers, such as accountants, can help, but only if they work in the relevant area. Nonspecialists may confuse the issues since conventional business thinking is not geared for high-risk, high-potential plays.

Find fellow entrepreneurs who know the ropes and can help you find similar valuations. It is reasonable to ask the venture capitalist to cite specific examples of other companies and even provide referrals to other entrepreneurs in his or her network.

Knowing the market and pricing accordingly sets up later rounds. Overpriced early money may give entrepreneurs a larger share of the company on paper, but it makes future financing more difficult. Though no one wants a "down round," prolonged battles to maintain artificially high prices can slow development and create discord. Usually, market pricing prevails and early-round gains get ratcheted back.

On the other hand, the entrepreneur should not get too little. The venture capitalist must keep in mind what is "fair" compensation for the start-up team, whose members are expected to devote their "lives" to the enterprise. If founders own 1 percent and investors 99 percent, the entrepreneurs are likely to use the capital for an education and start their own company when they figure out how to make money.

It's a good idea to talk to several venture firms with appropriate industry experience or similar portfolio companies. They should be able to provide references to CEOs and scientists/investors at other companies. They should also have expertise at investing at your level of development. As you work through the process, you will find that, despite what appears to be a rather subjective valuation process, most experienced venture capitalists arrive at similar terms and conditions for an investment.

NEGOTIATING WITH VENTURE CAPITALISTS

Negotiations are most successful when a good fit between entrepreneurs and a venture firm results in growing trust on both sides. The discussion usually revolves around the following issues:

- The process of developing the valuation.
- The management of multiple offers (if available) without offending the top choice.
- The optimization of financing terms and conditions to minimize risk and maximize comfort.
- The relationship between timing, stages, and share price.

When you negotiate with a venture capitalist, focus on the size of the opportunity and the percentage ownership needed to achieve a reasonable return for the money.

Talking to numerous venture capitalists will probably not be helpful. If word gets out (and the venture industry is a very small community) that you are shopping the deal heavily in the search of the highest bidder, the best venture groups are likely to lose interest. If you are fortunate enough to entice more than one high-quality venture group into coming on board, you can expect some improvement in price through competition, but a more likely scenario is that two or more of the groups will get together to syndicate the investment and share the risk.

While valuation is often thought of in terms of price, the ultimate end point of the process is really percentage ownership. This involves additional variables, which are the quantity of money invested and the timing of the investment. If you are having difficulty arriving at an acceptance price with a potential venture partner, you might try adjusting these other variables.

Reducing the capital needed can certainly help achieve your desired percentage ownership goals. But remember, the venture investor will want to ensure that you have sufficient funding to achieve development milestones, such as an issued patent, hiring of key personnel, proof of technology, initial sales, or other results, to attract a higher price from the next-round investor. The investor is also likely to have a minimum-size investment to make the process worthwhile.

Consider, as well, the relationship between timing and the evolving price. By investing money in multiple tranches, negotiated in advance and taken down over time, the venture investor can evaluate specific milestones that reduce risk and increase valuations (and price) at each tranch. Because this investor avoids putting in the total contribution at the initial and highest risk point, the result can be a higher overall price than if all the stock were purchased at the front end.

Naturally, if you miss the development milestones, the later tranches will come in at lower prices than negotiated. If you are confident of your ability to make your development plan work, a phased financing can be an excellent way to lower the risk for the venture investor and raise the price for you, the entrepreneurs.

When you negotiate with a venture capitalist, there are a few approaches I would not recommend. An elaborate argument based on discounted cash-flow revenues projected five years in advance will not carry much weight. Neither will it serve you well in having the accountant or consultant who built the model lecture the venture group on financial models and discounted cash-flow analyses.

Avoid hardball negotiations on the projected numbers. Conventional business rules for a "fair" return simply don't apply in the venture community, given the level of risk assumed and "human capital" contributed.

THE ROLE OF FINANCIAL MODELS

If discounted cash flow is not the preferred model valuing venture start-ups, what role do financials play? More important than the numbers themselves are the assumptions behind the model. The modeler can arrive at any number that justifies the investment. The underlying assumptions determine the validity of those numbers.

A venture capitalist wants to see conservative, defensible numbers but with three- to five-year projections. The only thing known for sure is that the actual numbers will be different. The venture investor develops a feel for the quantitative structure of the business by understanding how the model is constructed and how it responds to "sensitivity analysis." As that model evolves and is tested throughout the development of the company, it becomes a more reliable indicator of financing needs and potential valuation for the company.

Financial projections are fundamental to the understanding and operation of an early-stage business. However, the longer the time to significant cash flow and the higher the level of uncertainty associated with the financial model, the lower the value that the model plays in establishing the price of the early equity. In biopharmaceutical companies, financial projections have little bearing relative to the dimensions of the overall market opportunity. In health-care device and service opportunities that are closer to the market, models play a more significant role earlier in the process.

Though most entrepreneurs worry about who controls the magical 51 percent of the equity, few venture capitalists want control, per se. They would much prefer that the management team runs the company.

However, these investors are vitally concerned that control resides in the hands of those committed to maximizing shareholder value. This usually means a group of experienced entrepreneurs rather than management teams that may put more emphasis on preserving their jobs, pursuing a Nobel Prize, or another nonbusiness goal. Instead of outright control, the investor will insist on covenants that give venture interests voting control over basic issues regarding the company's future, such as the decision to sell, go public, or liquidate.

Investors want to ensure that management cannot cut a sweetheart deal with a would-be buyer that rewards employees at the expense of shareholders.

THE BOTTOM LINE IS MORE THAN A NUMBER

Coming to terms on your company's valuation is the cornerstone of concluding a successful initial venture investment. Price is important in determining your ultimate share of the pie. Even more important is the ultimate size of the pie. To maximize long-term value, the first task is finding the right venture investors and forging the right entrepreneurial business development team. The price you arrive at with your first venture investor is only hypothetical because private equity is not tradable. The price that counts is the one you receive upon liquidation.

The primary goal of seed- or early-stage financing is to select a partner to work with who builds the value that both share. A great deal of bonding goes into the venture evaluation process. Even if you knew the right price on the first day, it takes time to develop the requisite trust and respect needed for your venture team to be effective in the very challenging process of building a company. More important than getting the top dollar for your equity is getting the strongest partner.

STANDISH M. FLEMING
President and CEO
Forward Ventures Services Corporation

Standish M. Fleming has over 15 years of experience in the health-care venture capital industry and is a Co-Founder of Forward Ventures, which currently manages over $135 million in funds. As President and CEO of Forward Ventures Services Corporation, Mr. Fleming directs the Firm's operations and guides investment strategies. Since its founding in 1993, Forward has invested $45 million in 27 early-stage companies. Those companies currently have a market value in excess of $12.5 billion.

Mr. Fleming earned his bachelor's degree from Amherst College and master's degree in business administration from the UCLA Graduate School of Management. He currently serves as a Director of Triangle Pharmaceuticals, Arizeke Pharmaceuticals, Nereus Pharmaceuticals, MitoKor, EndiCOR, and Tandem Medical.

The Role of the Board

VINCENT OCCHIPINTI

A Board of Directors has a very important role to play in the success of your venture and can be a real asset. Having a Board does not mean you have to relinquish control of your company. A good Board wants your management team to lead and run the company. Such a Board sees its role as providing crucial support and resources to help you succeed. It is very important to select your Board with care and actively work to maximize its value.

Woodside Fund has participated in many highly functional Boards since the Firm's founding in 1983. We have seats on the Boards of most of our portfolio companies because we are the lead or co-lead investor. In our role as Board Member, we continue to work closely with many talented entrepreneurs to help further develop their companies. It is a very gratifying experience for Woodside Fund and our portfolio companies.

This chapter will discuss the responsibility of the Board, how and when to establish a Board, what a productive company–Board relationship looks like, how to change the composition of the Board, and how to maximize the value of the Board.

THE RESPONSIBILITIES OF THE BOARD

Once a company is funded, the venture capitals (VCs) will require that the company establish a Board of Directors to protect the interests of the share-holders. The main role of the Board of Directors is fiduciary. The Board takes on the responsibility for the financial accountability of the company, including monitoring the day-to-day operations, budget, and performance against plan. A Board is likely to suggest the use of specific reporting tools so that everyone is focused on the most critical information in the most usable form. For example, at Woodside Fund we have our portfolio companies construct waterfall charts. These charts track monthly updates to an organization's operating plan, indicate actual results, and then measure variances from the organization's original plan. Typical applications for the waterfall chart are cash-flow forecasts, P & L forecasts, and headcount forecasts. The Board also helps raise the next round of funding.

A second role of the Board of Directors is to help you build your management team. It is crucial that you hire the right CEO and senior VPs. Your Board Members will draw on their large networks to help identify and recruit candidates. They can also recruit other Board Members who will bring in complementary skills and knowledge.

The Board contributes to creating a vision for the company and a positive corporate culture. As we work together with you to build your management team and fill key staff positions, we look for candidates with unquestionable integrity. The pivotal qualities of integrity and an openness to communicate foster both a healthy corporate culture and a good relationship with the Board. In terms of vision, the Board requires that the vision of the company be spelled out in a five-year plan. This document helps everyone in the company understand your goals and how you will accomplish them.

The third major area where a Board can be instrumental is in strategic business management. Board Members are typically experts in various fields and can coach the management team on key aspects of the business. When something is not working, a good Board has the sound judgment to assess the situation and, when necessary, suggest a way to refocus or re-invent the company. Examples of problems that may require quick adjustments are when perceived need is not tracking with the actual need in the market or perhaps the technology may be better applied elsewhere. The Board will also know when the time is right to go public, merge, or sell.

WHEN TO FORM A BOARD OF DIRECTORS

The timing of forming a Board is kind of a chicken-and-egg situation. Until you get funded, you may not have the stature and money to recruit qualified Board Members. However, given the value you can gain from your Board, the earlier you can put together the right Board, the better.

Many companies begin with a Board of Advisers before they establish a Board of Directors. A Board of Advisers is very useful in the early stages of the company for specific types of input, such as technical, business development, and marketing. Fiduciary responsibility is what differentiates a Board of Advisers from a Board of Directors. A Board of Advisers has no true accountability.

HOW TO FORM A BOARD OF DIRECTORS

After the first rounding of financing, whether it is from Angels or venture capital firms, most companies instate a five-person Board that includes two venture capitalists (typically, the lead plus a partner from the next-largest investor, or two co-leads), a management person such as the CEO, and one person from outside the company who can contribute specific desirable skills and abilities.

For the outside Board Member, it is useful to develop a specification identifying the characteristics you want in this person. He or she should be able to open doors for you and provide sound judgment. Consider targeting someone from one of the market leaders whom you believe would be interested in staying on the Board long term. Do your due diligence on all candidates and check references.

In constructing your Board, it is a balancing act between having a homogeneous group and creating some healthy diversity. What is key is the style of the players, so that they work well together and with your management team.

There are risks to asking a friend to join your Board. Put friends through the same screen that you use with other candidates before enlisting them. A friend may be supportive and bright but may not have the experience, sound judgment, and areas of skills you may need during the crucial early months and years of your company's development.

Because the lead VC typically gets one seat on the Board, it is extremely important to select your VC partner as carefully as you do anything else in your business. Venture capitalists typically have a long-term interest in the company in which they invest. If your funding is syndicated, meaning that the lead venture capital investor brings in other investor partners to participate in the round, it is extremely important that your lead VC knows how to select the firms that will add value to your specific company. When interviewing prospective lead investors, find out what additional VC firms they envision bringing in. No matter to whom the VC introduces you, take the opportunity to interview them and do due diligence on all of them. You should feel that you are the one making the selection of the VC partners. If the lead VC does not respect that, you should be wary of establishing a long-term relationship with that firm.

Woodside Fund has clearly defined criteria for investment partners when we bring them in. They must have the ability to relate to entrepreneurs by virtue of having been a founder or having operating experience. They must have domain expertise that will be of value to the company. And they must also be willing to be supportive in good and bad times.

Who should the Chairman of the Board be? Sometimes this role falls naturally to the lead VC. Or it could be the CEO. It does not matter, as long as the Board is functioning well. Making a founder the Chair or Vice Chair may work well if there is a good fit with leadership style.

THE TENETS OF A GOOD COMPANY–BOARD RELATIONSHIP

Two of the most important tenets of a productive relationship with the Board are open and honest communication between the company and the Board, and a Board that contributes in appropriate and constructive ways.

It is important for the Board and company management get to know each other, in order to trust and communicate openly with each other. Woodside Fund uses a process we developed, called the "Org Chart Process," where we conduct individual interviews with members of senior management and learn how they assess the strengths of the organization and the management team. We learn a lot about what makes people tick in these conversations.

Ongoing communication between the company and the Board about progress, issues, and problems keeps everyone moving ahead together. Informing the Board about problems early on is especially crucial so that they may be resolved quickly.

Board Members can be most effective when they are good listeners and coaches. They should avoid overreacting or imposing decisions on company management. The best results are achieved when Board Members help the entrepreneur look at options and support a decision, as opposed to telling an entrepreneur what to do.

SOME ADDITIONAL WAYS TO MAXIMIZE THE VALUE OF YOUR BOARD

In addition to establishing a productive and respectful relationship with your Board, you can increase the productivity of Board meetings by sending out all the reports to Board Members prior to the meeting. A call to each Board Member before the meeting to review what you will present and discuss is useful.

Use the strengths of your Board. A good Board has tremendous knowledge, good judgment, and valuable resources, including large networks. Call upon the Board to contribute as individual members, as well as a group.

Behind the scenes, experienced Board Members with good judgment will work to see that the Board operates fairly and appropriately. These natural leaders will coach other members on how to conduct themselves and how to interact with company management, or they may dampen overreactions or unwarranted concerns of certain Board Members.

One technique to monitor the effectiveness of your Board is to have each Board Member write a few sentences about the effectiveness of the Board at the conclusion of each Board Meeting. Your review of these notes may reveal potential issues and suggest areas for improvement.

WHEN AND HOW TO CHANGE THE SIZE AND COMPOSITION OF THE BOARD

The ideal situation is clearly to have Board Members for the long term. It is very difficult to eliminate Board Members, and there is a tendency for the Board to continually expand because incoming VCs want a seat.

If a Board Member is not active, missing meetings, and more oriented to telephone conversations instead of face-to-face meetings, it is probably time to reevaluate that person's role. The question to ask her is, What is your interest? If the person is not committed, she may agree to move to Visitation Rights, which is a transitional role. As opposed to asking someone to leave, many companies add another member, typically at the next round of financing, then work toward moving a member out.

HOW BOARD MEMBERS ARE COMPENSATED

What do you have to give to receive the services of a Board? There are several different ways to compensate your Board Members. The first is to offer a stock option plan. In the case of a start-up, the percentage is higher than if the company already has revenues and has established some traction. Offering less than 1 percent is common. Offering more than 1 percent is rare but does happen, depending on the circumstances.

Alternatively, in lieu of stock options, a Board Member may be paid a negotiated fee for attending each meeting or be paid a lucrative consulting fee.

In conclusion, chosen wisely, a Board of Directors can be one of the greatest assets of a young company. It is up to the senior executives of the company to manage this important resource and maximize the value of the contribution of its Board of Directors. Boards will grow over time, and the key is to start out with people who have a commitment to the long term and with whom you can see yourself working and enjoying success in the years to come.

VINCENT OCCHIPINTI
Managing Director
Woodside Fund
Vincent Occhipinti has been intimately involved in the management and success of Woodside Fund and its portfolio companies. He is Chairman of the conferences of the Early Stage Venture Capital Alliance (ESVCA) and has a bachelor of arts degree from Stanford University.

Venture Leasing

Richard C. Walker

Equipment Leasing

Equipment leasing is a source of capital for financing equipment acquisitions. The equipment lease is a contract by which the owner/lessor provides the use of the equipment to the user/lessee for a specified period of time in exchange for periodic rental payments. The basic rationale for equipment leasing is that equipment should be paid for *while* it produces revenues and not *before* it produces revenues.

Leasing companies in the United States now acquire over $210 billion of equipment annually on behalf of their clients. This is roughly one third of all capital equipment sold in the United States.

History of Equipment Leasing

In 1963 the U.S. Controller of the Currency permitted banks to own and lease personal property, and in 1970 an amendment to the Bank Holding Company Act allowed banks to form holding companies. Very soon, almost every large bank in the country had formed a holding company that had a leasing subsidiary. Names like Citibank, Chemical Bank, and Manufacturers Hanover Bank dominated the industry. Credit decisions were based largely on historical cash flow.

The banks made three major contributions to the leasing industry when they became involved. First, they added substantial liquidity and volume. Second, they brought legitimacy to an industry that had previously been regarded as the lender of last resort to businesses about to fail. Third, they exported their expertise abroad and created a worldwide network of leasing companies, all operating with structures similar to the U.S. model.

Contemporaneously, independent leasing companies were being formed that were dedicated to a single product or industry. Most of these had short, active lives that paralleled the rapidly growing popularity of the industry they served. Classic examples were Itel Leasing in the container industry and IMF in the computer industry. A more successful example was U.S. Leasing, which pioneered the vendor leasing industry and survived until the year 2000. Given this history, ponder the future of the plethora of e-leasing sites gracing the Internet.

WHY IS LEASING SO POPULAR?

The bottom-line reason why equipment leasing continues to grow is that leasing meets the needs of so many types and sizes of companies. For example, mature, profitable companies may lease equipment to keep bank credit lines open for other purposes. Young, start-up companies lease to conserve cash, while firms requiring state-of-the-art technology lease equipment to avoid technological obsolescence and to preserve the ability to upgrade. The needs of each company are different and leasing meets those different needs.

Leasing has demonstrated a unique ability to modify its focus or products in reaction to changes in the economic environment and thus always have appropriate and timely products for the marketplace. The industry took aim at containers in the 1960s, mainframes in the 70s, software in the 80s, and personal computers/desktops in the 90s. During these decades, it adapted its structures to meet the ever-changing tax regulations originating from both federal and state sources.

Among the many reasons given by customers for using leasing are:

Technological considerations, such as a natural obsolescence hedge, takeovers, rollovers, and upgrades.

Financial reporting reasons, such as off-balance sheet financing, improved reported earnings, and increased return on assets.

Cash management considerations, such as affordability to lessees, improved cash forecasting, circumventing capital budget constraints, and reimbursement policies (especially contractors and subs).

Income tax motivations, such as lower taxes with faster write-offs; or, by using the lessor's higher tax rate, lower leveraged lease rates, deductibility of rentals, and negative impact of additional purchases (AMT and 40 percent fourth-quarter rule).

Ownership aspects, such as use versus ownership, ownership not available or feasible, avoiding stranded assets, lessee's potential for ownership.

Flexibility and convenience to the lessee, in lease structuring, bundled services, planned replacement of equipment, excessive use of leased equipment, and priority delivery.

Economic reasons, such as diversification of financing sources, additional source of debt financing, less-restrictive form of financing, or lower cost.

STRUCTURE OF THE LEASING INDUSTRY

In order to remain competitive in an ever-changing business and financial environment, the leasing industry has had to create new and better products to meet the needs of its customers. In the case of both new products mentioned further on, changes in the infrastructure have made them possible. Without substantial advances in personal credit information collection, sorting, and evaluation, the "Credit Application Only" lease would not be possible. Similarly, without a healthy venture capital community composed of multiple participants with varying appetites at various developmental stages, the "venture lease" would never have been viable.

The categories listed in the following sections are neither exclusive nor exhaustive. They change and overlap. As an example, the purest category now is the venture lease. However, as venture-funded companies become profitable, the venture lease will phase into a conventional lease.

Conventional Leases

Conventional leases continue the historical pattern discussed earlier of the leasing industry's adaptation to market needs. They come in all sizes but are found predominately between $100,000 and $10 million. They are most commonly used to finance new equipment under a favorable tax structure for the lessee. Credit decisions are usually based on cash flow plus additional support from either a solid balance sheet, a substantial personal guarantor, or equipment with substantial and predictable residual value. In order to evaluate a request, the lessor requires a full financial package that resembles the information provided to a bank when one requests a bank loan. Typical terms are 36 to 60 months, depending on the equipment and the lessee's objectives. For large leases of long-lived equipment (machine tools, generators, etc.), terms of up to 10 years are not uncommon. Rates in this sector are comparable to bank term-loan rates, except that they are fixed for the duration of the lease. Rates will also vary with credit quality and the size of the lease, with larger leases receiving lower rates.

The predominant volume of leasing today is in conventional leases. Most leasing companies offer them. Even some leasing companies specializing in other formats will also offer conventional leases, since there is so much demand for this product.

Credit-Application-Only Leases

Credit-application-only leases involve a simplified application process whereby the lessee can apply for a lease by completing just one or two pages of a credit application. These leases tend to be smaller than conventional leases and rarely exceed $100,000. Exceptions are made for certain industries (e.g., medical) with excellent payment histories or equipment with strong residual values.

Unlike the process of approving a conventional lease, where the lessor examines the operating results of the lessee, here the lessor deals almost entirely with derivative information supplied by third-party reporting agencies. The lessor obtains the personal credit information of key owners or executives. This is often in the form of a numerical rating that is plugged into a scoring formula. The lessor also obtains a Dun & Bradstreet report on the company, which may include both a score of the lessee's overall financial strength and a score of how promptly the lessee pays its bills. Finally, the lessor will check with the lessee's trade references and bank to verify the emerging picture of the lessee. Some lessors have a rigid scoring formula that determines who is accepted or rejected for credit, while others "eyeball" the information and make a more subjective decision.

Because personal credit is so important to these leases, a personal guarantee of the lease by owners and management is almost always required. An exception exists for what are called "corp only" leases. The exception is usually based on a combination of factors that can include professional management, diversified ownership, a long time in business, combined with demonstrated financial strength, and so on.

Typical terms for credit-application-only leases are 24 to 60 months, with the smaller leases having the shorter terms. Terms rarely exceed 60 months. Rates for these leases tend to average 3 to 5 percent higher than conventional leases, due to the smaller size and higher credit risk created by the relative lack of information about the lessee's finances. The sector has grown from nothing over the past 25 years. It was pioneered by Colonial Pacific Leasing, which was recently acquired by General Electric Credit Corp. A large number of leasing companies throughout the United States specialize in these leases, and many conventional leasing companies offer a credit-application-only product.

The Venture Lease

The venture lease breaks all the rules of credit extension. Not only do the lessees generally not have positive cash flow or net profits, many do not even have revenues. However, the companies that receive venture leasing all have one common element: a venture capital investor with deep pockets, long arms, and a proven track record of supporting its investments. Despite commonly made declarations to the contrary, the venture lessor is not basing its investment decision on the probable success of the lessee. That is just part of the analysis. It is really basing its investment on the probability that the venture capital investor(s) will keep the company alive long enough to pay off the lease. Thus, a venture capital firm with a poor record of portfolio support or no record is unlikely to have many of its portfolio companies secure venture leasing. On the other hand, those venture capital firms with strong track records of support have venture lessors clamoring to invest in their portfolio companies.

Minimum size for a venture lease tends to be around $250,000 because the due diligence required is considerable, even though the final decision is made based on the venture capitalist. In order to maintain a well-diversified portfolio, most venture lessors historically have kept the maximum size under $5 million. However, this limit is being exceeded with increasing frequency, due to the increasing size of venture leasing portfolios.

Venture leasing terms are shorter than conventional leases in order to mitigate the risk. Terms of 24 to 36 months are common, and 42 months is considered exceptionally long. This is even true for long-lived manufacturing equipment. Rates also tend to be higher due to the risk. Lessors in the venture arena seek yields of 15 to 20 percent, depending on the quality of the venture capitalist and the perceived credit risk. In addition to the base yield, most venture lessors seek warrants in order to participate in the success of the company and cover the losses of those lessees that do not complete the lease term.

Unlike most lease approvals that are written for specific pieces of equipment, venture leasing approvals are generally in the form of a "leasing line of credit," which is valid for 12 months and under which certain prespecified categories of equipment can be included. Usually, the lessee collects invoices on qualified equipment until some predetermined minimum is reached and then "batches" them and sends them to the lessor, which generates a lease "schedule" to be signed and repaid to the lessee. This level of interchange between lessee and lessor places a burden on the back offices of both. The lessee's due diligence in venture leases should always include the checking of current references regarding the lessor's back-office capabilities.

A unique application of the credit-application-only lease occurs in a sector of the venture space. It can occur in several ways, depending on the developmental level of the lessee and the willingness of its officers/owners to personally guarantee the leases.

A lessee may be able to obtain up to $75,000 on a "corp only" basis if it can show the following:

- No individual with significant equity ownership.
- 10 years in business.
- Comparable "corp only" credit from bank, lessor, and so on.
- Good corporate payment history.

A lessee may be able to obtain up to $100,000 with personal guarantees by owners/management if it can show the following:

- At least two years time in business.
- Guarantors have good personal credit.

- Five-figure bank account.
- Trades report payments as agreed.
- No D & B reports showing losses, negative retained earnings, and so on.

A lessee may be able to obtain up to $30,000 with personal guarantees by owners/management, although it has less than two years in business, if it can show:

- Guarantors have good personal credit.
- Management has a history in business/industry.
- A bank account has been opened.

Because venture leasing is a relatively new phenomenon in the leasing industry, there are probably less than two dozen companies providing the product. They tend to be grouped in Silicon Valley and the major financial centers. The industry is quite volatile. During the year 2000 alone, three previously active practitioners have exited the industry.

The Sale and Lease-Back

The sale and lease-back differs from all other leases in that the lessee is also the vendor. This means that at the completion of the documentation phase, the lessor writes a check to the lessee/vendor for its equipment. The purpose of the sale and lease-back is to raise cash for the lessee. Many of the companies that provide conventional leases also provide sale and lease-backs.

The absence of an independent vendor creates an equipment-valuation problem for the lessor. As a consequence, unless the equipment is less than a year old, an independent appraisal is usually required. The amount of the lease is usually some percentage of the appraised value.

Companies usually employ the sale and lease-back to generate cash in order to take advantage of an opportunity or to cover what management feels is a temporary cash flow shortage. In either case, the implication is that the business is not generating sufficient cash flow. As a consequence, the equipment in a sale and lease-back becomes essential to the lessor's credit decision and is identified as one of the primary sources of repayment. This means that only hard assets are considered as equipment in sale and lease-backs.

Rates for sale and lease-backs tend to reflect the quality of the credit proposed and, given the purpose of the lease, that quality is often relatively low. Terms tend to be shorter, usually 24 to 48 months, reflecting the fact that the equipment is used. However, sometimes the quality of the equipment will overcome the fact that it is used, and longer terms will be awarded.

VARIABLES IN A LEASING CONTRACT

The leasing contract between lessee and lessor may be composed of several dozen different documents in addition to the basic lease agreement. Despite this abundance of paperwork, only four key variables in the lease agreement directly affect the cost of each and every lease. This is not to say that lessors cannot increase their yields by some creative artifice in another area of the lease contract. They can. But these four variables appear in every lease, and each one must be agreed upon before the lessee can know if he has an acceptable proposal.

Term

Lease terms are determined by several factors. Most important is the useful life of the equipment. The general rule is: the longer the useful life of the equipment, the longer the lease term. There are several reasons for this, depending on your perspective. From the perspective of lessors, they do not want economically obsolete equipment as collateral in the event the lessee defaults and they have to sell the equipment. From the lessee's perspective, if the lessee undertakes a 60-month lease on equipment that is obsolete and has to be replaced in 36 months, the lessee could have to undertake a second lease that would run during the final 24 months of the initial lease, causing lessee to have to make two payments for only one production unit. In fact, this used to happen frequently with computers, when salesmen pushed longer terms (60 months) in order to sell the lower payment. Now, most lessees are more sophisticated and rarely accept terms exceeding 36 months for standard office desktops and laptops.

Another factor is lease amount. The general rule here is: the smaller the lease, the shorter the term. The reason is administrative costs and the fact that it costs less to send out 36 invoices than to send out 60. Some lessors will not write a lease under $10,000 for more than 36 months.

Lessee credit quality can also affect the term. Sometimes a lessor will be willing to approve a transaction for 24 months but not for 48 because it is concerned that the lessee may not survive for 48 months. This factor can work in reverse because a strong lessee can pretty much name its term.

Standard leasing terms are 24 to 60 months. Shorter terms are not encouraged by the lessors, whose sales, credit investigation, and booking costs are difficult to recoup in the short period. Longer terms are common on long-lived equipment and for larger transactions.

Monthly Rentals

The amount of the monthly rental is primarily determined by three factors: the cost of the equipment, the yield objective of the lessor, and the lease term. Since the monthly rental repays both the cost of the equipment and the cost of lessor's money, the longer the term, the lower the payment since each payment will contain a lower component of capital repayment.

Lease rentals are fixed for the term of the lease. Unlike bank loans that fluctuate with some reference rate (prime, libor, etc.), leasing rates are fixed from the first to the last payment. This allows leasing companies to advertise that the customer knows exactly what the equipment will cost under a lease. If interest rates rise, the loss is absorbed by the lessor. In the late 70s, some leasing companies, along with banks and savings and loans, were caught lending long and borrowing short, with the same disastrous results.

Lease rates are often expressed as "rate factors." A rate factor (e.g., .0234) is a shorthand way to express the lease payment, and when multiplied by the equipment cost, it gives the monthly payment. When comparing rates, smart lessees ask the leasing companies to quote in rate factors because the rate factor is a hard number. The rate factor can be compared to interest rates, which tend to be soft numbers because there are so many of them (simple, compound, discount, nominal, stream, etc.) and definitions are not uniform.

Advance Rentals and Timing

Lease payments are usually made in advance. The exception to this rule is government leasing (municipal, state, and federal), where payments are made in arrears. Often, one or more payments will be collected in advance, most commonly at the time the lease is signed. This has the effect of increasing the lessor's yield and reducing its risk. Without the advance payments, the rate factor would probably be higher so that the lessor would receive its desired yield.

The timing of lease payments is critical to the lessor's yield calculation. Any time the lessor can advance the time a payment is made, its yield will increase and the lessee's cost will increase. Prepaid purchase options are huge yield enhancers for lessors.

If advancing the timing of receipts enhances a lessor's yield, it stands to reason that delaying payments will have the same effect. The largest single payment that lessors make is paying for lessee's equipment. Reputable lessors will honor a lessee's terms with its vendor so long as documents are completed in a timely manner.

"Interim rents" are another yield-enhancing device used by some lessors. Interim rents are collected by a lessor that only books leases on one or two days a month, to cover the payment from the time the lease closes with the lessee until the lease books internally. Interim rents enhance the lessor's yield because they are composed of both principal and interest and yet do not reduce the term of the lease. Thus, the lessee pays principal beyond the lease term for whatever period it is paying interim rents.

Residual/Buyout

The residual is the final element of the lease that must be determined in order for the lessee to know the cost of the lease and the lessor to know its yield. Most lease programs allow for the lessee to choose its desired residual. Residuals are traditionally $1.00, 10 percent, or fair market value (mV). This choice should be made before the lease begins and should be unambiguously stated in the lease. Any unwritten statement by the lessor or a salesman that contradicts the lease should be ignored.

Many factors can enter into the choice of a residual. If the lessee seeks the lowest possible monthly payment, one way to reduce that payment is to select the largest possible residual. In this case, the lessor will write the residual as a "put," requiring the lessee to make that final payment since it is factored into the lessor's yield. The nature of the equipment can also influence the residual. Lessees should always be aware of the probable market value of their equipment at lease termination if they choose an mV residual. An mV residual with high residual value equipment can result in a lessee paying twice for the equipment—once in the monthly payments and once again buying it back at lease termination.

SOURCES OF EQUIPMENT LEASING

Equipment leasing is provided by a variety of different types of institutions. This section is intended as a brief review of the most prominent, with a few comments on the benefits and weaknesses of each.

Banks

Banks were late in entering the leasing industry, but they have embraced it fully, and now most banks with footings exceeding $1 billion have either a leasing division in the bank or a leasing subsidiary in the holding company. Bank leasing divisions often only provide leasing to existing clients and well-screened prospects. Holding company subsidiaries usually market to the local community and often buy leases nationally.

The good news about bank leasing companies is that the rates are usually pretty low. The bad news is that the leasing section is usually run like the bank. This means that credit will be evaluated to bank standards, and the lease approval may come with a requirement to open an account at the bank. Note that the longer a bank has been in the leasing business, the more likely it will have a relatively independent leasing operation, with the benefit of cheap money and the advantage of independence from the bank.

Independent Lessors

The independent lessors have historically driven this industry and, once again, an independent lessor, GECKO, is the largest lessor in the world. The independents tend to specialize. CHIT, for example, is known for its expertise in hard assets. GECKO has become an exception to this rule because it has acquired so many smaller leasing companies that it now offers just about all the products to all the markets.

Because independents must borrow their money from banks or the public markets, their cost of funds tends to be higher than that of the banks. They overcome this disadvantage by specializing in particular types of equipment and industries where their expertise makes up for the higher cost of money.

Brokers

Brokers are financial intermediaries who arrange leases for their customers with either banks or independent lessors. They are paid by their founders. The broker category is not exclusive, in that many bank leasing companies and independent lessors also have broker desks whose purpose is to syndicate leases that do not fit the institutional profile.

A broker comes with two built-in advantages. First, the broker does not get paid unless the lease closes, and thus the broker and the lessee are united in purpose. Second, the broker has multiple funding sources and can access these until a funder is identified for the lease. The disadvantage of using a broker is that injecting an additional party into the transaction may slow down the process by a day or so. Contrary to popular belief, using a broker is not more expensive than going directly, since the broker only receives what would otherwise be paid to the lessor's salesperson.

Vendors

Equipment vendors often offer their own leasing programs. These may be offered directly by the vendor that has set up its own leasing operation or through an agreement with a third-party leasing company. These programs usually offer a limited number of alternatives geared to the vendor's equipment and may not allow for the leasing of other vendors' equipment that is acquired at the same time.

The primary advantage of vendor programs is that sometimes the rates will be below normal market rates. This happens when the vendor buys down the rate in order to offer leasing as an incentive to acquire its equipment. Automobile companies have been doing this for years. Another advantage may be simplicity, in that the vendor will make acquiring the lease as simple as possible. The disadvantages are that often the rates are not competitive and the vendor is just using leasing as an additional revenue source. Kick-backs and sales spiffs are common in vendor programs, especially with office equipment. These costs must be recouped in the lease rate.

How to Select a Leasing Company

Potential lessees should approach selecting a leasing company with the same seriousness that they would employ in choosing a bank or accountant. All are service providers whose expertise will influence the lessee's success.

Equipment leasing is an unregulated industry. Unlike banking, anyone can enter the leasing business. Lessees need to remember this when they receive unsolicited cold calls from "leasing companies," particularly those from out-of-town. With this in mind, here are three easy steps to selecting a leasing company.

1. Get referrals from your banker, accountant, and attorney. There should be some overlap here and that is good.
2. Besides the standard questions that should be asked of all service providers, ask what leasing associations they belong to and how many Claps (Certified Lease Professionals) they have on their staff.
3. Trust your instincts. If the person you are dealing with does not feel right, he probably isn't.

Summary

Through the years, equipment leasing has financed equipment for wars, equipment for peace, equipment for the Industrial Revolution, and equipment for the Technology Revolution. With ever-accelerating technological change signaling the need to constantly update and modernize our infrastructures, equipment leasing will continue to be the financing vehicle of choice well into the future.

RICHARD C. WALKER
President
Capital Equipment Leasing

Richard Walker is the Founder and President of Capital Equipment Leasing, which provides equipment leasing for conventional lessees, high-technology companies, and venture-backed companies. His company leverages the scarce equity of high-tech companies at all stages of development through leasing. Some of Capital Equipment Leasing's clients are Ensemble Communications, TriPort Technologies, Inc. (Printable.com), Yahoo! (SimpleNet Communications), and VistaInfo.

Mr. Walker received his bachelor's degree from Stanford, his master's degree in business administration from Harvard, and his law degree from the University of Southern California.

Business Incubation
An Evolving Model for Launching Successful Enterprises

L. TYLER ORION

Incubation: the process of keeping in a favorable environment for hatching or developing.

OVERVIEW

Business incubation is the dynamic process by which early-stage ventures are offered a proactive, supportive environment in which to grow. Contrary to popular belief, business incubation is not an outgrowth of the Internet economy. In fact, as an industry, business incubation predates e-commerce and dot-com business models by nearly 20 years. Incubation evolved as a result of the economic downturn experienced by Rust Belt communities during the late 1970s and early 1980s, but experienced a sharp spike in growth during the late 1990s, as venture capital–backed incubation emerged. The overriding presumption in incubation, which has been borne out by experience, is that this process allows entrepreneurs to beat the start-up odds, which at last report were still stacked against success. While the data is difficult to track precisely, the U.S. Small Business Administration estimates that between 50 and 80 percent of all start-ups fail within the first five years. According to *Business Incubation Works,* under incubation, a documented 87 percent of start-ups have survived to year five, which serves in startling contrast to national statistics.

Incubation, as an informal process, has probably been conducted since the very beginnings of commerce, and capital providers and other stakeholders continue to incubate their portfolio companies without formalizing the process itself. Incubation only became organized as a business model during the late

20th century, and Best Practices are still being developed and tested. The track record of the early incubators was tenuous, however, due in part to the participation of nonbusiness interests—universities, government agencies, and economic-development professionals, which looked to incubation to solve specific community problems.

Although there are several major models and myriad variations in service delivery, some fundamental elements can be cited as the commonly accepted value-added contributions of incubators to their client firms. Despite their differences, business incubators serve a singular mission—sustainable new business development. Incubator programs:

- Increase the likelihood of business success during the first crucial years.
- Significantly reduce the "time to launch" for many companies.
- Enable business owners to focus on their core product development.
- Provide assistance with a wide variety of operational matters.
- Encourage and teach entrepreneurship.
- Create wealth, thereby generating job growth and an increase in the tax base of a community or a significant return to investors.

Business incubators add value. In a benchmark study published in 1997, just prior to the explosion of private, venture capital–backed incubation, the National Business Incubation Association (NBIA) and research partners studied the outcomes of incubators that were at least 10 years old. Thus, 126 incubated companies, representing 50 bona fide incubator programs, were examined. This inquiry yielded the following conclusions:

- High survival rates: In 1996, 87 percent of incubator graduates had passed the five-year benchmark and were continuing in business.
- Community contribution: In 1996, 84 percent of graduates were still in the same community as their incubators.
- Incubator programs showed high returns on public investment: In 1996, incubators showed a return of $4.96 for every $1.00 in subsidies.
- The businesses in the incubator programs produced substantial increases in average annual sales and full-time jobs.

BRIEF HISTORICAL PERSPECTIVE

According to the NBIA, the first incubator appeared in Batavia, New York, during the 1970s, and incubation began to become an industry in and of itself during the 1980s. (In 1980, there were 12 incubators in the United States.) During this period, several government agencies, most notably the Economic Development Administration of the Department of Commerce (EDA) and the

National Science Foundation (NSF), developed programs to subsidize incubator development. In 1996, the NBIA estimated that there were 530 incubators in the United States. In August 2000, that estimate had grown to 900 in the United States, with as many as 2,500 such programs estimated to be in operation internationally. In a study conducted by the Harvard Business School in 2000, it was estimated that 350 of these incubators were operating along the venture capital–backed "accelerator" model, to be discussed shortly.

In the late 1990s, business incubation saw an unprecedented expansion. Several of the factors that were possible contributors to this expansion include, in no particular order:

- The Wall Street boom, which resulted in the availability of abundant investment capital, and which simultaneously raised the stakes for investors, ratcheted up the definition of early-stage investment, and offered incentives for speed-to-launch business models.
- The need for larger valuations in the early stages left many start-ups without sources of seed funding.
- The need for velocity and momentum, which became a major differentiator in the development of successful Internet ventures.
- The success of firms such as CMGI and Internet Capital Group, which created "ecosystems" of portfolio companies and achieved record stock valuations.
- The tremendous market buzz generated by several of the early dot-com companies "hatched" by ideaLab!, one of the pioneers of incubation-for-equity.
- The complexity and cost of the technology infrastructure required to launch e-enabled companies.
- The revolution in the global economy, which resulted in the validation of entrepreneurship as a component of economic expansion.
- The proliferation of new start-ups, whose founders had significant experience in technologies or products and services, but who were not veterans of business or had little or no experience with the basic components of management.

FACTORS FOR SUCCESS

Incubators owe their success to a combination of factors, which include:

Selectivity: Although the missions of the various incubators differ substantially, and selectivity is relative to those objectives, most will only accept clients with a viable business concept and some of the necessary characteristics for success.

Accountability: Most incubators require that companies meet their milestones for development and have instituted a process for holding companies accountable for progress.

Access to capital: Whether by providing direct investment and access to growth capital or by establishing channels for financing, it is currently recognized that this crucial component for enterprise growth is an essential element of successful incubation, regardless of whether the incubator is a nonprofit or an equity/profit–based model.

Access to growth level–specific (scalable) resources on a just-in-time basis: These resources may include facilities, Internet access and e-commerce support, office equipment, legal and accounting services, management and staff recruiting, or industry-specific resources such as prototyping, packaging, alliance development, or distribution assistance. The incubator can pre-screen vendors for quality and appropriateness, thereby assisting the entrepreneur in what can be a complex selection process.

Assistance in developing non-core business components of the enterprise: By supplying resources, either in-house or through an extended network, incubators enable their client firms to focus on their core business and product development objectives while gaining access to the most appropriate assistance.

Qualified mentoring, coaching, or training: Entrepreneurs in incubators are offered the value of wisdom and experience, either by individual mentors, advisory groups, training programs, Board creation, or direct staffing by experts in various business functions.

Creation of synergy and reduction of "the loneliness of the entrepreneur": Incubated entrepreneurs benefit by informal peer-level relationships, and some incubators actively develop a "keiretsu" or "ecosystem" model of attracting companies, with alliance creation as an objective, in order to strengthen their collective ventures.

THE TRADITIONAL INCUBATORS

Traditional is a new use of a phrase that distinguishes nonprofit or community/ university–based incubators from venture capital–backed efforts. Generally nonprofit corporations or programs linked to either universities or research institutions, these incubators often have a specific community or technology mission. Traditional incubators generally offer services to start-up or early-stage businesses, based on entry and exit criteria as defined by their mandate, and offer mentorship rather than direct management of client or tenant firms. Within the traditional classification are: technology incubators; empowerment or microenterprise incubators; and industry-focused and mixed-use incubators.

- Technology incubators are often linked to a source of technology, such as a university or federal laboratory, and support the growth of companies involved in developing or commercializing emerging technologies or R & D efforts.

- Empowerment or microenterprise incubators focus either on the growth of businesses located in areas that face difficult economic situations, such as high unemployment and neighborhood deterioration, or on support to low-income, minority-, and women-owned businesses.
- Industry-focused incubators are developed to support new enterprises in a related industry, which may range from specialty foods, software, arts enterprises, or wireless technologies.
- Mixed-use incubators support the growth of a variety of businesses and are not focused on a particular industry or business cluster.

Traditional incubators generally charge a fee for service, which is often linked to space occupied or lease-plus-value payment terms. Many traditional incubators generate about one-third of their operating revenues from incubated clients (or tenants) and develop alternative funding sources, including sponsorships or subsidies and fee-for-service programs, in order to remain fiscally viable. While a few do establish equity or royalty relationships, this is more the exception than the rule within the nonprofit incubation sector.

VENTURE ACCELERATORS

Venture accelerators, which generated considerable interest in the late 1990s and early 2000, are generally backed by venture capital, either by a single firm or by an alliance with a professional investment fund that has targeted early- or seed-stage investments. Although some charge a fee for venture development services while others offer equity-only arrangements, these incubators often take a significant ownership position in their portfolio companies. Accelerators (referred to by many names, including "catalysts" or "venture labs") may, in fact, "incubate" concept-stage ventures, taking a very active role in the development of the business models.

One of the earliest-noted innovators in the development of seed-stage incubation is Safeguard Scientifics, which serves as a holding company for numerous business-to-business enterprises. CMGI and Internet Capital Group operate in a similar model, although there are many variations as well. Also during this period, large manufacturing conglomerates, such as Panasonic and Sony, developed corporate incubator models, in order to encourage outsourced research and development efforts and to "seed" potential future investment and acquisition opportunities.

While there have been some spectacular early results produced by the accelerators, the model was stimulated by the stock market valuations of 1999 and early 2000. Large numbers of investors, many of whom were not experienced in new venture development, launched incubators in order to capitalize on what were essentially unsustainable valuations. This "silly season" ended in the spring of 2000, however, with many of the so-called "build-to-flip" incubators closing. What emerged, though, were some very credible new models of incubation that, as of this writing, have not been in operation long enough to have produced a significant track record but show great promise.

Most of the accelerators work from the concept stage, generally with credentialed scientists or engineers, although some take advantage of the energy and innovative thinking of college-age entrepreneurs. Although, as is the case with the traditional incubators, there are almost as many models as there are incubators, yet some common components exist.

The accelerators generally:

- Are highly selective and seek business concepts or technology applications that promise to yield market capitalizations in the $100 million range by year three.
- Take an equity stake in the start-ups, which can range from 15 to 75 percent, depending upon the accelerator's perceived value-added model, as well as the accelerator's own business model and growth strategy.
- Manage, or have direct access to, a seed-stage venture capital fund, so that its fledgling ventures have immediate access to capital.
- Provide stylish facilities in which high-bandwidth and sophisticated e-commerce tools are in place.
- Have alliances with top-tier professional firms for legal, accounting, insurance, benefits, and recruiting services.
- Have access to capital markets for subsequent rounds of funding.
- Provide management teams to directly staff the market validation and growth phases of the enterprises; some actually employ the founders directly, until the business can be effectively launched.
- Include, in the senior management of the accelerator, individuals who have achieved significant business success, such as those with extraordinary careers in technology ventures or with major public companies.
- Utilize the "keiretsu" or "ecosystem" model, or have a specific, narrow industry focus, in order to build in a synergistic value to the enterprise overall.

Although a number of notable new accelerators are not facilities-based, most seem to be. Also, several of the more well-known models are either public corporations or intend to become public. Because this model of multiple investments can resemble a mutual fund, accelerators planning an IPO are crafting their investment models to avoid this consequence with the Securities and Exchange Commission (SEC). This lends itself, however, to the need for accelerators to reserve a majority ownership position in their portfolio companies.

Because the value of the accelerator model is closely linked to the ability to launch and grow companies either for public markets or for other significant liquidity events, these new accelerators are inextricably linked to the idiosyncrasies of capital markets. I believe that it is too early in the development of the accelerator model to objectively assess its effectiveness.

It should be noted that certain private, for-profit incubators have been operated successfully in the mode of traditional incubators. Also, some nonprofit incubators that are targeted to launch fast-growth companies have assisted their client firms in securing large venture capital investments.

MAKING AN INFORMED DECISION

An entrepreneur considering an incubator relationship would be advised to become informed about the specific entry criteria and value-added services of the incubators/accelerators in his community. Although the availability of capital and the cost of participation are major differentiators, there are many other significant factors for the entrepreneur to review. These include:

- The capabilities of the incubator or accelerator, weighed against the company's perceived needs, both immediately and over the next 12 to 18 months.
- Capital: Is there an investment fund or access to seed capital?
- Facilities: Are the facilities hospitable and flexible enough for growth?
- E-Infrastructure: Will the in-house Internet and e-commerce services be appropriate and sufficient?
- Telecom: Is the telephone service flexible enough for expansion?
- Business and professional services: Are they accessible, affordable, and appropriate for the company's immediate and future needs?
- Mentoring and professional development: Will the incubator add significant value?

The track record of the incubator and management staff:

- Industry knowledge: Is there sufficient depth of understanding of the entrepreneur's specific industry?
- Business and management skills: Can the incubator help the company fill crucial gaps?
- Previous successes: What is the successful launch record of the incubator and its management team?

The intangibles:

- The synergy with other incubator clients.
- The chemistry with key service providers, mentors, and incubator management.
- The image or buzz surrounding the incubator itself.
- The ability of the incubator to add value, champion the client, and support successful execution of the company's business model.

On the other hand, incubators and accelerators are selective. The ability to pay for services or the need for investment capital are not generally sufficient to ensure acceptance. The entrepreneur will generally need to meet a certain level of business "viability" standards and be "coachable." If there is an industry focus, the entrepreneur will need to be qualified to work in that particular domain in order to be a candidate.

Finally, there is the cost-value proposition. The entrepreneur must weigh the cost, whether it is in the form of an equity relationship or a monthly service fee, against the value-added services that the incubator offers. For the entrepreneur with few real gaps in experience, who can secure needed services, capital, and support without the aid of a "facilitating infrastructure," then incubation might not be a compelling strategy. If, on the other hand, it is a choice between a high probability of failure or an enhanced likelihood of success, then the incubator environment might be an appropriate choice.

AN INDUSTRY IN EVOLUTION

Business incubation is indeed an industry in evolution. As long as the economic landscape continues to encourage start-up activity, incubation is likely to play a role in new venture development. Presently, traditional incubators are becoming increasingly more business-like and the accelerator models are testing their own theories. In all fairness, it is too early in this process to posit realistic projections, much less draw conclusions. Time will tell.

L. TYLER ORION
Director
Orion Enterprise Development

Executive Director
PIN: Pacific Incubation Network
Orion Enterprise Development (OED) is a respected San Diego business-development firm that provides strategic mentoring and business-model development for emerging and early-stage technology companies and develops the facilitating infrastructure that enables business incubators to successfully sustain multiple new ventures.

In addition to her responsibilities at OED, Ms. Tyler serves on the Executive Board of the Regional Technology Alliance and on the Oversight Board of the San Diego Chapter of the MIT Enterprise Forum. She is a member of the National Business Incubation Association (NBIA) and a Founding Charter Member and Executive Director for PIN: Pacific Incubation Network. Ms. Tyler is a frequent guest speaker at conferences and entrepreneurship seminars.

Critical Employment Issues for Start-Ups

Jennifer A. Kearns

In today's ever-evolving, fast-paced business climate, the primary focus of most entrepreneurs is raising capital. And naturally so, for a company cannot operate and flourish on goodwill and great innovative ideas alone. But many start-ups fail to focus at an early stage on key employment issues that ultimately can impair their ability to raise additional funding or to gain the interest and confidence of underwriters. A common refrain heard from many start-ups is, "We'll deal with human resource issues once we're larger." Another is, "We're too busy." A third is, "We don't want 'formal' policies."

A start-up that fails to address key employment issues from the beginning of its existence may be likened to an ostrich with its head firmly planted in the sand. And when the ostrich finally pulls its head out of the sand and shakes the grains from its cloudy eyes, it may gaze upon a box—one commonly known as Pandora's box.

It is easy for emerging-growth companies to focus their energies on the aspects of the business that are exciting and dynamic—the development of technology, the raising of capital, and the marketing of product. When there are only 24 hours in a day, it can be difficult to allocate time to the mundane processes involved in setting up an employment infrastructure. However, a failure to engage in this important task at the early stages of a company's development can contribute to the emergence of legal problems that can be fatal to a growing company working on tight margins.

In the following pages, I will discuss several of the key employment-related issues that start-ups should focus upon at the earliest possible juncture. Addressing these issues creates a necessary infrastructure within the company and demonstrates to investors that the principals have done their homework, recognized and anticipated potential problems, and taken proactive measures to minimize the likelihood of their occurrence.

EMPLOYMENT AT WILL

Many states recognize the concept of at-will employment. At-will employment means that either the employer or the employee may terminate the work relationship at any time, with or without "cause" and with or without notice. One caveat is in order. Even if an employment relationship is on an at-will basis and no cause is required for termination, the company may not terminate any employee's employment for a reason that is illegal (e.g., unlawful discrimination) or that otherwise violates public policy (e.g., terminating an employee in retaliation for having engaged in whistle-blowing activity). In California, for example, all employment that is for an unspecified period of time is presumed to be on an at-will basis.

So what is the problem? The problem is the distraction of effort and the expense of litigating a wrongful termination case. Suppose that the start-up employer just could not be bothered to develop a human resource infrastructure. Employees are hired without offer letters, or offer letters that are issued are inconsistent. A terminated employee sues, alleging that there was an implied promise that he would not be terminated without good cause. To make matters worse, the suit is filed and served shortly before the company was set to close on a round of financing. The suit is likely a disclosable event.

Let us rewrite the scenario. The company creates a human resource infrastructure from the beginning. All offers of employment are made in writing, and a standard form of offer letter is used. The offer letter contains a clear, concise affirmation of the fact that the employment relationship is at will and explains exactly what that means. The letter also makes clear that promotions, stock option grants, verbal assurances of job security, length of employment, and the like, will not change the at-will nature of the employment relationship. The letter contains a legal provision known as an "integration clause." The company requires each person who accepts the company's offer of employment to sign his offer letter. How does this structured process change the outcome?

In the event that the company is sued upon the theory that good cause was required for the employee's termination, the company now has a piece of ammunition in its arsenal. The company may now be in a position to seek dismissal of the suit on the basis that the parties had an integrated at-will agreement. The existence of such an agreement may deter many plaintiff's attorneys from even taking on the employee's case.

The utilization of a good, standard at-will offer letter takes little effort on the company's part and can be an important tool. At-will offer letters should be reviewed by company counsel to ensure that key provisions are included and that other terms and provisions of the offer letter do not contradict the at-will provisions.

USING INDEPENDENT CONTRACTORS

Ask a principal affiliated with start-ups how many employees her company has, and you may hear, "None—everyone is a consultant." This is a big red flag. There is almost no circumstance under which a company can legitimately justify treating *every* worker as a "consultant" or "independent contractor." Some companies do so in order to avoid the expense and administrative burdens inherent in managing employees. Others do so at the demand of the workers themselves, who may insist upon being paid as independent contractors.

A company that inappropriately characterizes workers as independent contractors is creating potential liabilities for itself. First of all, if the company is audited by taxing or labor authorities and it is determined that workers should have been treated as employees rather than as contractors, the company may owe substantial sums in unpaid tax withholdings, plus penalties and interest. If the worker should have been classified as a nonexempt employee (more on exempt versus nonexempt status later), the company may be liable for unpaid back overtime. If the worker suffers a workplace injury (including a claim of workplace-induced stress), the company may be liable for failing to cover the worker under a workers' compensation insurance policy. As recent cases have demonstrated, persons who have been classified as independent contractors may claim that they were de facto employees, and that, as such, they should have been granted stock options and other employment benefits. In short, a misclassification of workers can lead to a wide variety of legal problems. So how does a start-up company determine whether a worker is an employee or an independent contractor?

The Internal Revenue Service and other administrative agencies look at a wide variety of factors in making the determination whether a particular worker is an employee or an independent contractor. As is the case with many legal matters, the determination is largely dependent upon the facts of the specific case. A key test that is employed is the "right to control" test. This test looks at whether the hiring person or entity has the right to control the means and manner in which the worker performs the work or instead has control only over the results of the work. Control of means and manner usually indicates an employer–employee relationship. In addition to the "right to control" inquiry, courts and administrative agencies may also consider other factors in determining the nature of the work relationship. Some of the other factors that are considered include whether the relationship is terminable at will or whether the right to terminate the relationship is dependent upon the attainment of specified objectives or results; whether the worker is engaged in a distinct occupation or profession; whether the worker holds herself out as an independent contractor, and whether she is actually engaged in performing work for other companies;

the amount and type of skill required in the occupation in which the worker is engaged; whether the worker or the company supplies the tools, instrumentalities, and location for the work to be performed; whether the worker is paid by the job (per project) or by time; whether the work performed is part of the regular business operations of the principal; whether the worker has an opportunity for profit or loss, other than through the payment of wages; whether the worker hires his own employees; whether the worker holds a license for the type of work performed; or whether there is evidence that the parties intended to create a specific type of relationship.

No single factor is dispositive. Thus, even if the parties enter into a written "independent contractor agreement," this does not guarantee that a court or administrative agency will concur. It is strongly recommended that start-ups using "independent contractors" review each such situation with counsel to ensure that proper classifications are being used. This is so even when it is the *worker* who insists upon an independent contractor classification.

EXEMPT AND NONEXEMPT EMPLOYEES

Another pitfall common among start-ups is treating all employees as "exempt" from federal and state wage and hour laws. Federal and most state wage and hour laws presume that workers are entitled to be compensated at one-and-a-half times their regular hourly rates for all hours worked in excess of 40 in a week. And, in California, year 2000 heralded a return of daily overtime laws—nonexempt workers are entitled to time and a half for all hours worked beyond eight in one day.

The key exemptions under wage and hour laws are for "bona fide executive, administrative, or professional" employees and outside salespersons. Determining whether a specific job meets any of the exemptions is on a case-by-case basis. One factor that is usually important is whether the individual exercises "independent judgment and discretion" in matters of significance to the company, and whether she does so as a substantial and regular part of the job. Job titles are not determinative. And, contrary to the popular belief (or hope!) of many, merely paying a worker on a salary basis, rather than hourly, does not make her "exempt."

One of the legal liabilities that can arise from improper employment classification is the nonpayment of overtime wages due. If it is found that the company has failed to pay overtime to a worker who was improperly treated as exempt and that the failure was willful, actual damages (i.e., the unpaid overtime) may be doubled as a penalty. And there is always the danger that one misclassification could lead an administrative agency to embark upon an audit of the company's full workforce.

STOCK OPTION ISSUES

Many start-ups use stock options as alternative forms of compensation or to lure workers. And many start-ups grant stock options fairly indiscriminately. But stock options should not be viewed as an unlimited resource. A company needs to be careful about the number of options granted to employees, particularly in early stages of operation, as investors often discount the value of companies that have optioned large percentages of their equity.

Another stock option issue of which start-up principals need to be aware is a trend that is developing in the wrongful termination arena. Many companies grant options to all employees as an incentive. Many companies ultimately conclude that a particular employee is not performing to expectations. And unfortunately, this conclusion is sometimes reached just a short time before the employee is scheduled to vest in some of his stock options! In recent years, a growing number of cases arose in which employees who were terminated just prior to vesting in options asserted that they were terminated in order to prevent them from vesting. Any employment lawsuit can be expensive and lengthy, but a case in which an employee's nonreceipt of stock is in issue presents special problems. Suppose that at the time the fired employee sues, the company is still privately held. The case takes the usual year or so to progress through the legal system. During that year, the company has its initial public offering (IPO). The stock in which the employed person would have vested is now worth millions of dollars. This illustrates only *one* of the problems in evaluating and managing the risk of litigation. Bear in mind that the existence of a pending lawsuit, particularly one involving issues pertaining to stock, can complicate the IPO process, even if the suit has no merit.

A further issue that start-ups need to be aware of relates to agreements to accelerate stock options in certain circumstances. Sometimes executive employment agreements provide that if the executive is terminated under certain circumstances, all of her unvested options will be accelerated and immediately exercisable. Other times, a termination agreement will provide that an employee's options will be accelerated. In either event, the acceleration of an employee's options may constitute a significant financial event for the company and may result in significant accounting charges. This financial impact should be quantified and considered *before* the commitment is made to accelerate.

Sometimes, in negotiating separation agreements, companies agree to allow the departing employee a longer window of time after termination within which to exercise vested options. Such an agreement may or may not be permissible, depending upon the specific terms of the controlling stock option plan. Persons negotiating such arrangements on behalf of the company should not do so until they have confirmed that an extension of the option exercise window is permissible under the terms of the operative plan.

The foregoing points certainly do not cover the whole host of issues that can arise in connection with stock options, but they should demonstrate the need for start-ups to be mindful that commitments concerning stock options are not to be made lightly.

RECOGNIZING AND PREVENTING UNLAWFUL HARASSMENT

Start-ups often delay implementation of formal human resource procedures, including the publication of employee handbooks and personnel policies and conducting employee training. The usual explanation given is that these issues will be addressed when the company is larger. In many states, companies are covered by laws prohibiting unlawful harassment and discrimination when they have as few as a handful of employees. In California, an employer with *one* employee is covered by laws prohibiting unlawful harassment.

In many states, however, an employer has an affirmative obligation to take proactive steps to ensure that unlawful harassment and discrimination do not occur. Having a policy that describes the types of conduct that are prohibited and that informs employees of the complaint and dispute resolution procedure to be followed is a bare minimum. A start-up company should consider holding a mandatory all-employee meeting at which these issues are explained and discussed by a person qualified to do so. Holding such training, and ensuring that all employees attend, is helpful in demonstrating the company's commitment to a workplace free of unlawful harassment and discrimination. It is also helpful in educating employees about what does (and what does *not*) constitute unlawful behavior.

The overall objective is to prevent the types of behavior that can lead to suits alleging unlawful harassment or discrimination. When such cases are filed, they can be difficult to evaluate. A lawsuit that alleges merely that the employee did not receive a job benefit promised (e.g., salary for a specified period of time or even stock options) is one in which the company's exposure can usually be quantified. But actions based upon unlawful discrimination and harassment are cases in which a successful plaintiff may recover damages for emotional injury, in addition to any damages for actual economic loss. In many jurisdictions, the amount of emotional distress damages that may be awarded to a plaintiff lies solely within the discretion of the jury. To make matters worse, in most unlawful discrimination and harassment cases, the plaintiffs seek awards of punitive damages. Again, the amount of punitive damages that arguably could be awarded is not easily quantifiable. And finally, these cases are generally brought under statutes that provide for awards of attorneys' fees, in addition to any damage awards! In summary, the "smart start-up" will take steps to educate its employees about unlawful harassment and discrimination and to minimize the likelihood that it will ever be the subject of a suit based upon such conduct.

PERFORMANCE EVALUATIONS

Many start-ups delay conducting performance evaluations, usually due to the press of other types of business. But this can be a crucial mistake, particularly when the company wishes to terminate the employment of an underperforming employee. If no performance feedback has been given, the employee may have a legitimate complaint that he was not informed of his shortcomings and was not given a meaningful opportunity to improve. In essence, the employee may make a "fairness" argument. And if the start-up has not adequately documented at-will status, it may find itself having to justify to a judge or jury its decision to fire an employee for "performance reasons," without having ever informed the employee that a problem existed.

Another mistake that many start-ups (and mature companies) make is soft-peddling or sugar-coating performance feedback. The usual justification offered in support of such a practice is that positive feedback will motivate the employee. However, when performance does not improve, the company has not only failed to inform the employee of problems but has even created an impression that the company is pleased with her performance!

PROTECTING INTELLECTUAL PROPERTY

In most start-ups, intellectual property is the foundation of the business. All companies whose success depends upon the successful exploitation of such property *must* take steps to protect their intellectual property from the outset.

All employees who work in such a company should execute intellectual property agreements upon the commencement of their employment. A good intellectual property agreement should define what the company considers to be intellectual property and/or trade secrets. It should contain provisions by which the employee assigns ownership rights in intellectual property developed during the employment to the company. The agreement should also indicate what, if any, intellectual property developed during the employment period will remain the employee's property. For example, in California, an employer cannot require an employee to sign away his ownership rights to intellectual property which is developed on the employee's own time; is unrelated to the employer's business; and did not involve the utilization of any of the employer's tools, instrumentalities, or facilities. It should require the new employee to identify any intellectual property in which he claims a prior interest. The same process should be followed with contractors and consultants who perform work for a company and who are exposed to the company's intellectual property, although in different forms to avoid any implication that such persons are de facto employees.

NONCOMPETITION AND NONSOLICITATION AGREEMENTS

The competition for top-notch candidates is at an all-time high. Start-ups are often tempted to require all new employees to sign "noncompete" agreements as part of the initial employment process. However, before doing so, the company should determine whether such agreements are enforceable. Enforceability varies from state to state. Requiring employees to sign agreements that are unenforceable under applicable law is simply not good practice and could be used as evidence of an absence of the employer's good faith.

Another circumstance in which a noncompete agreement may be implicated is the situation in which the start-up is hiring a candidate who may owe a noncompete duty to a former employer. The start-up hires the candidate, learning only after she arrives that there is this noncompete obligation. The former employer company then sues the individual for violation of her noncompete obligation and also sues the start-up, seeking to enjoin the new employment relationship. Suddenly, the start-up finds itself ensconced in litigation. To make matters worse, the noncompete agreement may have had a "forum selection clause," pursuant to which the employee may have expressly agreed that disputes involving the noncompete clause would be litigated in some other state. One can easily see how the litigation costs and distraction factors could escalate rapidly.

The solution is a targeted inquiry process by which candidates are screened for prior noncompete or nonsolicitation obligations. When candidates do have such obligations, they can sometimes successfully negotiate with their former employers to be relieved of such obligations or to have them narrowed in scope. Even if the start-up determines that the candidate is critical, with his noncompete baggage, it is prudent for the company and the candidate to determine their respective rights and responsibilities in the event that the other company elects to sue them both. These determinations can be made only if the start-up *knows* about the candidate's other obligations!

CONCLUSION

The foregoing should demonstrate that a number of employment related issues will arise in nearly every start-up and should receive early-stage attention. If the start-up is not yet prepared to hire an in-house human resources director or a VP, there are many skilled HR consultants who specialize in working with emerging-growth companies. Utilizing the services of experienced employment counsel is another option. Most start-ups find that the cost of a little proactive counseling is money well spent and that a close, interactive relationship with outside counsel can be effective in squiring the company through the field of employment land mines.

JENNIFER A. KEARNS
Partner
Brobeck, Phleger & Harrison, LLP
Jennifer A. Kearns is a Partner in the law firm of Brobeck, Phleger & Harrison, LLP, and heads up the Labor & Employment Group in the Firm's San Diego office, where she has practiced since 1987. Ms. Kearns specializes exclusively in employment law, representing companies and individual executives. Her practice primarily encompasses counseling and advising companies, both small and large, on a full range of employment-related issues and representing them in administrative and court actions. She is primarily outside labor counsel for several prominent biotechnology and high-technology companies.

Ms. Kearns obtained her undergraduate degree from the University of California, San Diego, and her law degree from the University of San Diego.

Venture Capital Marriage— Until Money Do Us Part?

Ben R. Neumann

I have been raising venture capital, either as an entrepreneur or as a venture capitalist, for many years and on several continents. This has included, but is not limited to, raising capital for my own businesses as well as helping others to raise capital for their new ideas and ventures or existing businesses.

A venture capitalist (VC) brings the cash to the party. Although it may seem as if the venture capitalist lives in the promised land, there's no such thing as a free ride. Between entry and exit, there is coexistence. There are people issues, business development issues, and financial reporting. And while trading highs can look after themselves, trading lows can prove testing. "Living" with a VC feels a little bit like a marriage. It's a close, but sometimes tricky, relationship. There are ups and downs, parties and arguments, and you need to constantly nurture the relationship to keep it going the right way.

RAISING CAPITAL

Besides requiring intelligent interaction with your VC, raising venture capital is both a marketing and a sales challenge in that, to ensure your success, you must both develop a product that a large-enough market wants to buy, and you must have the selling skills to convince the dogs that they should eat your particular brand of dog food. Most professional venture capitalists are essentially in the business of screening, qualifying, and selecting venture capital investments from as large a source of quality deal flow as they can muster. A few venture capitalists are essentially entrepreneurs themselves and can work with an entrepreneur to start and develop a new company. Those are the most valuable relationships to build.

Increasingly, the start-up variety of venture capitalist is hard to find, in that over the past decade, most venture capitalists now have so much money to manage that they cannot afford the time or effort required to help develop and then invest in a start-up. For all but the very few, start-up capital will not come from the professional VC but rather from the D.F.F. market—doctors, family, and friends—or from personal savings and credit. Some states have incubator programs or incubator venture funds that will provide small amounts of capital ($50,000 to 300,000), but once again, generally only the few, the persistent, and the lucky will qualify.

To successfully raise professional venture capital, particularly for a start-up, your venture will need to address a large, rapidly growing market with a unique product, which is very tough to duplicate and for which there is little or no known present competition. Your product needs "compelling economics"—twice as fast, twice as cheap, twice the margins, and twice the appeal. If the potential product is likely to gain rapid favor in the stock market after an initial public offering (IPO), all the better. The good news is that the D.F.F. market is about $60 billion annually. The professional VC market is only $35 billion. There are definitely more friends and family than venture capitalists.

You also need a very good management team, not neglecting scalability. Ask yourself: How will the business grow and how quickly? Larger companies are far more able to resist customer pressure to reduce prices than smaller ones are. This is one of the reasons why more and more deals are getting bigger. VCs tend to check businesses against a template they have built for each sector. It shows them what a star business in each sector would look like and compares their benchmark businesses against that. However, since sectors are always changing, it is hard to say exactly what a VC is looking for in the first place.

Your exit strategy needs to be razor-sharp and defined. VCs look for people who could name the people who would buy their business three years on. They want to see that management is thinking about this.

Use the following checklist as a guide to raising venture capital and to assess the likelihood of your success.

Management

Outstanding management is probably the single most important test that any growth enterprise needs to meet. Management should have substantial experience in the industry in which the company expects to compete. Working in the industry is a great way to learn (and make mistakes) on someone else's budget. Strong relevant experience is usually a prerequisite since investors are often unwilling to fund the education of inexperienced entrepreneurs, even those with "great" ideas.

In addition to strong topical experience, an ability to stomach the psychological, management, and marketing challenges that arise in developing a growth company is another important attribute of good management. The entrepreneurial path is not for the faint of heart. Many ultimately successful companies go through long periods of uncertainty, even come to the edge of bankruptcy, at times in their development.

Good venture managers are able to keep their employees motivated and customers loyal during the difficult times. Psychologically, they must be able to handle the overwhelming stress and pressure of wearing many hats and being responsible for the success of their company and the employees that depend on them. Accomplishing this under normal circumstances might be difficult enough, but since the payoff for all these efforts is far from guaranteed, the necessary commitment is almost superhuman. Entrepreneurs need to have a strong vision and the heart and determination to follow through. The former track records of the management team members are also crucially important. For example, members who have successfully grown and realized proceeds from a former company are likely to find investors easier to court the second time around. My personal track record has made it possible for me to raise capital for plenty of different projects without any problems. Correspondingly, former failures can count as one strike against a particular venture. However, many entrepreneurs have experienced failure at some point, so an important mitigating factor is the circumstances surrounding past failures and how management dealt with challenges in the past. A seasoned and connected Board of Directors can also be used to add to the strength of the management team.

The reason venture capitalists focus so much on people is that the companies that they finance are based on ideas and plans that can only become valuable if they overcome the challenges of competing in and adapting to the marketplace. Netscape Communications Corporation is worth a few billion dollars today. Most venture capitalists would agree, however, that a different team with less experience and the same idea might not have been so successful. Since history suggests that the only thing businesses can count on is to plan for and expect change, the right people are also the venture investor's first and only defense against unanticipated changes in the original business plan.

In summary, potential entrepreneurial companies should honestly assess themselves to see if their executives have the flexibility, experience, drive, and commitment to be successful with an entrepreneurial company. If holes are identified, recruiting additional team members and directors may be a useful or necessary step.

Growth Potential

Growth potential is another extremely important characteristic shared by most start-up and emerging-growth companies. Ideally, venture-stage companies should be able to address large markets and, if things go well, have the ability to become major companies. One rule of thumb suggests that a venture candidate should be able to achieve revenues of between $50 and $100 million within five years of the first financing (assuming other rounds are provided as needed).

Many business ideas inherently fail to measure up to such high growth hurdles. Although these businesses can often be successful for the owners and are usually financed by nontraditional sources of risk capital, they are often inappropriate for "conventional" venture financing. Fortunately, the nontraditional sources like Angel investors and the D.F.F. market are significantly more varied and are larger, in total, than the "conventional" venture funds.

Although many venture capitalists do not start out with specific industry criteria, the growth requirement explains why so many investments are directed toward technology, biotechnology, specialty retail, and a few other areas. As a result, almost 80 percent of the venture dollars invested between 1998 and 1999 by venture capital funds went to companies in the technology or life sciences categories.

Proprietary Element

Many successful venture-backed companies also feature a novel and proprietary product or service. It is very difficult to become a major player in a market where the business plan calls for the new company to displace the existing products of an established (and probably better-capitalized) competitor. Successful venture-stage companies must often rely on a strategy that gives them the lead in their new or emerging market. Entrepreneurs should think about how people currently survive in the absence of their proposed contribution and what changes in existing patterns of behavior would be necessary to make the new product or service wildly successful. A leading market position, when available, can and should be protected by patents and trademarks, preferably filed by experienced intellectual property counsel. The need for protection is especially important in a time such as ours, when an increasing amount of the value created and held by companies (and indeed society) takes the form of intellectual property and other intangible assets. Companies that are first can often fail and are surprised by how quickly competitors are able to emerge to change the composition of what may have been an empty arena. Entrepreneurs should always assume that success will rapidly breed imitation and should plan, from the beginning, to anticipate a competitive response.

Next Steps

Assuming that you have identified a team and an opportunity that meets all of the previous criteria, the next step is to create a business plan that can capture and communicate the story in a way that will attract the attention of potential investors and demonstrate the financial opportunity available to investors.

It'll Cost You

The price of financing through venture capital firms is high. Ownership demands for an equity interest in 30 to 50 percent and more of the company are not uncommon even for established businesses, and a start-up or higher-risk venture could easily require transfer of a significantly greater interest. Although the investing company will not typically get involved in the ongoing management of the company, it will usually want at least one, but typically more than one, seat on the target company's Board of Directors and involvement, for better or worse, in the major decisions affecting the direction of the company. The ownership interest of the VC firm is usually a straight equity interest or an ownership option in the target company, through either a convertible debt (where the debt holder has the option to convert the loan instrument into stock of the borrower) or a debt with warrants to a straight equity investment (where the warrant holder has the right to buy shares of common stock at a fixed price within a specified time period). An arrangement that eventually calls for an initial public offering is also possible.

Once everybody agrees on the fine print and is interested in closing the deal, things usually go fairly quickly. It is important to understand that once the funding is received, the VC relationship is just the beginning. Although some of my remarks may seem rather discouraging, I would actually like to encourage anybody with a potentially great idea or business to start the search for some venture capital before someone else does it faster than you.

BEN R. NEUMANN
President and CEO
Ad-Ventures, LLC

Born and raised in Krefeld, Germany, Ben R. Neumann studied marketing and business administration at the Gerhard-Mercator University.

After running several successful ventures in Germany, Mr. Neumann and his wife, Andrea, relocated to Southern California. In 1994 he founded Magic Logo, a small Los Angeles-based design company. At a time when only gurus knew what a domain name was, Mr. Neumann rented a small Web server, WWW Top Business Mall, which was soon filled with virtual tenants. In 1996, the company incorporated into B.N. Technology, Inc., dba Internet Communications (Icom). Today, Icom is one of the largest Wed-hosting providers in the U.S.

What to Be Prepared for—
The Inside Story

Nick Desai

The day we went to meet our first venture capitalist (VC), we already had a product out and had raised $1.5 million from private investors. Still, I had little idea what to expect. The VCs liked our idea, and we had what is known as a "term sheet" the next day. When you sign a term sheet, some due diligence happens and then you get your money. I knew all that, but I did *not* comprehend the basic notion that at some point you get a big, fat check. This is exactly what happened. We got two separate checks, each for $1 million.

I swallowed hard that day. I guess I never understood that people actually give you huge checks (or wire transfers) of millions of dollars. *That* is what you have to be prepared for, pure and simple, to run a real company, with real, professional outside expectations. When you get VC money, the expectations are daunting. It's not your little pet project anymore. It's the real thing, and there is *no* turning back. You can't change your mind, you can't walk away. I have been told it's like getting married and actually putting the ring on your finger. I wouldn't know—I have been too busy running companies to actually get married.

The bottom line is this: You have to be prepared for a level of responsibility and commitment you have probably never had in your life. I cried the day we got funded. Then I got scared to death. I cried because I realized that a prominent venture fund wanted to put millions of dollars into my idea. I was scared because even though I had run a business before, I had little concept of what would come next.

WHAT HAPPENS

First, a comment about due diligence. What is due diligence? It has been referred to, in humor, as "meeting your maker." It really isn't that bad. Mostly, it's paperwork. A part of it is your investors' making sure that you aren't a felon, that you won't steal the money, that your idea is really yours, that what you say actually works and who you say works for you actually does, and so on. But that is the easy part. It really is. Assuming you are not a fraud or a felon, and you haven't lied in your VC pitch, it's actually pretty straightforward.

The rest is contracts. Things like subscription agreements, articles of incorporation, stock certificate issuance, and so on. All are important documents that are the foundation and governance of your company. At the end of the day, those papers will truly determine your future. For due diligence, you need to do two things: First, get a really good corporate lawyer. Find one from a large firm who has *personally* done venture financing documents before. A lot of them. Get to know this person and trust him. Let this person understand your specific situation. Second, understand the process yourself. You can't leave this up to the VC or the lawyer. If you're like me, you want to get past all this nonsense and get to making your company. Great. But get books on your state and federal securities laws, on corporations, on governance, and so on. Read them from cover to cover. Understand the issues. This is really, really important.

I know founders who have lost millions because of the paperwork. It's not even that the VCs are bad, it's that the paperwork is the only thing that matters.

The Money

You have your money. What to do, what to be prepared for?

The most important thing is communication. You now have an actual Board of Directors, perhaps consisting of one or two of your fellow founders or other key employees, plus your VC. Schedule regular, frequent meetings and communicate *real* issues and the real state of affairs. Give people an accurate picture of the good and bad that is going on, and seek their advice. At the very least, let them know.

This is important to point out, because until that check clears, you are in sales mode. And in sales mode you naturally tend to accentuate the positives and minimize the issues. Fine. But once the venture capitalist is "in," your best bet is letting him know the situation. He is behind you now and wants to fix things as quickly as possible.

This kind of regular, open communication is *vital* to the success of your company and to the continued good relationship between you and your VC.

Also, remember, as with a marriage, there is a honeymoon period. The VC has just given you millions. His firm has invested in your company. His Partners must like you, and a lot, too. And so they will glow about you for a while. Don't get lost in that. Because it's easy to, and you miss your first revenue projections, and all of a sudden the VC wants to kick your tail, and rightfully so. *That* is his job. Along the way, if you can truly communicate your issues and setbacks (and believe me, they will come) to the VC, then the VC will be informed and able to help, which is his job.

- The number one thing to remember is that getting financed is the beginning.
- Having a company that fails is worse than not having a company. I know so many companies that have failed because the management and founders got too excited about the fact that they got their VC money. This is especially true when it comes from "known" VCs.
- So, what do you do?

Understand Your Role

Let's hope you have discussed this ahead of time with your VC, but you have a role in the company. A founder is a wonderful thing to be, but that doesn't make you a great manager. Maybe you don't want to be a manager, maybe you can't. Maybe, if you are a technology company, you are the technologist who invented the widget. Maybe you can sell the heck out of it. Maybe you can run a company. Understanding your role and place in the company is vital because it allows you to recruit the missing pieces.

Understand the Board and Its Role

A Board of Directors is a governing body that watches over the broad steps a company takes. It approves major hires, sets goals, reviews CEO-level performance, guides strategy, and approves major financial transactions. The CEO reports to the Board. The Board has voting authority on issues and will follow the result of the vote.

The Board is a *key* asset to your company. If not managed and run correctly, it's a major liability, too. The Board's make-up is important, as well. In early-stage companies, typically, two kinds of people are on Boards: VCs and founders/key employees. Remember, you want as much of "your team" on the Board as possible. You and your key employees should have the same goals and visions. Your VC represents his firm's interests and the interest of "nonworking" shareholders. Your company is made up of both those who work for money (you) and those who don't work in your company day to day. It is vitally important to add outside Board members who provide credibility, guidance, and an unbiased perspective to your Board. These are often industry experts and known names for your company. Don't bring in a friend of yours just because he is a friend. More important, don't let the VC pick someone by himself, either. That is vital. Otherwise, you are just giving his firm another vote.

Remember that a Board and its rules are all negotiated and set by you and your VC in your corporate by-laws. Things like "What happens in a tie vote?" or "Can I be removed from the Board?" or the kinds of issues the Board votes on are *all* negotiated. You, as founder, should push (in most cases) to be Chairman of the Board and to break tie votes. There are myriad issues here, so just get good help and don't be hurried to get through this. Set agendas, and ask the questions you want answered. Control the discussion.

You and Your Company Are *Not* the Same Thing

You need to understand that your "garage project" has now grown up. Just as you can't make decisions for an adult child, you can't make solo decisions for your company, because it isn't *your* company—it belongs to the shareholders, of whom you are one. You may be a major shareholder, but you aren't the only shareholder. A company is a separate, living, legal entity. You have to be very careful with finances, accounting practices, legal issues, representations that you make, and so on. Emotionally, it's hard to let go, but remember, this is necessary.

Get an Accountant

And get a really good one. The lack of accurate financial reporting will kill your company and get you into deep hot water. Quickly. If you don't understand how to read a P & L and a balance sheet, *learn.* Review the books. Weekly. I don't care if you have a CFO and your brother is the accountant. Be involved. The flow of money is the number-one indicator of a well-run company. Don't relinquish check-signing authority to anyone, and double-check everything.

Prepare for Professional Management

Even if you are in the CEO role, you must seek to hire professional managers. This is, frankly, a necessary evil. These people are not entrepreneurs like you. They are paid professionals who come in to do a job. They are risk-averse and will most certainly make more money than you do. They are politically savvy and have *no* real love for you or your dreams. They just care about making money, on to the next big pay raise. There are rare exceptions of founders who find great long-term CEOs, but those people truly become partners with the founders, more than hired hands. Understand this, and accept that you will need these people.

All this being said, good professional management is what it takes to build a great company. Take, for example, two companies. Same idea, same brilliant founder, same money. The company with management wins, every time. Be involved, and before you hire, ask, Does this person *understand* your company, industry, product, and so on? Does he understand you? Has he taken the time to get to know you? Has he done the job before? Does he understand a start-up? Be careful and select wisely. Just as good management can make a company, bad management can kill it.

Second, set real boundaries and explain roles specifically so that there is no misunderstanding. Make sure each person understands his responsibilities and is held accountable to them. Command respect.

Employees Are Not Your Friends

They just aren't. They aren't founders. They don't want the same things you do. Your most loyal employee will ditch you at the worst possible time— because the company isn't theirs, it's yours, even if things seem otherwise. You can be good to your people, push them, reward them, and make them part of a team, but never close your eyes, never be fooled, always keep that distance, and always be objective.

Work Selflessly but Not Too Selflessly

Remember, no one is watching your interests but you. Because you think of the company as your own, it is hard for you to "ask" for anything from the company. A raise, more stock, whatever. Don't make that mistake. Have contracts *on paper.* Get regular raises, more stock. Take as much out as you can now. Everyone else is doing it, too. You deserve it. Don't be unfair and overly demanding, but push for what you want. The Board will give it to you, provided that you deserve it and you ask for it.

Whatever Can Go Wrong, Will

This old adage is true. You will take more time than expected to develop products; the market will change; the largest company in the world will start doing what you are doing, but better and cheaper; your best employee will quit when you need him the most; your VC will have an ugly divorce and take it out on you. It will happen. All of it at the worst times, too. Trust me. We attempted to raise our third round and lost our COO, our largest customer, and two key employees while the NASDAQ plummeted hundreds of points over a few months. The question is *not* whether this will happen; the question is how will you react to it, and even more, how will you prepare for it? First and foremost, you can't let it get to you. You really can't. It's not personal. It's a business. You can love it, but it won't love you, not always anyway. Second, understand that you have a plan, and you have to hold firm. What defines great companies is their ability to react to adversity. Period. And that is what will define you as a leader. Third, be malleable. Having a plan is great, but as market and outside conditions change, be adaptable and open. It doesn't matter if you build the widget you've always dreamed of, if no one wants to buy it. That is the difference between a project and a company. When things go wrong, ask this question: Why did it happen and what can we do about it now and in the future? Learn. If you know *nothing* about running a company on day one, but if you ask yourself that question every day and in every case, and you are honest and open, you will achieve greatness. Because the hardest thing to do is say, "I blew it, I was wrong."

Your Friends and Family Won't Understand

They just won't. My family doesn't, despite running a family business. Yours won't, either. Just get used to it.

You Will Need More Money Than You Think

You will need more money than you think! *Always keep raising money! Never, never, never stop.*

The Hardest Thing

If the business works, everyone gets credit. If it doesn't, you take the blame. That's how it goes. If you don't like it, then don't do it.

SUMMARY

In the final analysis, what you have to expect is the unexpected. You are a founder. An entrepreneur. In modern society, you serve the most important role in the world. Bill Gates, Larry Ellison, Michael Dell, Jerry Yang. You are one of them now. Have pride and hold your head high. Very few people can do what you do.

Expecting the unexpected is the key. You started your company with an idea or an insight—something you figured out that no one else did. Ever. Think about that. You already expected the unexpected—the need for your product or service. Whether you did it by accident or by design does not really matter. You did it. So when things change or don't go your way, do what you do best. Look inside, and pull the rabbit out of the hat. You can do that, and others can't. The mistake that founders make, especially after funding, is that they stop being founders. They really do. They get so caught up in running a company, they forget the path they took to get there. The role of a founder is forever. Always be founding, always be creating, always be leading. Those are unending tasks. Empires have been destroyed without that role being filled.

The hardest thing for me is the emotional drain. It's a nonstop process. It's like having a baby. You can get a baby-sitter, but you don't stop worrying about your kid. It's the same with your company. What you have to learn is this: You did something great already, but if you succeed in building a great business, you will make others jealous. If you don't succeed, they will say I told you so.

Being a founder of a company is the greatest high I know of. It is the confluence of creation and execution that drives me, the fact that no two days are the same, that I learn every day and do my best, and the vision and company are mine. I can't think of a fate in the world better than running a company that I founded.

Good luck.

NICK DESAI
Co-Founder, Chairman, and CEO
Zkey.com

Nick Desai is the creator of the Zkey vision and the designer of the core platform, which launched in 1999. He is a visionary and product designer who anticipates market requirements and keeps business and product planning several steps ahead. As Chairman, he is central to core business strategies, long-term strategic vision and design, business development, and attracting investors.

Mr. Desai possesses the unique combination of technological understanding and business expertise and has spoken at several prominent venues. He received his master's degree in electrical engineering from the University of California, Los Angeles, with an emphasis in compound semiconductor device physics.

Danger Ahead: Success

DAVID A. KAY AND MICHAEL DEDINA

You have worked like a Trojan to make your business happen. It was your dream and now it is your baby, and you protected it from any and all dangers. For months and years you have prepared for this day—the launch. But, hey, no wonder! Your business is based on a great idea—your idea! They said it couldn't be done, but now it's on the verge of happening. And are you proud? You bet.

One of the greatest dangers that you face is the one you want the most: success. The trouble with success is that it leaves you thinking that you can do no wrong. After all, you have been getting all this adulation and money—so obviously, you can walk on water, right?

TOP OF THE WORLD AND BACK

This is a story of a guy I love very much—my dad, Andy Kay. Growing up, I got accustomed to his hard-driving perfectionism. His intense ambition was something I grew to admire.

Andy is a genius who invented the digital voltmeter and the miniaturized oscilloscope. He and I rocketed Kaypro Computers to $120 million in sales in 1984 and, unfortunately, to bankruptcy in 1990. We made serious management mistakes—mistakes that I want you to avoid.

We were the darlings of Wall Street. What happened?

What happened was that Dad could not accept advice from anybody. Not from his Board of Directors; not from me. When we had disagreements, I took it in stride. After all, Kaypro, like many other ventures, was bound to be risky. Besides, it was his investment capital, so I made the best of it.

At first, Kaypro Computers was the right product at the right time. The media loved the product. The stock soared. Toward the end of Kaypro, one of the few remaining dealers was compelled to ask that Dad write a letter asserting that he would not shut Kaypro down. The customer was worried that Kaypro would not be able to fulfill his large order. The dealer needed the letter to persuade the customer to allow him to submit a bid. That's how low the Kaypro name had sunk.

Sales went to a high of $120 million in 1984. Sales were $78 million the following year—a drop of $42 million. Stock went from an initial $10, when Kaypro went public, to 6 cents five years later.

What went wrong at Kaypro? That's what we'll discuss here.

Dad fired many of the staff members I had hired. He hired his old buddies—most were over 60. Dad kept many of these pals employed, even though their expertise was mostly analog and Kaypro was all about digital. But because of a good core relationship, we could disagree without resentment.

Our hiring practices were lax. Previous employment was never verified. In one example, we hired a top manager who told us she had an MBA from an Australian university. Under her care, Kaypro grew to have *six* incredibly intricate sales commission plans. What a mess! Orders got lost. Her MBA was a sham. Her "university" was a boy's school that only went to junior high. After I fired her, she sued Kaypro for paying her less than men.

Our company communication was a mess. We issued policy changes with no forewarning. Outside salespeople were confused by conflicting messages from headquarters. Questions about inventory remained unanswered. Salespeople found it impossible to get help for our 900 independent dealers—our most valuable asset.

Unrealistic sales quotas were set. Our new salespeople had to produce in their first three months. A new manager was ordered to fire eight sales reps on his first day on the job. Some of those eight guys deserved to get fired, but some of them should have been kept aboard. It takes at least half a year for a new sales rep to establish a tie with an independent dealer.

We had inventory problems, technological issues, fulfillment problems. Dad would never install an experienced professional management team, though his Board of Directors begged him to. Dad viewed professional management teams as a waste of money.

In 1988, in an attempt improve Kaypro profit margins, Dad decided to sell directly to consumers. As president of the company I had been in contact with many of our 900 independent dealers. I was certain they would perceive this as a betrayal. The Board and I pleaded with Dad not to do it. We would be competing with our 900 loyal independent dealers—our greatest asset. The dealers did not learn about it until they, like everybody else, saw our ads in computer magazines. Across the country, Kaypro computers were yanked off the shelves. Yearly sales went from a $100 million run rate to $0 for two months.

Dad fired me the day before the direct sales ads hit. Dad re-hired a marketing director whom I had fired. Thus began a public relations and ad campaign that blamed me for the company's state of affairs. Although this was a difficult time for my Dad and me, I perceived it as an opportunity to pursue a company that I had dreamed of since I was a teenager.

Over the next year and a half, Dad led Kaypro, a company that had been valued at $300 million (real money back then), into bankruptcy. When he did that, he lost not only $300 million but also the millions more that Kaypro could have gained in value, plus the sales that would have been generated over the years. Kaypro could have remained a powerhouse in the PC industry.

My dad is very intelligent, yet he drove a successful company into the ground. The moral of the piece is: If it happened to the great Andy Kay, it could happen to you.

WHAT CAN YOU LEARN FROM THIS CAUTIONARY TALE?

- Do not hire your friends only because you like and trust them. Get the best people you can, friends or not.
- Do not spend recklessly. Your employees will notice and emulate the boss.
- Hire professional managers as soon as you can afford to and delegate.
- Get the best directors you can get on your Board and listen to them.
- Don't believe your own public relations.
- When success comes, remember that you really can't walk on water.

Where is Dad now? Last year, at the age of 80, he started a new high-tech company. That's my dad—after all these years, he's still got the entrepreneurial spirit.

LESSONS LEARNED

Now, let me tell you how I have structured things differently at WordSmart. For starters, WordSmart's recent success has been my real dream. Since I was a teenager, I've wanted to create a profitable growing business that would improve lives in this fundamental way.

In my new company I am the sole founder. I licensed core technologies instead of taking on partners who could provide the necessary elements of the WordSmart software product. Through this structure I would have control over the quality of the product, at least in the early stages of the company's growth. Most educational software does not even attempt to be part of the core curriculum. WordSmart is at the very foundation of all curricula, so it was critical that the design integrity of the software not be compromised for any reason.

Now that WordSmart has achieved market penetration at the retail level and is nicely profitable, it is time for aggressive expansion into a huge new market—the computer labs of schools. With our school version finally fully networked and greatly enhanced for ease of use by teachers and students, forecasts of WordSmart sales to schools are exciting.

At our Web site, www.wordsmart.com, you can test your entrepreneurial mettle by clicking on the WordSmart Challenge and taking a five- to ten-minute vocabulary test. Free of charge, you will get a list of predicted occupations and the best, most efficient WordSmart volume to begin improving your chances of being a successful entrepreneur. Be fairly warned: If you do not score above our mid-level volume, volume E, your chances of achieving entrepreneurial success without improvement of this key trait are very slim indeed.

DAVID A. KAY
Founder and CEO
WordSmart Corporation

David A. Kay, CEO and Founder of WordSmart Corporation, has more than 19 years of experience in the microcomputer industry. In 1981, as Vice President of Marketing and Product Development for KayPro Inc., Mr. Kay developed the Kaypro II.

After leaving Kaypro in 1988, he began pursuing his lifetime vision of building a company based on intelligence research conducted by the Johnson O'Connor Research Foundation. In 1994, this creative effort led to the founding of WordSmart Corporation and the WordSmart product: a series of CD-ROMs designed to improve performance on IQ and all other standardized tests.

MICHAEL DEDINA
Founder
eDUALCITIZEN.com

Michael Dedina, a French-American dual citizen, is the founder of eDUALCITIZEN.com, a projected money-making business-to-consumer service for 40 million dual citizens in the United States and millions more in foreign markets.

Mr. Dedina is a published novelist. He has launched film/video production facilities and trained personnel in Central America and North Africa for the United Nations and the U.S. Agency for International Development.

Mr. Dedina has a master of arts degree in Radio and Television from San Diego State University.

What It Takes to Lead Your Company from Start-Up to Liquidity

ROBERT J. HARRINGTON

Frank Williams started his business out of his home with a little money and a lot of hard work. Three years later he had a booming business and 75 employees on the payroll. The problem was that, recently, the company's financial results had declined and the organization was in a state of chaos. Things that used to be simple to handle had become difficult, slow, and inefficient. The company had numerous opportunities for expansion but was unable to take advantage of them because it struggled to keep up with existing business. Frank was working as hard as ever but had a difficult time staying on top of things.

Then came the February Board meeting, where Frank was informed that he would no longer be needed as CEO. A new executive was being brought in by the venture firm that had provided funding to expand the business. *How could this happen?* Frank wondered. He had built the company to what it was, and they had no right to take the job away from him in his own company.

The scenario outlined here is much more common than many entrepreneurs realize. The management skills required to lead a company through the growth phase of its life cycle are quite different from the management skills required in a start-up. Few entrepreneurs realize this until they find themselves in a situation similar to Frank's.

Entrepreneurs are accustomed to being in control and overseeing all aspects of the business. As the company grows, it becomes more difficult for the CEO to stay involved in everything. Thus, a company requires proper structure and effective, efficient business processes and procedures to successfully expand and operate—all of which are rarely found in a start-up.

MANAGEMENT SKILLS

How do you know whether you have what it takes to lead your company in an incredibly competitive business environment? Should you aspire to be in charge all the way through, or should you consider stepping aside and bringing in someone who has the set of skills to take the company to the next level? Identifying the skills that are important and learning how to obtain them could be the difference between leading the company or just being a shareholder. Today, many investors and advisers look at management as being just as important as the business model and potential market. My belief is that management is the *most* important element.

The management skills required to lead companies in the New Economy and the Old Economy are similar, as evidenced by the number of Old-Economy managers who successfully lead New-Economy companies. In the New Economy, some additional skills are important, particularly in the early stages, such as the abilities to trust the intuitive leap, to create a business, and to communicate its potential effectively.

Here are some additional management skills that will help you lead your start-up through the rapid-growth phase of the business:

Quick as a Cat

Fast-moving leadership is essential for today's companies. Being able to make quick decisions and revise your business model as market conditions change is a must. In the information economy, your business model can be rendered obsolete with the development of a new technology or change of an existing technology. Therefore, today's leaders must move quickly to respond to the changing dynamics of the New Economy.

Change Is Good

Change is everywhere and it is increasing at a frenetic pace. Cultivating change-oriented management is an important part of the leadership process. Your business model might be a success now, but will it be next year? There is no road map to the future; it is up to leaders to define the future business world.

Passion

Being passionate about what you do and communicating it in a compelling way is essential to getting people to follow you. In today's tight labor market you need to recruit people by inspiring them with your vision and passion—not by the inducement of wages and options. In a start-up you are asking people to take a risk with you, and they must buy into your vision and passion.

Leadership

Hiring great people and supporting them with the tools and resources they need to be successful is a critical skill. Great leaders know how to get out of their people's way and measure their contribution based on results. The larger the company grows, the more day-to-day decision making needs to be pushed down to the lower levels of the organization. I recently witnessed a CEO who was interrupted during our meeting so that he could approve the title that was being put on the card of an administrative assistant. It was a classic example of a manager who had centralized all of the decision making at the top. This won't work in a large and rapidly growing organization.

If you have mastered the previous skills, you may have what it takes to lead your company from start-up through the rapid-growth stage. However, this is more the exception than the rule. If you don't have the leadership skills and are not interested in developing them, you may need to bring in a new executive to lead the business.

REALITY CHECK

Many entrepreneurs have great ideas but lack the capital to make the visions become a reality. Bringing in outside capital means you also must have a plan for those shareholders to liquidate their investment in the future. If starting a company is more of a lifestyle decision, in which you simply are interested in being your own boss, you had better think twice about raising capital from outside investors. Once you have investors, you no longer work for yourself—you are responsible for maximizing the return on their investment. That is where conflict can develop. Most investors would like to achieve liquidity in five years or less. If that's the case, the company must be developed to a point where it is a candidate for an initial public offering, a recapitalization, or a sale to a strategic buyer. To achieve that liquidity event requires leadership with the management skills listed earlier. If you do not have the skills to build the business to a successful liquidity event, investors might begin to ask for changes in the management team. You should be willing to step aside if it is in the best interest of the company and the shareholders. If a new CEO can get the company to a liquidity event faster and at a higher valuation, everyone benefits.

HIRING AND WORKING WITH A NEW CEO

Bringing in a new executive to lead the company is one of the most important decisions you will make. Once the decision is made, how do you find your new CEO? If you are a venture-backed company, the venture firm will usually want to participate in the process. In some cases it will handle the entire search for you. It is crucial that you get professional assistance in identifying, recruiting, and selecting your new CEO. Hiring the wrong person can set you back years, so it is wise to invest the money and have a professional assist you with this process.

When the new CEO is hired, it is important that you clearly define the CEO's role and yours, as well. As an entrepreneur, you may find it difficult to give up control of the company. However, failure to do so defeats the purpose of hiring a CEO. Your task should include facilitating a smooth transition and making it clear to the rank and file that the CEO is now in charge of running the company.

Management changes happen not only at the top but throughout the organization. When a new CEO is brought on board, that is usually just the beginning. The entire management structure will be scrutinized as to whether it will support the new CEO and the vision of the company. Changes should be identified and documented. Once the needs of the organization are identified, the existing management team is evaluated to determine if it fits the requirements of the new management organization. This is the point where objective decisions need to be made quickly so as to avoid the prolonged tension that already exists as a result of the new CEO being brought on board.

Remember that your interests should be closely aligned with those of your shareholders. Don't let your ego get in the way. In deciding whether you and your existing management team are the ones to lead the company through your growth to liquidity, you must set aside the desire to be in charge. It may help to confide in some trusted advisers and get their opinion of what would be best for the company. If bringing in a new management team is the answer and you do that in a thoughtful way, everybody wins in the end, including you.

ROBERT J. HARRINGTON
President and CEO
The T Sector, Inc.
Robert J. Harrington is a Founder of *The T Sector, Inc.,* a San Diego–based technology magazine and Internet site (www.theTsector.com) that covers the local technology community. Prior to founding *The T Sector, Inc.,* he was the Consulting Director for a national CPA and consulting firm, where he directed a staff and assisted companies in strategic planning, organization planning, and executive compensation. Mr. Harrington has a bachelor's degree from Purdue University.

A Biotech CEO's Perspective

WALTER H. MOOS, PH.D.

There are many trials and tribulations in building a company from the earliest stages to a more substantial critical mass. While much of the discussion in this article can be applied to any start-up or business, it contains a biotechnology slant, for that is my area of expertise. I have tried to use specific examples in this article, and you will find a somewhat random commentary targeting various points of interest.

COMPANY FOUNDATIONS AND MILESTONES

Visions and Champions

It should go without saying that the founders of any company must have some vision in mind, a vision that must captivate both investors and early employees. However, while some kernel of the original vision will likely follow the company to either success or to the grave, most companies change directions dramatically from their early ideas. Witness Amgen (www.amgen.com) and its original ideas to fade or soften blue jeans using recombinant enzymes, and its ultimate success with recombinant therapeutics. Chiron (www.chiron.com) represents a company true to its original visions, striving for almost two decades to prevent, diagnose, and treat disease through its vaccines, diagnostics, and therapeutics. Throughout, a company requires champions who will persevere to achieve success.

Technologies Versus Products

A large percentage of technology based companies fail to recognize the importance of products. Many technology-based organizations recognize the error of their ways too late in the game and thus fall prey to richer corporations and/or lower their expectations as service providers.

Sometimes the technology platform requires such a long time frame to be validated that only a few companies survive. Few of the original antisense companies, for example, are left. Indeed, it is often true in therapeutics development that the timelines (an average of 15 years and $500 million per marketed product) are so long that almost everyone loses hope several years before the first success. The lesson here is that you must be willing to see your idea through—completely.

This is not to say that product companies are always the winners. There are clearly far too many companies that are effectively one-trick ponies; they have bet the farm on the off chance that one idea or element will prove effective. The recent up-tick in mergers and acquisitions, which integrate ideas, products, and companies that often complement each other, may bode well for the future.

It is worth noting that the early biotechnology companies all seemed to target becoming FIPCOs (fully integrated product companies) as the desired model. After a large number of failures, most companies decided to pursue less grandiose plans. The models evolved to include, among others, FIDOs (fully integrated discovery organizations) and RIPCOs (royalty income product companies). Some might say the RIPCOs should "Rest in Peace," that is, the royalty model does not work and is dead. However, given the extremely long timelines for drug development and the relatively recent emergence of chemistry-based biotech companies, in my opinion, we need to wait a few more years before deciding whether the model works or not. A reasonable royalty on a blockbuster small molecule drug that reaches the market could easily generate $50–200 million per year of revenues for a RIPCO.

Differentiation and Competition

Investors and companies frequently act like lemmings, all jumping off the same cliff at the same time. Apparently, for some people there is comfort in knowing that if you fail, others fail, too. Yet the real innovators are those who run in the opposite direction and wait for the members of the pack to look over their shoulders and realize that they need to turn around to follow the lone wolf. But differentiation taken to its extreme can require inordinate effort to educate the world, and validation is a much more tortuous path. Moreover, having a major competitor can often be a major motivating force.

Validation Steps

At the end of the day, validation is often the key to future success. Just as having an Ivy League education provides immediate validation in some circles, having premier venture capitalists (VCs) investing in one's company can be crucially important. In addition, the top VCs have gotten there by being shrewd judges of character, excellent advisers, and more. The earlier the stage of the company, the more important it is to heed their advice. Many VCs continue to show their business value into the initial public phase of the company and beyond. Validation comes further through the receipt of major competitive grants; publications in top journals; a broad and deep patent portfolio; the recruiting of well-respected employees, both scientific and otherwise; and lucrative alliances with large corporations such as big pharma.

Location

Just as in real estate, there is an element of "location, location, location" in biotechnology. Biotech companies have largely concentrated around major academic centers such as the San Francisco Bay Area, Boston and its surroundings, and metropolitan San Diego. The founders are often part of the local academic scene. The location of top VC firms coincides with these concentrations of talent. This provides ready access to skilled workers and advisers, financial sources, but less and less affordable housing and more and more difficult commutes. The latter points should force significant new concentrations of companies in more livable locales.

ORGANIZATIONAL DEVELOPMENT

Timelines and Breakpoints

In developing and executing a business plan, a company's management team should remember that there is a clear "time value of money" component to their overall equation. If one compares two companies that achieve similar success financially, the one that gets there first provides a higher rate of return on their investment. A top company might go public or be acquired by another firm within several years of its founding. A lesser company might take 5 to 10 years to provide liquidity to its investors and employees. Though the time course to liquidity may not be a predictor of long-term success, it is surely a consideration of some importance to the early investors.

While every situation is different, I have found over the years that many evolutionary processes in companies follow a 1-, 2-, 5-, or 10-year schedule. For someone running a significant operation, it takes a year or so to figure out which way is up. It takes another year to point things in the right direction and feel like progress is being made and is sustainable. It takes 5 years to fully master a new situation. At this point, if one has outstanding colleagues, and if one is a good teacher, there may not be a profitable role for a chief executive to play unless there is a major new direction to be taken. Similarly, at 10 years, it is hard to imagine that a chief executive hasn't reached the "80:20 rule" of diminishing returns. Too many chief executives continue at the helm well past their useful corporate lifetimes.

As the organization grows, there are several natural points of tension. The initial 10 to 20 people often bond together as an extended founder group. Once the company grows to 40 to 60 people, the extended founder group may feel lost or at least less special, even exhibiting animosity to newcomers—the extended founders' connection to each other and the senior management team will naturally become weaker over time. The company is also big enough at 40 to 60 people to begin seeing fights over turf. In addition, at 40 to 60 people, the employees may, for the first time, see that the company's direction is not one that they feel comfortable with, and thus turnover can be high at this stage. This can be painful but healthy for the long term. Another breakpoint comes around 200 to 300 employees, after which it is hard to keep people motivated and organized, except in rare situations. In this sense, the old analogy of big pharma being like super tankers, with their many thousands of employees, and a small biotech being able to turn on a dime, is quite apt.

Recruiting and Retention

There is often a cultural fit among people who join small companies fresh out of school and a different profile for those who go to large corporations instead, and never the twain shall meet. Some very successful entrepreneurial founders of small companies probably wouldn't last a year at a big company (and vice versa). In general, fewer employees of small companies leave to join big companies than the other way around. Successful large-company employees can effectively train at their companies, with so many different situations to watch, and later in their career make the move to smaller companies. However, they often must unlearn certain big-company habits in order to be successful in the smaller-company setting. Given all of this, it is rare to lose a small-company employee to a large corporation, but the competition among small companies can be fierce. Chief executives who are located close by have learned to be gentlemanly in pilfering others' stables of talented employees, usually stopping at around two hires from a competing company in a given period of time.

Particularly for senior-level hires, recruiting firms ("head hunters") can be invaluable. These firms and their principals can readily identify top candidates, ferret out honest reference checks, and act as mediators in securing a deal that both the candidate and the company can live with.

Compensation will at one time or another rear its ugly head. There is an intrinsic level of conflict between investors and employees over spending the former's money on the latter's careers. Early in the development of the biotech industry, founders made large sums of money on stock. Many founders were able to double or triple dip, having an academic position as their safety net for employment; receiving royalties on licensed patents as inventors at the university, as well as consulting fees and laboratory support; and also receiving salaries, bonuses, and stock options for working at their companies. During the past decade, however, big pharma have done so well that biotech compensation has lost ground. If the recently reopened initial public offering (IPO) window stays open, the compensation levels may reach a better balance, but if not, then biotech will have to open its pocketbooks wider in the future or risk having "B teams" (with the "A players" working in big industry).

Board of Directors

The Board of Directors plays many important roles, which should naturally evolve during the different phases of a company's life cycle. In the earliest stages of a company's formation, Directors may help to manage the company on a day-to-day basis. Over time, the Directors usually take on more strategic, less operational roles. For traditional venture capital–funded companies, the initial composition of the Board will be heavily weighted toward investors and will include founders and one or more members of the company's top management team. Having several experienced investors around the table who can easily commit to or pull in the necessary funding when needed can be very important. Over time, a mixed Board evolves, bringing more independent outside Directors into the fray, typically individuals who have specific experience in areas of importance to the company. This mix might include pharmaceutical executives, chief executives from other biotechnology companies, and others who add value through their experience, insight, and connections. There are, of course, normal group dynamics issues to consider. Thus, a Board of five to eight people can be much easier to work with, for obvious reasons, such as staying in touch between Board meetings and making sure that everyone has a chance to make their points during discussions at Board meetings.

FINANCIAL AND RELATED MATTERS

Financings and Burn Rates

In the "old days," the amounts of capital raised and the valuations at different stages were reasonably standardized. In very round numbers the seed round would raise up to $1 to 3 million with a post-money valuation below $5 million. The second round would raise $5 to 10 million, and the third round would raise $10 to 20 million, each with progressively higher pre-money valuations. And then the company would go public, raising $20–30 million with a valuation around $100 million.

Indeed, in the earlier days of biotechnology, it often seemed to be sufficient to form a company around a research idea, recruit a respected set of scientific advisers and an impressive Board of Directors, file or license a few patent applications, go public within a very short period of time, and then cash out—with the company having no viable long-term strategy for success and sustainability. However, the marketplace has matured and now demands more substance than hype. The Internet companies have just gone through such a transition with many Web-based hype- and frenzy-driven "business models" (or the lack thereof) failing rapidly this year, and only the more substantial ventures surviving. Over the past couple of years, though, following a period of time referred to as a financing "nuclear winter" (credit to Dick Schneider of Domain Associates [www.domainvc.com] for this phrase), the money raised and the valuations have risen much higher. Early rounds started yielding $15 to 30 million or more.

Despite all of this money, most everyone still looks at controlled net burn rates (money in minus money out, on a monthly basis). Some companies spend money like it is burning holes in their pockets. Others are more conservative. Both can be quite successful from every perspective. I favor conservative spending and a "pay-as-you-go" mentality. Some VCs look at monthly net burn rates in the few hundreds of thousands of dollars. Crossing $5 million in net burn rate for a full year can be a milestone in a company's development, but remember that it will be many years until profitability is reached—so, be careful with spending. (I believe that profitability will be elusive for over 90 percent of the biotech industry for many years to come.) Distilling this to an easily remembered set of guidelines, one of our major investors, Jean Deleage of Alta Partners (www.altapartners.com), has three commandments for his companies: (1) be good at science; (2) be good at raising money; and (3) be good at keeping money.

Investment Banks, Bankers, Analysts

As a company matures, it needs to become a known quantity to investment banks and their bankers and analysts. These are the people who will take the company public, thus achieving liquidity and access to additional capital needed to build the corporation. There are several accepted tiers of banks, from top groups like Lehman Brothers (www.lehman.com) and UBS Warburg (www.ubsw.com) to smaller "boutique" banks like Gerard Klauer Mattison & Co. (www.gkm.com). Analysts, who write about the company once it is public and thus can have undue impact on the price of one's stock, can be outstanding regardless of their bank, but obviously the Morgan Stanleys (www.msdw.com) and Goldman Sachses (www.gs.com) of the world have more clout than smaller entities.

Discussions with the bankers and analysts inevitably lead to questions about strategy and business models. However, because so few companies have achieved success in the same way, it is hard to say that there is any clear path to business success during the early days of a start-up's life cycle. Thus, albeit unsophisticated, the "whatever works" model may gain popularity in many camps over the long term.

OTHER MATTERS

Founders

Founders are the essential parents of the company. Unfortunately, as the company grows and its directions change, it is common for the founders to become disenfranchised. Some expect financial returns far beyond the norm. Some seek fame to go with their fortune. Some are never able to give up control to successors. However, unless the founder takes an operating role at the company, leaving his or her other job(s), the outcome is predictable. Namely, there will be a distancing of the founder(s) from the company and its employees over the years.

Investors

Investors are essential, too, as validation, as advisers, and as sources of funding. They range from being silent to trying to run the company. VC firms may be solely venture capital in their make-up, or they may be divisions of corporations that have broader interests. While VCs have been referred to as "vulture capitalists," the vast majority serve helpful roles on Boards and otherwise. They have "been there and done that" many times before, and thus the CEO who ignores their advice does so at his own risk.

Business Development

For biotechnology companies, the crucial financial and validation aspects of corporate alliances with big pharma make the business development function a key position throughout a company's life cycle. (In the later stages of a company's development, the role of business development will often change from predominantly selling to buying technologies and products, though there are aspects of both at all stages.) Buying and selling require very different mindsets, and few people do both well. Selling is the usual emphasis in small companies, and the business development function must understand what is being sold in order to determine how best to sell it and which groups would most likely buy it. Moreover, it has become increasingly difficult to sell deals to big pharma. There are a number of reasons for this, including the recent wave of mega-mergers in the pharma sector, which if nothing else decreases the number of potential partners for small companies. Senior scientific staff participate in the business-development activities, and many CEOs are directly involved. Some people in business development are more focused on getting the deal terms right, while others are more intent on closing the deal (even if the terms are not yet quite right). The former individuals would be better off if they worked with a greater sense of urgency, and the latter would be stronger contributors if they gave away less as the negotiations proceeded.

Legal Counsel

A well-established company will typically have a stable of in-house lawyers, covering both contract law and intellectual property, in addition to having relationships with multiple outside law firms. Small companies, however, will usually start with no internal legal employees, only outside counsel. Picking the right firms can be important, as they will assist in many ways over time, keeping the company out of trouble, getting it out of trouble once it has misstepped, or helping to establish and interpret the numerous confidentiality agreements, research contracts, and the like, that are encountered on a weekly basis. Often, a company will select one firm to handle general law and one to handle intellectual property portfolio.

Consultants and Advisers

Outside experts can play important roles in all stages of a company's evolution by actually doing work in the early days while always offering skilled experience and access to a broader network of potentially helpful individuals. The scientific advisory board (SAB) can also play a role in validating a company's approach, though a group functioning only as "figureheads" has lost favor in most companies.

Academic Interactions

Most small companies end up collaborating with academic labs for a variety of reasons. Certainly, it is cheaper at the outset to do work at a university, with the "slave labor" indigenous to graduate student and postdoctoral ranks. It shifts the risk a bit, but ultimately option fees, royalties, and other payments may be required in order to extract the rights from the more financially savvy academic faculty and institutions. Collaborations also engage the professor in the company's programs in a gainful manner. Sometimes the work is done in a founder's laboratory, but conflicts of interest must be reviewed to make sure that this is appropriate.

Public Relations

Throughout, there will be contact with the outside world, some good and some bad. Public relations (PR) firms can help to get the message packaged appropriately and out the door. Packaging one's message can be a long-term process, since the early story is too technical for most to understand. The company needs to be able to tell its story in progressively more persuasive and concise ways, ultimately in 20 to 30 seconds (during a stock sales call). With today's graphics capabilities, it is easier and easier to portray complex stories in a way that educates the lay public. PR firms can also help with damage control during times of crisis. There is a delicate balance in pushing a company's message, versus pushing it too hard or too early. Go with your gut feelings in the early stages of the company, but don't go out too early with an unfinished story that will require revision or even correction near term.

For the chief executive, there is at times a direct conflict between satisfying what can be competing and occasionally diametrically opposite desires among the various constituencies: the investors, the employees, the public good, and the chief executive. To satisfy all simultaneously means making everyone unhappy much of the time. Counterintuitively, satisfying each one in turn can be a more successful path. Most of the time, this is a delicate line to walk. If one keeps the company afloat long enough, then success will eventuate most of the time. But this is no mean feat. Different CEOs accomplish this in different ways, from in-your-face to low key. Whatever your approach, to your own self be true. Under-promise and over-deliver, even when the results aren't coming along fast enough.

ACKNOWLEDGMENTS

I thank Jerry Weisbach for carefully reading a draft of this manuscript and making a number of helpful suggestions.

WALTER H. MOOS, PH.D.
Chairman and CEO
MitoKor
Walter Moos joined MitoKor as Chairman and CEO in 1997.

Mr. Moos's extensive experience in business and corporate development, as well as in mergers and acquisitions, makes him a credible source in the business development arena. He also has many years of experience managing business units and has served as a Director on the Boards of CMPS, Onyx, and Rigel. Mr. Moos has held adjunct faculty positions at the University of Michigan, Ann Arbor, and the University of California, San Francisco.

Hear This! What You Must Know When Raising Venture Capital

R. MICHAEL JONES

The days of easy and fast financing for start-ups are gone. However, investors still make substantial investments in start-ups every day, so it is up to you to find a source of capital for your business.

KEYS TO FINANCING YOUR START-UP

There are three keys to successfully financing your start-up. The first is to understand the characteristics investors are looking for and to structure your deal accordingly. The second is to realize that there are literally thousands of sources of capital. This book can help you understand which sources are the best candidates for you to approach with your deal. The third key is to develop a funding strategy that matches your deal characteristics to the funding source.

TYPES OF INVESTORS

Each investor has his own agenda. This agenda determines that person's approach to investing and whether or not he will be interested in your deal. For example, venture capitalists (VCs) manage pools of capital that they invest in a group of investments. These funds may specialize in a particular industry or they may be organized in other ways. Some funds are interested only in follow-on funding, which is to say that someone else has made the initial investment. Others invest only in debt instruments, while others only provide funding to companies at certain stages. An example would be a bridge fund, which invests in or makes loans to companies that are in-between funding events. All funds have minimum and maximum amounts they will invest.

Venture Capitalists

Venture capitalists are the largest source of funding for start-ups. Venture capitalists typically manage venture funds, which essentially are a type of mutual fund. The fund raises money from investors, whether they be high-income individuals, institutions, corporations, or other types.

To understand venture capital, it is necessary to understand portfolio theory. Portfolio theory provides a way of diversifying risk by investing in a portfolio of deals. Some, perhaps most, deals will be losers, but others will be winners. The maximum probable return on the winning deals determines the minimum acceptable average return. This minimum return determines the type of deals in which any particular fund will invest.

To find out which VC funds you should approach, you need to do a lot of work. First, read everything you can get your hands on about VCs. Books such as this one, which provide a directory of funds, are especially helpful. Next, you should check the fund's Web site for information and investment criteria. Get input from your advisers and other entrepreneurs. Last, you can call and ask the fund for investment criteria and general information.

Angels

Angels are another important source of funding for start-ups. *Angel* is a catchall term that generally applies to any individual investor who actively seeks investment opportunities in start-up companies. Angels may operate on their own, or as part of a group, such as the Band of Angels in the San Francisco Bay Area, Tech Coast Angels in Orange County, California, or the Aztec Angel Network in San Diego. Some Angels invest in a lot of deals, and others only invest in one. Angels frequently are former entrepreneurs and may be interested only in certain industries.

Individual Investors

Individual investors are the largest and most important type of investor. Collectively, they provide the foundation for the entire venture industry. Individual investors make up the "friends and family" round of investment that nearly every company will need to tap before it moves on to an Angel or VC round.

CHARACTERISTICS OF YOUR BUSINESS

In large part, the characteristics of your business and the background of the founders and management team will determine the route you choose to fund your new venture. Some start-ups are easy to fund and others are very difficult. What are the characteristics that investors look for? Here are some important characteristics that will determine the route you will use to finance your start-up.

Technology

Technology is the single most important characteristic. First and foremost, investors will look to the technology that your start-up will employ in its proposed business. Technology has become, and will continue to be, the growth engine of the 2000s.

Management

Management is the second most important characteristic. The background and track record of the management team of your start-up is critical. You will often hear that it is the *most important,* and this is true with respect to any particular start-up. However, management is really the number two factor, simply because management can be changed.

Industry

Whether your start-up is a vortal or a biotech makes a difference. That's not to say that either is not fundable. Many VCs target certain industries, so you need to do some homework. It doesn't make much sense to pitch your sports vortal to a fund that only finances biotech. Different industries are hot at different times and in different geographical regions. Wireless and optic networking technologies are now hot in California, but something else may be in current favor on the East Coast.

Potential Market

Whether your maximum target market is $100 million or $100 billion makes a big difference. You will have a difficult time convincing a professional investor of your ability to move in and immediately capture a huge slice of any market. It is generally regarded as easier, and more realistic, to project a modest penetration of a huge market.

Business Model

Your business model and, specifically, how you will generate revenues and when you will become profitable are extremely important elements.

Track Record

The track record of management is important, but the track record of the founder is also a primary factor in any investment decision by a professional investor.

Prior Investments

The amount and structure of prior investments and having "smart money" involved at an early stage are critical. In fact, many VC's will tell you that taking care of these elements is the best way to help yourself in the follow-on rounds and in getting to the initial public offering stage. Smart money comes from an investor who brings something to the table other than money, such as expertise and connections that the VC or other investor brings to your deal. This can make a huge difference in how far your deal will go.

FUNDING STRATEGIES

There are as many different ways to fund start-ups as there are different types of start-ups. Although this is not profound, it is true. Everyone knows that before the market sell-off in April 2000, it was relatively easy to attract funding and that it is more difficult to do so today. The days of hastily putting together a business plan, immediately attracting a strong VC investment, and then launching your initial public offering (IPO) soon after are gone, at least for most start-ups. Most companies will have to take other steps to finance their businesses. Described in the following sections are three models for doing your deal. Your deal may not fall squarely into one of these models—don't fret, these are only concepts.

The Grand Slam

The grand slam goes directly from business plan to major venture capital funding, in excess of $20 million, and heads directly for IPO or additional follow-on funding. How long it takes to complete the grand slam varies. In late 1999 and early 2000, many grand slams were completed, from start to finish, in as little as a few months. The grand slam is the deal that every entrepreneur dreams about, and though it has become truly rare, it still exists and indeed is important as a model.

To hit a grand slam, you will need:

- *Technology* that is revolutionary; solves a major problem and has been proven to be economically feasible; is protected by multiple patents; and is scalable.
- A *business plan* that details the rapid deployment of the technology; is within the budget imposed by available funding; is into a billion-plus dollar market; and supports strong entry into an industry targeted by the funding source.
- A *management team* that has a preexisting relationship with the funding source, including a major recent success in which the funding source invested; has already made or attracted a significant seed investment into the company; and has the experience, qualifications, and motivation to successfully manage the business and implement the business plan.
- Finally, to hit a grand slam, the proper *conditions* must exist, including stable general economic conditions and interest rates; a receptive attitude on the part of underwriters to the technology and business; a strong investment demand for the technology; and perfect market conditions for emerging companies.

The Home Run

The home run is a great deal but is not a grand slam, because the entrepreneurs need additional time and funding to meet one or more of the grand slam characteristics. The home run deal typically has gone through a seed round and several rounds of VC funding. The entrepreneurs have invested in the company. Simply put, more time is spent developing the home run company than the grand slam company. Nevertheless, the outcome is the same. The favorable outcome may be in the form of the IPO or a sale of the business.

The Base Hit

The base hit is a deal that is under construction. This start-up needs to raise interim funding while the founders work toward the ideal of the grand slam. The base hit needs money and time to develop and refine the business plan, attract or complete the management team, develop and protect the technology, and perhaps wait for the right conditions. Today's base hit may become tomorrow's home run. For example, voice-activated technology is hot today and is attracting the interest of VCs. This is due in large part to the development and refinement of wireless devices that will become the platform for voice recognition.

The best way to fund the base hit is incrementally. You start with a Founders' Round, and then go to a Friends and Family Round. In the Friends and Family

Round, you raise enough money to retain and pay necessary service providers, complete your business plan, and pay for the essentials every start-up needs. These essentials include business cards, phone bills, and perhaps a modest travel and promotion budget. Remember to keep essentials to a minimum. You don't need and can't afford to pretend you have much money at this point. The essentials are a means to an end—to help you obtain additional funding and to keep your deal alive.

The next step after the Friends and Family Round is the Seed Round. If you are making progress and have many of the attributes listed in the Characteristics section but still need some critical ingredients such as management, an Angel investment is a good goal for the Seed Round. An Angel may have connections to help you attract management or may help you meet other Angel investors or even provide introduction to VCs. The idea is to use your present investors as a way to attract other investors through referrals and introductions.

SECURITIES LAWS

Do not forget that you must comply with state and federal securities laws. There are plenty of reasons this is important. First, if you do not comply, you provide investors with a "put option" that allows them to demand rescission. Second, your deal will not be able to later pass the "due diligence" that a VC or an underwriter will insist on performing.

FINAL WORDS

Commit to success! In order to successfully fund your start-up, you must commit to a funding strategy. Don't hesitate to refine your strategy as you move forward—but commit to getting your deal done.

R. MICHAEL JONES
Founder
Startup Law Center at Higgs, Fletcher & Mack LLP
R. Michael Jones recently founded the Startup Law Center at Higgs, Fletcher & Mack LLP to serve the needs of start-up companies. Mr. Jones's practice is concentrated in the areas of venture development and finance, corporate, and securities law.

A member of the California State and San Diego County Bar Associations, Mr. Jones earned his bachelor of science degree in Business Administration from Regis University at Denver, his master's degree in Business Administration in International Business from the University of Colorado, and his law degree from the California Western School of Law.

What It Means to Take VC Money—Is the Vision Still Yours?

Nick Desai

I have been involved in business my whole life and am currently running my second start-up, for which I raised just under $20 million in three rounds from private investors and major Silicon Valley, East Coast, Japanese, and European venture capitalists (VCs) and investors. In the process, I talked to over 100 different venture capital companies.

The year I started raising money was the best year in NASDAQ history, and every initial public offering (IPO) with the term *dot-com* after it went through the roof. This year, the market has receded and dot-com is dead. My company was here before and is here now. I have over 80 private investors in my company, some of whom have never used our product or, for that matter, the Internet. My discussion, therefore, comes from experiences with my company and related in general to the high-tech VC community and mindset. Some of my advice is largely and broadly applicable, but it is certainly more applicable to the technology sector.

When you choose to take VC money, you have an equity partner in your company and in your vision. If, and only if, you work closely with the venture capitalist firm to manage expectations, set goals, and understand each other, then you can truly have a symbiotic relationship in which your vision evolves only slightly to accommodate the VC's needs and you build a great company together. To get to that point, it is important to understand and be prepared for the various factors that affect the VC mind-set and expectations. I expand on those in the following sections.

How the Process Works

Venture capitalists invest money in exchange for equity in start-up type companies. A venture capitalist operates under the home run model. Venture capitalist firms don't want a bunch of companies generating 20 percent returns for them; they want companies that generate thousands of percent return. One eBay or Yahoo! makes up for a lot of bad guesses along the way.

As with every other industry, venture capital has competition. There are better VCs and lesser VCs. Venture capitalist firms get their money from corporations, mutual funds, trusts, and wealthy individuals. They get money in funds that are a specific size. As you might expect, the performance of one fund is a key indicator to prospective investors in a subsequent fund.

Let's say a VC has a $100 million fund and it invests $10 million in each of 10 companies. In each case, it buys 25 percent of the company for $10 million, making each company worth $40 million post-money. Now, let's say one of those companies has Yahoo! or eBay–like success and becomes worth $1 billion. Let's assume, for simplicity, that no other dilution occurs. And, let's say the other nine companies fail completely. Finally, let's assume that this process took one year to work out. Then, the VC has turned $100 million into $250 million (its 25 percent of the $1 billion company). That is a 250 percent return. Pretty nice. And this is with 9 out of 10 companies failing totally.

Reality Check

This is not to say that VCs hope or want 9 of 10 companies to fail, it's just that they likely will. That is the reality of business. As an aside, the worst mistake you can make is to assume that just because you got VC money, and good VC money, you have accomplished anything. Other than taking money from people and raising expectations, you have accomplished *nothing*. Remember that every day.

Given that mind-set, most VCs are run as partnerships, in which the Investing Partners let the Managing Partners make investment decisions. The Partners generally have (or claim to have) certain expertise. They tend to invest in areas they know something about, or in industries that are growing. In 1998 it was e-commerce. In 1999 it was optical networking. In 2000 it is the mobile Internet industry. Once they pick an industry, they let business plans come to them, for the most part, and pick a company to get behind.

Now, I will say something that may sound contradictory. VCs pick a company to get behind and then *get behind* it, but they won't build a business. That is to say, your company doesn't have to be perfect to get funded, but it does have to be better in the same space as the other companies that the VC is looking at. When we received our first venture financing, our VC was looking for a company in our space. We walked in, had a better model than most that its Partners had seen, and we had a term sheet literally the next day.

Then they looked at our company, saw its issues and areas of concern, and helped us with those.

Another factor I mentioned is that VCs are run by Partners. Partners are people. And people are not perfect. VCs make as many mistakes as anyone else—in fact, more so. They really do. Talk to any major venture capitalist and ask him about the companies he passed on. The list will be long and will likely include names of companies you will recognize. Not just that, venture capitalists are prone to two kinds of biases: personal biases and industry biases. Their personal biases, which run the gamut, will directly impact their investment decisions—for example, if they have been burned in one area, or if they like one area, or if they have a friend who likes one area, or if they are having a bad hair day. There is almost no objectivity in this process, and what one venture capitalist will consider a great company, another might consider a dog.

Then there are industry biases. Two years ago, e-commerce was all the rage. VCs were investing in anything dot-com in which a product was being sold, all wanting to have the next Amazon. VCs will see between a few hundred and a few thousand business plans a month. Based upon this review, and their personal biases, they will choose the "buzz area" that makes sense for them and their fund and portfolio of companies.

And let's not forget the "who's who" factor. Chances are, if you are reading this book, then, like me, you were not famous before you started the company. When the CEO of big company X leaves to start a company focused on X, and he knows major I-banks and so on, the VC money comes tumbling in. These high-profile start-ups are not really start-ups, because their founders are often not "hungry." While there are certainly serial entrepreneurs who have done well repeatedly, a surprising number of high-profile start-ups are not as successful as you might think.

Most VCs have previous investments. They call it their portfolio. VCs are loyal to and influenced by their portfolio companies, almost as if the companies were family members. Remember, once a venture capitalist firm gets behind a company, it is truly behind that company. Given that, VCs will sometimes realize that you have a better company or model, but because they are behind a previously chosen company that is in a similar space, they will stick with their initial choice. If you have true first-mover advantage, then it's a different story, but few companies have this anymore.

VC MANAGEMENT STYLE

When you think about the Partners who run VCs, they come from a range of backgrounds. Some are consultants, some investment bankers, others simply rich individuals. If you are an entrepreneur, you are probably not a venture capitalist. There are some notable exceptions, but this is mostly the case.

Always remember that you are the visionary, not the venture capitalist. There are hands-off VCs and hands-on VCs. Again, chances are, if you are reading this book, you are in an earlier stage. And you are relatively new to running a business. The hands-off VC will give name, money, and guidance when you ask for it, as well as occasional direction and introductions. A good hands-on VC can be an indispensable asset in the early growth of your company. The firm can help set strategy, attract customers, raise money, hire management, and much more. A bad hands-on VC can kill your company.

But VCs don't want to run your company. The Partner from a good VC that is involved in your company is also involved in a *lot* of other companies. These Partners have limited time and energy. If you think them leaving you alone is a good thing, and that everything is great, this is not always true. They may have left you alone because you don't listen or because they are just plain busy with other things. It is *your* job to communicate and involve the VC. If everything is fine, most VCs will pull back, since they don't want to get in the way. If everything isn't fine and they know it, they will be all over you.

"THE OPERATION WAS A SUCCESS, BUT THE PATIENT DIED"

The final factor in all this is that your definition of success and a VC's definition of success may differ. This can manifest itself in two ways. Let's say you start a company. It happens to be in a "hot" area. You build up revenues, and your VC got in early enough to help you. You IPO the company. Your stock goes up, not by a huge amount, but say 50 percent in the first year. The VC sells its holdings in your company. It makes a *lot* of money. But your company is fundamentally flawed and your stock goes in the toilet. The VC's fund return looks great, and you have a dying company. The VC's interests can often be more short term than yours, since you are attached to your company for life (even if you walk away), and the venture capitalist firm is attached only to the numbers. This happens all the time. The entire cycle can take two years, and the VC is long gone.

It is important to point out here that a good VC (and our VCs are outstanding) may have all these factors but is nevertheless a *vital* part of the growth and success of your company. Remember, the VC owes you nothing. You are going there to ask for a *lot* of money to pursue your vision. What more can you want?

VISION MAKERS OR TAKERS?

We started to answer the question, Is your dream your own? Understanding the previous factors, you can appreciate that when a VC invests in your company, it becomes part "owner" and partner. The dream is now a collective. Yours and theirs.

This is usually a good thing. Your dream has some merits, of course. A VC wouldn't give you money otherwise. But, you're not perfect, you don't have all the answers, and you don't know everything. You *should* listen to qualified VCs and be open to guidance. Remember, venture capitalists look at thousands of business plans. Their comments come with insight that you can't get easily otherwise. For example, if a venture capitalist tells you, "Yeah, but 10 other people are doing the same thing," and you haven't come across this in your market research, it's probably because they have seen 10 business plans that you haven't. And, VCs have seen the mistakes and pitfalls, especially early in the company life cycle.

The important question is this: What can you do, given all the previous factors, to ensure that you and your VC manage to make everyone happy? If you do this, you and your VC will be great together; if not, you won't. You must:

Manage your own expectations and understand that there are alternatives. You can get private money, you can borrow money, you can finance a business from sales, whatever. When you choose the VC route, you should actively make the decision to build a company a certain way. You should be open to outside involvement. You should be open to "reporting" to a Board, controlled by your VC.

Understand what the venture capitalist wants. Understand the VC mentality in general, but also the specific venture capitalist firm and the specific person you are dealing with. What is the firm's background? Who are the Partners? What are the firm's other companies? (Most good VCs will provide references of portfolio companies.) What is the firm's investment philosophy? Knowing the VC and the Partners (more on this later) are key factors. You should, of course, talk to everyone, but the more synergies you find, the better off you will be. And the more likely your paths are to become one.

Communicate your vision. The fact that you have "always wanted to do this" is not a good reason for a VC to give you money. Understand your vision. Communicate it to the firm, and be honest. Do you want to be a CEO? Are you an idea person who doesn't have any real interest in running a company? What are you scared of? Where do you see yourself in five years? When do you *"have to"* start making some money from this thing? Knowing the answers to these types of questions and explaining your real reasons for doing this are important, too. Sure, it's for the money, but, as you already know, it's more than that. I told our first VCs that

I wanted to build something that changed people's lives. In whatever simple way, my widget was to be a life-changing tool. I also told them that I have the unique luxury of not thinking short term financially.

Know who you are dealing with. In an early stage, a Partner from the VC will take a Board seat on your company. *Who is this person?* Do you respect him? Does the person respect you? What is his background? You don't want to work with a duplicate of yourself, but you do want someone you can trust and respect, and vice versa. Ask yourself this: Would you go out for pizza with this guy? Or to a ballgame? That is a real indicator of your level of comfort. If the answer is "no," you may have reason to be concerned. Remember, though, you don't want (and trust me, you won't get) a "yes" man. Someone disagreeing with you or challenging you is a really good thing. At our first VC meeting, the senior Partner made us sing the *Brady Bunch* theme song—to see if we were "confident." At a recent VC meeting, we spent 10 minutes on our company and two hours on the state of an industry only tangentially related to what we were doing. Don't be put off by that. That venture capitalist wanted to know how I think, and whether I will just "cave" or offer my true opinions. You have to get to know the person and be comfortable taking direction, advice, and even a scolding from him.

Believe in something. Don't just suck up. The one thing that will kill your chances with a venture capitalist is saying yes to everything he says. If you want to start a company, you'd better believe in something—something real, and something you are willing to convince the world of, one person at a time. When you can do that, and *when* you can convince someone of that with passion and energy, then you may have a shot. Maybe. A good venture capitalist will bait you, test you, ask you random questions. You can't be rattled. And a venture capitalist will say (to your company making cookies), "Well, I think you're a great guy, but you should make donuts." If you say yes, you'll make donuts, it's over. You went there to sell a cookie business, so sell a cookie business. If you are that unsure of yourself, you have no business in a venture capitalist's office, and no business starting a business. Listening and being open to advice is one thing. Not believing is yet another.

Have a good idea and a good company. In Hollywood they have a saying: "A good movie will get made." Similarly, a good business will get funded. You can cry all the sob stories you want; if you don't have a good business, you won't get money, and if you do, you will.

Understand how your vision will change. Ask the venture capitalist about his firm's expectations, past performance, level of involvement, size of fund, and so on. Ask if he and his Partners like IPO companies or if they are open to acquisitions, too.

GETTIN' THE MONEY

Okay, so you understand the VC. You are prepared to change your vision to meet the VC's needs. What is it going to take to get the money?

You. You are the most important factor. VCs invest in founders. I have heard this line a thousand times in the last two years from VCs: "We figure that if we invest in good people who will die before they let their company die, and they are at least pretty smart, then they'll do something worthwhile," in some form or another. It is true. The market will change. Business models will change. You have to be the driving force, pure and simple.

A broad market vision. If you want to build the corner lemonade stand and it's going to be great and perfect and make money from day one, the VC doesn't want any part of it. If, however, you want to build 1,000 corner lemonade stands, based on your understanding that 10 million 16- to 20-year-olds want lemonade as their first beverage, *great.* Now the VC will listen, at least.

Expertise in your business area. If you're a lemon grower, it's great to start a lemonade stand. If you're an astrophysicist, probably not. Have some expertise in what you do, or the venture capitalist will say, "Great idea; why you?" It's a fair question. It can be technical, it can be business, it can be customers, whatever. Know your industry firsthand.

A business plan. Just saying that something is a great idea, the market is "everybody," and the money is "unlimited" won't work. Have a specific plan and projections. Everyone with an IQ over 7 understands that start-up revenue projections are total bunk. It doesn't matter. What does matter is your ability to do research and form a cohesive plan. Your ability to build a plan of this kind is a vital skill.

A solid management team. Either have a team in place or plan to bring a team in to help make your vision a reality. Even Michael Jordan needed four other players on the court. Who are they? Where do you plan to get them? When? The fact that someone is your friend is a really bad reason to make this person your COO. Chances are, if you are reading this book, you aren't a proven, experienced manager. Great. What are you good at? What are you *not* good at? Answer these questions before they are asked of you.

Understanding the competitive landscape. Do people want what you are making? A lot of people? And is the world's largest company making the same thing? As in, "Why will people buy it from you?" If you sell it, they won't come, unless there is a really good reason to. As you explain the competition to your prospective VC, remember one thing: Your competitors are not just the companies making the same stuff, but also the companies selling different stuff to the same customers you plan to sell to.

So, that is it. You have a vision. The VC has a vision. If you are willing to do what it takes, the two of you can work beautifully together. Good luck.

NICK DESAI
Co-Founder, Chairman, and CEO
Zkey

Nick Desai is the creator of Zkey vision and the designer of the core platform, which launched in 1999. He is a visionary and product designer who anticipates market requirements and keeps business and product planning several steps ahead. As Chairman, he is central to core business strategies, long-term strategic vision and design, business development, and attracting investors.

Mr. Desai possesses a unique combination of technological understanding and business expertise and has spoken at several prominent venues. He received his master's degree in electrical engineering from the University of California, Los Angeles, with an emphasis in compound semiconductor device physics.

PART THREE

Indexes

Investment Terms

KURT L. KICKLIGHTER

The following are terms that are often used in venture capital and other investment agreements and negotiations.

Accredited Investor. This is an entity or person who meets a sophistication test set forth in SEC Regulation D. Under the current rule, a natural person who has a net worth of at least $1 million, or annual income for the last two years and expected annual income in the current year of $200,000 ($300,000 with the person's spouse), meets the test. The test is more complex for trusts, partnerships, and other entities.

Anti-Dilution Provisions. These are provisions that limit the issuance of additional shares by the company. Sometimes these are flat prohibitions against issuing shares over some threshold or at prices less than some target. Sometimes they call for adjustments in the event that shares are issued for less than the consideration paid by the investor.

Blue Sky Laws. These are the state securities laws regulating the issuance and sale of securities.

Cliff Vesting. This is a term that refers to a complete vesting of options or stock ownership at a particular point in time.

Cumulative Dividends. Refer to dividends on preferred stock that are required to be paid at particular times and, if not paid in a timely manner, continue to be an obligation of the company. Noncumulative dividends, on the other hand, are scheduled to be paid, but if not declared by the Board of Directors in the appropriate period, they are not required to be paid later.

Demand Registration Rights. These are rights to "demand" registration of securities. It is generally difficult for holders of restricted securities to sell their shares, either privately or publicly. A party with demand registration rights can demand that the company register her shares for sale to the public.

Drag Along Right. This is a right to require that specific shareholders participate with the company or another shareholder in a sale of shares in order to preserve the percentage interests of the respective shareholders.

Forced Conversion. This refers to the ability of the holder of convertible stock or the company to require that it be "converted" into common stock. Usually, this is to the company's benefit so that the preferred stock is eliminated.

Founder Agreement. This is typically an agreement with the founder of a company restricting his rights to sell shares of the company, granting registration rights, and containing other provisions regarding the equity ownership of the founder.

Indemnification. A complicated concept that in the investment context usually refers to a company's agreeing to pay the legal fees and other losses of an investor that result from specific types of misconduct by the company.

IPO. Initial public offering. It is the first offering to the public of shares of the company directly by the company, usually with the assistance of underwriters.

Issuer. Refers to the company that is "issuing" shares or that has issued the shares that are being referred to.

Kickers. This is a generic term that means any participation in the increased value of the company above the return on capital or investment an instrument would otherwise provide the investor. Kickers include profit participation payments, bonus interest payments, warrants, and so on.

Lock-Up or Market Stand-Off Agreement. This is an agreement not to sell shares following a company's IPO. These agreements may require that securities not be sold during the first six months following the IPO, although the timing may vary. This is to permit the underwriters to establish a stable trading market following the IPO.

Milestones. These are particular events, the occurrence of which causes rights to arise or be eliminated. Typical milestones for a company, for instance, would be full operation of a beta site or performance of new technology, FDA approval of a drug or process, or gross revenues from sales exceeding a specific threshold.

Overallotment. This refers to additional shares issuable in an IPO beyond the stated number of shares. It permits the underwriter in an IPO to sell more shares if demand for the shares is sufficient. This is sometimes referred to as a "Green Shoe," named for the first transaction where an overallotment was taken.

Piggyback Registration Rights. These are rights granted to an investor to participate in the IPO or in any primary offering of securities by a company. This means that the investor can sell at the offering price alongside the company, directly to the public.

Pooling. This refers to an accounting treatment that allows two companies to be combined without revaluing the assets of either of the companies. If the assets of a target company are revalued, this could adversely affect the combined earnings of the companies because of higher amortization and depreciation expense. This treatment is not likely to be available for transactions closing after 2000, although the date for expiration is not clear at this time.

Pre-Emptive Rights. These are rights to maintain percentage ownership in the event of sale of shares by a company. Sometimes an investor will want to retain the right to keep its percentage interest, provided that it pays the same consideration as any new investor to the company.

Public Company. A company that files public reports with the SEC under the Securities Exchange Act of 1934. A company becomes obligated to file such reports in one of two ways. If a company conducts an IPO that is registered with the SEC, for a period of time thereafter, it is obligated to file these reports. If a company registers its shares for trading under the Securities Exchange Act of 1934, it is obligated to file these reports.

Primary Offering. An offering of its stock by a company to the public, either directly or through an underwriter.

Put-Call Provision. This is a provision that permits one shareholder to "put" its shares to a second shareholder for purchase. However, the second shareholder can elect to "call" for purchase of his shares at the same price as the "put" if he does not want to sell.

Redemption. Refers to the payment in cash (usually) by the company for its shares. The shares are generally then available for reissue by the company. Redemption may be "mandatory" or "optional" under specific circumstances, depending on the terms of the transaction.

Registration. When shares are "registered" with the SEC and "qualified" or "registered" with appropriate state securities authorities. Registration is a lengthy and expensive process under which the company, usually with the assistance of underwriters, files detailed disclosures and a prospectus with the SEC and state authorities. When the registration is "effective," the shares of the company may be sold to the public. Registration of shares of the company or insiders for purposes of selling directly to the public is accomplished under the Securities Act of 1933. Registration of shares for purposes of allowing the public generally to trade in securities of the company is accomplished under the Securities Exchange Act of 1934.

Restricted Stock. This generally refers to any stock issued, except stock issued in an IPO or in another registration that is not held by insiders. Thus, shares issued to the investors and to employees under a stock option plan will generally contain a legend to the effect that the shares are not subject to resale except if they are registered for sale or exempt from registration.

Rights of First Refusal. These are rights to purchase securities when offered to a third party, usually at the same terms. As a practical matter, these provisions make negotiations with a second potential investor group difficult in many cases.

Rule 144. A "safe harbor" rule that permits insiders and others holding restricted stock to sell shares in the public markets if the company is a public company. It imposes holding period requirements and timing and volume limitations on sales of such stock.

Secondary Offering. This is a term that seems to have different meanings to different people in the investment community. A secondary offering is generally an offering to the public of shares owned by existing shareholders. However, some people use the term to refer to any offering occurring after an IPO.

Securities Act of 1933. This is the federal act regulating the registration of securities for sale to the public. Securities may be sold privately under specific exemptions in this act.

Securities Exchange Act of 1934. This is the federal act regulating the public trading markets. Registration under this act permits a company's shares to be traded by the public in the public securities markets. Registration is required if a company has a number of shareholders over an applicable threshold.

Senior Debt. Debt that by definition is superior to specific types of creditors of the company. Usually, this debt is senior to all debt, other than that of vendors, and is secured. Sometimes it also includes some kind of kicker, such as a warrant.

Subscription Agreement. This is the agreement signed by an investor in a company, usually in a private offering, under which the investor agrees to purchase shares or other securities on particular terms. Sometimes restrictions on resale are contained in the agreement, and the company provides registration or other rights in the agreement to the investor.

Subordinated Debt. Debt that by definition is subordinate to the general creditors of the company. Subordinated debt is often accompanied by or incorporates some kind of kicker, such as a warrant.

Suitability Questionnaire. A suitability questionnaire seeks to elicit information that will help a company determine whether an investor is adequately sophisticated and meets the other qualifications for investment in a private placement.

Supermajority Provisions. These are provisions, usually in the articles of incorporation or bylaws, that require more than a majority vote of the Board or shareholders for particular corporate transactions. Typical transactions covered would be a sale, merger, or reorganization, where the price or terms meet or fail to meet specified parameters.

Tag Along Right. This is a right held by a shareholder to participate in the sale by the company or another shareholder (usually a manager of the company) in sales of shares to a third party.

Warrants. Essentially options to acquire additional shares. They are typically granted as a "kicker" for a loan or with preferred stock. The strike price is often higher than the fair market value of the shares at the date the warrants are issued so that the holder of the warrants participates in the appreciation of the shares only after a threshold is exceeded.

KURT L. KICKLIGHTER
Partner
Luce Forward & Scripps
Over his nearly 20 years of practice, Kurt L. Kicklighter has focused on helping businesses and individuals reach their financial objectives. He assists a wide range of enterprises, including technology companies, financial services companies, and family businesses in raising capital, acquiring and disposing of ventures, and accomplishing their strategic goals. This assistance includes representation of public companies before the Securities Exchange Commission (SEC) and other regulatory agencies.

Funds in Alphabetical Order

A

ABN AMRO Private Equity, 3
ABS Capital Partners, 3–4
AC Ventures, 4–5
Acacia Venture Partners, 5–6
Accel Partners, 6
Access Venture Partners, 7
Advanced Technology Ventures, 7–8
Advent International Corporation, 8–9
Ad–Ventures, LLC, 9
Alexander Hutton Venture Partners, 9–10
Allied Capital Corporation, 10
Alloy Ventures, 10–11
Alpine Technology Ventures, 11
Alta Partners, 11–12
Altos Ventures, 12–13
AltoTech Ventures, LLC, 13
American River Ventures, LP, 13–14
American Securities Capital Partners, L.P., 14–15
Amerimark Capital Corporation, 15
Ampersand Ventures, 15–16
Anila Fund, 16
Antares Capital Corporation, 16–17
Anthem Capital, L.P., 17
Apex Venture Partners, 17–18
Applied Technology, 18–19
APV Technology Partners, 19
Aqua International Partners, L.P., 20
Arbor Partners, LLC, 20–21
ARCH Venture Partners, 21
Aspen Ventures, 21–22
Asset Management Company, 22
Associated Venture Investors, 23
Austin Ventures, 23–24
Axiom Venture Partners, L.P., 24
Aztec Venture Network, LLC, 25

B

Bachow & Associates, Inc., 25–26
BancBoston Ventures, Inc., 26
Batterson Venture Partners, LLC, 26–27
Battery Ventures, 27–28
Bay Partners, 28

Benchmark Capital, 28–29
Berkeley International Capital Corporation, 29
Bertelsmann Ventures, 30
Bessemer Venture Partners, 30–31
BioVentures West, 31
Blue Capital Management, L.L.C., 31–32
Bluefish Ventures, 32
Boston Financial & Equity Corporation, 33
Boston Millennia Partners, 33–34
Boulder Ventures Limited, 34–35
Brad Peery Capital Inc., 35
Brantley Partners, L.P., 35–36
Brentwood Venture Capital, 36
Bristol Investment Group, Inc., 37
Broadview Capital Partners LLC, 37–38
Burrill & Company, 38

C

Callier Interests, 38–39
Cambria Group, The, 39
Canaan Partners, 39–40
Capital Insights, 40
Capital Network Incorporated, The, 40–41
Capital Southwest Corporation, 41
Capitol Health Partners PL, 41–42
Capstone Ventures, 42
Celerity Partners, 43
Centennial Ventures, 43–44
CenterPoint Ventures, 44
CEO Venture Fund, 45
Chanen & Co. Ltd., 45–46
Charterway Investment Corporation, 46
Chase Capital Partners, 46–47
Chisholm Private Capital, 47
Chrysalis Ventures, 47–48
CIVC Partners, 48–49
Claremont Capital Corporation, 49
Clarion Capital Corporation, 49–50
CMEA Ventures, 50
CMGI @Ventures, 51
Coast Business Credit, 51–52
Collison Howe & Lennox, LLC, 52
ComVentures, 52–53

Comcast Interactive Capital, 53–54
Commercial Bridge Capital, LLC, 54–55
Community Technology Fund, Boston University, 55–56
Compass Technology Partners, 56
Comstock Partners, LLC, 56–57
Conning Capital Partners, 57–58
Consolidated Firstfund Capital Corp., 58
Convergence Partners, 59
Coral Ventures, 60
Corporation Acquisitions, Inc., 60–61
Crescendo Ventures, 61
Crosspoint Venture Partners, 61–62
Crystal Internet Venture Funds, 62–63
CS Capital Partners, LLC, 63

D
Davis, Tuttle Venture Partners, 63–64
Delphi Ventures, 64
Delta Capital Partners, LLC, 64–65
DigitalVentures, 65–66
Doll Capital Management Co., LLC, 66
Dolphin Communications Partners, L.P., 67
Domain Associates, LLC, 67–68
Dominion Ventures, Inc., 68–69
Dorset Capital Management, LLC, 69
Dougery Ventures, 69–70
Doyle & Boissiere, LLC, 70
Draper Fisher Jurvetson, 70–71
Dresner Capital Resources, Inc., 71–72
DynaFund Ventures, 72

E
Earlybird, 72–73
Edelson Technology Partners, 73
Edgewater Funds LP, 74
El Dorado Ventures, 74
Elvey Partnership, The, 74–75
Empire Ventures, 75–76
Encompass Ventures, 76
Endeavor Capital Management, 76–77
Enterprise Partners Venture Capital, 77–78
EuclidSR Partners, 78

F
Fidelity Ventures, 79
Financial Broker Relations, 79–80
Financial Resources Corporation, 80
Financial Technology Ventures, 80–81
First American Capital Funding, Inc., 81
First Analysis Venture Capital, 81–82
First Capital Group, 82
First Manhattan Capital Partners, 83
Flemming, Lessard & Shields, LLC, 83–84

Fluke Venture Partners, 84
Forrest Binkley & Brown, 84–85
Forward Ventures, 85–86
Foundation Capital, 86
Freeman Spogli & Co., 86–87
Fremont Ventures, 87–88
Friedman Fleischer & Lowe, LLC, 88
Fulcrum Venture Capital Corporation, 88–89
Full Circle Investments, Inc., 89
Fuqua Ventures, LLC, 89–90

G
G.A. Herrera & Co., 90
G–51 Capital LLC, 90–91
GE Capital–Equity Capital Group, 91–92
Gemini Investors LLC, 92
General Atlantic Partners, LLC, 92–93
Generation Partners, 94
Geneva Venture Partners, 94–95
Genstar Capital, LLC, 95
Geocapital Partners, LLC, 95–96
Glynn Capital Management, 96–97
Grace Internet Capital, 97
Granite Capital Partners, 97–98
Granite Ventures, 98–99
Grayson & Associates, Inc., 99
Great Hill Equity Partners, 99–100
Greylock, 100–101
GRP, 101
GTCR Golden Rauner, LLC, 101–102
GulfStar Group, 102–103

H
Halpern, Denny & Company, 103–104
Hamilton Technology Ventures, 104
Hammond, Kennedy, Whitney and Co., Inc., 105
Harvest Partners Inc., 105–106
HealthCare Ventures LLC, 106–107
Hellman & Friedman, LLC, 107
Hickory Venture Capital Corporation, 107–108
High Street Capital II, LLC, 108
Highland Capital Partners, 108–109
HLM Management Company, 109–110
Hook Partners, 110
Housatonic Partners, 110–111
Howard Industries, Inc., 111
Hudson Ventures, 112
Humana Ventures, 112
Hummer Winblad Venture Partners, 113
Huntington Holdings, Inc., 113

I
Idanta Partners, Ltd., 114
IDG Ventures, 114–115

iMinds Ventures, 115
Imperial Bank, 115–116
Indosuez Ventures, 116
Industrial Growth Partners, 117
Infinity Capital, 117–118
ING Furman Selz Investments, 118
IngleWood Ventures, 118–119
InnoCal, 119
Innovest Venture Partners, 119–120
Insight Capital Partners, 120–121
Institutional Venture Partners (IVP), 121
Integra Ventures, 122
Integral Capital Partners, 122–123
International Capital Partners, Inc., 123
Interprise Technology Partners, LP, 123–124
InterWest Partners VIII, 124–125
ITU Ventures, 125–126
IVP (Institutional Venture Partners), 126–127

J
J. F. Shea Venture Capital, 127
JAFCO Ventures, 127–128
JatoTech Ventures, 128
Jefferson Capital Partners, LTD., 129
JK & B Capital, 129–130
Johnston Associates Inc., 130–131
Josephberg Grosz & Co., Inc., 131

K
Kansas City Equity Partners, 131–132
KB Partners, L.L.C., 132
KBL Healthcare Ventures, 132–133
KECALP Inc., 133–134
Kettle Partners LP, 134
Keystone Venture Capital, 134–135
Kleiner Perkins Caufield & Byers, 135
Kline Hawkes & Company, 136
KLM Capital Group, 136–137
Kohlberg & Company, L.L.C., 137–138
Kriegsman Group, The, 138–139

L
Labrador Ventures, 139–140
Ladenburg, Thalmann & Company, Inc., 140
Lake Shore Capital Partners, Inc, 140–141
Lambda Management Inc., 141
Lawrence Financial Group, 141–142
Lazard Technology Partners, 142
Lehman Brothers Incorporated, 143
Leonard Green & Partners, L.P., 143–144
Leong Ventures, 144
Levine Leichtman Capital Partners, Inc., 144–145
Liberty Venture Partners, 145
Libra Mezzanine Partners, L.P., 146

Lombard Investments Inc., 146–147

M
Macadam Capital Partners, 147
Madison Dearborn Partners, 147–148
Marquette Venture Partners, 148
Marwit Capital, LLC, 148–149
Mason Wells, 149–150
Matrix Partners, 150
Maveron, LLC, 150–151
MDS Venture Pacific, Inc., 151
MedTech Ventures, Inc., 152
MedVenture Associates, 152–153
Mellon Ventures, Inc., 153
Menlo Ventures, 154
Meritage Private Equity Fund, LP, 154–155
Meritech Capital Partners, 155–156
meVC, 156
Meyer Duffy Ventures, LLC, 156–157
MidMark Associates, Inc., 157
Millennium 3 Venture Group, LLC, 157–158
Mission Ventures, 158–159
Mitsui & Co. (U.S.A.), Inc., 159
MMC Capital C&I Fund, 160
Mohr, Davidow Ventures, 160–161
Montgomery Associates, Inc., 161–162
Morgenthaler, 162
Multimedia Broadcast Investment Corporation, 162–163

N
National Corporate Finance, Inc., 163
Needham Asset Management, 163–164
NeoCarta Ventures, 164–165
New Enterprise Associates, 165
New World Ventures, 165–166
New York Partners, LLC, 166
Newbury Ventures, 166–167
Newtek Ventures, 167–168
NewVista Capital, 168
NIF Ventures USA, Inc., 168–169
Nokia Ventures, 169–170
North Hill Ventures, LP, 170
Northwood Ventures LLC, 170–171
Norwest Venture Partners, 171
Novak Biddle Venture Partners, 171–172
Noveltek Capital Corporation, 172
Novus Ventures, LP, 173
Nth Power Technologies, 173–174
NU Capital Access Group, Ltd., 174

O
Oak Investment Partners, 174–175
Odeon Capital Partners, LP, 175

Olympic Venture Partners, 176
OneLiberty Ventures, 176–177
ONSET Ventures, 177
Opportunity Capital Partners, 177–178
Orion Partners, L.P., 178
Ovation Capital Partners, 178–179
Oxford Bioscience Partners, 179–180

P
Pacesetter Growth Fund, L.P., 180
Pacific Corporate Group, Inc., 180–181
Pacific Horizon Ventures, 181
Pacific Mezzanine Fund, 182
Pacific Northwest Partners SBIC, L.P., 182
Pacific Venture Group, 182–183
Palomar Ventures, 183–184
Paradigm Capital Partners, LLC, 184–185
Partech International, 185
Petra Capital Partners, LLC, 186
Pinecreek Capital Management, L.P., 186–187
Point West Ventures, 187
Polaris Ventures Partners, 187–188
Premier Medical Partner Fund L.P., 188–189
Primedia Ventures, 189
Primus Venture Partners, Inc., 189–190
Prism Venture Partners, 190–191
Putnam Lovell Capital Partners Inc., 191

R
Rader Reinfrank & Co., LLC, 191–192
Ravenswood Capital Venture Fund, 192
Redleaf Group, Inc., 193
Redpoint Ventures, 193–194
RedRock Ventures, 194–195
Richland Ventures, 195
Ridge Ventures, 196
Ridgestone Corporation, 196–197
Riordan, Lewis & Haden, 197
River Associates LLC, 197–198
Rocket Ventures, 198
Rocky Mountain Capital Partners, LLP, 199
Royalty Capital Management, Inc., 199–200
RRE Ventures, 200
RWI Group, 200–201

S
Salix Ventures, 201–202
Sand Hill Capital, 202
Sanderling Ventures, 203
Sandlot Capital, LLC, 203–204
Santa Barbara Technology Incubator, 204
Schroder Ventures Life Sciences, 204–205
Scripps Ventures, 205–206
SeaPoint Ventures, 206
Selby Venture Partners, LP, 206–207

Sentinel Capital Partners, 207–208
Sequoia Capital, 208
Seven Hills Partners, LLC, 208–209
Sevin Rosen Funds, 209
Shaw Venture Partners, 209–210
Sienna Holdings, 210
Sierra Ventures, 211
Sigma Partners, 211–212
Signal Equity Partners, 212
Signature Capital, LLC, 212–213
Silicon Valley Bank, 213–214
Silver Creek Technology Investors, 214
SOFTBANK Venture Capital, 215
Sorrento Associates, Inc., 215–216
Southwest Merchant Group, 216
SpaceVest, 216–217
Spencer Trask Securities Inc., 217
Sports Capital Partners, 218
Spray Venture Partners, 218–219
Sprout Group, 219–220
St. Paul Venture Capital, 220
Staenberg Private Capital, LLC, 220–221
StoneCreek Capital, Inc., 221
Summer Street Capital Partners, LLC, 222
Summit Partners, 222
Sutter Hill Ventures, 223
Svoboda, Collins LLC, 223–224

T
TA Associates, 224
TAT Capital Partners Ltd., 224–225
TD iCapital, 225
Technology Crossover Ventures, 225–226
Technology Funding, Inc., 226–227
Technology Investments, 227
Technology Partners, 227–228
Techno–Venture, 228
TechSpace Xchange, 228–229
Telecommunications Development Fund, 229
TeleSoft Partners, 230
Telos Venture Partners, 230–231
Third Eye Ventures, LLC, 231
Thoma Cressey Equity Partners, 231–232
Thompson Clive, Inc., 232–233
Thorner Ventures, 233
Three Arch Partners, 233–234
Timberline Venture Partners, 234
TL Ventures, 234–235
Tondu Corporation, 235
Toucan Capital Corp., 235–236
Trans Cosmos USA, Inc., 236–237
Trellis Partners, 237
Trident Capital, 237–238
Trinity Ventures, 238–239
Triton Ventures, 239

TSG Equity Partners LLC, 240
Tullis Dickerson & Co., Inc., 240–241
TVM Techno Venture Management, 241–242

U
U.S. Venture Partners, 242–243
Union Atlantic Capital, L.C., 243
UV Partners, 243–244

V
Valley Ventures, L.P., 244
Vanguard Venture Partners, 244–245
Vector Fund Management, 245–246
Vencon Management, Inc., 246
Ventana, 246–247
Venture Funding, Limited, 247–248
Venture Growth Associates, 248
Venture Management Associates, 248
Venture Strategy Partners, 249
Ventureplex, 249–250
Versant Ventures, 250
Vertex Management, Inc., 251
Vision Capital, 251
Viventures, 252

W
W.B. McKee Securities, 252–253
Walden Capital Partners L.P., 253
Walden VC, 253–254
Wasatch Venture Funds, 254–255
Wasserstein Adelson Ventures, L.P., 255
WebVestors Equity Partners, LP, 255–256
Welsh, Carson, Anderson & Stowe, 256–257
Western States Investment Group, 257
Western Technology Investment, 257–258
Weston Presidio Capital, 258
Whitney & Co., 259
WI Harper Group, 259–260
Windamere Venture Partners, LLC, 260
Winston Partners, 260–261
Winward Ventures, 261
Woodside Fund, 261–262
Worldview Technology Partners, 262–263
WRF Capital, 263

Z
Zone Ventures, 263–264

Funds by Industry Preference

Consumer Products/Services

AC Ventures, 4–5
Advent International Corporation, 8–9
Ad-Ventures, LLC, 9
Allied Capital Corporation, 10
American Securities Capital Partners, L.P., 14–15
Amerimark Capital Corporation, 15
Antares Capital Corporation, 16–17
Aqua International Partners, L.P., 20
Aspen Ventures, 21–22
Bachow & Associates, Inc., 25–26
Bertelsmann Ventures, 30
Boston Financial & Equity Corporation, 33
Brad Peery Capital Inc., 35
Brantley Partners, L.P., 35–36
Callier Interests, 38–39
Cambria Group, The, 39
Canaan Partners, 39–40
Capital Insights, 40
Capital Southwest Corporation, 41
CEO Venture Fund, 45
Chrysalis Ventures, 47–48
CIVC Partners, 48–49
Commercial Bridge Capital, LLC, 54–55
Comstock Partners, LLC, 56–57
Conning Capital Partners, 57–58
Davis, Tuttle Venture Partners, 63–64
Dominion Ventures, Inc., 68–69
Dorset Capital Management, LLC, 69
Doyle & Boissiere, LLC, 70
Edgewater Funds LP, 74
Enterprise Partners Venture Capital, 77–78
Fidelity Ventures, 79
First Capital Group, 82
Flemming, Lessard & Shields, LLC, 83–84
Freeman Spogli & Co., 86–87
Friedman Fleischer & Lowe, LLC, 88
GE Capital-Equity Capital Group, 91–92
Gemini Investors LLC, 92
Glynn Capital Management, 96–97
Granite Capital Partners, 97–98
Great Hill Equity Partners, 99–100
GTCR Golden Rauner, LLC, 101–102

Halpern, Denny & Company, 103–104
Harvest Partners Inc., 105–106
Hellman & Friedman, LLC, 107
HLM Management Company, 109–110
Housatonic Partners, 110–111
Huntington Holdings, Inc., 113
Idanta Partners, Ltd., 114
ING Furman Selz Investments, 118
Jefferson Capital Partners, LTD., 129
Josephberg Grosz & Co., Inc., 131
Kansas City Equity Partners, 131–132
Kettle Partners LP, 134
Kohlberg & Company, L.L.C., 137–138
Kriegsman Group, The, 138–139
Ladenburg, Thalmann & Company, Inc., 140
Lake Shore Capital Partners, Inc, 140–141
Lambda Management Inc., 141
Leonard Green & Partners, L.P., 143–144
Libra Mezzanine Partners, L.P., 146
Lombard Investments Inc., 146–147
Madison Dearborn Partners, 147–148
Mason Wells, 149–150
Matrix Partners, 150
Meritech Capital Partners, 155–156
Needham Asset Management, 163–164
North Hill Ventures, LP, 170
NU Capital Access Group, Ltd., 174
Partech International, 185
Petra Capital Partners, LLC, 186
Putnam Lovell Capital Partners Inc., 191
Ridgestone Corporation, 196–197
Rocket Ventures, 198
Sports Capital Partners, 218
Sprout Group, 219–220
TA Associates, 224
TD iCapital, 225
Thoma Cressey Equity Partners, 231–232
Trans Cosmos USA, Inc., 236–237
Trident Capital, 237–238
TSG Equity Partners LLC, 240
U.S. Venture Partners, 242–243
Venture Funding, Limited, 247–248
Venture Growth Associates, 248

W.B. McKee Securities, 252–253
Weston Presidio Capital, 258

Environmental
AC Ventures, 4–5
Advent International Corporation, 8–9
Allied Capital Corporation, 10
American Securities Capital Partners, L.P., 14–15
Antares Capital Corporation, 16–17
Aqua International Partners, L.P., 20
ARCH Venture Partners, 21
Capital Insights, 40
Capital Southwest Corporation, 41
Commercial Bridge Capital, LLC, 54–55
Comstock Partners, LLC, 56–57
Davis, Tuttle Venture Partners, 63–64
First Manhattan Capital Partners, 83
Friedman Fleischer & Lowe, LLC, 88
Glynn Capital Management, 96–97
GulfStar Group, 102–103
Industrial Growth Partners, 117
Josephberg Grosz & Co., Inc., 131
Kriegsman Group, The, 138–139
Lake Shore Capital Partners, Inc, 140–141
Lambda Management Inc., 141
Leonard Green & Partners, L.P., 143–144
Lombard Investments Inc., 146–147
Nth Power Technologies, 173–174
NU Capital Access Group, Ltd., 174
River Associates LLC, 197–198
Tondu Corporation, 235
Vencon Management, Inc., 246
Venture Funding, Limited, 247–248
Venture Growth Associates, 248
W.B. McKee Securities, 252–253

Information Technology
ABN AMRO Private Equity, 3
AC Ventures, 4–5
Advanced Technology Ventures, 7–8
Advent International Corporation, 8–9
Allied Capital Corporation, 10
Alloy Ventures, 10–11
Alta Partners, 11–12
Altos Ventures, 12–13
American Securities Capital Partners, L.P., 14–15
Antares Capital Corporation, 16–17
Anthem Capital, L.P., 17
Apex Venture Partners, 17–18
Applied Technology, 18–19
APV Technology Partners, 19
ARCH Venture Partners, 21
Aspen Ventures, 21–22
Associated Venture Investors, 23
Austin Ventures, 23–24
Axiom Venture Partners, L.P., 24
BancBoston Ventures, Inc., 26

Benchmark Capital, 28–29
Boston Millennia Partners, 33–34
Boulder Ventures Limited, 34–35
Broadview Capital Partners LLC, 37–38
Canaan Partners, 39–40
Capital Insights, 40
Capital Southwest Corporation, 41
Capstone Ventures, 42
CMEA Ventures, 50
ComVentures, 52–53
Commercial Bridge Capital, LLC, 54–55
Community Technology Fund, Boston University, 55–56
Comstock Partners, LLC, 56–57
Coral Ventures, 60
Crescendo Ventures, 61
DigitalVentures, 65–66
Doll Capital Management Co., LLC, 66
Dominion Ventures, Inc., 68–69
Draper Fisher Jurvetson, 70–71
DynaFund Ventures, 72
Earlybird, 72–73
Edgewater Funds LP, 74
El Dorado Ventures, 74
Elvey Partnership, The, 74–75
Encompass Ventures, 76
Endeavor Capital Management, 76–77
Enterprise Partners Venture Capital, 77–78
EuclidSR Partners, 78
Fidelity Ventures, 79
Friedman Fleischer & Lowe, LLC, 88
GE Capital-Equity Capital Group, 91–92
Gemini Investors LLC, 92
General Atlantic Partners, LLC, 92–93
Genstar Capital, LLC, 95
Geocapital Partners, LLC, 95–96
Glynn Capital Management, 96–97
Granite Ventures, 98–99
Great Hill Equity Partners, 99–100
GTCR Golden Rauner, LLC, 101–102
Hickory Venture Capital Corporation, 107–108
Hudson Ventures, 112
Humana Ventures, 112
iMinds Ventures, 115
ING Furman Selz Investments, 118
Insight Capital Partners, 120–121
Institutional Venture Partners (IVP), 121
Integral Capital Partners, 122–123
Interprise Technology Partners, LP, 123–124
InterWest Partners VIII, 124–125
JAFCO Ventures, 127–128
Jefferson Capital Partners, LTD., 129
JK & B Capital, 129–130
Josephberg Grosz & Co., Inc., 131
KB Partners, L.L.C., 132
KLM Capital Group, 136–137
Kriegsman Group, The, 138–139

Labrador Ventures, 139–140
Lake Shore Capital Partners, Inc, 140–141
Lambda Management Inc., 141
Leonard Green & Partners, L.P., 143–144
Liberty Venture Partners, 145
Lombard Investments Inc., 146–147
Marquette Venture Partners, 148
Meritech Capital Partners, 155–156
Mitsui & Co. (U.S.A.), Inc., 159
MMC Capital C&I Fund, 160
Mohr, Davidow Ventures, 160–161
Morgenthaler, 162
NeoCarta Ventures, 164–165
New World Ventures, 165–166
NewVista Capital, 168
Nokia Ventures, 169–170
Norwest Venture Partners, 171
NU Capital Access Group, Ltd., 174
Odeon Capital Partners, LP, 175
OneLiberty Ventures, 176–177
ONSET Ventures, 177
Pacific Venture Group, 182–183
Palomar Ventures, 183–184
Paradigm Capital Partners, LLC, 184–185
Partech International, 185
Petra Capital Partners, LLC, 186
Point West Ventures, 187
Polaris Ventures Partners, 187–188
RedRock Ventures, 194–195
Richland Ventures, 195
Rocket Ventures, 198
RRE Ventures, 200
RWI Group, 200–201
Salix Ventures, 201–202
Sanderling Ventures, 203
Sandlot Capital, LLC, 203–204
Shaw Venture Partners, 209–210
Sienna Holdings, 210
Signal Equity Partners, 212
Silver Creek Technology Investors, 214
SOFTBANK Venture Capital, 215
Summit Partners, 222
Svoboda, Collins LLC, 223–224
Technology Funding, Inc., 226–227
Technology Investments, 227
Technology Partners, 227–228
Telos Venture Partners, 230–231
Thoma Cressey Equity Partners, 231–232
Timberline Venture Partners, 234
TL Ventures, 234–235
Toucan Capital Corp., 235–236
Trans Cosmos USA, Inc., 236–237
Trident Capital, 237–238
Triton Ventures, 239
TVM Techno Venture Management, 241–242
U.S. Venture Partners, 242–243
UV Partners, 243–244

Valley Ventures, L.P., 244
Vector Fund Management, 245–246
Venture Funding, Limited, 247–248
Venture Growth Associates, 248
Venture Strategy Partners, 249
Vision Capital, 251
W.B. McKee Securities, 252–253
Wasatch Venture Funds, 254–255
WebVestors Equity Partners, LP, 255–256
Welsh, Carson, Anderson & Stowe, 256–257
Whitney & Co., 259
WI Harper Group, 259–260
Winston Partners, 260–261
Woodside Fund, 261–262
Worldview Technology Partners, 262–263
Zone Ventures, 263–264

Internet

ABN AMRO Private Equity, 3
AC Ventures, 4–5
Accel Partners, 6
Access Venture Partners, 7
Advent International Corporation, 8–9
Allied Capital Corporation, 10
Alloy Ventures, 10–11
Altos Ventures, 12–13
American River Ventures, LP, 13–14
American Securities Capital Partners, L.P., 14–15
Antares Capital Corporation, 16–17
Arbor Partners, LLC, 20–21
ARCH Venture Partners, 21
Asset Management Company, 22
Austin Ventures, 23–24
Aztec Venture Network, LLC, 25
Bay Partners, 28
Benchmark Capital, 28–29
Bluefish Ventures, 32
Brad Peery Capital Inc., 35
Brentwood Venture Capital, 36
Capital Insights, 40
Capital Southwest Corporation, 41
Capstone Ventures, 42
CenterPoint Ventures, 44
Chrysalis Ventures, 47–48
CMEA Ventures, 50
CMGI @Ventures, 51
ComVentures, 52–53
Comcast Interactive Capital, 53–54
Commercial Bridge Capital, LLC, 54–55
Community Technology Fund, Boston University, 55–56
Compass Technology Partners, 56
Comstock Partners, LLC, 56–57
Convergence Partners, 59
Crosspoint Venture Partners, 61–62
Crystal Internet Venture Funds, 62–63
DigitalVentures, 65–66

Doll Capital Management Co., LLC, 66
Dorset Capital Management, LLC, 69
Dougery Ventures, 69–70
Earlybird, 72–73
Elvey Partnership, The, 74–75
Empire Ventures, 75–76
Fidelity Ventures, 79
First Manhattan Capital Partners, 83
Foundation Capital, 86
Friedman Fleischer & Lowe, LLC, 88
G-51 Capital LLC, 90–91
General Atlantic Partners, LLC, 92–93
Generation Partners, 94
Geneva Venture Partners, 94–95
Geocapital Partners, LLC, 95–96
Glynn Capital Management, 96–97
Grace Internet Capital, 97
Granite Ventures, 98–99
Hamilton Technology Ventures, 104
Highland Capital Partners, 108–109
Hudson Ventures, 112
IDG Ventures, 114–115
iMinds Ventures, 115
Imperial Bank, 115–116
Indosuez Ventures, 116
Infinity Capital, 117–118
Institutional Venture Partners (IVP), 121
Integra Ventures, 122
Interprise Technology Partners, LP, 123–124
InterWest Partners VIII, 124–125
IVP (Institutional Venture Partners), 126–127
Josephberg Grosz & Co., Inc., 131
KB Partners, L.L.C., 132
KBL Healthcare Ventures, 132–133
Kettle Partners LP, 134
Kleiner Perkins Caufield & Byers, 135
Kline Hawkes & Company, 136
Kriegsman Group, The, 138–139
Labrador Ventures, 139–140
Lake Shore Capital Partners, Inc, 140–141
Lambda Management Inc., 141
Lazard Technology Partners, 142
Leonard Green & Partners, L.P., 143–144
Liberty Venture Partners, 145
Lombard Investments Inc., 146–147
Maveron, LLC, 150–151
Menlo Ventures, 154
meVC, 156
Mission Ventures, 158–159
Mitsui & Co. (U.S.A.), Inc., 159
Morgenthaler, 162
NeoCarta Ventures, 164–165
New World Ventures, 165–166
New York Partners, LLC, 166
NewVista Capital, 168
NIF Ventures USA, Inc., 168–169
North Hill Ventures, LP, 170

Norwest Venture Partners, 171
Novus Ventures, LP, 173
NU Capital Access Group, Ltd., 174
Oak Investment Partners, 174–175
Odeon Capital Partners, LP, 175
Olympic Venture Partners, 176
Ovation Capital Partners, 178–179
Petra Capital Partners, LLC, 186
Primedia Ventures, 189
Primus Venture Partners, Inc., 189–190
Prism Venture Partners, 190–191
Rader Reinfrank & Co., LLC, 191–192
Ravenswood Capital Venture Fund, 192
Redleaf Group, Inc., 193
Redpoint Ventures, 193–194
RedRock Ventures, 194–195
Rocket Ventures, 198
RRE Ventures, 200
RWI Group, 200–201
Santa Barbara Technology Incubator, 204
Scripps Ventures, 205–206
SeaPoint Ventures, 206
Selby Venture Partners, LP, 206–207
Seven Hills Partners, LLC, 208–209
Sienna Holdings, 210
Sierra Ventures, 211
Signature Capital, LLC, 212–213
SOFTBANK Venture Capital, 215
Sports Capital Partners, 218
Sprout Group, 219–220
St. Paul Venture Capital, 220
Staenberg Private Capital, LLC, 220–221
Summit Partners, 222
TA Associates, 224
TD iCapital, 225
Technology Crossover Ventures, 225–226
TechSpace Xchange, 228–229
TeleSoft Partners, 230
Telos Venture Partners, 230–231
Third Eye Ventures, LLC, 231
Thoma Cressey Equity Partners, 231–232
Thorner Ventures, 233
TL Ventures, 234–235
Trans Cosmos USA, Inc., 236–237
Trinity Ventures, 238–239
Triton Ventures, 239
TSG Equity Partners LLC, 240
Tullis Dickerson & Co., Inc., 240–241
UV Partners, 243–244
Valley Ventures, L.P., 244
Vanguard Venture Partners, 244–245
Venture Funding, Limited, 247–248
Venture Growth Associates, 248
Viventures, 252
W.B. McKee Securities, 252–253
Walden Capital Partners L.P., 253
Walden VC, 253–254

Wasatch Venture Funds, 254–255
Wasserstein Adelson Ventures, L.P., 255
Weston Presidio Capital, 258
Winward Ventures, 261
Woodside Fund, 261–262
Worldview Technology Partners, 262–263
Zone Ventures, 263–264

Life Sciences
ABN AMRO Private Equity, 3
AC Ventures, 4–5
Acacia Venture Partners, 5–6
Advanced Technology Ventures, 7–8
Advent International Corporation, 8–9
Allied Capital Corporation, 10
Alloy Ventures, 10–11
Alta Partners, 11–12
American Securities Capital Partners, L.P., 14–15
Antares Capital Corporation, 16–17
Anthem Capital, L.P., 17
ARCH Venture Partners, 21
Asset Management Company, 22
Axiom Venture Partners, L.P., 24
BancBoston Ventures, Inc., 26
Berkeley International Capital Corporation, 29
BioVentures West, 31
Blue Capital Management, L.L.C., 31–32
Boston Financial & Equity Corporation, 33
Boston Millennia Partners, 33–34
Boulder Ventures Limited, 34–35
Brentwood Venture Capital, 36
Burrill & Company, 38
Callier Interests, 38–39
Canaan Partners, 39–40
Capital Insights, 40
Capital Southwest Corporation, 41
Capitol Health Partners PL, 41–42
Capstone Ventures, 42
CEO Venture Fund, 45
Chrysalis Ventures, 47–48
CMEA Ventures, 50
Collison Howe & Lennox, LLC, 52
Commercial Bridge Capital, LLC, 54–55
Community Technology Fund, Boston University, 55–56
Compass Technology Partners, 56
Comstock Partners, LLC, 56–57
Conning Capital Partners, 57–58
Coral Ventures, 60
Crescendo Ventures, 61
Davis, Tuttle Venture Partners, 63–64
Delphi Ventures, 64
Delta Capital Partners, LLC, 64–65
Domain Associates, LLC, 67–68
Dominion Ventures, Inc., 68–69
Earlybird, 72–73
Edgewater Funds LP, 74

Enterprise Partners Venture Capital, 77–78
EuclidSR Partners, 78
Flemming, Lessard & Shields, LLC, 83–84
Forward Ventures, 85–86
Friedman Fleischer & Lowe, LLC, 88
GE Capital-Equity Capital Group, 91–92
Genstar Capital, LLC, 95
Glynn Capital Management, 96–97
Granite Capital Partners, 97–98
Greylock, 100–101
GTCR Golden Rauner, LLC, 101–102
GulfStar Group, 102–103
Halpern, Denny & Company, 103–104
Hamilton Technology Ventures, 104
HealthCare Ventures LLC, 106–107
Hickory Venture Capital Corporation, 107–108
Highland Capital Partners, 108–109
HLM Management Company, 109–110
Hudson Ventures, 112
Humana Ventures, 112
Idanta Partners, Ltd., 114
Imperial Bank, 115–116
Indosuez Ventures, 116
Industrial Growth Partners, 117
ING Furman Selz Investments, 118
IngleWood Ventures, 118–119
InnoCal, 119
Integra Ventures, 122
Integral Capital Partners, 122–123
InterWest Partners VIII, 124–125
IVP (Institutional Venture Partners), 126–127
Jefferson Capital Partners, LTD., 129
Johnston Associates Inc., 130–131
Josephberg Grosz & Co., Inc., 131
KBL Healthcare Ventures, 132–133
Kleiner Perkins Caufield & Byers, 135
Kline Hawkes & Company, 136
Kohlberg & Company, L.L.C., 137–138
Kriegsman Group, The, 138–139
Ladenburg, Thalmann & Company, Inc., 140
Lake Shore Capital Partners, Inc, 140–141
Lambda Management Inc., 141
Lehman Brothers Incorporated, 143
Leonard Green & Partners, L.P., 143–144
Leong Ventures, 144
Liberty Venture Partners, 145
Lombard Investments Inc., 146–147
Madison Dearborn Partners, 147–148
Marquette Venture Partners, 148
MDS Venture Pacific, Inc., 151
MedTech Ventures, Inc., 152
MedVenture Associates, 152–153
Meritech Capital Partners, 155–156
Mission Ventures, 158–159
Mitsui & Co. (U.S.A.), Inc., 159
Morgenthaler, 162
Needham Asset Management, 163–164

Newbury Ventures, 166–167
NU Capital Access Group, Ltd., 174
Olympic Venture Partners, 176
OneLiberty Ventures, 176–177
ONSET Ventures, 177
Oxford Bioscience Partners, 179–180
Pacific Horizon Ventures, 181
Pacific Venture Group, 182–183
Paradigm Capital Partners, LLC, 184–185
Partech International, 185
Petra Capital Partners, LLC, 186
Polaris Ventures Partners, 187–188
Premier Medical Partner Fund L.P., 188–189
Primus Venture Partners, Inc., 189–190
Prism Venture Partners, 190–191
Richland Ventures, 195
Salix Ventures, 201–202
Sanderling Ventures, 203
Schroder Ventures Life Sciences, 204–205
Sequoia Capital, 208
Seven Hills Partners, LLC, 208–209
Sevin Rosen Funds, 209
Shaw Venture Partners, 209–210
Signature Capital, LLC, 212–213
Silicon Valley Bank, 213–214
Sorrento Associates, Inc., 215–216
Spray Venture Partners, 218–219
Sprout Group, 219–220
St. Paul Venture Capital, 220
Summit Partners, 222
Svoboda, Collins LLC, 223–224
TA Associates, 224
TAT Capital Partners Ltd., 224–225
Technology Funding, Inc., 226–227
Technology Investments, 227
Technology Partners, 227–228
Techno-Venture, 228
Thoma Cressey Equity Partners, 231–232
Three Arch Partners, 233–234
TL Ventures, 234–235
Toucan Capital Corp., 235–236
Tullis Dickerson & Co., Inc., 240–241
TVM Techno Venture Management, 241–242
UV Partners, 243–244
Valley Ventures, L.P., 244
Vanguard Venture Partners, 244–245
Vector Fund Management, 245–246
Vencon Management, Inc., 246
Venture Funding, Limited, 247–248
Venture Growth Associates, 248
Ventureplex, 249–250
Versant Ventures, 250
W.B. McKee Securities, 252–253
Walden Capital Partners L.P., 253
Wasatch Venture Funds, 254–255
Welsh, Carson, Anderson & Stowe, 256–257
Western States Investment Group, 257

Weston Presidio Capital, 258
Whitney & Co., 259
WI Harper Group, 259–260
Windamere Venture Partners, LLC, 260
Winward Ventures, 261

Manufacturing/Distribution

AC Ventures, 4–5
Advent International Corporation, 8–9
Allied Capital Corporation, 10
American Securities Capital Partners, L.P., 14–15
Amerimark Capital Corporation, 15
Antares Capital Corporation, 16–17
Aqua International Partners, L.P., 20
Bachow & Associates, Inc., 25–26
Blue Capital Management, L.L.C., 31–32
Brantley Partners, L.P., 35–36
Callier Interests, 38–39
Cambria Group, The, 39
Capital Insights, 40
Capital Southwest Corporation, 41
CEO Venture Fund, 45
CIVC Partners, 48–49
Commercial Bridge Capital, LLC, 54–55
Comstock Partners, LLC, 56–57
Delta Capital Partners, LLC, 64–65
Dorset Capital Management, LLC, 69
Doyle & Boissiere, LLC, 70
Freeman Spogli & Co., 86–87
Friedman Fleischer & Lowe, LLC, 88
G.A. Herrera & Co., 90
Glynn Capital Management, 96–97
Granite Capital Partners, 97–98
GRP, 101
GTCR Golden Rauner, LLC, 101–102
Halpern, Denny & Company, 103–104
Harvest Partners Inc., 105–106
Howard Industries, Inc., 111
Huntington Holdings, Inc., 113
Industrial Growth Partners, 117
ING Furman Selz Investments, 118
Johnston Associates Inc., 130–131
Josephberg Grosz & Co., Inc., 131
Kansas City Equity Partners, 131–132
Kohlberg & Company, L.L.C., 137–138
Kriegsman Group, The, 138–139
Lake Shore Capital Partners, Inc, 140–141
Lambda Management Inc., 141
Leonard Green & Partners, L.P., 143–144
Libra Mezzanine Partners, L.P., 146
Lombard Investments Inc., 146–147
Madison Dearborn Partners, 147–148
Mason Wells, 149–150
Needham Asset Management, 163–164
NU Capital Access Group, Ltd., 174
Pacesetter Growth Fund, L.P., 180
Paradigm Capital Partners, LLC, 184–185

Pinecreek Capital Management, L.P., 186–187
Ridgestone Corporation, 196–197
Sentinel Capital Partners, 207–208
TAT Capital Partners Ltd., 224–225
Technology Funding, Inc., 226–227
TSG Equity Partners LLC, 240
Valley Ventures, L.P., 244
Venture Funding, Limited, 247–248
Venture Growth Associates, 248
W.B. McKee Securities, 252–253
Walden Capital Partners L.P., 253
Weston Presidio Capital, 258
Winston Partners, 260–261

Materials
AC Ventures, 4–5
Advent International Corporation, 8–9
Allied Capital Corporation, 10
American Securities Capital Partners, L.P., 14–15
Antares Capital Corporation, 16–17
Brad Peery Capital Inc., 35
Capital Insights, 40
Capital Southwest Corporation, 41
Commercial Bridge Capital, LLC, 54–55
Comstock Partners, LLC, 56–57
Davis, Tuttle Venture Partners, 63–64
Friedman Fleischer & Lowe, LLC, 88
Full Circle Investments, Inc., 89
GE Capital-Equity Capital Group, 91–92
Genstar Capital, LLC, 95
Glynn Capital Management, 96–97
Howard Industries, Inc., 111
Huntington Holdings, Inc., 113
ING Furman Selz Investments, 118
Josephberg Grosz & Co., Inc., 131
Kohlberg & Company, L.L.C., 137–138
Kriegsman Group, The, 138–139
Lake Shore Capital Partners, Inc, 140–141
Lambda Management Inc., 141
Leonard Green & Partners, L.P., 143–144
Lombard Investments Inc., 146–147
Madison Dearborn Partners, 147–148
Mason Wells, 149–150
MMC Capital C&I Fund, 160
NU Capital Access Group, Ltd., 174
Pinecreek Capital Management, L.P., 186–187
Technology Funding, Inc., 226–227
Valley Ventures, L.P., 244
Venture Funding, Limited, 247–248
Venture Growth Associates, 248
W.B. McKee Securities, 252–253

Software/Hardware
AC Ventures, 4–5
Advent International Corporation, 8–9
Allied Capital Corporation, 10
Altos Ventures, 12–13

AltoTech Ventures, LLC, 13
American River Ventures, LP, 13–14
American Securities Capital Partners, L.P., 14–15
Antares Capital Corporation, 16–17
Apex Venture Partners, 17–18
Aspen Ventures, 21–22
Associated Venture Investors, 23
Austin Ventures, 23–24
Aztec Venture Network, LLC, 25
Bachow & Associates, Inc., 25–26
Battery Ventures, 27–28
Benchmark Capital, 28–29
Boston Financial & Equity Corporation, 33
Brad Peery Capital Inc., 35
Brentwood Venture Capital, 36
Broadview Capital Partners LLC, 37–38
Callier Interests, 38–39
Capital Insights, 40
Capital Southwest Corporation, 41
CenterPoint Ventures, 44
CEO Venture Fund, 45
Chrysalis Ventures, 47–48
CMEA Ventures, 50
ComVentures, 52–53
Commercial Bridge Capital, LLC, 54–55
Compass Technology Partners, 56
Comstock Partners, LLC, 56–57
Coral Ventures, 60
Crosspoint Venture Partners, 61–62
Crystal Internet Venture Funds, 62–63
DigitalVentures, 65–66
Dougery Ventures, 69–70
Empire Ventures, 75–76
Endeavor Capital Management, 76–77
Fidelity Ventures, 79
First Capital Group, 82
Flemming, Lessard & Shields, LLC, 83–84
Foundation Capital, 86
Friedman Fleischer & Lowe, LLC, 88
G-51 Capital LLC, 90–91
Geneva Venture Partners, 94–95
Glynn Capital Management, 96–97
Granite Capital Partners, 97–98
Granite Ventures, 98–99
Greylock, 100–101
Hamilton Technology Ventures, 104
Highland Capital Partners, 108–109
Hummer Winblad Venture Partners, 113
Idanta Partners, Ltd., 114
IDG Ventures, 114–115
Imperial Bank, 115–116
Indosuez Ventures, 116
IngleWood Ventures, 118–119
InnoCal, 119
Innovest Venture Partners, 119–120
Insight Capital Partners, 120–121
Institutional Venture Partners (IVP), 121

JK & B Capital, 129–130
Josephberg Grosz & Co., Inc., 131
KB Partners, L.L.C., 132
Kettle Partners LP, 134
Kleiner Perkins Caufield & Byers, 135
Kline Hawkes & Company, 136
Kriegsman Group, The, 138–139
Lake Shore Capital Partners, Inc, 140–141
Lambda Management Inc., 141
Lazard Technology Partners, 142
Leonard Green & Partners, L.P., 143–144
Lombard Investments Inc., 146–147
Mason Wells, 149–150
Maveron, LLC, 150–151
Menlo Ventures, 154
Meritech Capital Partners, 155–156
meVC, 156
Mission Ventures, 158–159
Mitsui & Co. (U.S.A.), Inc., 159
MMC Capital C&I Fund, 160
Morgenthaler, 162
Needham Asset Management, 163–164
NeoCarta Ventures, 164–165
New World Ventures, 165–166
NIF Ventures USA, Inc., 168–169
Norwest Venture Partners, 171
Novus Ventures, LP, 173
NU Capital Access Group, Ltd., 174
Olympic Venture Partners, 176
Ovation Capital Partners, 178–179
Palomar Ventures, 183–184
Pinecreek Capital Management, L.P., 186–187
Primedia Ventures, 189
Redpoint Ventures, 193–194
RedRock Ventures, 194–195
RWI Group, 200–201
Sandlot Capital, LLC, 203–204
Santa Barbara Technology Incubator, 204
Sequoia Capital, 208
Sierra Ventures, 211
Sigma Partners, 211–212
Signature Capital, LLC, 212–213
Sorrento Associates, Inc., 215–216
Summit Partners, 222
TA Associates, 224
Techno-Venture, 228
Third Eye Ventures, LLC, 231
Timberline Venture Partners, 234
TL Ventures, 234–235
Trinity Ventures, 238–239
Triton Ventures, 239
TSG Equity Partners LLC, 240
Valley Ventures, L.P., 244
Vanguard Venture Partners, 244–245
Vencon Management, Inc., 246
Ventana, 246–247
Venture Funding, Limited, 247–248

Venture Growth Associates, 248
W.B. McKee Securities, 252–253
Walden Capital Partners L.P., 253
Wasatch Venture Funds, 254–255
Wasserstein Adelson Ventures, L.P., 255
WebVestors Equity Partners, LP, 255–256
Western States Investment Group, 257
Winward Ventures, 261
Woodside Fund, 261–262
Worldview Technology Partners, 262–263

Technology

Alexander Hutton Venture Partners, 9–10
Alpine Technology Ventures, 11
AltoTech Ventures, LLC, 13
American River Ventures, LP, 13–14
American Securities Capital Partners, L.P., 14–15
Anila Fund, 16
Antares Capital Corporation, 16–17
Anthem Capital, L.P., 17
ARCH Venture Partners, 21
Asset Management Company, 22
Bachow & Associates, Inc., 25–26
Batterson Venture Partners, LLC, 26–27
Battery Ventures, 27–28
Benchmark Capital, 28–29
Berkeley International Capital Corporation, 29
Bertelsmann Ventures, 30
Bluefish Ventures, 32
Brantley Partners, L.P., 35–36
Callier Interests, 38–39
Capital Insights, 40
Capital Southwest Corporation, 41
CEO Venture Fund, 45
CMGI @Ventures, 51
Coast Business Credit, 51–52
Comcast Interactive Capital, 53–54
Commercial Bridge Capital, LLC, 54–55
Comstock Partners, LLC, 56–57
Conning Capital Partners, 57–58
Convergence Partners, 59
Coral Ventures, 60
CS Capital Partners, LLC, 63
Delta Capital Partners, LLC, 64–65
DigitalVentures, 65–66
Domain Associates, LLC, 67–68
Dougery Ventures, 69–70
DynaFund Ventures, 72
Edelson Technology Partners, 73
El Dorado Ventures, 74
Elvey Partnership, The, 74–75
Empire Ventures, 75–76
Financial Technology Ventures, 80–81
First Capital Group, 82
Flemming, Lessard & Shields, LLC, 83–84
Fluke Venture Partners, 84
Forward Ventures, 85–86

Foundation Capital, 86
Friedman Fleischer & Lowe, LLC, 88
Fuqua Ventures, LLC, 89–90
Generation Partners, 94
Geocapital Partners, LLC, 95–96
Glynn Capital Management, 96–97
Hellman & Friedman, LLC, 107
High Street Capital II, LLC, 108
HLM Management Company, 109–110
Imperial Bank, 115–116
Indosuez Ventures, 116
Infinity Capital, 117–118
InnoCal, 119
Innovest Venture Partners, 119–120
Institutional Venture Partners (IVP), 121
ITU Ventures, 125–126
J. F. Shea Venture Capital, 127
JatoTech Ventures, 128
Josephberg Grosz & Co., Inc., 131
KB Partners, L.L.C., 132
Keystone Venture Capital, 134–135
Kriegsman Group, The, 138–139
Ladenburg, Thalmann & Company, Inc., 140
Lake Shore Capital Partners, Inc, 140–141
Lambda Management Inc., 141
Lazard Technology Partners, 142
Lehman Brothers Incorporated, 143
Leonard Green & Partners, L.P., 143–144
Liberty Venture Partners, 145
Lombard Investments Inc., 146–147
Marquette Venture Partners, 148
Matrix Partners, 150
Maveron, LLC, 150–151
Meritage Private Equity Fund, LP, 154–155
Meyer Duffy Ventures, LLC, 156–157
Mission Ventures, 158–159
Mohr, Davidow Ventures, 160–161
Multimedia Broadcast Investment Corporation, 162–163
NeoCarta Ventures, 164–165
New World Ventures, 165–166
New York Partners, LLC, 166
Newtek Ventures, 167–168
NIF Ventures USA, Inc., 168–169
Norwest Venture Partners, 171
Novus Ventures, LP, 173
NU Capital Access Group, Ltd., 174
Oak Investment Partners, 174–175
Odeon Capital Partners, LP, 175
Olympic Venture Partners, 176
Pacesetter Growth Fund, L.P., 180
Polaris Ventures Partners, 187–188
Rader Reinfrank & Co., LLC, 191–192
Redleaf Group, Inc., 193
Ridge Ventures, 196
Ridgestone Corporation, 196–197
River Associates LLC, 197–198

Sand Hill Capital, 202
Sanderling Ventures, 203
Santa Barbara Technology Incubator, 204
Selby Venture Partners, LP, 206–207
Sevin Rosen Funds, 209
Shaw Venture Partners, 209–210
Sigma Partners, 211–212
Signature Capital, LLC, 212–213
Silicon Valley Bank, 213–214
Silver Creek Technology Investors, 214
SOFTBANK Venture Capital, 215
Sorrento Associates, Inc., 215–216
SpaceVest, 216–217
Spencer Trask Securities Inc., 217
Sports Capital Partners, 218
Sprout Group, 219–220
St. Paul Venture Capital, 220
Staenberg Private Capital, LLC, 220–221
Summit Partners, 222
Sutter Hill Ventures, 223
TA Associates, 224
TAT Capital Partners Ltd., 224–225
Technology Funding, Inc., 226–227
Technology Investments, 227
Technology Partners, 227–228
TechSpace Xchange, 228–229
Timberline Venture Partners, 234
Trellis Partners, 237
Trinity Ventures, 238–239
Triton Ventures, 239
TSG Equity Partners LLC, 240
TVM Techno Venture Management, 241–242
U.S. Venture Partners, 242–243
Valley Ventures, L.P., 244
Ventana, 246–247
Venture Funding, Limited, 247–248
Venture Growth Associates, 248
Venture Management Associates, 248
Venture Strategy Partners, 249
Ventureplex, 249–250
Vertex Management, Inc., 251
W.B. McKee Securities, 252–253
Wasserstein Adelson Ventures, L.P., 255
WebVestors Equity Partners, LP, 255–256
Western States Investment Group, 257
Western Technology Investment, 257–258
Weston Presidio Capital, 258
WI Harper Group, 259–260
Winston Partners, 260–261
Winward Ventures, 261
Woodside Fund, 261–262
WRF Capital, 263

Telecommunications
ABN AMRO Private Equity, 3
AC Ventures, 4–5
Accel Partners, 6

Access Venture Partners, 7
Advent International Corporation, 8–9
Ad-Ventures, LLC, 9
Allied Capital Corporation, 10
Altos Ventures, 12–13
AltoTech Ventures, LLC, 13
American River Ventures, LP, 13–14
American Securities Capital Partners, L.P., 14–15
Anila Fund, 16
Antares Capital Corporation, 16–17
Anthem Capital, L.P., 17
Apex Venture Partners, 17–18
Applied Technology, 18–19
Asset Management Company, 22
Associated Venture Investors, 23
Austin Ventures, 23–24
Axiom Venture Partners, L.P., 24
Aztec Venture Network, LLC, 25
Bachow & Associates, Inc., 25–26
Battery Ventures, 27–28
Bay Partners, 28
Benchmark Capital, 28–29
Bertelsmann Ventures, 30
Blue Capital Management, L.L.C., 31–32
Bluefish Ventures, 32
Boston Financial & Equity Corporation, 33
Boston Millennia Partners, 33–34
Brad Peery Capital Inc., 35
Broadview Capital Partners LLC, 37–38
Capital Insights, 40
Capital Southwest Corporation, 41
Centennial Ventures, 43–44
CEO Venture Fund, 45
Chrysalis Ventures, 47–48
CIVC Partners, 48–49
CMEA Ventures, 50
Coast Business Credit, 51–52
ComVentures, 52–53
Commercial Bridge Capital, LLC, 54–55
Community Technology Fund, Boston University, 55–56
Comstock Partners, LLC, 56–57
Coral Ventures, 60
Crescendo Ventures, 61
Davis, Tuttle Venture Partners, 63–64
Doll Capital Management Co., LLC, 66
Dolphin Communications Partners, L.P., 67
Dominion Ventures, Inc., 68–69
Dougery Ventures, 69–70
DynaFund Ventures, 72
Earlybird, 72–73
Endeavor Capital Management, 76–77
Enterprise Partners Venture Capital, 77–78
First Capital Group, 82
First Manhattan Capital Partners, 83
Flemming, Lessard & Shields, LLC, 83–84
Foundation Capital, 86

Friedman Fleischer & Lowe, LLC, 88
GE Capital-Equity Capital Group, 91–92
Generation Partners, 94
Geneva Venture Partners, 94–95
Geocapital Partners, LLC, 95–96
Glynn Capital Management, 96–97
Granite Ventures, 98–99
Great Hill Equity Partners, 99–100
Greylock, 100–101
GulfStar Group, 102–103
Hamilton Technology Ventures, 104
Hellman & Friedman, LLC, 107
Hickory Venture Capital Corporation, 107–108
Highland Capital Partners, 108–109
Housatonic Partners, 110–111
Howard Industries, Inc., 111
Hudson Ventures, 112
Indosuez Ventures, 116
Industrial Growth Partners, 117
Infinity Capital, 117–118
IngleWood Ventures, 118–119
InnoCal, 119
Innovest Venture Partners, 119–120
Institutional Venture Partners (IVP), 121
IVP (Institutional Venture Partners), 126–127
JK & B Capital, 129–130
Josephberg Grosz & Co., Inc., 131
Kansas City Equity Partners, 131–132
KB Partners, L.L.C., 132
Keystone Venture Capital, 134–135
Kleiner Perkins Caufield & Byers, 135
Kline Hawkes & Company, 136
KLM Capital Group, 136–137
Kriegsman Group, The, 138–139
Ladenburg, Thalmann & Company, Inc., 140
Lake Shore Capital Partners, Inc, 140–141
Lambda Management Inc., 141
Lazard Technology Partners, 142
Leonard Green & Partners, L.P., 143–144
Lombard Investments Inc., 146–147
Madison Dearborn Partners, 147–148
Menlo Ventures, 154
Meritage Private Equity Fund, LP, 154–155
Meritech Capital Partners, 155–156
Mission Ventures, 158–159
Mitsui & Co. (U.S.A.), Inc., 159
MMC Capital C&I Fund, 160
Morgenthaler, 162
Multimedia Broadcast Investment Corporation, 162–163
NeoCarta Ventures, 164–165
New World Ventures, 165–166
Newbury Ventures, 166–167
NIF Ventures USA, Inc., 168–169
North Hill Ventures, LP, 170
Norwest Venture Partners, 171
Novus Ventures, LP, 173

NU Capital Access Group, Ltd., 174
Olympic Venture Partners, 176
OneLiberty Ventures, 176–177
Ovation Capital Partners, 178–179
Pacesetter Growth Fund, L.P., 180
Palomar Ventures, 183–184
Paradigm Capital Partners, LLC, 184–185
Petra Capital Partners, LLC, 186
Point West Ventures, 187
Primus Venture Partners, Inc., 189–190
Prism Venture Partners, 190–191
Rader Reinfrank & Co., LLC, 191–192
Richland Ventures, 195
Ridgestone Corporation, 196–197
Rocket Ventures, 198
RRE Ventures, 200
RWI Group, 200–201
Sandlot Capital, LLC, 203–204
Santa Barbara Technology Incubator, 204
SeaPoint Ventures, 206
Sequoia Capital, 208
Shaw Venture Partners, 209–210
Sienna Holdings, 210
Sierra Ventures, 211
Sigma Partners, 211–212
Signal Equity Partners, 212
Signature Capital, LLC, 212–213
Silver Creek Technology Investors, 214
SOFTBANK Venture Capital, 215
Sorrento Associates, Inc., 215–216
Sprout Group, 219–220
St. Paul Venture Capital, 220
Staenberg Private Capital, LLC, 220–221
Summit Partners, 222
TA Associates, 224
Technology Investments, 227
Technology Partners, 227–228
Techno-Venture, 228
Telecommunications Development Fund, 229
TeleSoft Partners, 230
Third Eye Ventures, LLC, 231
Timberline Venture Partners, 234
TL Ventures, 234–235
Trinity Ventures, 238–239
Triton Ventures, 239
TSG Equity Partners LLC, 240
TVM Techno Venture Management, 241–242
UV Partners, 243–244
Valley Ventures, L.P., 244
Vanguard Venture Partners, 244–245
Ventana, 246–247
Venture Funding, Limited, 247–248
Venture Growth Associates, 248
Venture Strategy Partners, 249
Ventureplex, 249–250
Viventures, 252
W.B. McKee Securities, 252–253

Wasatch Venture Funds, 254–255
Wasserstein Adelson Ventures, L.P., 255
WebVestors Equity Partners, LP, 255–256
Western States Investment Group, 257
Weston Presidio Capital, 258
Whitney & Co., 259
WI Harper Group, 259–260
Winward Ventures, 261
Woodside Fund, 261–262
Worldview Technology Partners, 262–263

Funds by Geographical Area of Interest

Asia

AC Ventures, 4–5
Advent International Corporation, 8–9
Alta Partners, 11–12
Aqua International Partners, L.P., 20
BancBoston Ventures, Inc., 26
Berkeley International Capital Corporation, 29
Brad Peery Capital Inc., 35
Chanen & Co. Ltd., 45–46
Chase Capital Partners, 46–47
Crystal Internet Venture Funds, 62–63
Doll Capital Management Co., LLC, 66
Dolphin Communications Partners, L.P., 67
Fidelity Ventures, 79
General Atlantic Partners, LLC, 92–93
Glynn Capital Management, 96–97
Grace Internet Capital, 97
IDG Ventures, 114–115
Innovest Venture Partners, 119–120
Insight Capital Partners, 120–121
Josephberg Grosz & Co., Inc., 131
KECALP Inc., 133–134
Kettle Partners LP, 134
KLM Capital Group, 136–137
Ladenburg, Thalmann & Company, Inc., 140
Lehman Brothers Incorporated, 143
Lombard Investments Inc., 146–147
Meritage Private Equity Fund, LP, 154–155
Newbury Ventures, 166–167
NIF Ventures USA, Inc., 168–169
Nokia Ventures, 169–170
Nth Power Technologies, 173–174
Partech International, 185
Redleaf Group, Inc., 193
Schroder Ventures Life Sciences, 204–205
Sports Capital Partners, 218
Techno-Venture, 228
Thompson Clive, Inc., 232–233
Tondu Corporation, 235
Vencon Management, Inc., 246
Venture Management Associates, 248
Vertex Management, Inc., 251
Western Technology Investment, 257–258

Whitney & Co., 259
WI Harper Group, 259–260

East

CEO Venture Fund, 45
Hickory Venture Capital Corporation, 107–108
Lambda Management Inc., 141

Europe

AC Ventures, 4–5
Advent International Corporation, 8–9
Alta Partners, 11–12
Aqua International Partners, L.P., 20
BancBoston Ventures, Inc., 26
Berkeley International Capital Corporation, 29
Brad Peery Capital Inc., 35
Capitol Health Partners PL, 41–42
Chanen & Co. Ltd., 45–46
Chase Capital Partners, 46–47
ComVentures, 52–53
Crystal Internet Venture Funds, 62–63
Doll Capital Management Co., LLC, 66
Dolphin Communications Partners, L.P., 67
Dresner Capital Resources, Inc., 71–72
Fidelity Ventures, 79
Full Circle Investments, Inc., 89
General Atlantic Partners, LLC, 92–93
Geneva Venture Partners, 94–95
Geocapital Partners, LLC, 95–96
Glynn Capital Management, 96–97
Grace Internet Capital, 97
GRP, 101
Harvest Partners Inc., 105–106
IDG Ventures, 114–115
Insight Capital Partners, 120–121
Josephberg Grosz & Co., Inc., 131
KECALP Inc., 133–134
Kettle Partners LP, 134
Ladenburg, Thalmann & Company, Inc., 140
Lehman Brothers Incorporated, 143
Leonard Green & Partners, L.P., 143–144
Meritage Private Equity Fund, LP, 154–155
MMC Capital C&I Fund, 160

Newbury Ventures, 166–167
NIF Ventures USA, Inc., 168–169
Nokia Ventures, 169–170
Noveltek Capital Corporation, 172
Nth Power Technologies, 173–174
Partech International, 185
Redleaf Group, Inc., 193
Schroder Ventures Life Sciences, 204–205
Sports Capital Partners, 218
Summit Partners, 222
TAT Capital Partners Ltd., 224–225
Thompson Clive, Inc., 232–233
Tondu Corporation, 235
Trans Cosmos USA, Inc., 236–237
TVM Techno Venture Management, 241–242
Vencon Management, Inc., 246
Vertex Management, Inc., 251
Vision Capital, 251
Viventures, 252
Western Technology Investment, 257–258
Whitney & Co., 259

Latin America

Advent International Corporation, 8–9
Alta Partners, 11–12
Aqua International Partners, L.P., 20
BancBoston Ventures, Inc., 26
Berkeley International Capital Corporation, 29
Brad Peery Capital Inc., 35
Chanen & Co. Ltd., 45–46
Chase Capital Partners, 46–47
Crystal Internet Venture Funds, 62–63
Doll Capital Management Co., LLC, 66
Dolphin Communications Partners, L.P., 67
Dresner Capital Resources, Inc., 71–72
Fidelity Ventures, 79
Full Circle Investments, Inc., 89
General Atlantic Partners, LLC, 92–93
Glynn Capital Management, 96–97
Grace Internet Capital, 97
IDG Ventures, 114–115
Insight Capital Partners, 120–121
Josephberg Grosz & Co., Inc., 131
KECALP Inc., 133–134
Kettle Partners LP, 134
Ladenburg, Thalmann & Company, Inc., 140
Lehman Brothers Incorporated, 143
Meritage Private Equity Fund, LP, 154–155
Newbury Ventures, 166–167
Nokia Ventures, 169–170
Nth Power Technologies, 173–174
Partech International, 185
Schroder Ventures Life Sciences, 204–205
Sports Capital Partners, 218
Thompson Clive, Inc., 232–233
Tondu Corporation, 235

Vencon Management, Inc., 246
Western Technology Investment, 257–258
Whitney & Co., 259

Middle East

Alta Partners, 11–12
Aqua International Partners, L.P., 20
BancBoston Ventures, Inc., 26
Berkeley International Capital Corporation, 29
Brad Peery Capital Inc., 35
Chanen & Co. Ltd., 45–46
Crystal Internet Venture Funds, 62–63
Doll Capital Management Co., LLC, 66
Dolphin Communications Partners, L.P., 67
Fidelity Ventures, 79
General Atlantic Partners, LLC, 92–93
Glynn Capital Management, 96–97
Grace Internet Capital, 97
IDG Ventures, 114–115
Insight Capital Partners, 120–121
Josephberg Grosz & Co., Inc., 131
KECALP Inc., 133–134
Kettle Partners LP, 134
Ladenburg, Thalmann & Company, Inc., 140
Lehman Brothers Incorporated, 143
Meritage Private Equity Fund, LP, 154–155
Newbury Ventures, 166–167
NIF Ventures USA, Inc., 168–169
Nokia Ventures, 169–170
Nth Power Technologies, 173–174
Partech International, 185
Schroder Ventures Life Sciences, 204–205
Sports Capital Partners, 218
Thompson Clive, Inc., 232–233
Tondu Corporation, 235
Vencon Management, Inc., 246
Vertex Management, Inc., 251
Western Technology Investment, 257–258
Whitney & Co., 259

Midwest

ABN AMRO Private Equity, 3
Access Venture Partners, 7
Antares Capital Corporation, 16–17
Arbor Partners, LLC, 20–21
Capstone Ventures, 42
Chanen & Co. Ltd., 45–46
Chisholm Private Capital, 47
Chrysalis Ventures, 47–48
Clarion Capital Corporation, 49–50
Hickory Venture Capital Corporation, 107–108
Indosuez Ventures, 116
Kansas City Equity Partners, 131–132
KB Partners, L.L.C., 132
Kline Hawkes & Company, 136
Lawrence Financial Group, 141–142

Leong Ventures, 144
Levine Leichtman Capital Partners, Inc., 144–145
Marquette Venture Partners, 148
MedVenture Associates, 152–153
Millennium 3 Venture Group, LLC, 157–158
Mohr, Davidow Ventures, 160–161
National Corporate Finance, Inc., 163
Newtek Ventures, 167–168
Rocky Mountain Capital Partners, LLP, 199
TL Ventures, 234–235
W.B. McKee Securities, 252–253
Wasatch Venture Funds, 254–255

Nationwide
ABN AMRO Private Equity, 3
AC Ventures, 4–5
Acacia Venture Partners, 5–6
Accel Partners, 6
Advanced Technology Ventures, 7–8
Advent International Corporation, 8–9
Ad-Ventures, LLC, 9
Alexander Hutton Venture Partners, 9–10
Allied Capital Corporation, 10
Alloy Ventures, 10–11
Alta Partners, 11–12
Altos Ventures, 12–13
AltoTech Ventures, LLC, 13
American Securities Capital Partners, L.P., 14–15
Amerimark Capital Corporation, 15
Ampersand Ventures, 15–16
Anila Fund, 16
Anthem Capital, L.P., 17
Apex Venture Partners, 17–18
Applied Technology, 18–19
APV Technology Partners, 19
Aqua International Partners, L.P., 20
Arbor Partners, LLC, 20–21
ARCH Venture Partners, 21
Aspen Ventures, 21–22
Asset Management Company, 22
Associated Venture Investors, 23
Austin Ventures, 23–24
Axiom Venture Partners, L.P., 24
Aztec Venture Network, LLC, 25
Bachow & Associates, Inc., 25–26
BancBoston Ventures, Inc., 26
Batterson Venture Partners, LLC, 26–27
Battery Ventures, 27–28
Benchmark Capital, 28–29
Berkeley International Capital Corporation, 29
Bertelsmann Ventures, 30
Bessemer Venture Partners, 30–31
Blue Capital Management, L.L.C., 31–32
Bluefish Ventures, 32
Boston Financial & Equity Corporation, 33
Boston Millennia Partners, 33–34

Boulder Ventures Limited, 34–35
Brad Peery Capital Inc., 35
Brantley Partners, L.P., 35–36
Bristol Investment Group, Inc., 37
Broadview Capital Partners LLC, 37–38
Burrill & Company, 38
Callier Interests, 38–39
Cambria Group, The, 39
Canaan Partners, 39–40
Capital Network Incorporated, The, 40–41
Capital Southwest Corporation, 41
Capitol Health Partners PL, 41–42
Celerity Partners, 43
Centennial Ventures, 43–44
CenterPoint Ventures, 44
Chanen & Co. Ltd., 45–46
Chase Capital Partners, 46–47
Chisholm Private Capital, 47
CIVC Partners, 48–49
Claremont Capital Corporation, 49
CMEA Ventures, 50
CMGI @Ventures, 51
Coast Business Credit, 51–52
Collison Howe & Lennox, LLC, 52
ComVentures, 52–53
Comcast Interactive Capital, 53–54
Community Technology Fund, Boston University, 55–56
Compass Technology Partners, 56
Comstock Partners, LLC, 56–57
Conning Capital Partners, 57–58
Convergence Partners, 59
Coral Ventures, 60
Corporation Acquisitions, Inc., 60–61
Crescendo Ventures, 61
Crosspoint Venture Partners, 61–62
Crystal Internet Venture Funds, 62–63
CS Capital Partners, LLC, 63
Delphi Ventures, 64
DigitalVentures, 65–66
Doll Capital Management Co., LLC, 66
Dolphin Communications Partners, L.P., 67
Domain Associates, LLC, 67–68
Dominion Ventures, Inc., 68–69
Dorset Capital Management, LLC, 69
Dougery Ventures, 69–70
Doyle & Boissiere, LLC, 70
Draper Fisher Jurvetson, 70–71
Dresner Capital Resources, Inc., 71–72
DynaFund Ventures, 72
Earlybird, 72–73
Edelson Technology Partners, 73
Edgewater Funds LP, 74
Elvey Partnership, The, 74–75
Endeavor Capital Management, 76–77
Enterprise Partners Venture Capital, 77–78

EuclidSR Partners, 78
Fidelity Ventures, 79
Financial Broker Relations, 79–80
Financial Resources Corporation, 80
Financial Technology Ventures, 80–81
First Analysis Venture Capital, 81–82
First Capital Group, 82
First Manhattan Capital Partners, 83
Flemming, Lessard & Shields, LLC, 83–84
Forrest Binkley & Brown, 84–85
Foundation Capital, 86
Freeman Spogli & Co., 86–87
Fremont Ventures, 87–88
Friedman Fleischer & Lowe, LLC, 88
Full Circle Investments, Inc., 89
G-51 Capital LLC, 90–91
GE Capital-Equity Capital Group, 91–92
Gemini Investors LLC, 92
General Atlantic Partners, LLC, 92–93
Generation Partners, 94
Geneva Venture Partners, 94–95
Genstar Capital, LLC, 95
Geocapital Partners, LLC, 95–96
Glynn Capital Management, 96–97
Grace Internet Capital, 97
Granite Capital Partners, 97–98
Granite Ventures, 98–99
Grayson & Associates, Inc., 99
Great Hill Equity Partners, 99–100
Greylock, 100–101
GRP, 101
GTCR Golden Rauner, LLC, 101–102
GulfStar Group, 102–103
Halpern, Denny & Company, 103–104
Hamilton Technology Ventures, 104
Hammond, Kennedy, Whitney and Co., Inc., 105
Harvest Partners Inc., 105–106
HealthCare Ventures LLC, 106–107
Hellman & Friedman, LLC, 107
Hickory Venture Capital Corporation, 107–108
High Street Capital II, LLC, 108
Highland Capital Partners, 108–109
HLM Management Company, 109–110
Housatonic Partners, 110–111
Howard Industries, Inc., 111
Hudson Ventures, 112
Humana Ventures, 112
Hummer Winblad Venture Partners, 113
Idanta Partners, Ltd., 114
IDG Ventures, 114–115
Imperial Bank, 115–116
Industrial Growth Partners, 117
Infinity Capital, 117–118
ING Furman Selz Investments, 118
Insight Capital Partners, 120–121
Institutional Venture Partners (IVP), 121
Integra Ventures, 122

Integral Capital Partners, 122–123
International Capital Partners, Inc., 123
Interprise Technology Partners, LP, 123–124
InterWest Partners VIII, 124–125
ITU Ventures, 125–126
IVP (Institutional Venture Partners), 126–127
J. F. Shea Venture Capital, 127
JAFCO Ventures, 127–128
JatoTech Ventures, 128
Jefferson Capital Partners, LTD., 129
JK & B Capital, 129–130
Johnston Associates Inc., 130–131
Josephberg Grosz & Co., Inc., 131
Kansas City Equity Partners, 131–132
KBL Healthcare Ventures, 132–133
KECALP Inc., 133–134
Kettle Partners LP, 134
Keystone Venture Capital, 134–135
Kleiner Perkins Caufield & Byers, 135
KLM Capital Group, 136–137
Kohlberg & Company, L.L.C., 137–138
Kriegsman Group, The, 138–139
Labrador Ventures, 139–140
Ladenburg, Thalmann & Company, Inc., 140
Lake Shore Capital Partners, Inc, 140–141
Lazard Technology Partners, 142
Lehman Brothers Incorporated, 143
Leonard Green & Partners, L.P., 143–144
Liberty Venture Partners, 145
Libra Mezzanine Partners, L.P., 146
Lombard Investments Inc., 146–147
Madison Dearborn Partners, 147–148
Marquette Venture Partners, 148
Marwit Capital, LLC, 148–149
Mason Wells, 149–150
Matrix Partners, 150
Maveron, LLC, 150–151
MDS Venture Pacific, Inc., 151
MedTech Ventures, Inc., 152
Mellon Ventures, Inc., 153
Menlo Ventures, 154
Meritage Private Equity Fund, LP, 154–155
Meritech Capital Partners, 155–156
meVC, 156
Meyer Duffy Ventures, LLC, 156–157
MidMark Associates, Inc., 157
Mission Ventures, 158–159
Mitsui & Co. (U.S.A.), Inc., 159
MMC Capital C&I Fund, 160
Morgenthaler, 162
Multimedia Broadcast Investment Corporation, 162–163
Needham Asset Management, 163–164
NeoCarta Ventures, 164–165
New Enterprise Associates, 165
New World Ventures, 165–166
New York Partners, LLC, 166

Newbury Ventures, 166–167
NewVista Capital, 168
NIF Ventures USA, Inc., 168–169
Nokia Ventures, 169–170
North Hill Ventures, LP, 170
Northwood Ventures LLC, 170–171
Norwest Venture Partners, 171
Novak Biddle Venture Partners, 171–172
Noveltek Capital Corporation, 172
Novus Ventures, LP, 173
Nth Power Technologies, 173–174
NU Capital Access Group, Ltd., 174
Oak Investment Partners, 174–175
Odeon Capital Partners, LP, 175
Olympic Venture Partners, 176
OneLiberty Ventures, 176–177
ONSET Ventures, 177
Orion Partners, L.P., 178
Ovation Capital Partners, 178–179
Oxford Bioscience Partners, 179–180
Pacesetter Growth Fund, L.P., 180
Pacific Corporate Group, Inc., 180–181
Pacific Horizon Ventures, 181
Pacific Mezzanine Fund, 182
Paradigm Capital Partners, LLC, 184–185
Partech International, 185
Pinecreek Capital Management, L.P., 186–187
Point West Ventures, 187
Polaris Ventures Partners, 187–188
Premier Medical Partner Fund L.P., 188–189
Primedia Ventures, 189
Primus Venture Partners, Inc., 189–190
Prism Venture Partners, 190–191
Putnam Lovell Capital Partners Inc., 191
Rader Reinfrank & Co., LLC, 191–192
Ravenswood Capital Venture Fund, 192
Redleaf Group, Inc., 193
Redpoint Ventures, 193–194
Red Rock Ventures, 194–195
Richland Ventures, 195
Ridge Ventures, 196
Ridgestone Corporation, 196–197
River Associates LLC, 197–198
Rocket Ventures, 198
Royalty Capital Management, Inc., 199–200
RRE Ventures, 200
Salix Ventures, 201–202
Sand Hill Capital, 202
Sanderling Ventures, 203
Sandlot Capital, LLC, 203–204
Santa Barbara Technology Incubator, 204
Schroder Ventures Life Sciences, 204–205
Scripps Ventures, 205–206
SeaPoint Ventures, 206
Sentinel Capital Partners, 207–208
Sequoia Capital, 208
Seven Hills Partners, LLC, 208–209
Sevin Rosen Funds, 209
Shaw Venture Partners, 209–210
Sienna Holdings, 210
Sierra Ventures, 211
Sigma Partners, 211–212
Signal Equity Partners, 212
Signature Capital, LLC, 212–213
Silicon Valley Bank, 213–214
Silver Creek Technology Investors, 214
SOFTBANK Venture Capital, 215
SpaceVest, 216–217
Spencer Trask Securities Inc., 217
Sports Capital Partners, 218
Spray Venture Partners, 218–219
Sprout Group, 219–220
St. Paul Venture Capital, 220
StoneCreek Capital, Inc., 221
Summer Street Capital Partners, LLC, 222
Summit Partners, 222
Sutter Hill Ventures, 223
Svoboda, Collins LLC, 223–224
TA Associates, 224
TAT Capital Partners Ltd., 224–225
TD iCapital, 225
Technology Crossover Ventures, 225–226
Technology Funding, Inc., 226–227
Technology Investments, 227
Technology Partners, 227–228
Techno-Venture, 228
TechSpace Xchange, 228–229
Telecommunications Development Fund, 229
TeleSoft Partners, 230
Telos Venture Partners, 230–231
Third Eye Ventures, LLC, 231
Thoma Cressey Equity Partners, 231–232
Thompson Clive, Inc., 232–233
Three Arch Partners, 233–234
Tondu Corporation, 235
Toucan Capital Corp., 235–236
Trans Cosmos USA, Inc., 236–237
Trellis Partners, 237
Trident Capital, 237–238
Trinity Ventures, 238–239
Triton Ventures, 239
TSG Equity Partners LLC, 240
TVM Techno Venture Management, 241–242
Union Atlantic Capital, L.C., 243
Vanguard Venture Partners, 244–245
Vector Fund Management, 245–246
Vencon Management, Inc., 246
Venture Funding, Limited, 247–248
Venture Management Associates, 248
Venture Strategy Partners, 249
Versant Ventures, 250
Vertex Management, Inc., 251
Viventures, 252
W.B. McKee Securities, 252–253

Walden Capital Partners L.P., 253
Walden VC, 253–254
Wasserstein Adelson Ventures, L.P., 255
WebVestors Equity Partners, LP, 255–256
Welsh, Carson, Anderson & Stowe, 256–257
Western States Investment Group, 257
Western Technology Investment, 257–258
Weston Presidio Capital, 258
Whitney & Co., 259
Windamere Venture Partners, LLC, 260
Winston Partners, 260–261
Woodside Fund, 261–262
Worldview Technology Partners, 262–263

Northeast
CEO Venture Fund, 45
Grace Internet Capital, 97
Lambda Management Inc., 141
New York Partners, LLC, 166
TL Ventures, 234–235
TSG Equity Partners LLC, 240
Walden Capital Partners L.P., 253

Northwest
Alexander Hutton Venture Partners, 9–10
Bay Partners, 28
Consolidated Firstfund Capital Corp., 58
Fluke Venture Partners, 84
Kline Hawkes & Company, 136
Macadam Capital Partners, 147
Mohr, Davidow Ventures, 160–161
Pacific Northwest Partners SBIC, L.P., 182
Staenberg Private Capital, LLC, 220–221
Thorner Ventures, 233
Timberline Venture Partners, 234
TL Ventures, 234–235
U.S. Venture Partners, 242–243
UV Partners, 243–244
Venture Growth Associates, 248
Venture Management Associates, 248
W.B. McKee Securities, 252–253
WI Harper Group, 259–260
WRF Capital, 263

Southeast
Antares Capital Corporation, 16–17
CEO Venture Fund, 45
Chrysalis Ventures, 47–48
Commercial Bridge Capital, LLC, 54–55
Davis, Tuttle Venture Partners, 63–64
Fuqua Ventures, LLC, 89–90
Hickory Venture Capital Corporation, 107–108
Richland Ventures, 195

Southwest
Access Venture Partners, 7
Bay Partners, 28

Davis, Tuttle Venture Partners, 63–64
Financial Broker Relations, 79–80
G.A. Herrera & Co., 90
Hickory Venture Capital Corporation, 107–108
Hook Partners, 110
Huntington Holdings, Inc., 113
Indosuez Ventures, 116
IngleWood Ventures, 118–119
InnoCal, 119
Kline Hawkes & Company, 136
Lambda Management Inc., 141
Lawrence Financial Group, 141–142
Leong Ventures, 144
Levine Leichtman Capital Partners, Inc., 144–145
MedVenture Associates, 152–153
Millennium 3 Venture Group, LLC, 157–158
Mission Ventures, 158–159
Mohr, Davidow Ventures, 160–161
National Corporate Finance, Inc., 163
Newtek Ventures, 167–168
Palomar Ventures, 183–184
Richland Ventures, 195
Riordan, Lewis & Haden, 197
Rocky Mountain Capital Partners, LLP, 199
Sorrento Associates, Inc., 215–216
Southwest Merchant Group, 216
Thorner Ventures, 233
Timberline Venture Partners, 234
TL Ventures, 234–235
Tullis Dickerson & Co., Inc., 240–241
U.S. Venture Partners, 242–243
UV Partners, 243–244
Valley Ventures, L.P., 244
Venture Growth Associates, 248
W.B. McKee Securities, 252–253
WI Harper Group, 259–260

West
Access Venture Partners, 7
Alpine Technology Ventures, 11
Alta Partners, 11–12
American River Ventures, LP, 13–14
Aspen Ventures, 21–22
Bay Partners, 28
BioVentures West, 31
Brentwood Venture Capital, 36
Capital Insights, 40
Capstone Ventures, 42
Chanen & Co. Ltd., 45–46
Charterway Investment Corporation, 46
Clarion Capital Corporation, 49–50
El Dorado Ventures, 74
Empire Ventures, 75–76
Encompass Ventures, 76
First American Capital Funding, Inc., 81
Forward Ventures, 85–86
Fulcrum Venture Capital Corporation, 88–89

Full Circle Investments, Inc., 89
Geneva Venture Partners, 94–95
Hook Partners, 110
Huntington Holdings, Inc., 113
iMinds Ventures, 115
Indosuez Ventures, 116
InnoCal, 119
Innovest Venture Partners, 119–120
Kline Hawkes & Company, 136
Lambda Management Inc., 141
Lawrence Financial Group, 141–142
Leong Ventures, 144
Levine Leichtman Capital Partners, Inc., 144–145
Libra Mezzanine Partners, L.P., 146
MedVenture Associates, 152–153
Millennium 3 Venture Group, LLC, 157–158
Mission Ventures, 158–159
Mohr, Davidow Ventures, 160–161
Montgomery Associates, Inc., 161–162
National Corporate Finance, Inc., 163
Newtek Ventures, 167–168
Pacific Venture Group, 182–183
Palomar Ventures, 183–184
Petra Capital Partners, LLC, 186
Rocky Mountain Capital Partners, LLP, 199
RWI Group, 200–201
Selby Venture Partners, LP, 206–207
Staenberg Private Capital, LLC, 220–221
StoneCreek Capital, Inc., 221
Thorner Ventures, 233
Timberline Venture Partners, 234
TL Ventures, 234–235
Tullis Dickerson & Co., Inc., 240–241
U.S. Venture Partners, 242–243
UV Partners, 243–244
Ventana, 246–247
Venture Growth Associates, 248
Venture Management Associates, 248
Ventureplex, 249–250
Vision Capital, 251
W.B. McKee Securities, 252–253
Wasatch Venture Funds, 254–255
WI Harper Group, 259–260
Winward Ventures, 261
Zone Ventures, 263–264

Index for Part Two

A

Academic interactions, 390
Accountability in business incubation, 345
Accountants. *See also* Financial advisers
    funding contacts of, 268, 276
    responsibilities and, 370
Accreditation of Angel investors, 272
Added value. *See* Value-added investors
Adversity, coping with, 371–372
Advisory board. *See* Board of Advisers
Affiliations, high–profile, 269
Agents. *See* Financial advisers
Alta Partners, 388
Amgen, 383
Angel investors, 271–279
    added value of, 275
    base hit strategy and, 398
    defined, 271
    drivers for investment decisions, 274–275
    finding, 276
    friends and family vs., 273
    investor presentation for, 275–276
    involvement in business by, 278–279
    "lead" Angels, 278
    nondisclosure agreements for, 276–277
    overview, 272, 279, 302, 394
    professional VC firms vs., 273–274
    return on investment for, 275
    size of investments from, 274
    time required for funding from, 277
    typical deal, 277
    valuation issues for, 278, 282–283, 302
    when to use, 268, 272–273
Attorneys
    due diligence review and, 268
    finding experienced firms, 283–284
    funding contacts of, 268, 276
    in-house vs. outside, 390
    need for, 390
At-will employment, 352

B

Bank Holding Company Act, 331
Banks
    as equipment leasing sources, 331, 339–340
    investment banks, 388–389
Barriers to competition, 268, 301
Base hit funding strategy, 397–398
Biotech companies
    academic interactions and, 390
    Board of Directors for, 387
    business development for, 389–390
    CEO timeline for, 385–386
    investment needs of, 317
    location issues, 385
    models for, 384
    scientific advisory board for, 390
    VC expectations for, 319
Blame for failure, 372
Blumenthal, Benjamin E. N., 307, 311
Board of Advisers
    for biotech companies, 390
    Board of Directors vs., 326
    described, 279
    developing, 285
    formation of, 326
Board of Directors, 325–329
    Board of Advisers vs., 326
    Chairman, 327, 370
    changing, 329
    communication with, 328, 368–369
    compensation for, 329
    composition of, 327, 329, 404
    corporate by–laws and, 370
    forming, 327
    importance of, 325, 329
    maximizing value of, 328
    monitoring effectiveness of, 328
    outside Board members, 327, 369
    responsibilities and roles of, 325–326, 369–370,
        387
    seats for investors on, 279
    tenets of good relationship with, 328
    tie votes, 370
    when to form, 326
Bradley, Wade, 281, 287
Bristol Investment Group, Inc., 311
Brokers, financial. *See* Financial advisers

Brokers for equipment leasing, 340
"Build and sell" business model, 269, 347–348
Burn rates, 388
Business characteristics, 395–396
Business development for biotech companies,
        389–390
Business incubation, 343–350
    empowerment or microenterprise incubators, 347
    evolution in, 350
    factors for success, 345–346
    historical perspective, 344–345
    industry–focused incubators, 347
    mission of, 344
    mixed-use incubators, 347
    overview, 343–344
    selecting an incubator, 349–350
    technology incubators, 346
    traditional incubators, 346–347
    venture accelerators, 347–349
Business Incubation Works, 343
Business model. *See* Business plans
Business plans
    for Angel investors, 276
    business characteristics and, 396
    business model risk, 295
    creating, 364
    elements of, 299–301
    elevator pitch (executive summary), 269, 275–276,
        299–300, 308
    grand slam strategy and, 397
    ingredients that attract funding, 268–269
    investment-screening criteria for, 293–294
    long-term value in, 269, 270
    other documentation requirements, 308–309
    percent seriously considered, 292, 299, 307
    professional consultants for, 268
    "time value of money" for, 385
    transformation into memorandums, 308
    value proposition, 300
    of Web-based businesses, 388
Buyout in equipment leasing, 339

C

Capital Equipment Leasing, 342
C corporations, 281–282
Celebrity affiliations, 269
Center for Venture Research, 272
CEOs
    change in, 381–382
    timelines for, 385–386
CGMI, 347
Chairman of the Board, 327, 370
Change-oriented management, 380
Characteristics of businesses, 395–396
Chemical Bank, 331
Chiron, 383

CHIT, 340
Citibank, 331
Commitment
    to Board membership, 329
    to management excellence, 268–269
    to vision, 269
Commodity, venture capital as, 267
Communication
    with the Board of Directors, 328, 368–369
    importance of, 376
    with new CEO, 382
    with VC Partners, 404
Community-based business incubators, 346–347
Compensation
    for Board of Directors, 329
    employee retention and, 386–387
    for founders, 371
    IPOs and, 387
Competitive barriers, 268, 301
Competitive risk, 295, 405
Computer graphic presentations, 276
Connectedness risk, 295
Consultants
    employment issues, 353–354
    need for, 390
Convertible debt instruments, 277, 283, 365
Corporate investors, 302–303
Credit-application-only leases, 333–334, 335. *See
        also* Equipment leasing
Customers, 268

D

Deal flow, 291–292
Dedina, Michael, 375, 378
Defining your business, 268
Delaware incorporation, 281
Deleage, John, 388
Desai, Nick, 367, 373, 399, 406
Development risk, 295
Devices. *See* Products or devices
Differentiation issues, 268, 384
Dilution, 282
Discrimination issues, 356–357
Diversification
    deal flow and, 291
    equipment leasing and, 332
    Labrador's guidelines, 291
    for risk management, 290–291
Documentation requirements, 308–309. *See also*
                Business plans
Domain Associates, 388
Due diligence review, 309, 318, 367–368, 398

E

Early-stage VC firms

benefits of using, 315–316
expectations of, 318–319, 400
later investors vs., 316–317
primary goal of, 322
typical investment format for, 317
venture accelerators, 347–349
when to use, 268
Economic Development Administration (EDA), 344–345
eDUALCITIZEN.com, 378
Elevator pitch (executive summary)
for Angel investors, 275–276
compelling, 269
guidelines for, 299–300
sections of, 308
Empire Ventures, 287
Employees. *See also* Management
at-will employment, 352
CEO change, 381–382
exempt and nonexempt, 353, 354
friends vs., 371, 376, 377
harassment and discrimination issues, 356–357
hiring managers, 370–371, 376, 377
independent contractors vs., 353–354
intellectual property protection issues, 357–358
leadership and delegation issues, 381
noncompetition and nonsolicitation agreements of, 358
performance evaluations for, 357
recruiting and retention of, 386–387
start-up employment issues, 351–359
stock option issues, 282, 355–356
as team partners, 283
Empowerment or microenterprise incubators, 347
Enterprise Partners Venture Capital, 267, 270
Entrepreneurs. *See also* Vision
cautionary tale about, 375–377
CEO change and, 381–382
companies vs., 370
control concerns for, 322
experience and risk management, 290
financial advisers vs., 309–310
first-time, 269–270
insider story for, 367–373
management skills needed for, 380–381
research necessary for, 267
responsibilities to outside investors, 381
role of, 369
WordSmart Challenge for, 378
Equipment leasing, 331–342
advance rentals and timing, 338–339
advantages of, 332
as capital source, 331
contract variables, 337–339
conventional leases, 333
credit-application-only leases, 333–334, 335
history of, 331–332

interim rents, 338–339
monthly rentals, 338
overview, 331, 341
rate factors, 338
rationale of, 331
residual/buyout, 339
sale and lease-back, 336
selecting a leasing company, 341
sources, 339–341
terms, 333, 334, 335, 336, 337
venture leases, 334–336
Exclusion lists for financial advisers, 308
Executive summary. *See* Elevator pitch (executive summary)
Exempt employees, 354
Exit strategies
Angel investors and, 273, 275
defining clearly, 362
VC firms' need for, 318
Experience
risk management and, 290
VC firm benefits, 315
Expertise, need for, 405

F
Family. *See* Friends and family
FIDOs (fully integrated discovery organizations), 384
Financable events (milestones), 304–305
Financial advisers. *See also* Accountants; Attorneys
capital-raising process using, 309–310
equipment lease brokers, 340
exclusion lists for, 308
need for, 307, 310
selecting, 308
terms of arrangement with, 308
Financial models, role of, 321–322
Financial responsibilities of the Board, 325–326
Financial risk, 294–296
FIPCOs (fully integrated product companies), 384
First-time entrepreneurs, 269–270
Fleming, Standish M., 313, 323
Flextronics, 279
Forward Ventures Services Corporation, 323
Founders
cautionary tale about, 375–377
CEO change and, 381–382
compensation for, 371
importance to VCs, 405
insider story for, 367–373
role of, 369, 372, 379, 389
track record of, 396
vision of, 383
Friends and family
Angel investors vs., 273
base-hit strategy and, 397–398

employees vs. friends, 371, 376, 377
  as sources of capital, 271, 302, 362, 394
  understanding by, 372
Fully integrated discovery organizations (FIDOs), 384
Fully integrated product companies (FIPCOs), 384
Funding strategies, 396–398
Fund-raising firms, 286

G
GECKO, 340
Gerard Klauer Mattison & Co., 388
Getting funded, 361–365
  business plan suggestions for, 268–269
  financial advisers for, 307–310
  funding strategies, 396–398
  on ill-conceived businesses, 270
  sources of venture capital, 271, 302–304, 393–394
Goldman Sachs, 388
Grand slam funding strategy, 396–397
Growing markets, targeting, 268, 293, 363–364

H
Harassment issues, 356–357
Harrington, Robert J., 379, 382
Home run funding strategy, 397
Human resources. *See* Employees

I
IMF, 332
Incorporation, deciding about, 281–282
Incubation. *See* Business incubation
Independent contractors, 353–354
Independent equipment lessors, 332, 340
Industry
  biases, 401
  business characteristics and, 395
Industry-focused incubators, 347
Industry Partner Programs, 292
Initial public offerings (IPOs), 271, 308, 387
Innovation, 364, 384
Institutional VC firms, 268
Intellectual property protection, 357–358
Interim rents in equipment leasing, 338–339
Internal Revenue Service, independent contractors and, 353–354
Internet Capital Group, 347
Investment banks, 388–389
Investor involvement in business
  by Angels, 278–279
  financial models and, 321–322
  incubation, 343–350
  for risk management, 296–297
  seed-stage vs. later investors, 316–317
  varieties of, 389

VC management style, 401–402
Investor lists
  developing, 309
  exclusion lists, 308
Involvement, investor. *See* Investor involvement in business
IPOs (initial public offerings), 271, 308, 387
Itel Leasing, 332

J
Jones, Michael R., 393, 398
Just-in-time resources, 346

K
Kay, Andy, 375–377
Kay, David A., 375, 378
Kaypro Computers, 375–377
Kearns, Jennifer A., 351, 359
Kibble, Robert F., 299, 305–306
Kirby, Bob, 290
Kubal, Larry, 289, 297

L
Labrador Ventures, 289, 290, 291, 297
Later-stage VC firms
  early-stage firms vs., 316–317
  expectations of, 318–319
Lawyers. *See* Attorneys
Leadership. *See also* Management
  cautionary tale about, 375–377
  emotional drain of, 373
  founder's role, 369, 372, 379
  hiring professional management, 370, 381–382
  preparing for adversity, 371–372
  skills required for, 380–381
Lead investor
  Angels, 278
  Board of Directors membership and, 327
  determining, 304, 327
Leasing. *See* Equipment leasing
Lee, David, 267, 270
Lehman Brothers, 388
Limited liability companies, disadvantages of, 281–282
Limited partnerships, disadvantages of, 281–282
Line of credit, leasing, 335
Liquidity events. *See also* Exit strategies
  Angel investors and, 273, 275
  VC firms and, 318
Local VC firms, advantage of, 303
Location issues, 385

M
Management. *See also* Investor involvement in business; Leadership

Board of Directors membership and, 327
Board of Directors' role in, 326
business characteristics, 395
in business plan, 300–301
CEO change, 381–382
change-oriented, 380
commitment to excellence in, 268–269
control issues, 322
founder's role and, 369, 379
grand slam strategy and, 397
hiring professionals, 370–371, 376, 377, 381–382, 405
risk, 295
skills required for, 380–381
timelines for, 385–386
track record of, 396
VC focus on, 362–363, 405
VC style of, 401–402
Manufacturers Hanover Bank, 331
Manufacturing risk, 295
Market
business characteristics, 395
in business plan, 301
investment-screening criteria for, 293
targeting growing markets, 268, 293, 363–364
vision and, 405
Marketing risk, 295
McDonald, Jack, 290
Mezzanine-stage VC firms
early-stage firms vs., 316–317
expectations of, 318–319
Microenterprise or empowerment incubators, 347
Milestones
for funding, 304–305
timelines and breakpoints, 385–386
Mission Ventures, 305
Mixed-use incubators, 347
Moos, Walter H., 383, 392
Morgan Stanley, 388

N
National Association of Securities Dealers (NASD), 308
National Business Incubation Association (NBIA), 344, 345
National Science Foundation (NSF), 345
NDAs (nondisclosure agreements), 276–277
Negotiating with venture capitalists, 320–321
Net burn rates, 388
Netscape Communications Corporation, 363
Networking
aggressive, for start-ups, 283
risk, 295
by VC firms, 304, 315–316
Neumann, Ben R., 361
New Economy, 267, 380–381

Noncompetition agreements, 358
Nondisclosure agreements (NDAs), 276–277
Nonexempt employees, 353, 354
Nonprofit business incubators, 346–347
Nonsolicitation agreements, 358
NSF (National Science Foundation), 345

O
Occhipinti, Vincent, 325, 329
Offer letters for at-will employment, 352
Orion Enterprise Development (OED), 350
Orion, L. Tyler, 343, 350
Outside Board members, choosing, 327, 369
Overtime wages, 354
Ownership
of companies, 370
equipment leasing and, 332

P
Partners of VCs, 400, 401, 404
Passion, need for, 380, 404
Performance evaluations, 357
PIN: Pacific Incubation Network, 350
Portfolio companies, 401
Post-money vs. pre-money valuation, 278
Presentations. *See also* Business plans
for Angel investors, 275–276
ingredients that attract funding, 268–269
Prior investments, 396
Product differentiation, 268
Products or devices
investment needs for, 317
investment-screening criteria for, 293
proprietary, 364
technologies vs., 383–384
VC expectations for, 318–319
Professional service providers, 268. *See also* Accountants; Attorneys; @INS:Financial advisers
Proof-of-concept investment, 317
Proprietary products and services, 364
Public relations firms, 391

R
Rate factors for equipment leasing, 338
Reality check, 381, 400–401
Referrals
for Angel investors, 276
deal flow and, 291
for equipment leasing, 341
importance of, 305, 307
for VC firms, 268, 305
Relatives. *See* Friends and family
Reporting
accountants and, 370

to Board of Directors, 328, 368–369
equipment leasing and, 332
tools for, 325–326
VC money and, 403
Residual in equipment leasing, 339
Responsibilities
accountants and, 370
of the Board of Directors, 325–326, 369–370
business incubation and accountability, 345
to outside investors, 381
term sheets and financial responsibilities, 367
Return on investment
Angel investors and, 275
VC expectations for, 318–319, 365, 400
for VCs vs. other investments, 290–291
RIPCOs (royalty income product companies), 384
Risk management, 289–297
challenges of, 289
deal flow and, 291–292
diversification for, 290–291
experience and, 290
for financial risk, 295–296
investment-screening criteria, 293–294
nurturing investments, 296–297
risk factors, 294–296
start-up risks, 290
Royalty income product companies (RIPCOs), 384

S
SAB (scientific advisory board), 390
Safeguard Scientifics, 347
Sales and lease-back, 336. See also Equipment
         leasing
Scalability risk, 295
Schneider, Dick, 388
Scientific advisory board (SAB), 390
S corporations, 281–282
Screening criteria for investments, 293–294
Securities and Exchange Commission (SEC)
financial adviser registration with, 307, 308
legal issues, 398
venture accelerators and, 348
Securities laws, 398
Seed-stage VC firms. See Early-stage VC firms
Selectivity in business incubation, 345
Self funding, 302
Series A Convertible Preferred stock, 277
Services
investment needs for, 317
investment-screening criteria for, 293
proprietary, 364
VC expectations for, 318–319
Small Business Administration, 343
Sohl, Jeffrey, 272
Startup Law Center at Higgs, Fletcher & Mack, 398

Start-ups. See also Business incubation; Early-stage
         VC firms; Employees
Angel funding for, 271
Board of Advisers for, 279, 285
business incubation, 343–350
corporate structure for, 281–282
dilution and growth of, 282
employment issues, 351–359
failure rate for, 343
foundations and milestones, 383–385
funding strategies, 396–398
fund-raising firms and, 286
law firms for, 283–284
networking for, 283
organizational development, 385–387
risk factors for, 294–296
risk management, 289–297
seed-stage vs. later investors and, 316–317
stages of raising capital for, 271
team building for, 285–286
valuation for, 278, 282–283
value-added investment partners for, 284–285
Stensrud, Bill, 267, 270
Stocks
as Board member compensation, 329
dilution issues, 282
employee stock options, 282, 355–356
Series A Convertible Preferred, 277
valuation, 278
Success
dangers of, 375–378
definitions of, 402
Sullivan, Joe, 271, 279

T
Targeting
growing markets, 268, 293, 363–364
investors, 269, 303–304
Taxes
equipment leasing and, 332
exempt employees and, 354
independent contractors and, 353–354
Team building for start-ups, 285–286
Technologies
business characteristics, 395
grand slam strategy and, 397
products vs., 383–384
Technology incubators, 346
Termination of at-will employment, 352
Terms
for equipment leasing, 333, 334, 335, 336, 337
financial adviser arrangements, 308
Term sheets
for Angel investors, 276
financial responsibilities and, 367
valuation and, 278

Time requirements
   for Angel-investor funding, 277
   for investment evaluation, 291–292
   for obtaining financing, 310
Timing
   for Board of Directors formation, 326
   leadership quickness and, 380
   of lease payments, 338–339
   for liquidity, 319
   milestones for funding, 304–305
   of nondisclosure agreements, 276–277
   for reports to Board of Directors, 328
   timelines and breakpoints, 385–386
Track record, 396
T Sector, Inc., The, 382
Twain, Mark, 300

U
University-based business incubators, 346–347

V
Validation, 384–385
Valuation, 313–323
   Angel investors and, 278, 282–283, 302
   bottom line for, 322
   convertible notes for, 277, 283, 365
   corporate investors and, 302
   defined, 278
   fairness issues for, 320
   financial adviser's role in, 310
   financial models and, 321–322
   methodologies for, 319–320
   negotiating with VCs, 320–321
   non-cash results of, 313–314
   overview, 314
   pre-money vs. post-money, 278
   process of, 314, 319–320
   rounds of financing and, 387
   VC expectations and, 317–319, 365, 400
Value-added investors
   Angel investors as, 275
   business incubators, 344, 350
   need for, 284–285
   VC firm benefits, 315–316
Value proposition, 300
VCs. *See* Venture capital firms
Vendor equipment leasing programs, 340–341
Venture accelerators, 347–349. *See also* Business
      incubation
Venture capital
   business incubation and access to, 346
   as commodity, 267
   funding strategies, 396–398
   issues for raising, 361–365
   returns on, 290–291
   sources of, 271, 302–304

   stages and ranges of investment, 317
   types of investors, 393–394
Venture capital firms. *See also* Early-stage VC firms
   Angel investors vs., 273–274
   benefits of, 315–316
   Board of Directors membership and, 327, 404
   considerations for choosing, 303–304
   defined, 271
   financial models for, 321–322
   management focus of, 362–363, 405
   management style of, 401–402
   need for, 314–315
   needs and expectations of, 317–319, 365, 400, 403
   negotiating with, 320–321
   net burn rates and, 388
   overview, 394
   Partners in, 400, 401
   portfolio companies, 401
   price of financing through, 365
   shopping the deal and, 320
   success defined by, 402
   targeting, 269, 303–304
   types of, 268, 393–394
   validation from, 384–385
   vision and, 399, 402, 403–406
   Venture Economics, 290
Venture leases, 334–336. *See also* Equipment leasing
Vision
   Board of Directors' role in, 326, 369
   broad market and, 405
   champions for, 383
   changing, 383, 404
   commitment to, 269
   outside investors and, 381
   VC money and, 399, 402, 403–406

W
Waterfall charts, 326
Williams, Frank, 379
Woodside Fund, 325, 326, 327
WordSmart Corporation, 377–378
Workers' compensation, 353
Wrongful termination cases, 352, 355

Z
Zkey.com, 373, 406

About the Author

Dante Fichera is the Managing Director and owner of Ventureplex, a life science and technology business refinery headquartered in San Diego. He has a degree in accounting from San Diego State University.

Mr. Fichera's first professional career venture was in public accounting. He subsequently launched a successful business consulting start-up, which assisted companies with developing business plans, networking, and obtaining capital. Eventually, his start-up was rolled into the services of Ventureplex, a much larger operation that provides promising early-stage companies with state-of-the-art facilities, access to capital, business development services, topical workshops, networking, and weekly investment forums. Visit their Web site at www.ventureplex.com.

The creation of *The Insider's Guide to Venture Capital* was a vision of Mr. Fichera's that originated years ago as a small pamphlet of local venture capital funds. First distributed at a local networking event, months later entrepreneurs were still carrying around those same pamphlets, holding them tight and applying them as one of their greatest resource tools. The need for a more comprehensive document was recognized. The result is *The Insider's Guide to Venture Capital.*

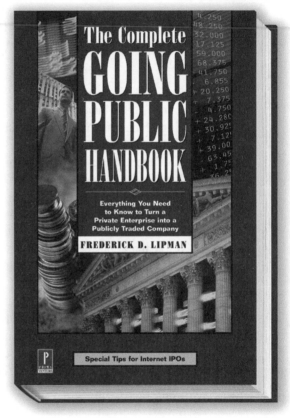

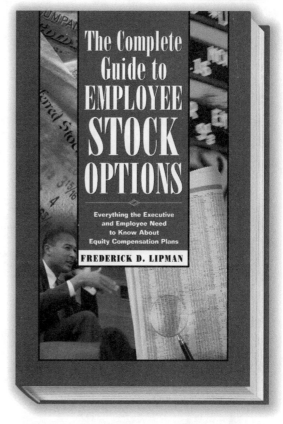